Praise for *Republic of Caste*

'Anand Teltumbde's *Republic of Caste* is a much-needed intervention in the politics of emancipation. It offers us a critique of the critique: introducing the various dimensions of appraising both the dalit and the left movements. It competently works out the possibility of reconfiguring transformative thinking and politics.' **Gopal Guru**

'Anand Teltumbde is a rare scholar who straddles the contrasting worlds of academia, business and civil rights activism. With his outstanding ability to think outside the box, he sheds new light on old subjects: from the relation between caste and class, and the meaning of secularism, to the nature of the Indian state, and the hindutva agenda. In this illuminating book, Teltumbde presents both an incisive critique of India's power structures and novel ideas for radical change. On both counts, he goes back to basics and places caste—and its annihilation—at centre stage. A timely and powerful wake-up call.' **Jean Drèze**

'*Republic of Caste* reflects Teltumbde's well-known expertise on dalit issues as well as his equally well-known sincerity and commitment. He shows that despite the abolition of untouchability, casteism is alive and well, with a resurgent Hindu nationalism legitimising it even further. Reviewing the attitude of various schools of thought towards the caste question—including those of the Indian left, Gandhi, and of the Congress, the BSP and AAP—Teltumbde makes it clear that nobody remains true to Ambedkar's principles in spite of trying to appropriate him, something the BJP is especially good at. Equally important, this book comprehensively discredits the claim that neoliberalism is solving India's caste problem with economic growth: the widening class inequalities only compound the fissures of an already hierarchical society.' **Christophe Jaffrelot**

Anand Teltumbde is a civil rights activist and a scholar. Among his many books are *Dalits: Past, Present and Future, Mahad: The Making of the First Dalit Revolt, The Persistence of Caste: The Khairlanji Murders and India's Hidden Apartheid* and the co-edited volume *The Radical in Ambedkar: Critical Reflections.* While serving as professor at the Goa Institute of Management, Teltumbde was incarcerated under the lawless law, the Unlawful Activities (Prevention) Act, on 14 April 2020 and is currently lodged in the Taloja Central Jail in Navi Mumbai. To know more about him visit www.realanandteltumbde.org

Republic of Caste

Republic of Caste

Thinking Equality in the Time of **Neoliberal Hindutva**

Anand **Teltumbde**

With a **foreword** by Sunil **Khilnani**

navayana

Republic of Caste: Thinking Equality in the Time of Neoliberal Hindutva
First published in hardback on 14 April 2018
First published in paperback in 2018, reprinted 2019, 2020, 2021, 2022, 2025
ISBN 9788189059866

Navayana Publishing Pvt Ltd
155 2nd Floor
Shahpur Jat, New Delhi 110049
Phone: +91-11-26494795
navayana.org

Typeset in Baskerville and Conduit ITC at Navayana
Printed by Sanjiv Palliwal, New Delhi

Distributed in South Asia by HarperCollins India

Subscribe to updates at navayana.org/subscribe
Follow on facebook.com/Navayana

To my unlettered mother, Anusaya,
who epitomized the value of struggle
and to Puka and Putch,
my well-educated daughters,
who, I hope, internalize it

Contents

Foreword

Sunil Khilnani

As conservative politics seem to take grip the world over, India finds itself at a decisive moment in determining its future as a republic. The inaugural promises of our democratic experiment have long sputtered, and even the rising hopes so palpable a little over decade ago—that economic growth might connect to popular struggles, finally delivering the benefits of growth to those at the back of the queue—seem to be from another age. With *Republic of Caste*, Anand Teltumbde tellingly dissects the complacent imagination of contemporary activism, and gets to the heart of what is at stake: 'our collective survival as a democratic republic'.

His book underlines the troubling disorientation that characterises our democratic politics. Across the land, we see surging movements for rights, justice, accountability, and for the freedom to speak and think as individuals: powerful in each local instance, together they reveal an episodic and fragmentary panorama. India's billion present-day mutinies find themselves disarmed by the onward rumble of a centralising political machine. Driven by ideological fervour, its informational antennae adept at eliciting and transmitting feelings of resentment and victimhood, the ruling dispensation is at pains to mutate Indians into a new religious conglomerate of digital Hindus.

The various strands of Teltumbde's analyses are united by a central concern: to examine one of the foundational ideals of the republic—the ideal of equality. The logic, shrewdness and passion of his writing reveal the multiple subversions of this ideal across our history, and why its realisation is now more distant than ever in an India caught in the throes of religious recapitalisation.

At the same time, efforts to mobilise and organise against inequality have been frustrated by what Teltumbde sees as an original flaw in the Constitution itself, and by the failures of analysis and judgment across India's progressive movements. These failures, ironically, are symbolised by the fate that befell the man who more than anyone put the value of equality at the centre of independent India's ambitions—B.R. Ambedkar. There is no questioning his status as a national icon, embraced—at least ostensibly—even by those whose privileges he sought to destroy. For the political elites, including the managers of hindutva, rituals of reverence for Ambedkar signal good intentions towards the downtrodden—and promise the electoral harvest of his followers. Perhaps inevitably, Ambedkar has become a stand-in for the particular causes and interests of anyone who chooses to appropriate him.

Yet, the dalit interests Ambedkar fought for remain unfulfilled and have become in many respects even harder to realise. Teltumbde's account of this decay is telling. While Ambedkar is given credit for shaping a Constitution that seemingly expunged caste, in reality, Teltumbde argues, 'the Republic of India has been constructed on the foundation of caste'. Even as untouchability was abolished by fiat, caste was infused into the Constitution by the legislative afflatus of reservations. Policies of reservations, Teltumbde agrees, have produced real gains for dalits. But they also gave the already privileged a pliant tool to manipulate caste categories—allowing them to maintain their dominance, not least by generating a self-cancelling politics of internecine conflict between subcastes.

The elite-induced transfer of caste from the social order, via reservations, into the juridical and administrative order recreated graded hierarchy within the state itself, now sanctioned by law. As a result, 'caste-related grievances and improvisatory forms of redress' have been amplified, leaving little room or energy for addressing the core dimensions of inequality. Simultaneously, those excluded from reservations have increasingly turned their envy into physical aggression, fuelling new waves of upper caste violence against dalits. As Teltumbde grimly notes, the growing presence of dalits in public office has done little to provide even the barest physical protection for dalits, let alone advance their economic and social interests.

Meanwhile, the main social forms of resistance to deepening inequalities—the left and dalit movements—anyway never very close, have only drifted further apart. Teltumbde writes astringently both of the Indian left's unwillingness to address caste, and of dalit unwillingness to imagine any more general forms of collective action, outside of categories of caste identity. The result is a dalit movement whose agitational vigour is quite out of proportion to its effectiveness, and a left whose torpidity is matched only by an excess of causes which should have, in reality, galvanised it.

Can a politics then emerge which is at once more universalist and effective? Recalling Ambedkar's own approach here is important, especially since he has been reduced 'to an inert godhead', a sectarian figure. In fact, as Teltumbde reminds us, while Ambedkar was not at all a Marxist, he was a universalist who tried always to find the underlying principles that could conjoin the energy of particular causes:

> Ambedkar was great simply because he genuinely strove to make this world a better place to live in... If Ambedkar had taken up cudgels for dalits merely as his own people, he would not qualify for greatness. He took up the cause of dalits because it was crucial to the ideals of human equality and democratisation, and necessary in the immediate sense to extricate Indian society from stagnation and degradation. It was an integral part of the struggle for liberation of human beings from the structures of exploitation and oppression.

As Ambedkar put it in 1952, the future of India's democracy was dependent on what he called 'public conscience'—a normative universalism. 'Public conscience', Ambedkar explained, 'means conscience which becomes agitated at every wrong, no matter who is the sufferer and it means that everybody whether he suffers that particular wrong or not, is prepared to join him in order to get him relieved.'

Teltumbde challenges us to recover that public conscience. It is a structure of thought and feeling all but erased in our current poisonous atmosphere, where the powerful feign victimhood even as they bludgeon the less powerful. It behoves those who do believe in such a public (and I would also call it, political) conscience, who are committed to respecting the diversities of want, need and choice across our society, to stand back and reflect on how these diversities can be integrated back into a shared vision of what India is.

Hindutva offers itself as one simplified version of that vision—a prescription with doctrinal clarity and apparent demographic weight. It is important to avoid an equally simplistic response to hindutva: that is, simply to push back with intense particularity, invoking counter, anti- and sub-nationalisms in hopes of disrupting the tinsel nationalism of the Sangh. Much harder, and more necessary, is to figure out a vision that sees our diversities as our advantage, not a threat. It took our founders huge effort, and some failure, in their attempts to do so: and it was and always will be a fragile vision. It is certainly not a vision innate to our civilisation, nor does it have great intrinsic virtue in itself. It is a politically created vision, and it's one clear advantage is that it can sustain the frame, the republic, in which our real struggles, for equality, universal rights, and addressing the serial wrongs of our history—the necessary struggles that Teltumbde gets us to think about—can advance to some better outcome.

Anand Teltumdbe's clear-eyed arguments won't bring comfort to anyone—but they need to be read and engaged with by all, for they urge us to think harder.

Introduction

Thinking Equality in the Time of Neoliberal Hindutva

Recently, one of my former students asked me, with some hesitation, how and why I began writing on caste, class and communalism, rather than the subjects I was formally trained in. While not the first person to ask me this, he was certainly the first among my students to do so. After a career in the corporate world, I have taught management at some of the premier institutes of the country. This is the professional trajectory that my training—a degree in engineering, followed by another from the Indian Institute of Management, Ahmedabad, and then a doctorate in cybernetics—had, strictly speaking, prepared me towards. My student's question was understandable and deserved a proper response.

After some thought, I asked him, using the jargon that he was familiar with, if we didn't all strive towards making some kind of a difference through our work. As it happens, I did publish in the manner and on the subjects he expected of me: research papers in the area of technology and management in scholarly journals. But the difference made by such research was to the greater good of the prevailing system. While modern science has the intrinsic capacity to drive society towards an egalitarian ideal, the capitalist relations of production that encompass it usurp new technologies to profit a few. The consequences of this—mass impoverishment and accentuated inequality—are sufficiently evident. Eighty-two per cent of the wealth created last year went to the richest one per cent of the global population, while the condition of the 3.7 billion people who make up the poorest half of humanity only worsened. It is imperative to change the framework and work towards one where the good of the people comes first. These concerns have guided me throughout my career. In addition to working within the status quo, I have had a parallel 'career' as an activist starting from my schooldays.

In the town of Wani in Yavatmal district, studying in the ninth grade, I led a struggle against the hegemony of the Rashtriya Swayamsevak Sangh in the government school. Some brahmin students wore black RSS caps in place of the white Nehru caps that was part of the uniform. One day, after discussing with a few close friends, I came up with a plan to counter the RSS boys. I had made some money painting cinema hoardings, and used it to buy one hundred blue caps. We distributed these to willing students across caste, and got them to wear it on a particular day. Seeing many of us in blue caps at the assembly, our games teacher—a dalit—created a fracas. I was taken to meet the headmaster, a Muslim. I told him that we had resolved to wear blue caps until he ensured that every student complied with the school uniform. He agreed, but pointed out that those boys were from rich and powerful families and he would have to talk to their parents. Whatever he did, the practice of the RSS boys wearing black caps stopped. Right from my formative years, I sought to work across caste lines and received support from others.

This approach helped me set a record in my engineering college student union election—I received all the votes barring nineteen out of the thousand-odd cast. In my adult life, organising contract workers in West Bengal, working among agricultural labourers in Gujarat, among Muslim slum-dwellers in Rajasthan, with the dalits in Tamil Nadu, and in diverse political struggles in Mumbai, my activism has always been at odds with what I did for a living. I have also had a long association with a civil rights organisation, the Committee for Protection of Democratic Rights, of which I am currently general secretary. Under the CPDR banner, I have been associated with numerous civil rights struggles over the last four decades.

Truth be told, I have enjoyed being at once in the belly of the beast and fighting it, of sitting in the board rooms of companies and also holding aloft red flags. The world outside threw far bigger challenges than the most complex problems I encountered in the cocooned corporate world. Experiencing both caste as well as class struggles, knowing dire poverty first hand in my village, being part of both the bourgeoisie as well as the proletariat, has led me to conclude that no radical change is possible in India without confronting caste. Contrary to the prevailing understanding of both the dalit and the left movements, I see class and caste as intertwined. Without the annihilation of caste, there can be no revolution in India, and at the same time, without a revolution there can be no annihilation of caste. I became aware of the necessity of confronting the orthodoxies of both positions even if it meant being misunderstood by either side: a lonely furrow to plough.

To the management student who was curious about my double role, both 'left' and 'dalit' were alien terms. In the gung-ho world of upwardly mobile Indians, such is increasingly the case. I was not sure whether he fully understood what I said. Perhaps he will read this book and come to reflect on how beneath the veneer of a modern, developing, superpower India remains a republic of caste.

This book is unusual in that I did not set out to write it. The credit for its conception goes to the Navayana team. In my monthly column for the *Economic and Political Weekly*, running for over a decade, I respond to events as and when they occur. The publisher noted thematic links between the hundred-odd essays and suggested recasting and updating them. This gave me an opportunity to expand, sharpen and augment my arguments, untrammeled by the limitations of a column. Slowly but surely, *Republic of Caste* emerged as a book. While we are given to believe that the Constitution helmed by Babasaheb Ambedkar created a republic that repudiates caste, in reality the republic of India has been constructed on the foundation of caste. Although the lawmakers outlawed untouchability in the Constitution, they skillfully consecrated caste which is the source of untouchability. Caste has thrived and prospered alongside the republic; this book tells you how and why. Each of the thirteen chapters in *Republic of Caste* looks at how inequality in India is deeply entwined with caste and religion, and how in our times, both caste and religious fundamentalism have colluded with the market to speak the language of majoritarianism. Concern about the outcome of these dire processes for the dalits, adivasis and minorities, and in a more general sense, the dispossessed masses, undergirds this book.

In the context of the Indian system, where caste and capitalism amalgamate, the biggest obstruction to the growth of a politics of change has been the growing divergence between the dalit and left movements. The cause of this rift lies in the dichotomy of caste and class, reflecting a misunderstanding of both categories. Caste is a concrete reality—the life-world of the people of the subcontinent. Caste often encompasses classes within it. Class, on the other hand, is a conceptual category; an abstraction based on one's relation to the means of production. It follows that a class analysis of Indian society cannot be done without taking cognisance of the overriding reality of castes. However, the communists who came from middle class and upper caste urban backgrounds used borrowed conceptual moulds from Europe to map a complex Indian reality. The much misused Marxian metaphor of 'base and superstructure' reinforced their misconception. They relegated caste to superstructure and trusted that it would go away when the economic base was changed—after the revolution. Consequently, they ignored the problem of caste and left its worst victims, the 'untouchable' dalits, to combat it alone. When the dalit movement gained momentum, the left developed an antagonistic attitude towards it and viewed it as something that fragmented the proletariat. The dalits, on their part, focused merely on their religio-cultural oppression by the castes placed above them. They neglected other aspects of their exploitation and developed a hostile attitude towards the communist movement. This internecine conflict did the two streams of the proletariat no good. The foremost challenge is to get them back on the track of convergence; if not, to reimagine them anew premised on a better understanding of both caste and class. This is what I write towards in the chapter, "The Caste and Class Dialectic".

The divergence of these movements assumed a doctrinaire character. The left swore by Marxism, and the dalits by Ambedkarism. While Marxism is universally recognised—notwithstanding its marginalisation by Leninism, Maoism, and later variants—as an integral body of thought with explanatory and predictive prowess, 'Ambedkarism' did not develop such universal claims. Insofar as Marxism drew from the theory of dialectical materialism, it was a way of examining the world from a scientific standpoint. Creatively extending dialectical materialism to the realm of social existence, Marx conceptualised historical materialism, a way of identifying the patterns in our collective life, thus enabling the possibility of breaking out of oppressive systems towards greater egalitarianism. Such theories aren't verifiable like physical phenomena and therefore should be held as tentative truth open to correction if new data so warrants. As a matter of fact, even in science every accepted truth remains tentative, continually evolving as new data is gathered. This is the crux of the scientific process. Unfortunately, Marx's theories were packaged by zealous adherents into an ism, as the dogma of a quasi-religious sect. They could not be interrogated without incurring the risk of excommunication. Marx execrated such a static conceptualisation of his theories, as he famously put in a letter in 1882 to Eduard Bernstein, 'ce qu'il y a de certain c'est que moi, je ne suis pas marxiste' (The one sure thing is that I'm no Marxist). As science welcomes new truth and assimilates it, Marxism should have been open to refining itself with new data generated by post-Marx capitalism as well as other pertinent research findings. However the Marxists, with their party apparatus, blocked that process. They did not hesitate to push doubters into the enemy camp, branded with labels like 'reactionary', 'renegade', 'capitalist-roader', 'revisionist', and so on.

Of course, the left movement in India today has little to do with this classical Marxism. It may not have much to do with Leninism and Maoism either. Among the Ambedkarite dalits, however, the stereotype of Marxism persists as a useful strawman to attack. They developed Ambedkarism in opposition to Marxism, pitching Ambedkar against Marx, as though they were born enemies. There can be no doubt that Ambedkar was no Marxist, and he did not conceal his reservations about Marxism, but can he therefore be construed as opposed to it? The essay "Ambedkar, Ambedkarites, Ambedkarism: From Panther to Saffron Slave" looks at the many curious byways that Ambedkarism travelled, the strange company it often kept, and the various political dead ends it reached. I argue that Ambedkar was essentially against any construction such as Ambedkarism. He did not believe that there could be any theory of history. Under the influence of John Dewey, his professor at Columbia University, he remained a pragmatist in dealing with history. If one examines his methodology, one cannot miss this philosophical strand. What is called Ambedkarism actually boils down to pragmatism, a way of practically resolving particular issues with available resources, rather than relying on grand narratives and a politics of overhaul.

The basic question to be asked is, what is the worth of these ideological identities, be it Marxism, Ambedkarism or any ism for that matter? Whereas natural science strives to achieve unanimous recognition for its propositions, the social sciences, even as they claim validity for their isms, sharply divide their practitioners into opposing camps. The promoters of these isms invariably undermine the vision of their progenitors, nowhere perhaps as starkly as in the case of the so-called Ambedkarites. Ambedkar's position on various issues may be debated with subjective interpretations but there cannot be a dispute about his basic struggle against caste as a system of oppression. Before Ambedkar appeared on the scene, movements of the subordinated castes had germinated all over India but none targeted the system in toto. Most efforts were directed at improving the situation of their 'own people' (jati), uplifting them culturally and economically, or in some exceptional cases like Ayyankali's (1863–1941), by rebelling against oppression. Ambedkar was the first who strove to theorise the problem and envisaged the annihilation of caste as its only solution. This culminated with his renouncement of Hinduism—the *source* of the caste system in his diagnosis—and conversion to Buddhism; there is no obscuring his core vision, mission and goal—that of the annihilation of caste. In contrast, the movements that rose in his name and the people who swear by his leadership have done everything possible to preserve castes. Ambedkar tried to bind all untouchable castes into a quasi-class, dalit. Today, the dalit identity itself is sought to be eroded by valorising its primordial constituent castes and subcastes.

When the dalit movement broad-based itself, it was on the basis of caste and community identities. It was in a way emulating the ruling class stratagem of using the caste–community arithmetic for electoral gains. The ruling classes certainly would not want caste to be annihilated, which they had transplanted from traditional terrain into the new Constitution. The tactic of the dalit parties, of using caste identity as a bargaining counter to negotiate alliances with the ruling class—paying the enemy back in its own coin—may yield short-term results, as is occassionally evident, but it is based on several flawed assumptions. The first is in terms of resource asymmetry; the ruling classes can control a patron–client relationship in ways not available to a dalit party—such as by splitting the dalits into rivals for patronage. Second, goal asymmetry; the goal of the ruling classes is to perpetuate the status quo, whereas the expected goal of a dalit party would be to smash it. Third, the silent metamorphosis of a dalit party into its antithesis, a ruling-class party, occurs further along this slippery slope, and unleashes a dynamic reinforcing of caste consciousness. The electoral success of the Bahujan Samaj Party so mesmerised Ambedkarite dalits, that it never crossed their minds that this process was antithetical to the annihilation of caste as conceived by Ambedkar. This is precisely what is discussed in the chapter "Assertion Not Annihilation: The BSP Enigma". The system they were joining in triumph was believed to be of Ambedkar's devising. Ambedkar had expected them to be enlightened (prabuddha) enough to discover the traps within it, but they would not heed even his own words—he had declared quite plainly in the Rajya Sabha in 1953 that he had been used as a hack in the writing of the Constitution.

It is one thing to live in an exploitative world while being conscious of the need to change it, and quite another to acquiesce with its arrangements. The behaviour of the dalit public betrays the latter tendency. They have been the willing prey of ruling class propaganda: that the system may have operational defects but is essentially perfect as designed by Ambedkar. This notion is propagated so energetically by the ruling classes and the dalit intelligentsia that even to suggest otherwise would be taken as blasphemy. The Constituent Assembly was overwhelmingly dominated by the Congress, its advisory committees which took final decisions on all major issues discussed by the subcommittees, were dominated by Nehru and Patel. Three-quarters of the resultant Constitution was simply the last colonial constitution, the India Act of 1935, poured into a new vessel. These facts, and the essential continuity of institutional structures of governance into the postcolonial period, should easily dispel the illusion that the Constitution handed over by Ambedkar to the chairman of the CA carried his writ. Ambedkar undoubtedly piloted each clause through assembly debate, protecting it from distortion by vested interests, and put the whole into legal language, but the substance of the Constitution comprises the decisions of the Congress party that emphatically represented the ruling classes. When he spoke in the Rajya Sabha disowning the Constitution, it was not an angry outburst, but a painful disclosure of the truth, and when he covered it up two years later by saying that the Constitution was a beautiful temple occupied by demons, it was a strategic retreat.

The only motive with which Ambedkar wanted to enter the CA was to preserve the safeguards he had earned for the dalits. Reservations comprised a major part of these. While reservations were basically carried forward from the colonial regime, the postcolonial ruling classes cunningly honed them into a choice weapon to perennially divide the people. Reservations became the pretext to conserve caste in the Constitution. The biggest cost the dalits have paid for the short-term gains of reservations is the compromise of their long-term goal of annihilation of caste. The opening chapter, "Reservations: A Spark and the Blaze", demonstrates how it has become a weapon in the hands of the ruling classes, it does not automatically mean that they are inherently bad and should be discarded. The test of my argument is that even if dalits were to demand their scrapping, the ruling classes would never let it happen. Again, it is important to remember that it is one thing to use them while knowing that they are traps, and quite another to treat them as heaven-sent solutions to a historical adversity. The cost of reservations far exceeds its benefits.

One of its costs is evident in the grudge against dalits in rural areas, which continually precipitates into violence against them. Paradoxically, rural dalit folks have hardly benefited from reservations but they keep paying its price with their blood. While reservations benefit an individual or at most that person's family, the fact that they are given in the name of caste means that the entire community bears the negativity that comes with it. Of course, reservations are not the only cause of growing violence against dalits. Contrary to the folklore that mass violence against dalits is as old as caste, it is distinctively a product of our postcolonial political economy. Castes being the life-world of people, humiliation, oppression and exploitation have been integral to caste relations throughout the history of the institution, and are internalised as such by all—evidenced by the jati names of untouchables (such as pariah, chandala or chamar) standing in for slurs. In such a situation, no additional spur is needed to orchestrate gory spectacles that disturb the settled order. Such happenings are distinctive features of a new order that arose in the later part of the 1960s.

Earlier, if a dalit violated the caste code, they would be punished instantly. Today, the violence is committed in a planned manner by a collective of caste Hindus against a collective of dalits, invariably with the motive that it would serve as a cautionary lesson to the entire community. It was with this motive that Surekha Bhotmange and her children were lynched to death in Khairlanji, in September 2007. The chapter "Violence as Infrasound: Khairlanji, Kawlewada, Dulina, Bhagana..." argues that this new genre of atrocity started in 1968 at Kilvenmani in Tamil Nadu, when forty-four dalit agricultural labourers who organised themselves under a communist flag were burnt to death by a powerful landlord. Unfortunately, Kilvenmani or Khairlanji are not the only atrocities, or even exceptional instances. There have been tens of thousands over the years. On an average, more than two dalits are murdered and more than five dalit women raped every day. As exceptions, particular atrocities provoke public uproar and are highlighted in the media. For the most part, they are taken as normal, as integral to India's cultural ecosystem. I explain the phenomenon of atrocities with a conceptual triangle, analogous to a fire triangle, necessitating the coincidence of three factors: a grudge against the dalits, an assurance that no harm would befall the perpetrator, and a trigger. The question, though, is not how but why these atrocities take place. Commonsensically, they should be inversely related to the representation of dalits in the state administration and hence should have shown a declining trend over the years. Instead, their numbers have consistently risen. Khairlanji presents an illustrative case. Almost the entire state machinery—from the district police chief, the inspector of the local station to the doctor who performed the postmortem—was staffed by dalits, most of them belonging to the same subcaste as the victims. Not only did they remain inert, some of them made matters worse. This should make dalits sit up and rethink the logic of representation that has been the pivot of their movement.

Dalits also need to rethink the concept of the state. The state that deprives them access to the basic wherewithal necessary for dignified living—like education, healthcare and sanitation—silently starves and kills them with its policies, blatantly violates constitutional guarantees, humiliates them, and discriminates against them to favour the rich, is still popularly cast as an impartial arbiter between them and society. The slightest sign of independent expression from dalits, and the state descends upon them with brute force, incriminates them as naxalites, incarcerates them for years, and even kills them with impunity. In the atrocity triangle, the state is the permanent agent that reassures various culprits that they need not worry about consequences. The courts often play along. Instead of actively addressing the growing incidence of atrocities, even the Supreme Court is tweaking the provisions of the PoA Act in favour of the accused. Hearing the case of harassment of a storekeeper by two 'Class One' officers at a pharmacy college in Maharashtra, the two-judge bench of A.K. Goel and U.U. Lalit ruled in March 2018 that the Act 'should not result in perpetuating casteism' and sought to protect potential aggressors from 'frivolous and motivated' charges. Yet, in the dalit universe, the state continues to be seen as a patron and benefactor, primarily because it provides reservations, affirmative action against the discriminatory attitudes of caste society. Reservations, thus, shroud an entire spectrum of contrary experiences of the dalits, not only those who are miles away from reservations but even its beneficiaries.

A trusting attitude towards the state is not confined to reservations—it extends to everything that bears the imprint of state authority. The dalit populace lionises those who occupy positions in officialdom, whether through reservations, elections or even the ignoble route of nomination—which should immediately raise suspicions instead. Thousands of committed activists genuinely working for them may pass unnoticed, but large crowds will assemble to felicitate some debauched person who is made a minister in the state. The dalit who is cherry-picked for even a ceremonial post instantly becomes great for the community. What gets passed over is the simple reasoning that if the state, which is an agent of dominant-caste interests, has picked a person from among them, it must be sure that they would serve its interests. Instead, crowds bear them on their shoulders. Conversely, those who oppose the state become an anathema to the dalits.

Once the state labels a dalit as naxalite, he or she gets automatically excommunicated. The naxalites languishing in prisons and killed in fake encounters mostly belong to the adivasi and dalit communities. But this has raised no alarms among the dalits. When Sudhir Dhawale, a dalit activist, was arrested in 2011 on the trumped-up charge of being a naxalite and incarcerated for nearly four years, there was hardly any protest from the community. Two forces were at work here: one, faith in the state, and; two, ideological antipathy to the left. Under the ruse of naxalism as a threat to its existence, the Indian state, notwithstanding its democratic mask, has resorted to the use of terror, as discussed in the chapter "Manufacturing Maoists: Dissent in the Age of Neoliberalism". The cases of Binayak Sen, Arun Ferreira, Sudhir Dhawale and G.N. Saibaba starkly exemplify this state terror but beyond these well-known instances involving urban professionals, unrestrained terror in vast rural areas, which hardly gets reported, has been unspeakable.

The dalit struggle against caste cannot be seen in isolation from other injustices unleashed across the world and the efforts to fight them. After the Great Depression in 1930, capitalism was facing a fatal crisis. It was saved from imminent collapse by what came to be known as Keynesianism, after the economist John Maynard Keynes (1883–1946).

His prescriptions assigned the dominant role in the economy to the state and inspired a model of welfare which became, in varying degrees, almost a reflexive choice for the entire world. Post–War capitalism thrived on the opportunity to reconstruct the world using the Keynesian model for over two decades. A booming demand–supply–employment cycle had restored the power of business houses and drew them into close alliance with political authority. However, this system inevitably slipped into crisis owing to overcapacity, stagflation and a falling rate of profit, and a wave of social unrest was unleashed all over the world by the late 1960s. In the wake of this crisis, the capitalist establishment adopted a hodgepodge theory of neoliberalism developed by three Austrians as a counter to the collectivism of the Soviet bloc. They were Karl Popper, a philosopher and ex-communist, who criticised all thinkers from Plato to Marx who valued the collective over the individual; Ludwig von Mises, an economist and former left-winger who migrated to the US and argued that socialism would necessarily lead to economic failure; and Friedrich Hayek who believed central planning was impossible because no person, however clever, knew what people wanted (see Jones 2012). It marked a shift from the liberal form of Keynesianism to the extremist form of laissez-faire capitalism.

Historically, the first book-length analysis of neoliberalism was by Jacques Cros in his doctoral thesis of 1950, the term having existed in French ('néo-libéralisme') since the nineteenth century (cited in Thorsen and Lie, 2011). Cros' main argument is that these neoliberals sought to redefine liberalism by reverting to a more right-wing or laissez-faire stance on economic policy issues, compared to the egalitarian liberalism of William Beveridge (1944) and Keynes (1936). Theories advocating a free market worked handily for a capitalist world raring to use its overcapacity and accumulated surplus to expand in the direction of postcolonial economies, or the 'third world'. They were packaged and pushed through the IMF and the World Bank which were created in the Bretton Woods Conference of 1944. The 1974 oil crisis, caused by the OPEC's (Organisation of the Petroleum Exporting Countries) quadrupling of oil prices, created acute indebtedness among developing nations, compelling them to approach the IMF/World Bank for rescue loans—now to be given with neoliberal conditions attached. The Soviet system, the last remaining obstruction to capitalist expansionism, which was in decline during these years, collapsed in 1991, and neoliberalism duly became the default ideology of global capital.

In India, the ruling classes essentially continued with the inherited colonial state apparatus, merely embellishing it with a constitutional flourish to cheat people. Not only did they preserve draconian colonial laws to suppress people but also significantly added to them. It took two decades for the people to realise the true character of the regime and rise against the state, encouraged by the worldwide unrest of the late 1960s. Starting with the Naxalbari uprising (1967), growing national disaffection took varying forms, be it the founding of the Dalit Panther (1972), or a range of student movements—Gujarat's Navnirman Yuvak Samiti and Navnirman Andolan (1973–75), Bihar's Chhatra Sangharsh Samiti (1974–75), and others in Delhi University and Jawaharlal Nehru University—or Jayprakash Narayan's call for Total Revolution (1974). These political churnings were answered with the declaration of Emergency in 1975 by Indira Gandhi. Voted out of power at the end of the Emergency (1977), she was back in office less than three years later. When she took a five billion dollar loan from the IMF in 1980, the biggest ever given by the latter until then, she paved the way for the influx of neoliberalism. In 1991, using the pretext of its balance of payments crisis, India formally embraced the Washington Consensus—a term coined by British economist John Williamson, encapsulating ten standard prescriptions of liberalisation delivered to developing countries—with a team from institutions like the IMF and World Bank in the saddle to implement it. Nothing in India would remain the same thereafter.

In *A Brief History of Neoliberalism*, David Harvey defines the concept as 'a theory of political economic practices that proposes that human well-being can best be advanced by liberating individual entrepreneurial freedoms and skills within an institutional framework characterised by strong private property rights, free markets and free trade' (2005, 2). The role of the state, he suggests, is to create and preserve an institutional framework appropriate to such practices. It follows that the state has to set up structures and functions required to secure private property rights and to ensure, by force if need be, the proper functioning of markets. Many social services traditionally provided by the state, such as water, education, healthcare, sanitation, social security, transport, etc. would be marketised—handed over to private capital—which naturally hits the majority of the poor, necessarily dalits, hardest. In order to contain their outcry against these policies, the state becomes intolerant of any dissent and turns authoritarian.

Such a fascistic state, some dalit intellectuals claim, is beneficial to dalits. Their view is based on the theoretical argument that markets do not recognise caste, and are therefore better than the ancient brahminic code of Manu, backed by the empirical claim that these policies have boosted entrepreneurial activities among certain dalits. Expectedly, they end by invoking Ambedkar as a monetarist or supporter of the market economy. The chapter "Slumdogs and Millionaires: The Myth of a Caste-free Neoliberalism" deals with these arguments. Neoliberalism is the economic face of social Darwinism, which according to its progenitors, Herbert Spencer and others in the late nineteenth and early twentieth centuries, is the notion that individuals, groups, and peoples are subject to the same Darwinian laws of natural selection as plants and animals (Claeys 2000). It is used to justify political conservatism, imperialism, and racism, and to discourage welfarist intervention and reform (Largent 2000). Although its postulations have been comprehensively debunked, social Darwinism still informs the neoliberal outlook. It is not difficult to refute all these arguments. The claim that markets are caste neutral is theoretically untenable. It is also empirically untrue that there has been a spurt in entrepreneurial activities among dalits, or that whatever is observed may be attributed to these policies. It is apparent that they have increased economic insecurity among the poorest people the world over, and no less in India. Thepredatory ethos of this capitalist offensive can be seen as injurious to people in inverse proportion to their social standing. In addition, it is evident that neoliberalism has catalysed the resurgence of religiosity, fundamentalism, and obscurantism the world over—as manifested by the rise of hindutva in India—which has been grossly injurious to dalit interests. The scholar Meera Nanda (2012) has shown how globalisation and Hinduisation have become lethally intertwined and neoliberal policies have worked to the advantage of the god market, creating a deadly 'State–Temple–Corporate complex'. Likewise the Marxist scholar Aijaz Ahmad has argued that 'the ideology of hindutva and the economics of liberalisation are not only reconcilable but complementary' (2002, 105).

One of the most adverse manifestations of neoliberalism is in the field of education. Education is the greatest instrument for moulding young minds, but it is also the biggest and relatively price-inelastic service market in the world. It was generally considered a public good because of its huge positive externalities, and was in large part publicly provided. Even if some private institutions came forward to provide it, they did so with philanthropic motivation. However, with the advent of neoliberalism, the price-inelasticity of the education industry—which makes it a producer's market—came to outweigh all other considerations. While elementary education, the basic qualifier for an individual to participate in the market, was made the responsibility of the state, higher education has increasingly come to be left to private capital. Given India's demography, its market of higher education is one of the biggest in the world (projected to touch $144 billion by 2020) and is being targeted by the global players. "The Education Mantra and the Exclusion Sutra" explains the neoliberal machinations around this vital instrumentality for human emancipation. It also illustrates how, for long, the ruling classes avoided including education as a fundamental right and pushed it to the ineffective part of the Constitution—the Directive Principles of State Policy; how they dodged the recommendations of the first education commission, the Kothari Commission (1964), and let education subside into a multi-layered system, that would—using the most secular of pretexts—succeed in excluding the poor from access to quality education; how even after the interpretation by the Supreme Court making education a fundamental right, they schemed to deprive 170 million children of the 0–6 age group and yet more in the 14–18 year range of this right; how they left the question of quality of education unaddressed, instead placating the people with their time-tested weapon of reservations (25 per cent) for students from financially disadvantaged backgrounds.

In the field of higher education, the government blatantly staged committees and commissions to echo the diktats of the World Bank. It unashamedly mandated a committee of the top businessmen of the country—the Birla–Ambani committee—to create a framework for reforms in education that expectedly carved out huge business opportunities in higher education. The government has since scaled up self-financing through substantial hikes in fees. While it was not politically feasible to completely dismantle the state financing of higher education, these moves did prepare the ground for offering up higher education to the WTO in 2005, under the General Agreement on Trade in Services. With the conclusion of the current Doha round, it may become an irrevocable commitment with far reaching consequences for the education of the poor and dalit/adivasi children. In addition, the current regime has been zealously working to saffronise education. They have mutated history to inject communal poison in young minds, de-emphasised rationality and a scientific outlook so that students become easy prey for fascist propaganda. To ensure organisational control over these processes, they have installed partisan vice-chancellors and directors, charged with eliminating dissent and campus democracy. All the while, as the onslaught of neoliberal policies proceeds, so does the apotheosis of Ambedkar.

The exacerbation of inequalities goes hand in hand with the present hindutva dispensation's frenzied iconisation of Ambedkar. To woo dalits, they have declared that grand memorials shall be raised to Ambedkar wherever he had set foot. It may be worth recalling that when Ambedkar, whom the ruling classes have now turned into their pet icon, died and his body had to be flown to Mumbai (the night of 6 December 1956), neither the state nor central government was ready to foot the bill. Eventually, half the cost of transportation had to be borne by the dalits; the payment was made by the Scheduled Caste Improvement Trust, then headed by Dadasaheb Gaikwad. For almost a decade, no monument came up in his memory at his cremation ground. His son, Yashwantrao Ambedkar, had to undertake a march from Mhow (Ambedkar's birthplace in present-day Madhya Pradesh) to Mumbai, collecting small change from people, to construct the modest structure at the Chaityabhoomi in 1967 that still serves as his memorial. For years, only a hundred odd people including his family would even visit the site on his death anniversary. The dalits had to undertake a massive countrywide jail-bharo struggle for almost a month to demand, among other things, that Ambedkar's portrait be put up in parliament; the one that hangs in the Central Hall was finally unveiled on 12 April 1990 to mark his birth centenary. Alarmed by the intensity of this agitation which was primarily a demand for land by landless peasants (and not just the memorial), the ruling establishment for the first time feared the dalits, and began to devise policies of co-option. The importance of 'Ambedkar' was reinforced by other developments too. The implementation of land reforms followed by the Green Revolution—a capitalistic agricultural programme—aimed to create a class of rich farmers out of the most populous band of the 'shudra' castes, creating valuable allies for the ruling party. The class contradiction between these capitalist farmers and rural dalits—proletarianised by the collapse of traditional jajmani relations—found its flashpoint along the axis of caste in the form of a new genre of atrocities, as illustrated by the Kilvenmani massacre in 1968. By then, the political ambition of this class had led to the emergence of regional parties, making electoral politics increasingly competitive. In the first-past-the-post system of electoral victory, it pushed up the value of vote blocs based on caste and community. Dalits being one such bloc, comprising one-sixth of the total electorate, their independent politics in disarray, became important to ruling class parties. On their part, faced with increasing atrocities, helplessness and an uncertain future, dalits became increasingly tied to Ambedkar, nostalgically and emotionally, as their only saviour. For the ruling classes, feigning love for Ambedkar was far easier than stemming atrocities, ensuring justice for its victims or addressing the material needs of the dalits. With the BSP showing the way, statues of Ambedkar sprung up everywhere, roads started being named after him, lands and funds were granted to put up his memorials.

Even the lynchpin of hindutva, the Rashtriya Swayamsevak Sangh could not remain unaffected. Representing a resurgent brahminism, the RSS is nothing but the ideological enemy of Ambedkar. It was always uncomfortable with his vitriolic criticism of Hinduism and his decision to renounce it. Although a decision was made to avoid getting into direct conflict with him, the discomfort of its ideologues and cadre only grew with Ambedkar's role in shaping the Indian republic on liberal democratic lines. In public it preserved a tepid, prudently non-committal stance towards him. During the long tenure (1973–94) of Madhukar Dattatraya Deoras, who became the Sangh supremo after the death of Madhav Sadashiv Golwalkar, the strategic imperative to broad-base the Sangh's appeal was realised, and Ambedkar was quietly included in the list of the Sangh's pratahsmaraniya (venerable persons to be remembered at daybreak). Efforts were initiated to saffronise him by launching a purpose-built vehicle, Samajik Samrasata Manch (social harmony platform), in Pune in 1983. Soon, a plethora of literature fraught with pure lies and half truths about Ambedkar entered circulation: now asserting that he was friends with Hedgewar and Golwalkar, now that he was all praise for the Sangh, stood for the Hindus and hindutva and against Muslims and so on. His utter contempt for Hinduism was neutralised by projecting him as the greatest benefactor of the Hindus. The near collapse of autonomous dalit politics and its ideological degeneration facilitated these inroads. Unctuous fawning over Ambedkar was to pay rich political dividends to the Bharatiya Janata Party: today most dalit leaders are within its fold. On the one hand, the hydra-headed Sangh parivar unleashed terror on the dalits to suppress their cultural expression (as in Gujarat in 1981, 1985, and 2016 in Una, among numerous other incidents, including the latest at Bhima-Koregaon, Maharashtra, on 1 January 2018), and on the other, it zealously promoted Ambedkar in order to hold the dalit masses in thrall. Ever since Narendra Modi, a seasoned pracharak of the RSS, took over the reins of power at the centre, the Sangh sees its dream of a Hindu rashtra within touchable range and has intensified its display of devotion towards Ambedkar to woo the dalits in larger numbers. Modi has been zealous in putting up gigantic memorials to him while curtailing the share accorded to dalits in successive budgets. These processes and their subtexts are the theme of "Saffronising Ambedkar: The RSS Inversion of the Idea of India".

Raw electoral considerations are complemented by a more sophisticated need to identify a suitable icon for neoliberal India. With his halo from the freedom struggle, Mohandas Karamchand Gandhi, the Mahatma, was the principal icon of postcolonial India. The Gandhi icon inspired generations with his vague ideas of a 'Ram rajya' that would magically harmonise the interests of all classes; but it ceased to fit the self-image of a consumerist neoliberal India that aspired to become a global superpower. For the ruling classes, Ambedkar—in his three-piece suit, with academic distinctions earned at world renowned universities, an economist favouring pragmatic reforms, with a published work on monetary policy that could possibly push him into the camp of monetarists—could replace the half-clad, nativist Gandhi. Coming from the lowest end of caste hierarchy and scaling the highest peaks of academics, politics, and various other walks of life, he becomes the best exemplifier of social Darwinism. His love of 'Liberty, Equality, Fraternity' (that could make him a libertarian), as also for democracy and constitutionalism, his tacit advocacy of regulation of peoples' conduct—the state as an external and religion the internal regulator—can all be used to cast him as a neoliberal icon. Above all, his 'dhamma pravartak' image—as a missionary of dhamma—offers a bulwark against communism, making him a perfect fit for the vacant niche of a patron saint to neoliberal India. The only people who could thwart this project are his own followers, by resurrecting him as the emancipator of the downtrodden and hence on the side of the resistance to neoliberalism. But when they themselves start to promote him as the greatest free market ideologue, the coast is clear for a right-wing takeover.

While the state promoted Ambedkar to outshine even the gods on his 125th birth anniversary, safai karamcharis (manual scavengers) were taking a Bhim Yatra across the country with the despairing slogan 'Stop Killing Us'. These dalits, estimated to be 1.3 million in 2000 (the government's risible figure being 679,000) still carry human excreta on their heads as their caste vocation and die in their thousands of asphyxiation in city sewers. Even as they struggle unavailingly to get the government to implement its own law (The Employment of Manual Scavengers and Construction of Dry Latrines (Prohibition) Act 1993), the government has launched its Swachh Bharat Mission (SBM), estimated to cost US $36.3 billion. Blithely disregarding the demands and inputs of the communities most urgently concerned with sanitary practices, the SBM is a vanity exercise aimed at garnering international applause and bolstering nationalist self-regard. It aims at ending open defecation and introducing practices of hygiene and sanitation across the country. Meant to be realised by 2019, the 150th anniversary of Gandhi's birth—for the parivar's government needs to appropriate the legacy of the man whom another pracharak shot dead—the programme is an overdue investment. As per the UN report of 2015 on the global costs of poor sanitation, co-authored by the charity WaterAid, nearly half of the country's population practised open defecation, accounting for over half of the 1.1 billion people across the world doing so, and introduced 65,000 tonnes of uncovered, untreated faeces into the environment in India every single day, causing around 117,000 deaths yearly among Indian children under the age of five. The cost to India's economy in terms of decreased productivity, expenditure on treatment, and premature deaths, is estimated at $106 billion per year, or over 5 per cent of its gross domestic product. However, SBM focuses solely on creating hardware (the construction of toilets) and neglects the software—the cultural aspects of the problem that perhaps constitute its crux. Cleanliness does have its economic side, but it is largely a function of culture. The caste system, that relegates the job of cleaning to people of a particular caste and further associates cleaning with lowliness, is bound to fail the project as explained in the chapter "No Swachh Bharat without Annihilation of Caste".

The insincerity of the government gets exposed when one looks at its apathetic responses to the decades-old struggle of manual scavengers. The Safai Karamchari Aandolan has for years struggled on several fronts against the government's lies, denials and indifference. A snarl of committees, commissions and legislation have deliberated but achieved little on the ground. Ignoring the SKA is expediental since the government's own departments have been the biggest culprits in sustaining the practice of manual scavenging. It is reported that wherever toilets have been installed under this mission, their cleanliness is delegated to contractors who employ manual scavengers for paltry salaries. In all probability, this mission is likely to aggravate the existing

problem of manual scavenging. As things stand, the government may well trumpet the successful completion of the mission on the eve of the next general election even as its quantitative targets are unlikely to be met; but, what's more, there may hardly be any impact on the ground in terms of hygiene and sanitation.

While the Swachh Bharat Mission gets accomplished on paper and the government could thereby officially negate the story of India's million-odd manual scavengers, there are hopeful signs that the dalits may adopt new forms of struggle in the coming times. Young dalits are coming forward to directly challenge their oppression and exploitation as shown by the Bhim Army in Uttar Pradesh. It reminds one of the birth of the Dalit Panther in 1972 in Mumbai, an angry response of the youth to the inaction of dalit politicians amid the growing incidence of atrocities. Like the Dalit Panther, the Bhim Army does not have programmatic clarity yet, and one hopes it would gain it in the course of its struggle. Another trigger for purposive politics came from Modi's Gujarat. The atrocity that took place in July 2016 at the village of Mota Samadhiyala in the Una taluka of Gir Somnath district sparked off a new kind of dalit struggle. Rather than projecting their weakness—in the plaintive mode that has marked dalit protests in the wake of any atrocity—the youth gave a focused direction to their movement by identifying their own strength and the weakness of the adversary. They resolved to give up caste vocations like dragging dead cattle and demanded five acres of land for each family instead. In order to drive home their point, they threw cattle carcasses into the collectorate compounds, the stink of which brought the administration to its senses. Una, the nearest town, to which four youths of a family had been dragged and where they were publicly flogged by cow vigilante goons, became the symbol of this new genre of struggle by dalits translating their cultural oppression into material issues, as explained in "Dalit Protests in Gujarat: Shifting Paradigms". While justice to the Una victims remains elusive, the struggle has forced the administration to expedite the handing over of lands allotted on paper to dalits three decades ago. The Una struggle did not waste breath in producing stereotypical rhetoric against the so-called upper castes, but identified the state as the culprit. It strove to unify all the oppressed without reference to caste. The ripple effect of Una is being felt all over the country, consolidating the unity of people along class lines. It has inspired youth to emulate a similar approach towards building class unity. The popularity of Jignesh Mevani, who emerged as the face of this struggle, testifies to the fact. While not relying much upon electoral politics—which has been a game of the ruling classes, played with money and muscle power—the struggle recognised the strategic need of contesting elections in order to intensify its impact on the ground. Mevani thus ran for office in the assembly elections from Vadgam constituency as an independent candidate and won by a comfortable margin in December 2017. His victory showed that one could go beyond caste and community, build peoples' unity and defeat the ruling classes at their own game.

Another unusual struggle unfolded in 2012–13, catapulting an extraordinarily shrewd ordinary man, Arvind Kejriwal, to the chief ministership of Delhi. In the wake of a series of corruption scandals that broke out during the United Progressive Alliance (UPA) II rule (2009–14), Kejriwal with some of his friends launched a movement under the banner of his NGO, India Against Corruption, using Anna Hazare, a small-time social worker from Maharashtra, as mascot. It was a canny move that played to the middle class self-image—combining an aseptic, 'post-ideological' politics with the rhetoric of the conscientious objector. The public ombudsman or 'Jan Lokpal' for which the movement was launched is not yet in evidence, but the issue helped in no small measure to launch both the BJP as well as Kejriwal into power, denouncing the corruption-embroiled reign of the Congress at the centre and the state. Kejriwal floated a party quite like a political start-up, fought elections to the Delhi assembly and managed to form government with the unsolicited help of the Congress. Even as chief minister, Kejriwal continued his agitational politics against the centre in the streets and endeared himself immensely to the people of Delhi. Actions like resigning from the chief ministership in just forty-nine days over the issue of the Lokpal Bill added to his appeal.

The support Kejriwal had received and his overweening ambition led him into the misadventure of contesting Lok Sabha elections all over the country. After a dismal showing in the general elections of 2014, Kejriwal and his party stunned every observer by winning sixty-seven seats out of seventy to the Delhi assembly in January 2015. His Aam Aadmi Party enthused progressive youths who saw it as a new model of politics. However, they were soon disillusioned and Kejriwal is fast slipping into the familiar mould of the politician. His party, increasingly identifiable as his personal vehicle, carries on, reportedly doing some good work but it is still a far cry from all that it promised to be. Reflecting Kejriwal's ambition, it has been fighting elections in most states but without success. What is behind the clicking of Kejriwal and his AAP in the political marshland of India? Do they really represent an alternative to established politics? Can there really be one within the present framework? Does transparency of personal finances make ideology redundant? All these and related issues are addressed in the last chapter "Aam Aadmi Party: A Political App for the Neoliberal Era".

If Kejriwal appeared as an aam aadmi (common man) who became khas (special), Rahul Gandhi was born khas but is at pains to appear aam. He comes across as a reluctant politician, a point the media never tires in making. It has been the fate of Nehru's descendants to assume leadership of the Congress, most times unprepared. To the dismay of observers, most of them managed to inhabit the role they donned, except Rahul, or at least until now. He is unlucky to some extent, being pitched against a formidable opponent in Narendra Modi—an astute politician with RSS training, backed by the well-oiled machinery of the parivar and the support of global capital. If the legacy of Congress governments—from soft hindutva to being widely identified with corruption and the neoliberal economy—has weighed Rahul Gandhi down, he seems wanting in political imagination too.

Staying overnight in the huts of dalits is all very well but his struggle to imagine himself into the shoes of the powerless and to articulate their aspirations has so far made for just low comedy, or painful viewing. "The Aerocasteics of the Congress, the Acrobatics of Ambedkarites" takes up one of his public utterances to probe the values and worldview of the man who is now president of the Congress party, his misunderstanding of caste a reflection of the persistent and unreformed casteism that has prevented the Congress from recognising dalits sans condescension over the decades since independence. Under assault from Modi's political sledgehammer, the Congress ought to have woken up to reality and devised a real counter to the BJP. But its conduct in the Gujarat elections of November 2017 may leave even an anti-BJP person seething with anger. Even critics of the Congress who hold it responsible for every ill that the country endures, would still support it to thwart the imminent danger of hindutva fascism. When Rahul Gandhi asserts his Hinduness unprompted, with much-publicised visits to temples during his campaign in Gujarat, projecting himself as a janeu-dhari (thread-bearing) brahmin, he exposes not merely his lack of imagination, but the reactionary core of his political position which his displays of love for dalits can barely shroud.

These essays are rooted in our times and deal with issues which may be taken as crucial for our collective survival as a democratic republic. The issues assume particular importance at a juncture of history where the very idea of India we cherished—if we also complained unavailingly at its non-realisation—may be lost forever. Today, as our institutions get saffronised, our cultures hinduised, our diversity undermined, we recognise the impact of hindutva forces as a setback to what little good was accomplished during the last seven decades. The democratic ethos stands destroyed as terror gangs are unleashed to accomplish what the government's coercive system cannot. The first four years of Modi's rule may just be a foretaste of what lies ahead.

His success also brings home to us many of our failures: the failure to comprehend the facts in systemic terms by taking every outrage as though it were a discrete occurrence or a manifestation of the personal infirmities of politicians; the failure to understand that this is a historical moment of triumph for the RSS with its most competent pracharak at the helm of state; the failure to recognise that what we see here is a working model of fascism in the neoliberal era. Some literal-minded analysts, dogmatic Marxists in particular, have occupied themselves with picking through the details to point out niggling differences between hindutva and the ur-model of 1920s fascism, as if fascism was an ahistorical and static phenomenon.

Modi's Gujarat model, which stands exposed today for its sell-out of state resources to global capital, done under the cover of a flashy rhetoric invoking a 'vibrant Gujarat' and Gujarati pride (asmita), proved more alluring to capital than what the Congress could show, particularly during its UPA II phase. Modi was skilful in convincing global investors of his management prowess. Despite the blot of being associated with the 2002 carnage of Muslims, he won successive elections while also managing to protect all involved in the pogrom. This amalgamation of strongman politics and neoliberal ethos was exactly what investors desired. The resultant compact with global capital was what enabled Modi to win the 2014 general elections. He has used his resources to tune up the party organisation, with unitary control of both the government as well as the party in his hands. He has fortified his position by consolidating his 'Hindu' constituency into bhakts (devotees) and rendered others helpless by decimating the opposition with a kind of TINA (there is no alternative) situation coming to prevail. However harassed people may feel by his policies, or disillusioned on realising that he has not delivered on any of his promises, they will continue to be deluded into voting for him. Modi's cultivation of a fascistic persona lends confidence to the RSS in realising its goal. If his international backers see unimpeded access to the spoils of India—its market and natural resources—on the horizon, that is where his domestic backers now see the sun rising on a Hindu rashtra.

The closest analogue of the Hindu rashtra is indeed the fascist model that operated in the 1920s and 1930s in Italy and Germany, and which so impressed the progenitors of hindutva, from B.S. Moonje and V.D. Savarkar to M.S. Golwalkar. There, an economy of efficiencies had combined cheerfully with primitive identity politics and state-sponsored civil violence; the erosion of rights and freedom ran parallel with evocations of a fictional past glory on the verge of return. Although previous sarsanghchalaks avoided mentioning it, the current one, Mohan Bhagwat, is emboldened by the political successes of the BJP to verbalise the connection. For instance, Bhagwat emphasised the need to bring about 'uniformity' in the country and explicated it with Golwalkar's phrase, 'one language, one nation, one God and one religion', echoing Nazi Germany's infamous 'ein Volk, ein Reich, ein Führer'.

For Bhagwat, India is already a Hindu rashtra. Strange as it may sound, the seeds of it were sown in the Constitution itself when the advisory committee headed by none other than Nehru rejected the decision of the subcommittee to include secularism in the Constitution. Instead, it was decided that the state should not have a religion but would treat all religions equally—expressed loftily in Sanskritic coinages, dharmanirapekshata or sarva dharma samabhava. It was not realised that a state constituted as a democratic polity, its government elected through the first-past-the-post system, is bound to be responsive to the will of the majority and in turn, their religion. It is an open secret that the rituals and customs of Hinduism—for instance, bhoomi pujan, or the consecration of land before the commencement of building works—are followed by the state as a matter of course. The Sanskrit formulation to which the early statesmen reflexively turned in articulating their vision of the future should have offered a clue. The myth that India is a secular country has lived on despite evidence to the contrary from within Nehru's own government. The Supreme Court, as custodian of the Constitution, went on to openly declare in 1995, 'Hindutva is not a religion, but a way of life and a state of mind,' and declined to revisit its stand when we (Teesta Setalvad, Shamsul Islam and I) challenged it in 2016. During the last three years, hindutva marauders have had a free run on minorities, terrorising critics into silence by selectively murdering figures like Dr Narendra Dabholkar, Comrade Govind Pansare, Dr M.M. Kalburgi, and recently, Gauri Lankesh. While the Goa-based Sanatan Sanstha openly equates these acts with slaying demons, applauds the murder of Dabholkar, and was linked to the accused in the Pansare case, it remains untouched even as scores of other organisations are banned on the fabricated charge of naxalite connections.

Given the pace with which the forces of darkness are scaling the ramparts, to persist in believing that technicalities such as constitutional barriers will prove any hurdle to them would betray monumental naïveté.

1

Reservations

A Spark and the Blaze

Caste and reservations: the two words are yoked together in public discourse. A conversation about caste in urban India ends up being about reservations. If the interlocutor happens to be privileged, he or she attacks the very idea as undermining 'merit'. History, reason and even the facts of the case are at issue, so that a defender of reservations begins on the back foot, having first to explain the idea of merit as birth into privilege and the opportunities opened up by unearned social capital. The arguments that ensue have no neat endings. Just as we see a casual denunciation of reservations, we also see practically all communities—right from the shudras to brahmins—staking a claim to backwardness and demanding some form of reservations or another, their share of what has reductively come to be seen as social justice.

The caste system, weathering challenges and change over centuries, continues in its essence to espouse the principle of hierarchy. Caste has worked on the principle of assigning certain tasks to certain people, as determined by their birth. While the brahmins had absolute monopoly over reading and writing—mostly through the rote learning of scriptural material—the untouchables typically dragged and flayed dead cattle to turn the skin into useful objects. It does not occur to the opponents of reservations that their much revered Hindu social order was based on reservations of the worst kind. Brahmins did not have to prove any merit to avail of all privileges and assume dominance over society; the untouchables did not have to commit any crime to be condemned for generations to a societal hell. Caste equations, never as static as they are made to appear, have undergone epochal changes over time. While the caste–occupation linkage has weakened in modern times, what Ambedkar called the ascending scale of reverence and descending scale of contempt remains largely in place. The untouchability that was supposed to have been abolished is still intact, not to speak of the discrimination that is pervasively practised against the dalits. A dalit millionaire or chief justice or chief minister or even president can be—and often is—the object of casteist slurs. The reservation of social dignity for certain groups, and against others, has played a major role in the caste dynamics of modern times.

It was in the colonial era that the idea of reservations—as a corrective to the debilitating effects of caste—came to be formally introduced. It was not the British who introduced it first, though their massive exercises of census and data gathering came to shape the demographic self-awareness of castes and religious communities, starting with the first census of 1871. Across the subcontinent, castes and religious communities became conscious of their numbers, and justice came to be seen as a share in employment and education, if not in the larger swathe of resources controlled by the upper castes and the state. Modern means of communication and transport also played a big role in germinating caste solidarities across the geography of the subcontinent.

Shahu Maharaj (1874–1922), the king of Kolhapur in Western India, pioneered the idea of reservations. Having experienced brahmin arrogance in the infamous 'vedokta' episode, wherein he was denied the recitation of the vedas in courtly ritual because he was a shudra, he wanted to dismantle the dominance of brahmins in his administration; in 1902 he reserved half the seats for non-brahmins. In order to promote education among the non-brahmins so they could avail of this reservation, he opened schools and hostels. Shahu even challenged the monopoly of brahmins over priest-craft and set up institutions to train and employ the non-brahmin marathas as priests. Reservations became the answer of the non-brahmin movement wherever it acquired strength.

After Kolhapur, it gained ground in the Madras Presidency in the 1910s and 1920s under the aegis of the Justice Party–led non-brahmin movement which developed the concept of proportional representation for non-brahmins in ministries and government jobs. As against Shahu Maharaj's bias towards the untouchables, the non-brahmin reservations were mainly monopolised by the relatively better-off shudra castes, to the exclusion of dalits. The pitfalls of the non-brahmin movement that later morphed into the bahujan movement, or of the caste-based movement at large, could be clearly seen in these subtle shifts. Even Jotirao Phule (1827–1890), an early pioneer and an inspiration to Shahu Maharaj, whom Ambedkar regarded as one of his three gurus (the others being Kabir and the Buddha), with all his desire for dalit uplift could not override the caste contradiction. At the condolence meeting held after his death in Pune, his shudra followers did not allow entry to the untouchables. In 1895, five years after Phule's death, the Samaj decided to ban chambhars, dheds, mahars, and mangs from their meetings (Kshirsagar 1994, 372).

In the South, under pressure from the non-brahmin movement represented by Praja Mitra Mandali, the king of the princely state of Mysore, Krishna Raja Wadiyar IV, appointed the Miller Committee headed by Sir Lesley Miller in 1918 to survey the state of the non-brahmin castes and suggest measures for their uplift. The Miller Committee's report of 1919 came up with the scheme of proportional representation. This report became the blueprint for subsequent policies and comprised one of the documents referenced by Ambedkar while framing policies for proportionate representation of the Depressed Classes at the national level. Similar schemes were adopted later by other princely states such as Baroda and Travancore. A section of the shudra castes was hugely empowered by these reservations for non-brahmins, but the benefits did not extend to the untouchables. Tamil Nadu today, for instance, has a whopping 69 per cent reservation for almost the entire spectrum of non-brahmin castes, which correlates to the hegemonic hold of the backward castes in the state.

Reservations for the Depressed Classes, as the untouchables were officially termed then, came with the Government of India Act of 1935. During the Round Table Conferences (1931–32), in fierce contention with Gandhi, Ambedkar had won the dalits separate electorates with reserved seats. However, Gandhi went on to fast against the Communal Award and pressured Ambedkar into signing away separate electorates. The resulting agreement—the Poona Pact, signed on 24 September 1932—increased reserved seats for the dalits from 71 to 147 in provincial legislatures and 18 per cent of the total in the central legislature. One of the clauses of the pact provided for securing fair representation to the Depressed Classes in the public services, subject to such educational qualifications as may be laid down for appointment (*BAWS* 18, Part I, 368–9). In order to enhance educational qualifications, it also earmarked a sum out of the educational grant of every province to provide facilities to the dalits. These provisions were accepted by the government as an amendment to the Communal Award and were included in the Government of India Act of 1935. This was the source of reservations for dalits in educational institutions and public employment. From 1935 to 1943, reservations operated as a preferment policy since there were not enough qualified candidates to make a fixed quota viable. In 1943, when Ambedkar was a member of the viceroy's executive council, he got this policy transformed into a quota system reserving 8.5 per cent seats for dalits (believed to be the proportion of their population to the total) in educational institutions as well in public employment. One could say that reservations for the dalits in the familiar form of a quota system came into being in 1943 on the basis of their belonging to an administrative category called 'Scheduled Caste'. This policy was based on the premise that the untouchables were a distinctively stigmatised community that suffered deep social prejudice in Hindu society. It was agreed that the larger Hindu society—which ghettoised dalits and extracted unpaid labour from them all over the subcontinent—could not be relied upon to represent their interests or render an honest account of their dues. Therefore, a kind of mechanism was needed to ensure that their self-representation.

After the transfer of power in 1947, the political condition of the country was precarious. The Constituent Assembly acted as the parliament—its members elected by the members of the provincial assembly, who in turn had been elected in March 1946 through a limited franchise that included just 28 per cent of the people. The wounds of partition were still fresh. The Hindu nationalists were trying their best to turn the prevailing communal strife to advantage. The armed struggles of the peasantry led by the communists had just been quelled into an uneasy silence. The political integration of over five hundred princely states was achieved but their socio-economic integration was under question. The Congress party had claimed to represent all Indian people since its transformation from a club of Western-educated elites to a mass movement under Gandhi in 1916, but this claim was a fig leaf to cover the party's bias towards the nascent industrial–capitalist class. Jawaharlal Nehru, who took over the reins of power, had a Fabian vision of India as a modern developed nation along capitalist lines. In such a situation, the Congress could ill-afford social unrest or any loss of face as the champion of the downtrodden; it was hardly in a position to reverse social justice measures that the dalits had won from the colonial power. Ambedkar's induction into the CA (after he lost his Khulna–Jessore seat in Bengal due to Partition) and his being made chairman of its most important committee—the drafting committee—were intended as a reassurance to the dalit audience, to make them feel like stakeholders in the Constitution. This Gandhian masterstroke has proved its efficacy in full measure. Despite Ambedkar's own disclosure—in a statement to the Rajya Sabha on 2 September 1953—that he was used by the Congress as a hack to write the Constitution, which was of no use to anyone, dalits by and large continue to swear by the Constitution.

The CA adopted the category of Scheduled Castes by replacing The Government of India (Scheduled Castes) Order, 1936, with one of its own: The Constitution (Scheduled Castes) Order, 1950. It wanted to extend safeguards and social justice measures to the adivasis and promulgated another order, The Constitution (Scheduled Tribes) Order, 1950. This initiative served the Congress by exhibiting its commitment to social justice but in reality diluted the only viable concept of reservation—as an exceptional measure for people in a historically exceptional position. There was little doubt that the dalits were people in a historically exceptional position, suffering the consequences of deep-rooted social prejudice, who would never receive their due unless it was secured by some countervailing force. The case of the adivasis was different. No doubt, large numbers of them were traditionally detached from the mainstream and living in remote locations, but they did not suffer social ostracism comparable to the untouchables. Some of their communities had established kingdoms in their history. And many of those who settled on the plains became part of caste society. Nonetheless, the majority of the adivasis were in an extremely pitiable state and looked down upon because of backwardness along secular indices of development. The decision to extend reservations to them, like the dalits, could be welcomed on these grounds; but, equally, they could have been included within the same schedule—suitably renamed and with due enhancement of the quantum of reservation. Combining dalits and adivasis would have diluted the social stigma associated with the schedule of the dalits, since the adivasis were not untouchables. The argument that a joint quota would not ensure that the adivasis accessed their rightful share applies also to the various groups, at varying levels of development, who make up the 'Scheduled Castes' bloc. It would have been a step towards the annihilation of caste. But it remained a step untaken. Instead, the government created a parallel schedule, replacing caste with tribe, and thus conserved the caste identity of the dalits.

This calculation was further extended to the OBCs. Article 340 of the Constitution mandated that the government identify 'classes' which were 'socially and educationally backward', and implement measures 'to remove such difficulties [so] as to improve their condition'. The catch in this innocuous seeming article is that backward 'classes' means 'castes' for all intents and purposes, while carefully sidestepping the word.

The political scientist, Christophe Jaffrelot, in his essay "The politics of OBCs" (2005), traces the origin and usage of the expression 'backward classes' to the early non-brahmin movement of 1870s in the Madras Presidency, and observes:

> When India achieved independence, Nehru gave them a new name, though hardly more satisfactory: 'other backward classes', implying classes other than the untouchables and the tribes. But the key word here is 'classes': even if he was not the first to use it, Nehru was clearly intending to distance himself from an approach in terms of caste (41–2).

It is not as if Nehru was so anti-caste or progressive that he shied from the word caste. He was cast in the liberal mould and saw caste as primordial. He sought to wish caste away by not naming it as such. Whatever the reasons, the euphemism of class for caste entered the Constitution and has created confusion, a confusion that has been duly taken advantage of by the political classes with reservations for 'class' groups being read into the Constitution mischievously. The point of intersection between these terms caste and class is the term 'backward'. In a country characterised by graded inequality, to use Ambedkar's phrase, all people could claim social backwardness because even subcastes of brahmins could prove their 'social backwardness' in relation to some other group. With regard to educational backwardness, even today, seven decades after independence—with barely eight per cent of the population graduating—almost all castes could meet this criterion. This article built and packed a can of caste worms; what's more, with a convenient lid that could be lifted by the ruling classes at any moment, to re-caste anew all of society.

The cardinal criterion for reservations in a country characterised by pervasive backwardness can only be insurmountable social prejudice, which leaves no other recourse other than an especial measure such as the countervailing force of the state. Quotas represent that force. This criterion cannot be diluted into backwardness. Special measures taken for other groups may be defended as aimed against backwardness in general, ensuring that developmental investments by the state do not further enrich the traditional elites at the expense of the masses. Despite the provision of reservations galore, this is precisely what did not happen in India, where the rich have gotten steadily richer and the poor poorer.

The key to fathom the reservations imbroglio is to understand the duplicity of the native rulers who succeeded the British and have been driving this policy in the service of capital behind a facade of social justice. The structural provision for it built into the Constitution skilfully consecrates castes and religion under the pretext of delivering social justice (read reservations) to the 'lower' castes and retaining scope for the state to implement reforms. Nobody notes that reservations did not require castes as they were based on a composite administrative category called 'Scheduled Caste' of which no equivalent obtained in the social world. When the lawmakers outlawed untouchability, castes also should have been outlawed. Being an aspect of caste, untouchability would not go away unless castes were destroyed. Instead, our legislative history presents the spectacle of continually reinforced caste identities through proliferating reservation, accelerated by the introduction of the criterion of backwardness. Since castes and religions have a proven mettle in dividing the working class, capitalists can only relish their survival. What's more, their interests coincide with those of the political class, as caste and religion provide handy levers to manipulate the people away from livelihood issues.

Invoking constitutional provisions, various commissions were appointed—starting with the first Backward Classes Commission established in 1953 under the chairmanship of Kaka Kalelkar—to identify and devise measures in favour of the backward communities. Kalelkar identified 2,399 backward castes or communities in the country, of which 837 had been classified as the 'most backward'. The commission reiterated 'caste as the criterion' to determine backwardness and recommended caste-wise enumeration of population in the census of 1961, and among other steps, the reservation of 70 per cent seats in all technical and professional institutions as also the reservation of vacancies in all government services and local bodies for the OBCs. This report was not accepted by the government as there was no political necessity to do so at the time. However, it became politically expedient to implement the recommendations of the second backward classes commission—the Mandal Commission. The Janata Party, in its election manifesto of 1977 had promised a 'policy of special treatment' in favour of the weaker sections of society and reservation for the backward classes to the tune of 25 to 33 per cent in all appointments to government services and educational institutions. The Janata government duly appointed a backward classes commission under the chairmanship of B.P. Mandal, a member of parliament, with a view to get definite recommendations by which it could implement its election promises. The Mandal Commission identified 3,743 castes and communities as backward, a number that swelled to 5,013 by 2006. The population of OBCs was estimated to be 52 per cent of the total population, and a reservation of 27 per cent (since the total quantum of reservation had been limited to 50 per cent by the Supreme Court) for them in jobs and educational facilities was recommended. Since there has not been a caste-based census after 1931, wide ranging estimates of the OBC population are afloat. For instance, the National Family Health Survey estimated it at 32.4 per cent in 2002, as against the Mandal Commission's 52 per cent in 1979. However, it is not the population or the quantum of reservation for the OBCs that matters here; it is the principle that is in question.

The Mandal Commission report gathered dust for a decade until V.P. Singh's minority government suddenly decided to implement its recommendations, tabling the report in parliament on 7 August 1990. V.P. Singh's political compulsions were not lost on anyone. He had fallen out with jat supremo Devi Lal and consequently lost the support of a significant chunk of the ahir, jat, gujar and rajput (AJGAR) alliance, which also left the Janata Dal governments in Uttar Pradesh and Bihar shaky. He needed to break the Congress monolith in North India with a new caste combination and also to puncture the BJP's Hindu consolidation. The Mandal recommendations could potentially achieve all these objectives in one shot. Singh's caste game also passed for social justice, making him a messiah of the backward classes. Such ruses are not new to Indian politics and reservations have been the prime move each time. From 1972 to 1978, Devraj Urs in Karnataka had employed the stratagem by wooing certain subcastes of lingayats into a political alliance with the vokkaligas and giving the new grouping 50 per cent reservations. Barring brahmins and vaishyas, the remaining 92 per cent of the state's population qualified as OBCs. In Tamil Nadu, the Dravida movement broke the Congress' caste alliance between brahmins and dalits, to create a new ruling elite of the vellalars, chettiars, naidus, and mudaliars for whom 31 per cent reservations were created.

V.P. Singh's declaration was met with a spate of fiery protests all over the country, mainly by college students belonging to the privileged castes. While these protests were engineered by political rivals of Singh, they were not so much against the government or reservations to the OBCs as they were against the concept of reservation itself. In fact, there was so much confusion about the OBCs that many belonging to that category participated in these protests and even beat dalits who had come out in support of reservations for them. Urban dalits, not versed in the contradictions between themselves and the OBCs in rural India, supported the Mandal recommendations because they imagined their constituency swelling with this new addition. All hues of the left vied with one another in supporting the OBCs to prove their leftism; myopia blocked their analytical faculties. They failed to see that this would lead to casteisation of society which would eventually prove detrimental not only to the dalits, but also and most particularly to the idea of class unity. No one noted the paradox that the very nationalists who had initially seen quotas as a colonial policy of divide and rule, had made a political plaything of a social justice measure, turning it into a weapon to divide people and destroy the nation. And no one paused to question the Constitution that enabled their doing so.

Reservations in operation

The concept of reservations in its present form started as political representation developing through preferment policies in educational institutions and public employment. All three forms of reservation differ in terms of modalities of operation and efficacy, and hence need to be discussed separately. Reservation in legislature is clearly informed by the logic of representation. Ambedkar's original scheme of separate electorates had envisaged it as such, with the rationale that only a person elected independently by dalits from among themselves could truly represent them. Additionally, the dalits had a vote in the general constituency, which guaranteed that they would not be neglected by the general candidates. Once the Poona Pact annulled separate electorates, dalit candidates from the reserved constituencies depended more on securing the good graces of the majority community and its votes than those of dalits. Naturally, in the event of winning, they would be obligated to the majority community and its party. Right here the logic of representation gets punctured. While Ambedkar expressed satisfaction with the outcome of the Poona Pact (*BAWS* 18 Part I, 368–9), he came to realise its evil import and was not very enthusiastic about its inclusion in the Constitution. However, it got included as a scheme limited to ten years, its renewal at the end of that period dependent upon the findings of a proper review. As we have repeatedly seen, reservation not only gets flatly implemented but also automatically renewed before its expiry after each ten-year period, even without any special agitation for it. This clearly establishes that its real beneficiaries are the ruling classes and not the dalits. In a first-past-the-post system, the so-called dalit representatives inevitably carry out the writ of the caste Hindu majority, to the detriment of dalit interests. Ambedkar himself lost two elections post-independence. Such a majoritarianism has failed in creating a proportionate representation of dalits in legislative bodies, and instead manufactures stooges by way of dalit representation..

Reservation in educational institutions is premised on the supply–deficit situation. If there is enough supply of 'equal quality' education to meet the demand, reservations will be rendered meaningless. In the prevailing system of multilayered education, it acquires meaning insofar as it guarantees admission to the dalit students in coveted institutions run with public funds. The increasing number of private institutions that rival public ones today in the volume of supply are exempt from the obligation to provide reservations. In public institutions, reservations are effected by depressing the criteria of selection in the case of dalit students. This is premised on the unequal material resource endowment of dalit students and the discrimination they face in evaluation. It is true that dalit students face numerous odds due to their socio-economic condition that lead to their getting inferior education compared to non-dalits. It is also true that they suffer discrimination in subjective evaluation, although an increasing number of them have emerged with flying colours, even as toppers. While reservation in educational institutes is, generally speaking, justified and empirically seen to benefit the dalits, sufficient attention is not paid to alternatives that might have reduced its necessity while sparing dalits the huge psychological burden of lifelong devaluation. The alternative was instituting free, compulsory and universal education through a neighbourhood school system for all students up to the age of 14 (as was eventually adopted in 2009, with the Right to Education Act) and the abolition of any commercial intrusion into the educational sphere. If this had been done, much of the need for reservations could have been eliminated. Interestingly, there is not a word of protest against the multi-layered school system that grew over the years, education shops that mushroomed at the secondary and higher secondary level, and the rampant commercialisation of higher education that has been happening in recent years, which finds a variety of secular pretexts to exclude dalits. (The chapter "The Education Mantra and the Exclusion Sutra" deals with these issues at length.)

The true picture of reservations in jobs emerges if one considers the distribution of India's labour. The country's organised sector stands at just 6 per cent of the total workforce, and the public sector (including all government jobs) is about 66 per cent of the organised sector. This leaves us with the potential domain of reservation at just about 4 per cent of the total workforce. If our yardstick is the typical distribution of public employment among reserved categories—1.7 per cent in Class A jobs, 3.3 per cent in Class B, 65 per cent in Class C, and 30 per cent in Class D—one would realise that a microscopic part (0.002 per cent, combining Class A and Class B) of jobs in the total workforce is what educated candidates in the reserved category are really aiming at. All the noise about reservation from practically every caste is actually over this diminutive and diminishing pie of public employment.

Ambedkar's projection for these reservations was the occupation of important positions in the bureaucracy by university-educated dalits to form a protective canopy over the dalit masses. Within his lifetime he lamented the emergence of a contrary aftermath. Those who reached bureaucratic positions got engrossed with the advancement of their own family and paid no attention to the community. They constituted a thin upper-class layer over the vast dalit masses and, being vocal and visible, misrepresented both their true condition and interests. Contrary to Ambedkar's expectations, as a few dalits get pushed up the socio-economic ladder, they become increasingly detached from the dalit masses. The biggest and most basic outcome of the prevailing reservation system is that it benefits an individual or their immediate family but its cost is borne by the entire caste, mostly by those who can hardly avail its benefits. The grudge against the dalits, reflected in atrocities, can to some extent be attributed to the perception of reservations by other caste groups.

While the dalits must make their own cost–benefit analysis of reservations and see whether in net terms they have benefited from them, casteist remarks by detractors of the institution need to be unequivocally condemned. It has to be kept in mind that reservations are not reparations that the dalits are asking for, for wrongs done to them over millennia, but a token safeguard extended to the victims of an ongoing racism. If reparations for historical wrongs were on the agenda, not illegitimately as one may think today, this country would have to be sold a million times over to raise the amount. Reservations are simply a mechanism to ensure dalit participation, not a measure of justice. If the non-dalits had not suffered from the sickness of casteism, there would not have been any need for reservations. Already reservations are limited to the public sector, as if the operations of the private sphere were free of both caste consciousness and public investment. The modalities of implementation apart, in principle there cannot be any dispute that the dalits must get their due share in every sphere of public life simply because the caste prejudice against them is all-pervasive.

The main argument of the detractors of reservation is that it favours the undeserving or unmeritorious over the meritorious. This cocksureness is amazing, given the patent falsity and ignorance on which the argument is founded. A cursory look at India's placement in the global comity of states reveals what the capable management of so-called meritorious people has yielded till date. India still ranks near the bottom on every index of human development. Moreover, every negative parameter—whether the indices of illiteracy, poverty, malnourishment, disease, infant mortality, incarceration, internal displacement, or what you will—shows its highest concentration among traditionally marginalised people. When traditional deprivation continues to be inflicted with full force on their customary victims, what more evidence is needed against the claim of a purported secular meritocracy? Tellingly, the champions of meritocracy descend into full-blown casteism soon enough, with victim blaming. It is as if the most deprived and vulnerable sections of the population have conspired to remain in poverty, for the perverse satisfaction of defaming the country and holding back its progress. And soon it follows that candidates are disbarred from running for office in local government if they do not have a toilet in their home or enough education under their belt—as took place in Haryana and Rajasthan, with the backing of the Supreme Court in 2015. The court's judgement of 10 December—incidentally the International Human Rights Day—was welcomed by both state governments that saw themselves as striking a blow for meritocracy and felt vindicated, a matter we shall return to in due course.

The argument for merit deserves scrutiny for another reason. It needs to be pointed out that marks scored with rote learning and bought through extra coaching and tuition do not constitute merit. On the other hand, when dalit children schooled in villages, frequently in a hostile atmosphere, come out to compete in towns and cities, it is an attestation of both merit and spirit. Even in terms of marks, it has been found often enough that dalit students who perform well in objective evaluation are pushed down the scale when they come face to face with the subjectivity of an 'upper' caste assessor. Such a case from the very first IAS examination conducted by the UPSC in 1950 was retrieved from the archives of the National Library in Kolkata by A.K. Biswas, himself an IAS officer ("Sorry, Mr Das: Merit, caste... a tale of two IAS candidates", *Outlook*, 30 May 2016). A dalit candidate, Achyutananda Das, alumnus of the Calcutta University and the first Scheduled Caste entrant to the IAS, had scored the highest marks in the written examinations but was given the lowest marks in the viva voce. Similar discrimination is revealed in the case of the first Scheduled Tribe candidate to enter the IAS, Nampui Jam Chonga from Assam, who cleared it in 1954. These discoveries are obviously not an accidental exception but indicate the general rot. If they have topped various exams in the country, it is despite this pervasive societal sickness.

Lacking in cultural capital and the material facilities their privileged counterparts take for granted, dalit and adivasi students often have to surmount several hurdles to make it to a university in the first place. Despite these hurdles, when 'quota' students fare well in the written entrance test, they are often 'shown their place' in the viva voce—this issue is at the heart of the struggles led by dalit students in elite institutions like Jawaharlal Nehru University. Muthukrishnan, a dalit MPhil scholar at the Centre for Historical Studies in Jawaharlal Nehru University, who committed suicide in March 2017, wrote in a Facebook post: 'There is no Equality in MPhil/PhD Admission, there is no equality in viva voce, there is only denial of equality'. Till 2016, JNU weighted the written exam and the viva voce at 70:30; while student bodies demand the viva voce to be reduced to only 15 per cent, JNU has adopted the University Grants Commission (Minimum Standards and Procedure for Award of MPhil/ PhD Degrees) Regulation, 2016, which converted the written exam into only a qualifying exam, and made the viva voce the final determinant of admission.

The angle of repose

Although the caste system is a continuum of hierarchy, from some subcaste of brahmins at the top of the heap to the lowest among the dalits at the bottom (both imprecisely defined), with its associated discriminations across castes, there is a kink, a point of inflexion, that divides caste and non-caste communities. There is social osmosis on either side but no contact across. This understanding of castes is vital to the understanding of reservations. In providing reservations only to the untouchables, the absolute nature of this social divide was acknowledged. After independence, however, when the CA adopted this policy from the colonial regime, it subtly introduced the criterion of backwardness into it (Clause 2 of Article 29 of the Constitution). While this was the result of pulls and pressures within the CA, it also betrayed the biases of the new ruling classes. As noted earlier, this is reflected in the way the Constitution uses the term class but means caste. None other than Ambedkar, during the debate on the Constitution (1st Amendment) Act 1951, had said the 'backward classes… are nothing else but a collection of certain castes'. In a backward country, mapping backwardness in terms of castes was always going to be a vexatious proposition. After all, the problem of pervasive backwardness could hardly be solved through reservations. When one speaks about forward and backward castes, it is in reference to their location in a graded hierarchy. When it comes to the criterion of 'educational and social' backwardness, it becomes a contentious issue to identify forward castes. Even the brahmin, admittedly the most forward caste, has its subcastes, some of which legitimately qualify as educationally backward. The Constitution makers failed to conceptualise the singularity of reservations, necessitated by the inability of the larger society to treat its own people as equal. They also failed to understand that any such policy should be self-terminating and should therefore orient themselves towards destroying the conditions that brought caste and discrimination into being. Had reservation for the dalits been rationalised as stemming from the inability of society to treat them as equal, and contingent upon the preservation of the status quo, the measure would have shamed society and given it the incentive to overcome its disability at the earliest possible time to do away with the anomalous provision. Dalits, instead of being apologetic about accessing reservations, would train their vision upon opportunities beyond the limited share secured through reservations. There would not be a vested interest for any party to preserve the policy as it stands. Reservations, as formulated and implemented, lacked these basic principles. As a result, a token gesture got projected as a remedy for the backwardness of the subject-castes. The policy and programme of reservations makes the dalits out to be a disabled people, and society their magnanimous benefactor. It induces inferiority in the dalits, makes them defensive and an object of disdain in society. It replicates the caste ethos that expects the dalits to show gratitude for what others have given them. The entire conceptual structure is inverted and serves to perpetuate the problem.

In 1991, India formally switched to neoliberal economic reforms—an extremist form of capitalism. This strain of capitalism manifests through the torrent of policies of liberalisation, privatisation and globalisation, which unleash multi-dimensional crises on the entire lower strata and makes the state increasingly repressive to contain the expression of discontent. Concurrently, it makes people turn inward, seeking shelter and security in the occult, which results in the resurgence of fundamentalism and religiosity. This has happened in varying degrees all over the world. In India, it assumed organised form as the hindutva movement, seeking to recreate a brahminical paradigm in the form of a Hindu rashtra. The deadly cocktail of neoliberalism and hindutva, its potency sustained by caste and religion, may very largely be traced back to the Constitution and its errors of omission and commission. Reservation and secularism became the constitutional proxies, or stalking horses, of this virulent politics. Interestingly, when the policy thrust of neoliberalism is shrinking the public sector and thereby reserved openings, whether in education or employment, there has been a spurt in the demand for reservations by every conceivable caste/community. There is even a muffled demand from the BJP for extending them to the economically poor of the forward castes, duly echoed by Mayawati after her transmogrification into a 'sarvajan samaj' leader. There are pending demands, far more legitimate than most others, from backward (pasmanda) Muslims and dalit Christians. Even in this impossible situation, people refuse to reconsider whether it is a measure of social justice at all, let alone an efficacious one.

It is inconceivable how anyone could devise a system to accommodate the growing claims for reservation by communities unless of course the entire pie is summarily distributed to all the castes and communities in the same proportion as they constitute the total population. Impracticable as it is, even if such a system is implemented it would aggravate rather than solve the problem, as can already be seen from all the claims and counterclaims that came flooding into the enlarged domain of reservation. Ignoring the unequal resource base of castes, to institute pervasive reservations negates even social justice, making a mockery of the idea that certain groups stand in need of them for the chronic, historically deep-rooted prejudice against them in society.

The maratha agitation

The maratha community that indisputably dominates the social, economic and political space in Maharashtra, has organised huge processions since July 2016 in various cities of the state, with reservation as one of its demands. This is not the first time that such a dominant caste has come out in the streets demanding reservation. Before it, the gujjars in Rajasthan, the jats in the Northern belt, and the patels in Gujarat, to name just the prominent ones, have had their run. The marathas have still baffled observers by their mode of expression (they call it a muk morcha, or mute front) and mobilisation.

The protests were triggered by a crime: the gang rape and murder of a fourteen-year-old schoolgirl belonging to the maratha caste by four drunk men belonging to a Scheduled Caste, at Kopardi village in Ahmednagar district, Maharashtra, infamous otherwise for atrocities against the dalits. All four culprits were arrested almost immediately.

In fact, in November 2017, within sixteen months of the crime, a special court pronounced the death sentence on the three accused dalits. The incident evoked statewide condemnation as warranted. During the monsoon session of the assembly, the leader of the opposition Radhakrishna Vikhe Patil, who hails from Ahmednagar, stressed the caste angle and attributed the incident to the shield of protection provided to the dalits by the Scheduled Castes and Scheduled Tribes (Prevention of Atrocities) Act (PoA), 1989. This was ludicrous, to say the least, as it suggested that the marathas were vulnerable to violence by the dalits. It was also malevolent because Vikhe Patil's own district has a shameful history of atrocities against the dalits perpetrated by the marathas. In January 2013, three men of a family in Sonai village were murdered; a fourteen-year-old dalit boy at Kharda in Jamkhed tehsil was lynched in April 2014; in October the same year, three members of a dalit family were killed at Javkheda. In fact, in the same week as the Korpadi verdict was delivered, in the trial of the murder of seventeen-year-old Nitin Aage, a dalit, over his love affair with a maratha girl in 2014, an Ahmednagar court acquitted all the nine accused who were marathas. These are but routine incidents of violence and miscarriage of justice. The Kopardi incident is an exception in that the victim was a maratha. Several protests and bandhs were observed across Ahmednagar in August 2016 to demand the speedy arrest of and death penalty to the culprits. After a month, the protests assumed very different form and content under the banner of the Maratha Kranti Morcha (Maratha Revolutionary Front)—which cultivates the image of being an unaffiliated organisation spontaneously created by the protest movement, to the extent of not divulging the date of its foundation. The demand for speedy justice for the victim was overtaken by the demand for reservation for the marathas in education and jobs, and for the repeal of the PoA Act. New demands were added in due course—like the building of a Shiv Smarak (a memorial to Chhatrapati Shivaji) in the Arabian Sea, and taking back the Maharashtra Bhushan award from the brahmin bard Babasaheb Purandare for having allegedly insulted Jijamata (Shivaji's mother) in his writings. Shivaji, who carved out an empire from the declining Adilshahi sultanate of Bijapur in the seventeenth century, is the ultimate maratha icon.

Marathas, the most populous community in the state and dominant in every sphere, came out in the streets in unprecedented numbers with unusual calm to present their grievances. There is no face yet to the leadership of these massive demonstrations. As several lakhs marched silently without a visible leader, with no speeches and no slogans, each successive rally larger than the previous one, this novel show of strength stunned political observers. Unknown youngsters, some in their teens—girls in large numbers—were pushed forward as the face of the agitation.

Given the defeat of many of the maratha leaders in the general and assembly elections of 2014, and with some of them facing charges of corruption, however spontaneous these massive rallies may appear, they seem to have the tacit support and instigation of the Nationalist Congress Party (NCP) behind them. Later, as maratha leaders from the BJP and the Congress expressed support to the movement, its ownership became more diffuse, along with its potential to generate significant electoral gains for any single party. Significantly, this was the point at which the movement began to lose its lustre. A planned rally to Delhi on 20 November 2016 had to be cancelled in the wake of demonetisation, and attendance started to dwindle at marches in Maharashtra's cities.

The chain of silent rallies was apparently supported by professionals such as doctors, engineers, lawyers, accountants, etc., and executed by faceless youth who would not allow the involvement of any established politician. The scale of public mobilisation, however, makes this assertion unconvincing. There has been intermittent mention in the media of certain unnamed NCP politicians admitting to logistical support. The people who conceived of this form of struggle and sustain it may not reveal themselves, but they do exist. It is a creative strategy, using the spark of Kopardi to create a single blazing expression of maratha power, hitherto affiliated across parties. While the marathas marched without any slogan and dispersed without any speeches being made, their placards and saffron flags bore a menacing message to the dalits. Through their silence the crowds effectively communicated their anger, and more importantly, forged a consciousness of victimhood, which would be a lasting political asset in the days to come. The violent protests that the marathas, with pride in their warrior past, have frequently resorted to—like the protracted violence of 1977–79 orchestrated against dalits who demanded renaming the Marathwada University in Auranagbad after Dr B.R. Ambedkar—did not achieve these objectives. Violent protests are not easy to scale up, replicate over large areas, sustain over long periods, or control, and are prone to repression by the state.

The marathas, who are almost one-third of Maharashtra's population, are not a homogeneous community. Historically, they evolved from the farming caste of kunbis who took to military service in medieval times and started assuming a separate identity for themselves. Even so, they claimed a hierarchy of ninety-six clans. Real differentiation came about with the post-independence development process that created classes within the caste. A tiny but powerful section of elites that secured control over cooperatives of sugar, banks, educational institutions, factories, and politics, called gadhivarcha (topmost stratum) maratha, has its own political outfit in the NCP. The next section comprising owners of land, distribution agencies, transporters, contracting firms, and those controlling secondary cooperative societies, is the wadyavarcha (well-off stratum) maratha, which is with the Congress and the BJP. The rest of the population of marathas comprising small farmers are the wadivarcha (lower strata) maratha, who identify with the Shiv Sena and the Maharashtra Navnirman Sena. Enthused by the patidar agitation forcing the removal of Anandiben Patel from the post of chief minister of Gujarat on 3 August 2016, the NCP, after its electoral drubbing in 2014, saw an opportunity to use maratha anger over the Kopardi incident to mobilise them through seemingly apolitical protests. Caste groups jockeying for dominance make up the barely concealed subtext of the movement. This is apparent when we consider that Maharashtra's BJP chief minister (at the time of writing) Devendra Fadnavis—whose grip on power was threatened by the unrest—is only the second brahmin, after Manohar Joshi in 1995, to occupy the post since the formation of the state in 1960, amid a long run of the marathas. A significant detail is that marathas make up only 38 per cent of Fadnavis' council of ministers, compared to nearly 80 per cent in the previous NCP–Congress coalition; and this at a time when Maharashtrian brahmin ministers—Nitin Gadkari, Suresh Prabhu, Manohar Parrikar and Prakash Javadekar—have been prominent faces in the central government. To set aside the technicalities of funding and orchestration, the main argument of the marathas is that a majority of them are backward. This argument applies universally to any caste or community, including brahmins, and uses the logic of backwardness as the basis for reservation. It is true that the majority of the marathas (basically kunbis) are small landholders. Taking pride in their sociopolitical dominance, they neglected education as well as the changing economic environment for too long. Over the years, with a mounting agrarian crisis, mainly due to the policies of the government, accentuated by crop failures in Maharashtra in three consecutive seasons in 2014–15, they experienced a severe erosion of their status. In contrast, the dalits with little or no land turned towards education, following Babasaheb Ambedkar, seeking jobs and relatively secure lives. As early as 1954, the literacy level among the marathas was estimated at 7 per cent, when it stood at 11 per cent for the mahars. Increasingly, as their insecurities mount, the marathas resent this trend, foreseeing a future when their overlordship of the dalits would no more remain unchallenged. They do not seem to hold their elites—who have dominated state power, the economy and educational sectors—responsible for their misery.

According to a report in the *Indian Express* (27 June 2014), since 1960, 'more than half of all MLAs have been from the maratha community. Almost 50 per cent of educational institutions are controlled by maratha leaders. Of the 200-odd sugar factories, the mainstay of the state's economy, 168 are controlled by marathas. Of the district cooperative banks, 70 per cent are controlled by marathas.' As a community, they still own the most land (the 32 per cent share of marathas in the state's population possesses in excess of 75 per cent of its agricultural land) and dominate all spheres of public life. They know that it will not be easy to establish their credentials as a socially and educationally backward community fit for inclusion in the OBC list. If this were done, the other OBCs would be up in arms against them; some already are, as evidenced by the Mali Samaj Mahasangh's counter rally against the maratha demands at Nashik on 3 October 2016.

The other demand, asking for the repeal of the PoA Act, is aimed directly at the dalits and is still less tenable. The oft-repeated argument of the misuse of the law based on acquittals is self-refuting. The fact is that the entire state apparatus is directly dominated by marathas; as case after case reveals, this has rendered the act toothless. The conviction rate under the PoA Act still hovers around single digits in Maharashtra—it stood at 1 per cent in 2016. The very fact that a dalit victim of atrocity, unless backed by their community or helped by an NGO or a movement, finds it impossible to get a complaint registered, shows the argument of misuse to be mischievous. There have been a few cases where maratha bigwigs have misused the PoA Act by positioning some dalit as compared to their caste rivals, but these are few and far between.

The maratha demand for reservation as an OBC group has twice been rejected through institutional processes. In 2008, the Maharashtra State Backward Class Commission, basing its decision upon the report of the Justice R.M. Bapat Commission, had declared that marathas did not meet the social, educational, economic or political criteria to be recognised as backward. In 2014, four months short of the state elections in October, when the Congress–NCP government tried to introduce 16 per cent reservation for the marathas, the Bombay High Court overturned the decision for the same reasons, apart from the fact that additional reservation would take the quota of reserved seats above the 50 per cent limit set by the Supreme Court. When the dominant community develops a sense of grievance, it can lead to systemic change, provided it transcends its community identity. If not, it portends societal strife.

The cream and the whey

It is not as if every community listed as a scheduled caste or tribe has benefited from reservations. In 2015, the Supreme Court dismissed a public interest litigation (PIL) filed by O.P. Shukla, a retired official of the Indian Legal Services, seeking the exclusion of certain caste and tribal groups from the benefit of SC/ST reservations as they had cornered 99 per cent of the quota meant for the advancement of 1,677 castes and tribes listed in the Schedule. The case may have been dismissed but the plaintiff's argument still represents the inevitable fallout of the caste-centric reservation policy as it has been implemented, as also the upsurge of the subcaste squabbles that broke out in Andhra Pradesh between the malas and the madigas in the 1990s, which took the form of a virtual war and inspired others to raise the issue of sub-categorisation within reservation. The demand for sub-categorisation in aid of the madigas and rellis of Andhra Pradesh is pressed to this day by the Madiga Dandora—the popular name of the Madiga Reservation Porata Samithi. The demand may not be feasible but cannot be dismissed as baseless or motivated. The point is that it lays bare the limitations of the policy, whereby the malas have benefitted disproportionately from reservation. Now it is mangs versus mahars in Maharashtra, arundhatiyars versus parayars and pallars in Tamil Nadu, chamars versus other minor castes in the Northern states, and so on. Cashing in on this politically clever and relatively risk-free mode of servicing 'social justice', Nitish Kumar, as chief minister of Bihar, in 2007 established the State Mahadalit Commission, enlisting eighteen jatis (subsequently expanded to twenty-one) under this category, arguing that only a few jatis had cornered the benefits.

In O.P. Shukla's case, his brahmin surname perhaps signifies that he did not want to be identified with his own community, balmiki. However, he professed to have worked for its welfare over the previous thirty-five years and intervened in many matters that affect its well-being. Appearing to be a one-man force, Shukla claims he presides over the National Coordination Committee for Revision of Reservation Policy, consisting of representatives of extremely backward communities of SCs and STs from all over India. The hundred-page PIL, filed in 2011 by what seems to be a letter-head organisation, contended that the reservation policy in force for the previous sixty-one years was lopsided and had failed in its objective of uplifting the SCs/STs. The PIL argued that castes such as chamar, mahar, mala, dusad (paswan), passi, dhobi, etc—could now be removed from the list of the SCs. It is an unfortunate but undeniable fact that people of some populous castes, as named in the PIL, have benefited disproportionately from reservations, although not to the exaggerated extent the case tried to represent. Was this unexpected, given the characteristic hierarchical structure of society? Besides, after these groups were weeded out, wouldn't there again be some four to five dominant castes among the remainder to reproduce the problem it sought to resolve? This argument of categorisation is specious for another reason: taking caste as our basis it may appear that certain castes have monopolised the benefits of reservation, but if one changed the comparator to the family, the same picture would emerge within each caste—the beneficiaries of reservations are concentrated among a few families, while the majority is excluded. This essentially intra-caste inequality may be observed among all the castes who are supposed to have cornered the benefits of reservation.

The solution to this problem cannot lie in blaming the beneficiary castes and excluding them from the Schedule as the PIL demanded. Contrary to assumptions, equity was never the objective of the policy. Rather, propping up a few individuals from among the SCs and STs would have been its real objective, for they—and here the Indian ruling class went by Macaulay's colonialist logic—would then act as agents of the system. Reservations never had the wherewithal to do away with existing social inequality. At best, they might have been expected to counter the aggravation of inequality in the domains of education and government employment. Second, reservation did not extend to promoting SC representation across the board in these spheres. The policy, as noted, did not extend to the large number of privately funded educational institutes or to employment in the private sector; nor, for that matter, to all parts of the public sector where—for instance, in defence and the higher judiciary—posts were excluded from the purview of reservation on the grounds of being highly specialised.

Given the hollowing-out of state institutions as avenues of public sector employment due to neoliberal policies, the demand arose from among dalits for reservations in the private sector, expressed for the first time at the Bhopal Conference organised on 12–13 January 2002. In principle, there cannot be any dispute over this demand because the so-called private sector is not really private and thrives on public resources. However, the demand betrays naïveté about the private sector's capacity to implement reservation. While it is admittedly large and growing, unlike the public sector it is structurally amorphous and ranges from small family enterprises to giant corporate groups. Even the latter do not have the fixed organisational structure required for implementing a quota system. Again, this reservation may only be relevant for professionally educated people and not for the non-management workers. In all probability, blue-collar workers are already employed in private companies in larger numbers than the reservation percentage may entail. Instituting caste-based reservation may even lead to reducing their numbers and stigmatising their status, at least in some companies.

An appropriate system might have been affirmative action, with the government mandating the requisite representation of specified communities. Although not without its own problems, the kind of affirmative action practiced in the US—which stresses equitable representation for specific communities—perhaps works better. India fails abysmally in any diversity test of management and board-level employment. Here, casteist cunning reflects in the diminishing percentage of SC/ST representation as one goes up the bureaucratic ladder; the top layers having practically zero representation. Moreover, the Indian system lacks accountability, with no punitive provisions for defaulters—unlike affirmative action in the USA. But whatever the system, it should lead to curing the main disease and not to preserve or aggravate it. Reservation, by design, has squandered this core goal for short-term gains.

People of Shukla's ilk argue that every caste could be assigned its proportionate share of the quota: say, the statutory 8 per cent distributed equitably among the 1,670 castes on whose behalf he filed his case. Assuming that once the current monopolists of reservation have been weeded out, all the remaining SCs are of equal size and endowment, the average share per group would work out to 0.005 per cent. When and how with such a hare-brained scheme would the weaker castes hope to benefit? And what would be left of the dalit identity at the end of this process of subdividing reservations?

Certain ongoing developments in Tamil Nadu further complicate the picture. A section of pallars have refashioned themselves as 'mallar', 'devendrar' or 'devendrakula vellalar', claiming they were a class of rulers in the mythical past. Saying they are descendants of 'Lord Devendrar', another name for the vedic god Indra, they now demand *exclusion* from the Schedule. The concern here is that reservation and their inclusion in the Scheduled Caste list makes them out to be untouchable by another name and they repudiate both labels—SC and dalit. The Devendrar Charitable Trust passed a resolution in 2015 imploring the state government to declare the seven SC subcastes—pallar, kudumbar, pannadi, kaalaadi, kadayar, devendrakulatar and vaadhiriyaar—spread across Southern Tamil Nadu as 'devendrakula vellalars'. These efforts have unsurprisingly earned the support of the BJP president Amit Shah, whose stated mission is the creation of a Hindu rashtra. Shah addressed their rally in August 2015. However, there is a further wrinkle in the fabric: for a while now, one of the sub-castes clubbed with the seven has been resisting its nominal uplift into the aristocracy. A report in the *Hindu* (25 February 2011) read that a group of vaadhiriyaar petitioned the Tuticorin district collector thus: 'We, members of vaadhiriyaan sect, appeal to the government to allow us to be in the 72nd position in the list of Scheduled Castes, as we are getting the State Government benefits as a SC, privileges of the Centre as OBC and the Christian vaadhiriyaan as BC.' If one sub-caste can be identified in so many different ways, it demonstrates how intractable and mindboggling the problem is.

The Lokur Committee report of 1965—cited reverentially by Shukla—was submitted by B.N. Lokur, a secretary in the union ministry of law. It merely stated what was in the Constitution: the need to periodically review the list of the SCs, which was indeed done by adding a few more castes. Subcaste manipulation first started in Punjab as early as 1972, by subdividing the quota between ravidasias on the one hand and balmiki and mazhabi Sikhs on the other. The next big upsurge was witnessed in the neoliberal era, most notably in Haryana (categorisation of claimant communities by priority, into A and B, as per the recommendation made in December 1990 by the Justice Gurnam Singh Commission), Andhra Pradesh (categorisation into A, B, C and D as per the recommendation of the Justice Ramchandra

Raju Commission in May 1997), and Bihar. All this, of course, at a time when reservations as an avenue of employment have been virtually exhausted by the continued shrinkage of the public sector, along with the hope of any radical change in caste society effectuated through the Constitution.

A rural reality check

Let us now turn to how reservations work or do not work in rural India, where close to 80 per cent of the dalit population and 70 per cent of the overall population live. Ambedkar, the architect of the reservation programme, did not of course romanticize the village. He minced no words when he told the Constituent Assembly on 4 November 1948: 'What is the village but a sink of localism, a den of ignorance, narrow-mindedness and communalism? I am glad that the Draft Constitution has discarded the village and adopted the individual as its unit' (in Das 2010, 176).

Although the village panchayat is flaunted as India's traditional governing institution, it was always a jati panchayat, in the manner of a khap panchayat, and did not have much to do with its current avatar. The roots of contemporary panchayati raj can be traced to the colonial logic of Ripon's resolution of May 1882, which aimed at involving the 'intelligent class of public-spirited men in the management of rural areas under the British rule'. It led to the setting up of district and taluka boards with nominated members to look after health, roads, and education, but failed to make the village the basic unit of local self-government. The Montagu–Chelmsford Reforms of 1919 revived the idea and in almost all provinces and native states laws were enacted for the establishment of village panchayats.

After independence, panchayati raj was re-inaugurated by Nehru in 1959, following the Balwant Rai Mehta Committee recommendations of 1957, but the scheme fell through, impelling scholars to declare by 1960 that panchayati raj institutions were 'the God[s] that failed'. By 1970, the

Nehruvian modernist project had fructified, but even as land reforms and the Green Revolution introduced capitalist relations of production in the agrarian sector—with machine-intensive monocultures of cash crops, large surpluses and market access—and brought huge gains to a section of the farming castes, they led in equal measure to the vulnerability of the dalits. The collapse of traditional jajmani relations, wherein the tiller or sharecropper had a share in the produce as well as autonomy in the tillage of a certain part of the landlord's fields, tilted the scales further. A class of middle and rich peasantry emerged out of the traditional farming castes, taking over the baton of brahminism from erstwhile upper caste landlords, aggressively pursuing more power and resources, leading to the rise of regional parties and the inauguration of an era of coalition politics. The Janata government, the first manifestation thereof in 1977, attempted to rejuvenate the panchayati raj institutions through the Ashok Mehta Committee—which submitted its report in 1978 with 132 recommendations to revive rural self-government—but without much success. Over the years, local interests became more varied and complex; in fact, too complex for a centralised polity to handle. Paradoxically, the Communist Party of India (Marxist)-led Left Front government in West Bengal was the first to realise the importance of panchayati raj for sustaining political power. The effective implementation of land reforms and the panchayati system there, since 1984, had buttressed the aspirations of the middle and rich peasantry and given them access to power and resources. This was the key factor behind the LF's lasting electoral success until 2011. Whereas at the centre, the implementation of the Mandal Commission recommendations became the strategy of choice to placate these sections.

It was only from the mid-1980s and formally from July 1991—the same month as the introduction of economic liberalisation by the then finance minister Manmohan Singh—that concrete steps were taken to implement the panchayati system. The strategy was to prepare for a diminishing role of the state by relegating governance of local issues to the local leadership. The legislation had the progressive veneer of anti-caste, anti-patriarchy provisions as seen in the 73rd and 74th amendments passed in 1993 for rural and urban self-government respectively, with one-third of all seats reserved for women, SC, ST and OBC members. This decentralising measure would focus rural political energies on local concerns and coexist with the new economic regime, ensuring its sustenance without in any way turning into a threat.

What about the social change it was meant to herald in the countryside? The ground reality is that in a substantial number of cases the candidates who have won panchayat elections are mere fronts for the old power holders. In case the reserved seat is for a woman, it is usually the wife or daughter-in-law of the old sarpanch who is made to sign papers while the husband or the father-in-law transacts all business. Where the reservation is for the SC/STs, it is the bonded labourer of the sarpanch who becomes his proxy. In other cases, some SC/STs may be lured to share the spoils with the power elite, under the tutelage of the latter. Only in exceptional cases have the dalits challenged and confronted the dominant classes/castes—often having to pay with their lives. Thus, it is rich peasants and landlords of the dominant castes that exercise de facto political power at the local level and control the institutions of panchayati raj.

Disincentives to the participation and leadership of dalits as well as women are built into the way the panchayati system operates. They have usually been applied through a localised violence, but are now also taking a statutory shape. In 2015, the BJP-ruled states of Rajasthan and Haryana introduced new criteria of eligibility to contest panchayat elections. Haryana mandated that unlettered people could no longer run for office, that a male SC candidate had to have completed Class 8 of his schooling and a female SC candidate Class 5, in order to be eligible—as if their illiteracy was self-willed and not a failure of the state. At one blow, 68 per cent of SC women voters and 41 per cent men were disqualified from standing for election. Challenged in the Supreme Court, a bench comprising Justices J. Chelameswar and Abhay Manohar Sapre upheld the new law in December the same year. The judges agreed that the new law created two classes of voters but found no merit in the argument that people do not choose to be illiterate, going on to assert that leaders had to serve as role models to society. For this reason, the court also upheld the Haryana government's stipulation that candidates must have a functional toilet in their homes, acceding to the argument of the defense that 'if people still do not have a toilet it is not because of their poverty but because of their lacking the requisite will'. The Rajasthan law had come into being earlier, in the form of an ordinance, before panchayat elections in December 2014, and was then enacted by the state legislature the following year. The stipulations about toilets and minimum educational qualifications had originated with the Rajasthan ordinance. In one dovetailed stroke of efficiency, the Supreme Court's judgement in the Haryana case secured the future for Rajasthan's law as well.

A steady constriction of participation and empowerment opportunities for SCs, STs and women—beneficiaries of reservation in local governments—has accompanied the operation of panchayati raj ever since its introduction. Even before Rajasthan and Haryana showed how this could be accomplished through legal measures, it operated on the ground—as it continues to do—through violent reprisals against elected dalit and female leaders.

Krishnaveni, a dalit woman of the arundhatiyar caste (a scavenging community, the third major dalit caste in the hierarchy after parayar and pallar in Tamil Nadu), a school dropout and mother of two, had contested the election in 2007 as an independent candidate in the Thalaiyuthu panchayat in Tirunelveli district, when it was declared reserved for dalit women candidates. She won by a margin of 700 votes and became the sarpanch. Her sincerity and work earned widespread respect. Her fellow-villagers spoke with admiration about how she had managed the construction of roads, the building of a library, and the speedy development of infrastructure. They also vouched for her integrity, and commended the way she had conducted herself in the face of continuing threats from the dominant castes. In recognition of her work, she received the Sarojini Naidu Award for 2009 from President Pratibha Patil for the best (district-level) implementation of the National Rural Employment Guarantee Scheme. Her accomplishments however came as a rubbing of salt to the wounded egos of the old power elites, who could not bear the fact that an arundhatiyar woman was their boss, winning accolades at that. Apart from their caste prejudice, their material interests were also affected as she would not allow panchayat funds to be siphoned off. Krishnaveni filed more than fifteen complaints against her aggressors, including the vice-president and ward members, who were obstructing her work. However, the district administration and police did not pay heed. Instead, the impression was created that she was quarrelsome and could slap cases under the PoA Act against her detractors.

On 13 June 2011, at around 10 pm, as she was returning from the panchayat office in an auto rickshaw, she was attacked murderously by a group of people. The immediate trigger was her plan to build a toilet for dalit women on some poramboke (common) land that was illegally occupied by a thevar, a dominant backward caste. She was hacked all over the body and left for dead. After days in the ICU—initially at Tirunelveli, and later moved to Chennai thanks to the efforts of young activists of the arundatiyar community—she survived fifteen stab wounds and a hacked ear. The activists also mobilised people to agitate in protest and managed to get established dalit leaders like Thol Thirumavalavan and John Pandian to support them. Still, they could not move the media and the state administration out of their habitual apathy towards dalit issues.

The case was strikingly reminiscent of two earlier incidents that took place in the same Tirunelveli district in 2006 and 2007, when the panchayat presidents of Nakkalamuthanpatti, P. Jaggaiyan and Maruthankinaru Servaaran, who also belonged to the arundhatiyar community, were murdered by members of the dominant castes. In a similar manner, in 1997, a dalit panchayat president, Murugesan, and six of his relatives were done to death near Madurai for having dared to contest the election. About the same time, the villages of Pappapatti and Keeripatti, also in Madurai district, made news by refusing to allow panchayat elections once these constituencies were reserved for dalits. A social diktat was enough to ensure that no dalit filed the papers, the execution of Murugesan and his six relatives in Melavalavu serving as a warning. Back then, the dominant thevars of the village had said, 'An untouchable may well be the president of India but in our villages we'll not suffer an untouchable president.' The allusion was to President K.R. Narayanan. It was only in 2006, after much effort by NGOs, dalit and left groups, that Pappapatti and Keeripatti relented to allow a dalit to represent them.

In all these cases, there was a recorded history of threats and harassment by the dominant castes and of the administration's persistent negligence in taking note of them. Jaggaiyan's case is a classic illustration of how panchayati raj becomes the de facto rule of the dominant castes. Before Jaggaiyan, when the post of sarpanch was reserved for women, the wife of Thirupathi Raja, a powerful landlord belonging to the kamma naidu (naicker) community, served as his proxy in the post of sarpanch. The next time, when the post was reserved for SCs, Raja financed Jaggaiyan's election, expecting his loyalty. However, when Jaggaiyan showed independence and defied Raja's dominance, he was murdered.

With no acknowledgement of the structural propensities under which power and domination play out in rural India, the rhetoric of the decentralisation of power—with its blanket eulogies to panchayati raj—simply encourages rural elites to establish and maintain control over subordinate groups. The wheel comes full circle when laws such as those passed by the Rajasthan and Haryana assemblies make it apparent that tokenism rather than empowerment is the object of reservation. A plethora of literature on panchayati raj suggests that formal regulations stipulating the participation of people like dalits and women have had minimal impact on the functioning of the panchayats. There is also evidence, albeit in limited cases, that decentralisation has helped these groups to make their presence felt in local political institutions, implying that when marginalised groups are empowered and panchayats made democratic, they can act as agents of social change. The state has a definite role and responsibility in this—inter alia, the district collector and superintendent of police should be made personally responsible for any instances of the violation of rights of the SC/STs and women. This is the least the state must do if it means to stand by its pronouncements on panchayati raj. However, the routine nature of atrocities against dalit sarpanches—who are prevented from even hoisting the national flag on Republic Day, as happened in 2012 with A. Kalaimani, a dalit woman panchayat president of Karu Vadatheru village in Pudukottai district, Tamil Nadu—provide stark validation of what Ambedkar had said decades ago about villages being a sink of localism and a den of ignorance. Office holders who do not buckle despite threats to their lives seldom have the backing of the state; they can only register a personal protest—as Krishnaveni did on Independence Day in 2007, by unfurling a black flag instead of the tricolour.

Skullduggery and cynicism

While eternally useful to politicians, the idea of reservations has been problematic with regard to its professed objective. Since reservation for the SCs and STs is premised on social prejudice, its outright abolition is out of the question while these prejudices are still visible. On the other hand, there is certainly a case for plugging the obvious lacunae. Applied flatly, reservations promote the interests of the better placed among the target population. As a result, while a small section of the population progresses, the rest gets left behind. At the time when reservations were conceived for the SCs and STs, these considerations were not material simply because there was no visible elite among them. Whoever came into prominence was to be a role model for the rest and was trusted to represent their interests. Now that the third and even fourth generation of beneficiaries are around, the evils of the system have surfaced clearly. Most issues of democratic representation sought to be addressed through reservations could perhaps be resolved better by an electoral system of proportional representation, as proposed by many analysts. In evaluating the present terrain, we must keep in sight the fact that someone like Ambedkar could never win an election in post-independence India. Rather than a reasoned debate on the shortcomings of reservations as a panacea, what we have witnessed instead is merely a clamour for its extension to various communities that claim backwardness. The inner compatibility of a deeply flawed system of reservation and parliamentary democracy with the caste system has given rise to various competitive claims to redress.

The judiciary has so far ensured that claimants to OBC status do not enjoy an easy passage, as the marathas have repeatedly discovered. However, with the central government's new Constitution (One Hundred and Twenty-Third Amendment) Bill, 2017, the National Commission for Backward Classes is set to acquire the same constitutional status as the commissions for SCs and STs—the NCSC and NCST, respectively. More importantly, the bill recognises parliament as the final arbiter of changes to the OBC list. Which way parliament will lean when confronted with the demands of wealthy and populous communities like the marathas, patidars and jats, is easy to predict. The agitations of gujjars, jats, patels, marathas and sometimes even sections of brahmins demanding reservations are, after all, encouraged by the electoral promises of parties. When the category of 'backward' became too bulky to accommodate new entrants, 'special' and 'other' species of backwardness were devised. At present, eleven states and union territories have a sub-categorisation for the induction of OBCs into their state services. These comprise Tamil Nadu, Puducherry, Karnataka, Andhra Pradesh, Telangana, Haryana, Jharkhand, Bihar, West Bengal, Maharashtra and Jammu and Kashmir. The system in Andhra Pradesh, cited twice by the Supreme Court in 1972 and 1993, inspired the NCBC to recommend that OBCs be divided into three categories: A, consisting of Extremely Backward Classes (EBC); B, of More Backward Classes (MBC); and C, Backward Classes (BC). The EBC in Group A would consist of aboriginal tribes, denotified tribes or vimukta jatis, and nomadic and semi-nomadic tribes. Group B would include vocational groups such as blacksmiths, brass smiths, weavers, carpenters, etc. Group C would have OBC communities with a business or agricultural background—or, if we prefer an Orwellian touch, the other Other Backward Classes. In a system of graded hierarchy, the possibilities of caste-related grievances and improvisatory forms of redress are endless. Reservation has been politically useful as a substitute for explicit exhortations to caste mobilisation—forbidden by the Constitution—and is being skilfully exploited by political parties. The sway of caste identities in influencing voter groups has intensified with the collapse of the hegemony of the national parties, the emergence of regional parties, and the rise of coalition politics. Reservations have become the operative via media to influence castes. The social justice pedigree of reservations imparts a progressive veneer to such rhetoric.

Let us now consider the skullduggery and cynicism that underlie the pieties mouthed by political parties on reservation, as illustrated in the ongoing agitation of gujjars in Rajasthan to get reservation as a Special Backward Class. Gujjars, a caste in the Northern, North-Western and Western parts of India were designated as STs in Jammu and Kashmir and Himachal Pradesh, but in all the other states in this region—Uttar Pradesh, Rajasthan, Haryana, and Gujarat—they are classified as an OBC. The British government had designated the gujjars as a criminal tribe in 1857 and they were duly brought under the Criminal Tribes

Act of 1924, repealed by Vallabhbhai Patel's Home Ministry in 1949, its 'criminal tribes' denotified in 1952. In Rajasthan, they had staked a claim to ST status in 1981 but a committee constituted by the then Congress government rejected it on the basis of criteria laid down for being an ST—only a minority of the community was found to live in the hills and ravines, and the majority was not cut off from mainstream society. The demand surfaced again in 2003, was expressed with mild protests in December 2006, and took the shape of a violent movement in the summer of 2007, when twenty-six people, including some policemen, lost their lives.

The gujjar agitation against the state inevitably provoked the meenas, a prominent ST community in Rajasthan that enjoys the greatest share of the ST reservation and would not brook gujjar inroads upon its domain. In December 2007, the gujjar demand for recognition as an ST was rejected again, this time by the four-member Justice Jasraj Chopra Committee which recommended a special package of welfare measures for the community instead, particularly in remote areas. This package of Rs 282 crore was duly prepared by the state's BJP government of the time, only to be rejected by the gujjar leadership. In December 2008, a new Congress government was formed, which tried to create a special reservation of 5 per cent for the gujjars. The decision was challenged in court and struck down by the Rajasthan High Court's verdict of December 2010. These events established the contours of the story which has proceeded along the same tortuous lines ever since, with sporadic outbreaks of protest and violence, changes of government, readjustment of demands, animosity between competing social groups, and court verdicts that pour cold water over the compromises struck between the gujjars and the state government. In December 2016, the High Court overturned the latest political accommodation of gujjar demands by the BJP state government that attempted to secure them a 5 per cent quota in employment by clubbing them together with four other groups, all deemed SBCs; the court struck down the SBC Reservation

Act passed by the state legislature the previous year. On its part, the gujjar leadership has accused the government of acting in bad faith by sabotaging its own case, and threatened to relaunch the movement.

Gujjars, as an OBC, do enjoy reservations in Rajasthan. Why then did they want to be designated as ST? There are three reasons. First, the proportion of reservations in the ST category, at 12 per cent, is generous vis-à-vis the proportion of gujjars in the population, seen against the 27 per cent quota for OBCs that falls way short of the claimed 52 per cent of OBCs in the state population and has given rise to intense competition. Well-off gujjars stand a better chance of bagging the reserved seats in employment and educational institutions as STs than as OBCs. In the latter category, they complain it is jats who corner all the benefits. Second, gujjars are already recognised as STs in two states. Third, there is a possibility of such inclusion as evidenced by the case of meenas, who secured it in 1954 and have since become a formidable community in the state. Getting SC status might equally have conferred these advantages and therefore it is pertinent to ask why the gujjars do not ask for that. The answer is that unlike any other reserved category, there is a social stigma associated with the SC status, which no non-SC caste would like to incur no matter what the benefit. In fact, during the first colonial-era censuses several communities that were subjected to untouchability—such as the toddy-tapper caste of ezhavas, or the shanans who refashioned themselves as nadars in South India—opted out of being classified as untouchable once they realised they were being slotted with castes perceived to be inferior. The other reason for gujjars not opting for the SC label is the more definitive criterion of belonging to an ex-untouchable caste to be an SC, unlike the relatively fluid criteria for being an ST.

We see that reservation-centric politics plays out along three main axes: one, demanding reservation for certain social groups such as dalit Christians, pasmanda Muslims, and so on; two, backing demands by certain castes to be included in the reserved categories; and three, inciting demands from certain subcastes for a split in the quota of a conglomerate reserved category (as raised by the madigas in Andhra Pradesh). All of these inevitably create inter-caste conflict, which is turned to their advantage by political parties.

After the basic schedules for the SCs and STs were prepared in 1936 and 1950 respectively, there have been many subsequent inclusions of caste groups within them. (For instance, in 2014, from Haryana alone the communities of aheria, aheri, heri, naik, thori, turi, hari, rai Sikh, banjara, dhobi and dhobirajak were recommended for inclusion in the list of Scheduled Castes, though not all made it. Each state makes such recommendations, but an amendment to the list of Scheduled Castes can be effected only by an Act of Parliament, in view of clause (2) of Article 341.) The meenas, who have come out in the open to oppose the demands of the gujjars, are an example of such inclusion as an afterthought. In Rajasthan, they constitute 10 per cent of the population and virtually monopolise the ST reservations. But the gujjars who constitute 7.5 per cent of the population have become important enough in the coalition era. This is why their demands have received a sympathetic hearing from both the major political parties of the state—later state governments have also attempted to see them through—with even the Samajwadi Party lately expressing its support to the gujjars.

The gujjar agitation highlights the devastating hold of reservations as a means of advancement on the political imagination of a community. Any caste can stake its claim, contend with other castes, grudge other castes getting more, and so on. It is dividing people in numerous ways and pushing the country to the edge of civil strife. When economic policies are fast reducing the size of the reservation pie itself, people invest caste-based reservations with panacea-like properties against their social and economic backwardness. The dogged pursuit of reservations, alongside the subtle and systematic distortion of the concept, has blinded people to recognise that the pie offers diminishing returns.

Thinking afresh

Is there a way out of this impasse? On 1 August 2009, the vidvatsabha (council of intellectuals), an initiative led by Prakash Ambedkar, organised a seminar in Mumbai on the unlikely subject of reservation within reservations. It suggested that reservations for the SCs, which have been disproportionately accessed by a single subcaste in every state, should be subdivided among all subcastes in the SC category to ensure that equitable benefit accrues to all of them. It had a ring of the sub-categorisation debate between malas and madigas that had cropped up in Andhra Pradesh during the mid-1990s and Shukla's PIL of 2015 discussed earlier. It was strange that echoes of this argument should resonate in Maharashtra years later, particularly when its prospects were blocked by the courts. Moreover, there was no happening in the recent past to prompt such a seminar. It still attracted more than a thousand people, which showed that the issue was resonant enough, no matter what the law said.

It was imagined, or so we were given to believe, that the SCs would be gradually absorbed into the mainstream, thereby eliminating the very need for reservations. Both, the assumption behind reservations and the expected outcome from it, were unrealistic, and insincere. It may be argued in its defence that at the time the policy was first mooted, the untouchables (as the SCs were then called) were not much differentiated. It was perhaps not possible to imagine their uniform socio-economic rise and hence one had to think of their representation by advancing a select few from among them. There were certain obvious costs associated with it, however. Since caste was used as the basis for reservation, individual caste consciousness would survive. The new administrative identity of SCs could not obliterate it. To achieve a functional unity of these castes as the quasi-class of the SCs, dampening individual caste consciousness was not entirely impossible but had to be worked towards. Such a unity did materialise among the dwija castes during the pre and postcolonial decades through capitalist development. The same process later extended this unity to absorb the upper layers of the shudra castes. The lead, in this regard, was taken each time by the castes that were relatively advanced. In traditional parlance, these were the castes of a ritually higher status. The consolidation of the populous shudra castes into a powerful political constituency changed the entire socio-political fabric of the country. Paradoxically, the castes labelled as backward are in social control of rural and semi-urban India, dominate politics and a significant part of the economy of the country. Today, the ritualistic distinctions between them and dwija castes are virtually extinct because of these developments. This dynamic has reduced caste to the divide between dalits and non-dalits. Although, many communities constituting the BC/OBC are as backward as the dalits and adivasis, the idiom of caste binds them with their more powerful members and prevents identification with the dalits and adivasis.

Among the SCs, the castes which were at the forefront of the Ambedkarite dalit movement were expected to perform this task of forging a composite unity. To know them by name, in Maharashtra it would have been the mahars, the malas in Andhra Pradesh, the jatavs in Uttar Pradesh, the pallars in Tamil Nadu, the holeyas in Karnataka, and so on. Sadly, they proved incapable of fulfilling this role. On the contrary, they evinced a consciousness of superiority over the other castes in the Schedule. A case in point would be the counter-argument made by the malas against the Madiga Dandora's demand in the late 1990s for a rightful share of the reserved quota in Andhra Pradesh. The mala leadership retorted that the madigas—with fifty-nine sub castes among them—should not grudge their progress because they had worked hard for it while the madigas just ate, drank and loafed. It is the defining prowess of the caste system that even its victim easily forgets their own victimhood and assumes the oppressor's posture vis-à-vis others when the opportunity arises. It is forgotten that what they are repeating is the anti-reservationist argument. The powerful castes have always justified their privileges on the basis of their 'merit', earned in the previous birth, or, as is said nowadays, by dint of hard work, efficiency, talent, and so on. The fact that the accident of birth in a social structure of differential privileges is more important than individual 'merit' is so well concealed that it may go unnoticed even by the victims. Nor is this mechanism confined to the privileged castes; it operates among the SCs as well. The son of a mahar IAS officer in Mumbai is certainly privileged, while the son of a mahar landless labourer in a remote village of Gadchiroli district is proportionately handicapped, in each case by the accident of birth.

There cannot be any caste-based solution to the problem of inequality. If one wishes to find a practicable solution, it will have to be a non-caste one. The vidvatsabha proposed one such solution, taking the nuclear family as its basic unit. The proposal suggests that the entire dalit population be divided into two categories of families: those that have availed of reservation and those that have not benefited from it so far. Reservation should be prioritised for the families that have not availed of it. The category that has already accessed reservations will now get it only after those who have not availed of it have had their turn, and obviously, only if some seats remain.

The greatest merit of this solution, besides its simplicity, is that it looks beyond the caste label to address the issue of access to benefits. It provides a solution to the inequitable distribution of the benefits of reservations not only among various castes within the SCs, but also within a single caste group. The solution could be refined keeping in view the various levels of reservations (class of job, level of education) and their category, too. This proposition would not have much difficulty in securing the approval of the majority among all castes since it transcends caste and proposes a just distribution of benefits to all. Moreover, there would be no conflict with the Constitution of the kind that took place over the categorisation issue when Shukla's PIL came to grief. It does not tinker with the constitutional provision of reservation to the SCs but only brings in a modality to ensure that its benefits reach all the potential beneficiaries. Most importantly, it would pave the way for the consolidation of all the subcastes of dalits into a class.

This solution could have been applied right at the inception of reservation. As argued, the entire scheme was faultily conceived and unimaginatively implemented, to result in the current mess. This may well have been deliberate because the records show how reservations and all the centrifugal caste turbulence they create have not benefited the dalits so much as the ruling classes. Had reservations been applied as an exceptional policy for an exceptionally deprived people, occasioned by the disabilities of the larger society, and implemented keeping in view the fact that it is not the caste but the family that benefits from them, and had this been coupled with a motivation towards the annihilation of caste, by now we might have seen a significant erosion of caste identities. Instead, post-independence politics has conditioned us to imagine both castes and reservations as eternal. It is a sad paradox that just when the base of reservation has been contracting with neoliberal reforms, the din over it is becoming louder and rationally thinking about it more difficult. It is in no one's electoral interest to take into account the quantifiable gains made through reservations by the purported beneficiaries against the cost extracted from them. Today, even the public sector openly resorts to management solutions such as business process outsourcing and subcontracting to dodge the obligation to ensure reservations. The ongoing privatisation of public sector undertakings will accelerate this process. The reservationists have no cogent solution to offer, just a rhetorical demand for instituting quotas in the private sector. The manipulation of expectations is their gameplan. It is to be hoped that coming generations of young dalits will overcome the inertia which is their political inheritance and prove capable of thinking afresh to put an end to this cynical game of the ruling classes.

2

The Caste and Class Dialectic

The Way In and the Way Out

A caste is an enclosed class.
—B.R. Ambedkar, "Castes in India" (1916)

Class is not this or that part of the machine, but the way the machine works once it is set in motion.
—E.P. Thompson, "Peculiarities of the English" (1965)

In the swirl of contradictions that envelops India, no other pair of terms has had as baleful a consequence for the politics and future of this country as caste and class. These two words have divided the working class movement into two camps—movements oriented towards class struggle and those against caste, each driven by the ideological obsessions of their protagonists through divergent paths that led to the eventual marginalisation of both. While caste and class are conceptually different, the similarity between the two is enough to build a unified emancipatory struggle—a potential that both these movements have failed miserably to realise. The price paid: both have been reduced to near irrelevance today. While caste movements, largely co-opted by the ruling classes, do not admit to the need for introspection, the class (left) movement finds itself isolated and threatened with decimation. On the other hand, since the rise of naxalism in the late 1960s with its roots in rural terrain, the left has amended both its theory as well as practice and attracted dalits in significant numbers, but still could not fully wipe out its theoretical and moral deficit in facing the challenge.

At the outset, I must say this dichotomy has always been anathema to me. As societies world over contend with issues of class disparity, why is India alone—with its caste system—to be exempt from this theoretical framework? Castes in India must be in some way a form of class as Ambedkar had rightly conceived, and classes may be seen as embedding castes. However, this spurious binary has given birth to many sterile theories and pontifications. To me, it is intellectual inertia to typecast Marx with class and Ambedkar with caste. Both sides, the so-called Marxists and the Ambedkarites, have contributed immensely to aggravate the divergence between their movements to their own self destruction.

The dichotomisation of the caste and class struggle can be traced to the brahminical outlook of the early communists and their obsession with the Marxian metaphor of base and superstructure as though it was some scriptural dictum. They still do not realise that it cost them a revolution. On his part, Ambedkar, the doyen of the anti-caste movement, demonstrated on the roads of Mumbai that both class and caste struggles could be organically unified. The communist and dalit movements have had their meeting points, and enough opportunities to mend their ways. Had they done so, they would have changed the course of history. However, they passed up these opportunities, leaving us to squander our energies in fruitless debate over the mistaken binary of caste and class.

It is true that class, constituted on an economic basis, is absolutely central to the materialist foundations of Marxist ontology and epistemology. Likewise, castes are central to Ambedkar, who saw them mostly in religio-ideological terms as sourced from Hindu religion. Beyond this superficial positioning, insofar as both Marx and Ambedkar strove for the emancipation of the proletariat and the dalits respectively, one must understand the reasons why this divergence came into being and its implications for the future course of struggle. Why does Indian society, with its castes, become the sole exception to Marx and Engels' view of all history as the history of class struggle?

Archaeology of caste

All ancient societies had stratified social structures; some of them strikingly similar to India's chaturvarna (four-varna) structure. Yet, no single society had anything resembling the immense and complex dynamics of the caste system. Historically, while many pockets in the world have had social groups similar to the untouchables—the Burakumin in Japan, the Osu in Nigeria, the Baekjeong in precolonial Korea, the Cagot in France—the systems underlying these did not prevail to a comparable geographic (subcontinental) or demographic (ubiquitous) extent, nor do they compare with the sheer endurance of India's hierarchical system with its religious sanction. Ambedkar tells us that while much may have changed, the practice of untouchability and the existence of untouchables has been a constant:

> It is true that Hinduism can absorb many things. The beef-eating Hinduism (or strictly speaking brahminism which is the proper name of Hinduism in its earlier stage) absorbed the non-violence theory of Buddhism and became a religion of vegetarianism. But there is one thing which Hinduism has never been able to do—namely to adjust itself to absorb the untouchables or to remove the bar of untouchability (*BAWS* 9, 195).

There is a plethora of theories on how castes originated as also on their definition; each one—like the six blind men describing the elephant—contains some truth, yet are far from the complex whole. While it is difficult to believe that a minority of brahmins could impose their writ with scriptures and hymns on a majority, several challenges to this ideology—including Buddhism that became a ruling class religion—could not dent the contrivances of the caste system. What is pertinent is that caste has survived despite continual streams of invaders from the Northern borders and easily assimilated them when they settled here. A major jolt to the caste system came during medieval times with the establishment of Islamic rule and the rise of Muslim society in the subcontinent. An egalitarian Islam, coupled with material opportunities created by the advanced feudalism that the rulers brought, caused artisanal and labouring castes to migrate in large numbers to the new urban centres. There was an exodus of sorts of the labouring castes to Islam, a demographic threat to the ordained social world of brahminism.

Later, British colonial rule brought in multidimensional changes in terms of modernisation, urbanisation and industrialisation, that proved immensely beneficial to the subordinated castes. The birth of the non-brahmin and dalit movements is directly attributable to these changes. The spread of capitalist relations in urban pockets also 'secularised' the dwija castes that consider themselves twice-born. Their interface with the capitalist economy significantly weakened their ritual bases. Far more consequential changes took place after the British left India. The countryside, the home base of caste, was permeated with capitalist relations in the guise of the Green Revolution; a class was carved out of the populous shudra landowners as the harbinger of these relations. The process of secularisation of castes that had begun with the dwija castes during colonial times now engulfed these rural castes, so that the caste system came to be primarily expressed as a dichotomy between castes and non-castes, or non-dalits and dalits. Caste still governed the material life of a majority of the lower strata as much as before.

The castes in existence today may be taken as archaeological remains of the classical castes. They are still birth-based identities; the rules concerning food and commensality may not be conspicuous but they are observed—especially in the private sphere—in both rural and urban settings. Occupational associations also are intact; 'lower' or menial jobs are still done by certain sub-castes of dalits; endogamy still stands as a general rule and the rules concerning status and untouchability are also extant, as survey after survey reveals. With the ritual and scriptural basis of castes provided by religion having almost disappeared, what survives of caste, sustained by politics and economics, is nevertheless as menacing as before, if not more than ever.

The term class is etymologically derived from the Latin 'classis', which was used to categorise citizens by wealth. By the late eighteenth century, as wealth and income began to replace hereditary characteristics as markers of status, class replaced previous classifications—such as estate, rank, station and order—that had served to organise society through hierarchical divisions. Two types of usage of class are in vogue in the social sciences, viz. Marxian and Weberian. The Weberian conception of class used by most non-Marxian liberals is based on Max Weber's three-component theory of stratification, which saw social class as emerging from the interplay between wealth, status and power. Weber believed that class position was determined by a person's relationship to the means of production, while status or power emerged from estimations of honour or prestige (see Weber 2015, 27–57). Weber contended, contrary to Marx's theories, that stratification was based on more than merely the ownership of capital. He pointed out that some members of the aristocracy lack economic wealth, yet might have political power whereas many wealthy Jewish families in Europe lacked in prestige and honour, on account of their religion.

Marx, in contrast, saw classes as the factors that actualised the universal law of dialectical materialism in the making of history. He was not content with the Weberian purpose of describing history, but more in unearthing its underlying processes, to bring about an egalitarian change. After examining the history of many societies, he came to the conclusion that all of them were divided into privileged and exploited classes. The real difference between classes lay in the manner in which one class laboured and produced wealth, while another, which exercised private rights of ownership over the means of production, lived more or less off the toil of the labourers. The contradiction between them manifested as class struggle which on reaching its zenith would usher in a qualitative change in society at an advanced phase. This is the crux of his theory of historical materialism as well as revolution. Ambedkar's position comes closer to Weber's but his concern to change society gives his analysis of caste a marked affinity with the Marxian conception of class.

While class is a pivotal conception in Marx's theory of revolution, the vehicle of the struggle through which the dialectics of history is effectuated, neither Karl Marx nor Friedrich Engels defined class explicitly. Rather, their usage of the term differed with the context each time. For instance, in *Capital: Critique of Political Economy*, Marx said that developed capitalist society has only two classes: a capitalist and a proletarian class. Later, he proposed a third class of landowners existing under European capitalism, which he believed to be sufficiently advanced for a communist revolution to occur. Thereafter, he applied the label of class to several other economic units, such as the petty bourgeoisie, peasants and farm labourers. In at least one instance—brought out by H. Meyer in "Marx on Bakunin: A Neglected Text" (1959)—he explicitly stated that farm labourers are proletarians, but whenever he uses the term in a focused way, it is always used of industrial workers.

At another point, Marx asserted that class is a 'product of the bourgeoisie,' but in the same breath he spoke of all history as the history of class struggle. 'Class' in Marxism is not just a label for groups carved out of society on the basis of a discernible set of standards, but also includes the implied interactions among them. For Marx, the meaning of 'proletariat', 'capitalist' and the like develops as their interaction with one another proceeds. The distinction is well captured by E.P.

Thompson's formulation, that class refers to the way the entire machine runs rather than to its individual parts.

Among the Russian Marxists, Nikolai Bukharin directly addressed the question of the difference between a social class and a caste. As he explained in "Historical Materialism: A System of Sociology" (1921), a class is a category of persons united by a common role in the production process, whereas a social caste is a group of persons united by their common position in the juristic or legal order of society. For instance, landlords are a class; the nobility are a caste. Economically speaking, this or that noble may be impoverished; they may only have the barest subsistence; they may be a slum-dweller; but their station remains that of a noble. Bukharin's use of the concept of caste is similar to Weber's conception of class; it serves to further distinguish Marx's conception of class from that of Weber. Although written against the European context, Bukharin's representation is accurate on how caste status functions in India. A brahmin might be poor, living in a slum, but they would still command their birth privileges. In his essay "The Future Results of British Rule in India" (1853), Marx himself had characterised castes as 'the most decisive impediment to India's progress and power.' He made it clear that there existed a causal connection between the archaic social formation of castes and relations of production. The point, however, is not anxiety over the difference between caste and class, but how to conceive of classes in a society in which people's lives are primarily governed by castes.

Lenin, who transmuted Marxism into practice, formulated a definition of class that appears in Volume 29 of his *Collected Works*:

> Classes are large groups of people differing from each other by the place they occupy in a historically-determined system of social production, by their relation (in most cases fixed and formulated by law) to the means of production, by their role in the social organisation of labour, and, consequently, by the dimensions of the share of social wealth of which they dispose and their mode of acquiring it. Classes

> are groups of people one of which can appropriate the labour of another owing to the different places they occupy in a definite system of social economy (1965, 421).

Although it may be faulted for its staticity, it largely captures what Marx and Engels meant by class.

To Marxist-Leninists, therefore, the class to which a person belongs is determined by 'objective reality', not by someone's opinion. What is the objective reality of India then? If one goes by the above definition, one would necessarily come closer to considering castes, especially lower ones, themselves as classes. Are dalits, for instance, not differentiated from non-dalits by the place they occupy in a historically determined system of social production, by their relation (in most cases fixed and formulated by law, the law of Manu) to the means of production, by their role in the social organisation of labour and, consequently, by the dimensions of the share of social wealth, and also their mode of acquiring it? This perhaps is the sense in which Ambedkar said that castes were enclosed classes. But there is obvious difficulty in considering dalits as a class because the law which made them different from non-dalits could also apply to the various castes within the category of 'dalit'.

While class potentially brings people together, the very nature of caste is to divide them by seeking hierarchy. The classes in India, therefore, are to be conceived with broad aggregation, in relation to the dominant mode of production—which means that class analysis in a caste-based society would necessarily subsume caste. For example, the proletariat would include most of the shudras and dalits, but they would not automatically form a class until the caste contradiction between them is eradicated. After all, even class interests are not conceived ab initio. They develop through the exposure of people occupying particular social positions in particular social circumstances, separate groups forming a class in so far as they make common cause against another class; remaining otherwise on hostile terms with each other as competitors. For Marx, class unity was never simply a given.

Communication and building solidarity was essential in actualising the working class as a cohesive entity.

If the communists in India had really understood Marxian theory, they would have conceptualised classes incorporating numerous castes, and internalised the need to wage a struggle against caste. It is, no doubt, a complex proposition, but this is the concrete situation they are to confront. If this had been done in the 1920s, the need for a separate dalit movement would not have arisen. It would have given a fillip to the anti-caste struggles and thereby advanced class struggle towards accomplishing both, revolution as well as the annihilation of caste.

Ambedkar on class

Like Marx, Ambedkar recognises classes as the basic constituents of society. In his very first research paper "Castes in India: Their Mechanism, Genesis and Development" read at an anthropology seminar in Columbia University in 1916, he observes:

> The atomistic conception of individuals in a Society so greatly popularised— I was about to say vulgarised—in political orations is the greatest humbug. To say that individuals make up society is trivial; society is always composed of classes. It may be an exaggeration to assert the theory of class-conflict, but the existence of definite classes in a society is a fact. Their basis may differ. They may be economic or intellectual or social, but an individual in a society is always a member of a class. This is a universal fact and early Hindu society could not have been an exception to this rule, and, as a matter of fact, we know it was not. If we bear this generalisation in mind, our study of the genesis of caste would be very much facilitated, for we have only to determine what was the class that first made itself into a caste, for class and caste, so to say, are next door neighbours, and it is only a span that separates the two. *A Caste is an Enclosed Class* (*BAWS* 1, 15, emphasis original).

While deliberating how these classes came to be enclosed, he, however, identifies non-material factors like 'customs and the social superiority arrogated by the priestly class in all ancient civilisations' as the originating factors behind this 'unnatural institution' founded and maintained through these 'unnatural means'. He calls the varna division essentially a class system, which became a closed-door caste system when the priestly class—brahmins—enclosed themselves into a unit with the characteristics of a caste. The other classes, being subject to the law of social division of labour, underwent differentiation, some into large, others into very minute groups. How this closed-door system was adopted by others is explained again in terms of non-material factors like psychological and mechanistic ones:

> This sub-division of a society is quite natural. But the unnatural thing about these sub-divisions is that they have lost the open-door character of the class system and have become self-enclosed units called castes. The question is: were they compelled to close their doors and become endogamous, or did they close them of their own accord? I submit that there is a double line of answer: *Some closed the door: Others found it closed against them.* The one is a psychological interpretation and the other is mechanistic, but they are complementary and both are necessary to explain the phenomenon of caste-formation in its entirety (*BAWS* 1, 18, emphasis original).

Ambedkar summarises his essay into four main points: '(1) that in spite of the composite make-up of the Hindu population, there is a deep cultural unity; (2) that caste is a parcelling into bits of a larger cultural unit; (3) that there was one caste to start with and (4) that classes have become castes through imitation and excommunication' (22).

In *Annihilation of Caste*, which he wrote twenty years after "Castes in India", he came to the painful realisation that social reform within the ambit of Hinduism was not possible (*BAWS* 1, 38). The developments of the 1930s, in terms of political reforms, impelled him to expand his social base from dalits to the working class. He began speaking of 'Brahmanshahi and Bhandawalshahi' (brahminism and capitalism) as an antagonistic duo and tried to appeal to the larger body of working classes. It led to the formation of the Independent Labour Party (ILP) in 1936, to fight the provincial assembly elections the next year as per the India Act 1935. This party was modelled after the party of the same name in England, strongly influenced by the Fabian socialists. The base of Ambedkar's ILP, however, hardly extended beyond his own caste. The candidates the party fielded in the 1937 elections were mostly mahars. The chronicler of the mahar (that was to become the dalit) movement, Eleanor Zelliot records that of the party's seventeen candidates, there was only one mang candidate fielded in 1937, while the other non-mahar was an untouchable from Gujarat (1970, 26–69). The chambhars, who were socially and economically better placed than the mangs and mahars, were hardly represented in the party. Christophe Jaffrelot says, 'Indeed Ambedkar met with many difficulties attracting the support of chambhars or mangs who considered him to be a mahar leader' (2005, 76–77).

Much later in 1946, when Ambedkar proposed a model of state socialism in the tract *States and Minorities*, he again came to use the idiom of class although the treatise itself was written on behalf of a caste-based party—the Scheduled Castes Federation.

One can easily see that while struggling against the caste oppression of dalits, Ambedkar avoided using a caste-based idiom and always referred to various communities as classes. It reflected his desire to bring all the untouchable castes together as Depressed Classes or dalits. Apart from this label, however, the content of his movement did not make much difference even to untouchable castes other than his own. The people of other castes who followed him remained a minuscule minority, an exception to the rule.

The difference between the conceptions of class by Marx and Ambedkar was due to their approach to the problem. Whereas for Marx class was an essential and universal element spiralling down history through revolutions, to Ambedkar it was a culture-specific interest group that could accomplish its goal by forcing through a series of changes in its situation. Marx tried to construct an integral theory which could be a guide to people to change the world wherein they would realise their 'species being'. In contrast, Ambedkar's approach was pragmatic. His training in Columbia and London School of Economics had taken place under the influence of Fabian philosophers. They believed that socialism could be brought about peacefully and gradually (as against violent revolution proposed by Marx). It would be accomplished by the enlightened middle classes (as against the proletariat who were to be the communist vanguard); and through the emancipation of land and capital (as against the emancipation of labour). The Fabian standpoint led Ambedkar to have serious misgivings about Marxism. Nowhere does he acknowledge this influence, except that of John Dewey (the well known American Fabian of his times, one of the prominent philosophers of pragmatism and the protagonist of progressive education) but it is reflected in his actions throughout, viz. the foundation of the ILP and the proposal of state socialism, if not the broad liberalism he practiced. It shows also in his writings. For instance, after the struggle at Mahad, Ambedkar had realised that

> the intellectual class is the class which can foresee, it is the class which can advise and give a lead. In no country does the mass of the people live the life of intelligent thought and action. It is largely imitative and follows the intellectual class. There is no exaggeration in saying that the entire destiny of a country depends upon its intellectual class. If the intellectual class is honest, independent and disinterested it can be trusted to take the initiative and give a proper lead in a crisis (in *Annihilation of Caste*, *BAWS* 1, 71).

Fabian influence shows clearly in the proposition that the middle classes take the lead; and more particularly the influence of Dewey, who emphasised the importance of intellectuals endowed with progressive education.

Ambedkar's views on Marx and Marxism have been enigmatic, yet it remained a continual reference point in his writings, if only in order to prove to himself that his decisions were superior to those of Marxist leaders. There is an implicit if back-handed compliment in this.

Ambedkar appears to acknowledge the Marxists as his competitors, the second best after himself; at the same time, there is no denying his warnings to his followers that the communist offer of emancipation was a spectre. Ambedkar did not find anything in Marx that could be of help to him in dealing with the problem of caste. There is no evidence that he ever tried to find out the applicability of Marxism to the Indian situation. He relied for evidence on the Marxism practiced by the (mostly brahmin) communists in Bombay. These Marxists had disregarded the caste question as a non-issue, whereas to Ambedkar it was the core issue. The communist attitude towards the anti-caste movement was one of arrogant dismissal on the grounds that it was unscientific, as well as resentment since they perceived it was dividing their 'proletariat'. This increasingly alienated Ambedkar from Marxism.

Marx on caste

Marx touched on the caste system in a number of places. See particularly his well known description of the Indian village community in *Capital*:

> Manufacture, in fact, produces the skill of the detail labourer, by reproducing, and systematically driving to an extreme within the workshop, the naturally developed differentiation of trades which it found ready to hand in society at large. On the other hand, the conversion of fractional work into the life-calling of one man, corresponds to the tendency shown by earlier societies, to make trades hereditary; either to petrify them into castes, or whenever definite historical conditions beget in the individual a tendency to vary in a manner incompatible with the nature of castes, to ossify them into guilds. Castes and guilds arise from the action of the same natural law that regulates the differentiation of plants and animals into species and varieties, except that when a certain degree of development has been reached, the heredity of castes and exclusiveness of guilds are ordained as a law of society (1974, 321).

Marx saw the caste system as a distinctive articulation of the problem of the division of labour before the rise of capitalism. Outside of the village community—in towns or in the trade of surplus goods between villages—castes traditionally functioned as hereditary guilds. Inside the village community, where Marx understood there to be no commodity trade at all, castes functioned as an 'unalterable division of labour' providing those necessary crafts and services too specialised to be done in individual peasant households (and which therefore could not be supplied by the domestic 'blending of agriculture and handicraft'). These service castes—the barber, the washerman, the potter, and so on—were 'maintained at the expense of the whole community'. So the caste system allowed each village to be self-sufficient, while at the same time maximising the surplus that could be extracted in the form of rent by the state.

Marx has not written any treatise on caste but, as his writings reveal, he was not unaware of it. One of the first references to caste appears in *The German Ideology* (1846). He referred to the caste system as a 'crude form of division of labour' (1976, 63). One finds half a dozen references in *Capital* (1867), alluding to it as a special division of labour. In 1847, Marx wrote *The Poverty of Philosophy*, a critique of Proudhon's book (*The System of Economic Contradictions, or The Philosophy of Poverty*, 1846), and referred to the caste system as a product of the conditions of material production, which were formalised into a code much later, something which was also observed by Ambedkar in his "Castes in India". Marx writes:

> Under the patriarchal system, under the caste system, under the feudal and corporative system, there was division of labour in the whole of society according to fixed rules. Were these rules established by a legislator? No. Originally born of the conditions of material production, they were raised to the status of laws only much later. In this way these different forms of the division of labour became so many bases of social organisation. (118)

There is also a passing reference in his 1859 work, *A Contribution to the Critique of Political Economy*: 'Or, legislation may perpetuate land ownership in certain families, or allocate labour as a hereditary privilege, thus consolidating it into a caste system' (1970, 201). Some of the observations of Marx on the Indian villages are surprisingly similar to Ambedkar's opinion:

> Now, sickening as it must be to human feeling to witness those myriads of industrious patriarchal and inoffensive social organisations disorganised and dissolved into their units, thrown into a sea of woes, and their individual members losing at the same time their ancient form of civilisation, and their hereditary means of subsistence, we must not forget that these idyllic village-communities, inoffensive though they may appear, had always been the solid foundation of Oriental despotism, that they restrained the human mind within the smallest possible compass, making it the unresisting tool of superstition, enslaving it beneath traditional rules; depriving it of all grandeur and historical energies (*New York Daily Tribune*, 25 June 1853).

Ambedkar called the village 'a sink of localism, a den of ignorance, narrow-mindedness and communalism'. In another article in the *New York Daily Tribune*, Marx observed the impact of the railway system in British India, which shows him thinking about the annihilation of caste. He imagines that capitalist modernisation due to the spread of the railway system will destroy the hereditary division of labour, which he identified as the caste system. Most people, reflecting lazily on this, might give a verdict on how wrong Marx was. But one might notice the changes in the caste configuration wherever capitalist modernisation has reached. For instance, during the colonial period, capitalist modernisation touched mainly the dwija castes and we find that at least the ritual divisions among them on caste lines have almost melted away. As mentioned before, in the 1960s when the Nehruvian state created a capitalist class of rich farmers, the shudra cart also appears to have got hitched to this dwija bandwagon, reducing the caste system to a class like formation of caste and non-caste or non-dalits and dalits. This may be a provocative observation, but this trend can be discerned wherever the wealth and power of shudra castes have risen.

It is clear that caste did not constitute the core concern of Marx and hence he did not elaborate on it in detail like Ambedkar did. Nevertheless, his insightful description of the caste system is impressive and anticipates Ambedkar's disdain for it; it also indicates that caste was not extraneous to the frame of his historical materialism. Equally, in his broad brush treatment, he explicates caste as a special case of the division of labour. Here Aijaz Ahmad's observation in *In Theory: Classes, Nations, Literatures* is pertinent. He writes in the chapter "Marx on India: A Clarification" that Marx's direct comments about the power of the caste system in the Indian village

> are, on the one hand, a virtual paraphrase of his comments on the European peasantry as being mired in 'the idiocy of rural life' and remind one, on the other hand, of the whole range of reformist politics and writings in India, spanning a great many centuries but made all the sharper in the twentieth century, which have always regarded the caste system as an altogether inhuman one—a 'diabolical contrivance to suppress and enslave humanity', as Ambedkar put it in the preface to *The Untouchables*—that degrades and saps the energies of the Indian peasantry, not to speak of the 'untouchable' menial castes (1992, 225).

Marx's solution can then seem merely a generic one, which has not fully materialised, despite the spread of capitalist relations in India.

Marx's metaphorical flight

The main factor that created the dichotomy of caste and class is the Marxian metaphor of base and superstructure, which, as understood by the so-called Marxists, valorised strictly economic struggles by classes and relegated all other factors to the superstructure. This concept, evolved in a small number of writings of Marx and Engels, had not been intended as a template for historical materialist analysis but came to be invoked as such, particularly by the Russian interpreters of communism.

The early communists in India were typically youth from the

educated brahmin middle class, inspired by the Bolshevik Revolution in 1917 and by their diet of literature and other resources smuggled from Britain and Russia. They naturally began their activities with trade unions, which, in fact, had cropped up much before the Communist Party of India was formally founded in 1925. Their confrontation with caste was limited to organisational contradictions within trade unions that included a small minority of dalit workers. The faultline of caste was something the communist leadership wanted at all costs to avoid facing or redressing. In the textile mills of Bombay, for example, where the communists had total control over the workers, dalits were debarred from jobs in the better paid weaving section as the non-dalit workers were repulsed by the prospect of being polluted if they touched threads that had been joined by dalits: before putting the thread into the machine for the first time as well as joining the broken thread thereafter, a worker had to wet the end of the thread with saliva. Also, untouchability was practised by keeping separate pitchers of drinking water for dalit workers in the mills. Even after Ambedkar pointed out these oddities, the communists did not act for fear of displeasing the caste Hindu workers. A decade later, Ambedkar would raise this issue in 1938 delivering the presidential address to the G.I.P. Railway Depressed Classes Workmen's Conference in Nashik:

> It is notorious that there are many avocations from which a Depressed Class worker is shut out by reason of the fact that he is an untouchable. A notorious case in point is that of the cotton industry. I do not know what happens in other parts of India. But I know that in the Bombay Presidency, the Depressed Classes are shut out from the weaving department in the cotton mills both in Bombay and in Ahmedabad. They can only work in the spinning department. The spinning department is the lowest paid department. The reason why they are excluded from the weaving department is because they are untouchables… (in Das 2009, 52).

Instead of seizing the gravity of the caste question and facing it, the communists took shelter under Marx's metaphor of base and superstructure, as though it was incontrovertible. They feared that confronting the issue of caste might lead to organisational break-up, quite like how bourgeois parties fear losing Hindu votes if they speak out against the hindutva excesses of the Sangh parivar.

Though castes were primarily rooted in the organization of production, the communists relegated them to the superstructure (culture, rituals, institutions) and took them as 'determined' by the 'base' of the economic structure (the forces and relations of production). The entire behaviour of the communist parties vis-à-vis castes is explained by their literalist and mechanical use of this metaphor. As Ambedkar pointed out, it led them to conduct a struggle for the rights of the working class but ignore that of the Depressed Classes. Even the working class was narrowly defined as industrial workers, to the neglect of workers in the countryside where casteism was rampant.

In 1941, the communists in Thanjavur began on their own initiative—not under the steerage of the central leadership—to organise landless peasants and press for their demands. While they were partially successful in overcoming castes in their struggle, they still shied away from putting forth any specific caste related demand (say, against obligatory unpaid labour) aside from seeking legislation 'protecting' untouchables with equal political and religious rights. It is only lately, notably after the eruption of the naxalite movement with its rural roots which had to confront caste in a big way, that rethinking this metaphor began. Most naxal factions have refined their stance towards the caste question and some of them have come around to seeing caste as part of both base and superstructure. None, however, has discarded the larger schema as useless.

The metaphor has a baffling history. In his early writings, Marx did not separate base from superstructure. In *The German Ideology* (1840) Marx alluded for the first time to an idealised superstructure. It was only in 1859, in the preface to *A Contribution to the Critique of Political Economy*, that he used this metaphor in the form of a relationship between the economic structure and the 'legal and political' superstructure. Marx used it to explain the dialectical relation between base and superstructure in history. But his followers enthusiastically employed it to sideline superstructural aspects. While superstructure is influenced by the base, it can also impact the latter.

By 1890, the incorrect usage of this metaphor had become so rampant that Engels had to intervene. In a letter of 25 January 1894, he wrote to the German economist Walther Borgius:

> Political, juridical, philosophical, religious, literary, artistic, etc, development is based on economic development. But [...]it is not that the economic situation is cause, solely active, while everything else is only passive effect. There is rather interaction on the basis of economic necessity which ultimately always asserts itself (Engels 1934).

Again in a letter to a German student Joseph Bloch (21–22 September 1890), he stressed this point saying,

> Marx and I are ourselves to blame for the fact that young writers sometimes lay more stress on the economic side than is due to it... According to the materialist view of history, the determining factor in history is, in the final analysis, the production and reproduction of actual life... Now if someone distorts this by declaring the economic moment to be the only determining factor, he changes that proposition into a meaningless abstract, ridiculous piece of jargon (Engels 1972).

In her book *Democracy Against Capitalism: Renewing Historical Materialism* political theorist Ellen Meiksins Wood observes, 'The base/superstructure metaphor has always been more trouble than it is worth. Although Marx himself used it very rarely and only in the most aphoristic and allusive formulations, it has been made to bear a theoretical weight far beyond its limited capacities' (2007, 49). The real problems began with the establishment of Stalinist orthodoxies which elevated—or reduced—the metaphor to the first principle of Marxist–Leninist dogma, asserting the supremacy of a self-contained economic sphere over other passively reflexive subordinate spheres.

This metaphor underwent transmutation for the worse at the hands of Russian Marxists, who happened to be the major ideological source of the Indian communists. Even before Stalin, Georgi Plekhanov (1856–1918), often referred to as the father of Russian Marxism, remodelled and rigidified the base–superstructure concept and then schematised it. In one of his early and important books (*The Development of the Monist View of History*, Chapter V, "Modern Materialism") Plekhanov stated, 'the very direction of intellectual work in a given society is determined by the production relations of that society.' In *Fundamental Problems of Marxism* (1907), he provided a schema to describe the development of the base–superstructure concept, wherein he stated that a superstructure composed of a sociopolitical regime, 'the psychology of man in society', and various ideologies reflecting this psychology are erected upon a particular economic foundation. While neither Lenin nor Leon Trotsky had made much use of the base–superstructure concept, Nikolai Bukharin devoted a full chapter to it in his book *Historical Materialism* (1925). In his hands, Marx's superstructure became more elaborate, hovering over a society's economic base. Such erroneous interpretations reinforced the notions of Indian communists that caste was to be excluded from class, as class was the governing condition, or base, while caste was the superstructure that would simply cave in when class relations were realigned.

Contention with Ambedkar

With this ideological orientation, the communists inevitably came into contention with the dalit movement led by Ambedkar, whose raison d'être was the abolition of caste discrimination and oppression. For dalits who essentially belonged to the working class, the communist conception of class or class struggle was an abstraction in contrast to the concrete and pervasive discrimination they suffered. They had principally decided that their struggle would be led by them alone and they had a leader of Ambedkar's calibre at the helm. The movement took off at Mahad in March 1927 asserting the right to access public places, with Ambedkar declaring: 'We are not going to the Chavadar Tank to merely drink its water. We are going to the Tank to assert that we too are human beings like others. It must be clear that this meeting has been called to set up the norm of equality' (in Dangle 1994, 225). To the communists, the struggles of the dalits were pointless as the superstructure of caste would not change without the economic base changing through revolution. Their response to Ambedkar's movement reflected this trivialising attitude which was no different in the eyes of dalits from that of orthodox upper castes—to which the communist leaders incidentally belonged.

Ambedkar, though not quite sold on Marxist theory, was attracted towards its goal and accomplishments. It may be purely symbolic, but his public life is bracketed by two instances that clearly mark his innate attraction to Marxism. The first is his essay, "Castes in India", with its definition of caste as an enclosed class, paving the theoretical grounds to unify the two in future struggles; and the second is his last (technically penultimate) lecture in Kathmandu in 1956 on "Buddha and Karl Marx", (*BAWS* 3) that generously acknowledged the goals of both Buddha and Marx as the same, but faulted Marx's method on two counts: one, its reliance on violence, and the other, dictatorship. Even between these bookends, there is huge evidence that testifies to his interest in Marxism. Right from *Mooknayak*—the first paper he had started (1920), even before formally launching the movement—to *Janata* (1927), the newspapers he oversaw carried laudatory stories and serialised important articles on Marxism and the Bolshevik Revolution in Russia. For example, while the Marathi translation of *Capital* appeared in the early 1960s, Ambedkar's *Janata* had carried a translation of *Wage, Labour and Capital* in Marathi as "Karl Marx che Majuri, Kam va Bhandwal" published in nine installments from 31 October to 3 December, 1932. It had also published an article on Karl Marx and Friederich Engels in its issue of 23 July 1932.

During the 1930s, Ambedkar actually tried his hand at class politics. He founded the Independent Labour Party on 15 August 1936 in the run-up to the 1937 elections to provincial assemblies. This party had a rigorously expressed class agenda; the word 'caste' occurred in its manifesto just once, in passing. The manifesto of the ILP noted that 'the word labour was used instead of the word Depressed Classes because labour includes the Depressed Classes as well.' The party advocated state management and ownership of industry and supported credit and cooperative societies, tax reforms to reduce the burden on agricultural and industrial labour, and free and compulsory education. For all that, as Eleanor Zelliot notes in *Ambedkar's World*, the ILP 'failed to secure a base among caste Hindu workers. The Depressed Class origin of the party worked against this' (2003, 184). Ambedkar formed the Mumbai Kamgar Sangh in 1935 and made efforts to organise dockyard workers and railway workers in 1948. Through the connected efforts at land reform and abolition of hereditary privileges in the countryside, these organisational efforts sought to forefront caste as a crucial factor for the working class movement. He led a massive agitation against 'khoti'—a kind of landlordism prevailing in the Konkan region—bringing together over twenty thousand dalits and kunbi peasants and landless labourers to march in a massive procession in Bombay. During this period, when Ambedkar was at his radical best, he addressed a number of conferences of peasants in and around the Bombay province. In sum, it was Ambedkar who really demonstrated that the struggle against caste could be embedded into a class struggle.

The communists, however, were not prepared to yield their theoretical fixation and remained confined to trade unions. Ambedkar's bitterness about Marxism/communism actually arose in response to this conduct of the communists. In the textile mills of Bombay, despite the communists' control over the workers, the practice of untouchability continued unabated. Such experiences thwarted the understanding between these two movements right from the beginning. When the communists called for a mill workers' strike in 1929, Ambedkar—in alliance with Frederick Stones, manager of the E.D. Sassoon Mills—asked dalit workers to resume work, breaking the strike, a move that drew the ire of the communists. They saw this action as of a piece with Ambedkar's breaking ranks with the nationalist movement in the previous year, to cooperate with the Simon Commission. Nonetheless, he later joined hands with the communists and led a massive strike of workers in 1938 against the Industrial Dispute Bill introduced by the Congress provincial government of Bombay that sought to curtail the workers' right to strike. In 1940, he adopted the red flag for the ILP with eleven stars in the upper left corner, symbolising the eleven provinces of India at the time. Thus, there is ample evidence to show that Ambedkar, while being vocal about the primacy of the caste question, sought to unify both caste and class struggles, whereas the communists self-righteously stuck to their class guns. Their dogmatic application of the base–superstructure concept, reducing it to a formula, is strongly redolent of brahminical theology with its shabda pramanya (paramountcy of the word). Given the predominance of brahmins in the leadership of the then Communist Party of India, this overflow of old reading practices into a new context is not surprising, nor is the way it turned Marxism into a quasi religion, not a blueprint for creative application but akin to veda vakya (scriptural authority) to be as mechanically endorsed as formerly the dharmashastras were.

Ambedkar was alert to this strain in Indian communism. In a protracted interview given to the American journalist Selig Harrison over the course of several months in 1953, he remarked:

> The Communist Party was originally in the hands of some brahmin boys—Dange and others. They have been trying to win over the maratha community and the Scheduled Castes. But they have made no headway in Maharashtra. Why? Because they are mostly a bunch of brahmin boys. The Russians made a great mistake to entrust the Communist movement in India to them. Either the Russians didn't

> want communism in India—they wanted only drummer boys—or they didn't understand (Harrison 1960, 190–1).

A stark instance of the CPI's wilful blindness to the issue of caste is M. Singaravelu's presidential address at the first Communist Conference at Kanpur in 1925. He belonged to the fisherman community, had been influenced by Ayothee Thasser Panditar and Periyar Ramasamy Naicker, and was almost unique among the party leadership in having known caste discrimination from close quarters. Nevertheless, Singaravelu blithely asserted, 'No sooner their economic dependence is solved the social stigma of untouchability is bound to disappear.' Entry into temples, tanks, and roads were non-issues. No targeted measures were called for at all. Being raised to economic independence alongside the other poor would vaporise untouchability. If a person with Singaravelu's background could say such a thing, the thinking of the other leaders, a majority of whom came from the brahmin caste, can be easily imagined. One of the reasons caste was seen as a niggling distraction was because some leaders of the CPI were in a hurry to get the revolution started, which would inaugurate a utopian society and solve all problems. M.N. Roy, among others, had proved to his own satisfaction that India had already been vaulted into late capitalism by sustained contact with Britain and the political and economic measures introduced by the colonial power. Caste was therefore no impediment at all and would land in the dustbin of history, alongside the remnants of feudalism, just as soon as the proletarian revolution was underway.

This attitude of the communists evoked hostility from Ambedkar. In the anxiety to prove their (base–superstructure) thesis wrong, he would write that history bore out the proposition that political revolutions have always been preceded by social and religious revolutions (*Annihilation of Caste*, *BAWS* 1, 44), inadvertently conceding their core argument that castes were indeed a superstructural matter. One may speculate that if the communists had not been doctrinaire, they would have appreciated Ambedkar's viewpoint and forged an approach to class analysis in India where the anti-caste struggle of the dalits would become an integral part of the proletarian class struggle. There would have been no need of a separate dalit movement and consequent internecine hostility. One of the manifestations of this hostility could be seen, as Zelliot observes in *From Untouchability to Dalit* (1992, 137), in Ambedkar's embrace of Buddhism, which was to serve as a bulwark against communism in India. Such is the cost of this dichotomy of caste and class that if it had been nipped in the bud, India could perhaps have seen a revolution instead of a mere change of guard in 1947.

One could lazily observe that both Marx and Ambedkar have failed to accomplish their goals: Marx in realising socialist revolution at all, much less one that conformed to his predictions, and Ambedkar in ameliorating the condition of dalits, much less the annihilation of castes. However, their failures cannot be classed together. Marx gave a scientific framework for revolution and a theory to bring it about. He provided analytical tools to understand the world around us and certain ideas to strategise our actions. Naturally, his goal was long term. In contrast, Ambedkar adopted a pragmatic method to make use of the available situation to accomplish his goal. His was essentially a short term approach, geared to yield immediate results, and not always in coherence with his long term goals. There are obvious problems with the pragmatic method vis-à-vis the scientific method of Marx, which is that the former is basically reactive. The advantage of the Marxist method is that at the level of its theoretical foundation, it has objective rigour while it also explains the past. However, the translation of it into practice has proved more than problematic.

Looking at the caste system as the life world of the Indian people that pervades every aspect of their social life, Ambedkar was broadly right in prescribing its annihilation while simultaneously recognising the task as well nigh impossible. Castes, as he himself said, were neither born out of religion nor sustained by religion alone. Religion was merely one of the contributors to their sustenance. The major factor was that it provided material power to the dominant castes, in a cascading manner, which gave the descending levels of the hierarchy a diminishing stake in its continuance. Castes are thus homomorphous with the social structure itself and have enough resilience to adapt to changes in it. Therefore, the annihilation of castes will necessitate a thoroughgoing democratic revolution, which has been fast slipping from sight. A meeting point between Ambedkar and Marx may occur yet in India's future: it is certainly needed.

3

Ambedkar, Ambedkarites and Ambedkarism

From Panther to Saffron Slave

If the number of busts and statues, pictures and posters, songs and ballads, books and pamphlets, conferences, seminars, or the size of congregations in memory of a person were to be taken as measures of greatness, there may not be another historical figure to rival Babasaheb Ambedkar. New places are continually added to the existing list of memorials. The present ruling dispensation under Narendra Modi has gone overboard commissioning grandiose projects of commemoration. Modi announced in 2016 that five places—Ambedkar's birthplace in Mhow (Madhya Pradesh), the building in London where he stayed while studying there, Deekshabhoomi in Nagpur, Mahaparinirvan Sthal in Delhi, and Chaityabhoomi in Mumbai—were being developed as 'Panchteerth' or five sites of pilgrimage. The two lavish memorials in Delhi—Dr Ambedkar International Centre on Janpath and Dr Ambedkar National Memorial at 26 Alipur Road—are mere links in the chain. The union minister of social justice and empowerment, Thawar Chand Gehlot, went further still, declaring that they would memorialise Ambedkar in a grand manner wherever he had set foot. What might lie behind this phenomenal zeal? There is no doubt that for dalits Ambedkar has been a messiah, and their gratitude for what he did for them is natural. It is one thing to revere a hero and quite another to approach him as pilgrims do god, particularly when the hero had curtly warned against his deification. The way Ambedkar is invoked by the political class, and even by dalit intellectuals—whether stemming from sheer ignorance or to gain traction with the ruling classes—reduces him to an inert godhead, merely to be worshipped. Or worse, a reactionary identity icon blocking any further enlightenment. Cheaper still, a coin in the trade of careerist transactions, easing the ascent of cynical climbers. The severe erosion of the dalit movement, persistent misery of the dalit majority and the growth of a reactionary stratum of self-serving dalit elites engendered by this bhakti cult over the last four decades have set in motion a vicious cycle of hopelessness, which reinforces the saviour syndrome all over again.

This outgrowth of adulation resulted from the way 'Ambedkarism' turned into an ideologically free-floating signifier along the diverse paths it has travelled since Ambedkar's death. Before turning our attention to these, it is important to take stock of the salient milestones of Ambedkar's life, to see if there is any indisputable theme or unique system of thought to be discerned amid its eventfulness; a system that could be plausibly presented as Ambedkarism.

Ambedkar's struggle

After the Mahad struggles in 1927, Ambedkar was disillusioned with the response of caste Hindus. He had imagined that if the dalits agitated for their civil rights, the advanced section of Hindu society would wake up to its duty and pursue reforms. The Mahad conference, which was conceived and planned by one young man—Ramchandra Babaji More, later to be known as Comrade More—was attended by three thousand dalits, mostly First World War veterans. The gathering was initially planned as just a Depressed Classes conference—'Depressed Classes' being the British administrative term for dalits from 1916 onwards. But it was decided that the participants would use the occasion to assert a civil right extended to them four years previously—in 1923, by the Bole Resolution of the Bombay Provincial Assembly—by marching together to the Chavadar tank and drinking its water. The Bole Resolution had stated that 'all public water sources, wells and dharamshalas which are built or maintained out of public funds [...] as well as public schools, courts, offices and dispensaries' should henceforth be open to the use of all without let or hindrance. Its provisions were later adopted by a special resolution of the Mahad Municipality. Addressing the gathered delegates on 20 March 1927, Ambedkar said, 'We are not going to the Chavadar tank to merely drink its water. We are going to the tank to assert that we too are human beings like others. It must be clear that this meeting has been called to set up the norm of equality.' However, on their return from the tank, the delegates came under attack from an orthodox Hindu mob. Twenty people received serious injuries, while sixty to seventy others, including women, were wounded. The brahmins then decided to 'purify' the 'polluted' Chavadar tank by pouring into it 108 earthen pots of cow-dung and cow-piss, milk, ghee and curd—what they called panchakarma—amidst vedic chanting. Ambedkar was incensed at this and planned another conference for nine months later, this time as a 'satyagraha'. This was the first struggle consciously planned as a satyagraha by the Depressed Classes and was attended by more than ten thousand volunteers. Even this time, however, the outcome was to be inconclusive as some caste Hindus obtained a court injunction against the satyagrahis by making the fraudulent claim that Chavadar was a Choudhary tank, a private property that could not be trespassed. It was at this second conference, on 25 December 1927, that a copy of the *Manusmriti*—the second-century CE text which Ambedkar called 'the book of the philosophy of brahmanism' enjoining the worst kind of proscriptions against untouchables—was burnt at the hands of Bapusaheb Sahasrabuddhe, a progressive brahmin.

Hereafter, Ambedkar gave up his efforts to bring about social reforms from within Hindu society and turned towards newly emerging opportunities in politics. Right after Mahad, he began to speak publicly about delivering the ultimate message to the Hindus by renouncing Hinduism. In one of his early speeches of 1928 at Jalgaon (Vidarbha), he exhorted dalits to become Musalmans and some twenty people followed through. His message now had a dual aspect, social as well as political. While the social message still targeted reform in Hindu society, the political content grew out of a claim pressed by the Muslim League in the course of the Morley–Minto reforms of 1909, that the untouchables and adivasis were not Hindus. The League had employed this contention to deflate the Congress' bid for a greater number of seats. Ambedkar would use it to construct his politics by claiming a separate identity for the dalits. Contrary to the commonplace notion, Ambedkar had by this point given up on the method of satyagraha, although he did not explicitly discourage his followers from undertaking any. The Parvati temple satyagraha (1929) at Poona as well as the long-drawn out Kalaram Mandir satyagraha (1930) at Nashik were organised and led not by him but his followers, P.N. Rajbhoj and B.D. (Dadasaheb) Gaikwad respectively. Ambedkar did lend them his moral support and even participated once in the latter.

When the British government sent the seven-member Simon Commission in 1927—to study constitutional reforms as promised at the time of the Montague–Chelmsford reforms of 1919—the Congress boycotted it on arrival, but Ambedkar decided to cooperate. On 29 May 1928, speaking on behalf of the Bahishkrita Hitakarini Sabha (Depressed Classes Institute) at Damodar Hall in Parel, he raised before the Commission issues pertaining to the state of education among the Depressed Classes in the Bombay Presidency. The Commission submitted its two-volume report in May 1930, recommending a round table conference of the government with representatives of various communities. Ambedkar and Rettamalai Srinivasan from the Madras Presidency were invited to London as the representatives of the Depressed Classes. Ambedkar used the opportunity to push for the recognition of a distinct identity for dalits and, in the teeth of Gandhi's vehement opposition, won them separate electorates with reserved seats in provincial assemblies. When the British prime minister Ramsay MacDonald announced the Communal Award on 16 August 1932, granting separate electorates to the Forward Castes, Muslims, Sikhs, Europeans, Indian Christians, Anglo-Indians, and untouchables, Gandhi took exception and declared a fast unto death against the grant to the dalits. The other separate electorates did not affect him. The result was that Ambedkar had to renounce his gains and accept joint electorates with the Hindus. The number of reserved seats was enhanced (148 against the previous 70) and a system of primary elections instituted, whereby dalits had exclusive rights to decide on a panel of four candidates, of whom one would be elected by the general constituency. The Poona Pact was signed on 24 September 1932, and came to be incorporated in the Government of India Act 1935.

Although Ambedkar seemed satisfied with the Poona Pact, when he was asked six months later by Gandhi for a greetings message for the inaugural issue of *Harijan* (11 February 1933), he sent the taunting reply that the Hindus would not treat a message from an untouchable with respect and asked that the journal carry a statement from him instead:

> The Out-caste is a bye-product of the Caste system. There will be outcastes as long as there are castes. Nothing can emancipate the Out-caste except the destruction of the Caste system. Nothing can help to save Hindus and ensure their survival in the coming struggle except the purging of the Hindu Faith of this odious and vicious dogma (in Mandal 1999, v).

The disaffection and combativeness in evidence here were a prelude to the tone he would take in *Annihilation of Caste*, which he wrote three years later. The text of his proposed speech to a 1936 conference at Lahore, *Annihilation of Caste* traced the roots of the caste system to the Hindu Dharmashastras and asserted that they would have to be dynamited for Indian society to achieve the title's objective. Ambedkar had been invited (and then disinvited) to speak by the Jat-Pat Todak Mandal, a maverick offshoot of the reformist Arya Samaj. The organisers of the conference having taken fright at his speech and reneged, Ambedkar bore the cost of its publication as a booklet in May 1936. On 31 May, he addressed a conference of the Mumbai Elaka Mahar Parishad of the mahars at Naigaum (in the suburb of Dadar), delivering his famous "Mukti Kon Pathe?" (What path to salvation?) speech in which he spelt out his reasons for favouring religious conversion. Pertinently, Ambedkar saw the struggle against religious oppression as a class struggle:

> This is not a feud between two rival men. The problem of Untouchability is a matter of class struggle. It is a struggle between caste Hindus and the Untouchables. This is not a matter of doing injustice against one man. This is a matter of injustice being done by one class against another. This class struggle has its relation with the social status… This struggle starts as soon as you start claiming equal treatment with others (Ambedkar 1988).

In the build-up to provincial elections under the terms of the India Act 1935, Ambedkar formed a political party—Independent Labour Party—in August 1936, which he defined as a workers' party. This was part of a strategy to broaden his appeal beyond the dalits, as demanded by electioneering, but was also the expression of his belief in the class unity of people. In the manifesto of the ILP published on the eve of the 1937 provincial elections, he addressed the material issues of workers and peasants under the rubric of class, while caste got just a single passing mention. However, Ambedkar was in the same period deeply involved in seeking a new cultural identity for the dalits. On 13 October 1935, in a conversion conference at Yeola in Nashik district, he had exhorted the dalits to leave Hinduism and had himself taken the famous vow, 'I had the misfortune of being born with the stigma of an Untouchable. However, it is not my fault; but I will not die a Hindu, for this is in my power.' Coming alongside such a resolute focus on caste and religion, the switch to class politics looks abrupt and limited in scope. A mutual resistance between class and caste politics would surface from time to time, as we will see.

During the ILP phase, he took up remarkable class struggles in the assembly as well as outside, as attested by a number of standout events—the founding of the Bombay Municipal Workers Union, the historic January 1938 peasants' march in Bombay for the abolition of the khoti system, the workers' strike of 7 November 1938 against the Industrial Dispute Bill, which was joined by the communists, to mention a few instances—but his fight against caste retained undiluted character. Rather, it would appear that he never saw any contradiction between class and anti-caste struggles, as he had termed capitalism and brahminism the twin enemies of dalits. The most remarkable of these cross-caste, or class-based, efforts was the about twenty thousand-strong march of peasants he led to the Council Hall in Bombay, with kunbi and mahar peasants along with landless labourers walking together under the ILP's flag. Shyamrao Parulekar, secretary of the ILP who was the MLA from Ratnagiri, played a key role in this mobilisation. Like More, he would eventually leave Ambedkar to join the Communist Party of India.

While Ambedkar did not recognise any essential contradiction in a class struggle with an anti-caste core, he was also not complacent like the communists in pretending that class politics would inevitably redress the injustices of caste. The ILP's influence among the working class had limitations that are reflected in both the pronounced mahar character of the party's base and the divisive influence of caste among the poor. As Jaffrelot notes, 'The party could hardly become the representative of *all* workers whereas it was based on a network of dalit activists.' The Samata Sainik Dal (The Equality Corps) which supplied the ILP with its most disciplined cadre and an effective local outreach, drew its members overwhelmingly from mahar youth and marched under its own blue flag. Moreover, Jaffrelot adds, the support base Ambedkar was trying to cultivate was thickly acculturated with caste: 'Even the poorest [of the peasantry and working class] considered themselves to be of a naturally superior rank to Untouchables' (2005, 79–80).

Given the immediate political circumstances and the lack of support from other parties to foregrounding the aspirations of dalits, Ambedkar's programme appeared to have reached an impasse. Also, as the end of British rule hoved into view, events set an exigent pace, unfavourable to the nurturing of new constituencies. The terms of political engagement were increasingly dominated by identitarian politics on behalf of a communal support base, rather than any secular agenda. In March 1942 came the report of the Cripps Mission (the Cripps Proposals or Formula), which did not take demands of the untouchables into account while proposing the election of a Constituent Assembly. On the other hand, Muslims were virtually guaranteed the prospect of a separate state, Pakistan, for which the demand had been formally raised by the Muslim League in 1940. Ambedkar was angry to see 'his community's interests sacrificed in this manner' (Jaffrelot 2005, 80).

In April 1942, he founded the All-India Scheduled Castes Federation. The replacement of the ILP with the SCF signalled a clear return to the centrality of caste issues. In July the same year, Ambedkar was invited to join the viceroy's executive council as labour member. He used his proximity to the viceroy to institute scholarships for dalit students to study abroad, and later, in 1943, to institute the quota system in public employment. He enacted many laws in favour of labour, notably the Indian Trade Unions (Amendment) Bill (1943), making the recognition of a union compulsory in every enterprise. However, his party could not make much political headway. After World War II, the British sent the Cabinet Mission to discuss the modalities of the transfer of power. The viceroy's executive council was reconstituted as the cabinet of free India and Ambedkar did not find a place in it. His pleas and representations were consistently ignored by all—the British, the Congress and the Muslim League. In the general elections of March 1946, his party contested fifty-one seats altogether (in Madras, Bombay, Bengal, United Provinces, Central Provinces, and Berar) but could win only two—one for J.N. Mandal from Bengal and the other for R.P. Jadhav from the Central Provinces and Berar. Ambedkar, who was highly critical of the Cabinet Mission Plan, calling it a 'shameful betrayal of the cause of sixty millions of untouchables' in a letter dated 17 May 1946 to Winston Churchill (cited by Cháirez-Garza 2017), was just as vehemently opposed to the manner in which elections were conducted to the CA that resulted from the Plan. Its members were indirectly elected via a system of proportional representation from the Congress-dominated provincial assemblies, which in turn had been elected in March 1946 on a restricted franchise consisting of about 20 to 24 per cent of the adult population. Eighty-two per cent of the elected members were from the Congress, and of the 83 per cent of Hindu members, 45 per cent were brahmin. Ambedkar, who was desperate to enter the CA, could not find a way of doing so. In this context, he set about the task of submitting a memorandum to the CA on behalf of the SCF, outlining his plan for state socialism, which would be later published as *States and Minorities*. His comrade from the Scheduled Caste Federation, Jogendranath Mandal, helped him get elected to the CA from the Khulna–Jessore constituency in East Bengal. But this was a short-lived triumph. With the announcement of the Mountbatten Plan of Partition, he would lose his membership.

In the meantime, he managed to patch up his relationship with the Congress. When Nehru presented his Objective Resolution to the CA, Ambedkar was invited to speak out of turn by Rajendra Prasad. He delivered a much-applauded speech giving clear indications that he would cooperate with the Congress. While making critical observations on the Objective Resolution, he implied that his sympathies lay with a plan of state socialism but that he would not champion it in the House. The truce with the Congress led to his getting elected from the Bombay assembly—for which purpose the Congress shelved its own plans—before the next session of the CA was convened. Around the same time, he was inducted as law minister in the first cabinet formed under the premiership of Nehru, and also made the chairman of the most important committee—the drafting committee—of the CA. Ambedkar would successfully pilot the draft, which was already prepared, and produce a Constitution which was very largely a rehash of the India Act 1935 (nearly 250 of its total 321 articles being adopted verbatim or with minor changes into the new Constitution which had 395 articles) along with additions from several other constitutions.

Amid the lavish praise he received as the chief architect of the Constitution, Ambedkar would exhort his followers to shun agitational methods, including satyagraha, and use constitutional methods to secure their demands. Later, in the sober hindsight of September 1953, he was to blurt out that he had been used as a hack by the Congress; the Constitution was no good to anyone and he would be the first person to set it aflame. Still later, in March 1955, he would explain away his outburst by suggesting that the Constitution was good—likening it to a temple built for devas or gods—but that it had been taken over by demons. He had already resigned from the Nehru cabinet in September 1951 on account of accumulated frustration, declaring that his decision was triggered by the failure of the Hindu Code Bill, a large-scale exercise in reform and codification of practices relating to Hindu marriage, divorce, adoption, and inheritance, to which opposition came from almost all Hindus. He managed to get elected to the Rajya Sabha but could never win elections in independent India. With rapidly failing health and seeing his most valued strategies deliver a contrarian result, he embraced Buddhism in October 1956, fifty-three days before his death.

To make a provisional summary, any faithful life sketch of Babasaheb Ambedkar would certainly underscore his extraordinary commitment to the cause of the dalits, his hatred of the caste system and of brahminism, its fountainhead; and his belief that constitutionalism and democracy were capable of bringing about revolutionary change without bloodshed. To him the institution of the state was a necessity, and the human agency shaping it all-important. The secular belief that it is human destiny to progress towards a society based on liberty, equality and fraternity, went alongside the conviction that religion serves to conserve the moral fabric of society—a love for Buddhism its best exemplar. His respect for Marxism was evident, as the only other ideology that foregrounds the exploitative nature of worldly relations and aspires to alter them, but so were his serious doubts regarding its claim to scientific truth: whether in the analysis of history or prognostications for the future. While accepting that society is always made up of classes, he did not accept that their relations are necessarily defined by conflict. He shared the goal of equality with the communists, but had reservations about the inevitability or desirability of revolution in bringing it about. In no case would he approve of violence, however desirable its goal. While accepting the aims of socialism, he had reservations about the re-appropriation of wealth without its owners being compensated for their property.

To discern and express the characteristic elements of Ambedkar's outlook in even such general terms may not be without controversy. In the course of a turbulent life, his opinions, decisions and actions kept changing, sometimes shifting to the opposite stand from one he had previously taken. It is not always simple to retrieve the elements that informed his thinking. What's more, he freely admitted to being inconsistent and derided upholding consistency as an absolute ideal. Much of what he said or wrote was also polemical, rooted in the heat and context of the moment—hence difficult to distil into certain lasting principles. At a broad level, it may be said with certainty that he was rooted in liberalism. Armed with no more than this sketchy picture of him and a permissive template, we may proceed to take stock of the Ambedkarite movement that has claimed to follow him after his death.

A Noah's ark

Following his personal defeat in the 1952 and 1954 elections, Ambedkar had begun contemplating a non-communist opposition party to the Congress and sounded out prominent socialist leaders like Ram Manohar Lohia, P.K. Atre, S.M. Joshi and others with this idea. To infuse fresh blood into the new party, he established the Training School for Entrance to Politics in Ahilyashram, Pune, in July 1956, with a first batch of fifteen students. Not much is known about what happened to the school or those students thereafter. On 30 September 1956, the executive committee of the Scheduled Castes Federation, chaired by Ambedkar took a decision to dissolve the SCF and form a new party, the Republican Party of India. This decision was later announced by Ambedkar to the congregation of people gathered for the conversion programme at Nagpur in October 1956. The dissolution of the SCF and foundation of the RPI was prompted by many factors: one, after conversion to Buddhism, there would be no Scheduled Castes; two, the 'republican' in the new name would refer to Lincoln's party in the USA as well as to the Buddha's nostalgia for the clan republics that preceded monarchy; and three, Ambedkar's own desire to revert to a broad-based constituency of the ILP era, in view of his poor experience with the SCF. The new organisation could not, however, be raised very quickly because of his death within two months of the announcement and the impending general elections two months thereafter. The SCF manifesto issued for the elections of February 1957 had indicated the change in the name of the party. Surprisingly, the proposed name in this instance was no longer the RPI but the Backward Castes Federation, so as to include the OBCs and adivasis in addition to the SCs (Jaffrelot 2000, 86). This betrayed a lack of unanimity among the SCF leadership. Interestingly, after converting to Buddhism the SCF—and thereafter RPI—leaders continued to belong to their Hindu castes to avail of political reservations. In deference to Ambedkar's wishes, however, his followers dissolved the SCF and formed the RPI on 3 October 1957 at

Nagpur. As R.S. Morkhandikar writes:

> Its programme was framed on the basis of an open letter to the people written by Ambedkar (and published posthumously). In the letter he elaborates the concept of democracy and wants the Republican Party of India to aim at a society free from oppression and exploitation of one class by another, freedom to each individual from fear and want, and equality of opportunity. Those who never had the opportunity to develop were to be given precedence. The whole letter is imbued with a faith in liberal democracy, freedom of the individual as the goal and the state as a means to the end. The party was to organise struggle only if social justice and equality were denied to the deprived. (Morkhandikar 1990, 586)

The RPI proved to be merely a new label for the old SCF. At the time of its foundation, it had been wisely decided that leadership would be collectively exercised through a presidium, there being no leader like Ambedkar who could command the confidence of all. But this experiment did not last long. Allying with the Samyukta Maharashtra Samiti (an ad hoc organisation aimed at creating a separate state for Marathi-speaking people), the RPI won thirteen seats in the 1957 assembly election. The very next year, the RPI saw its first split over the issue of what 'Ambedkarism' was. B.C. Kamble, one of the members of the presidium and an advocate by profession, contended that Ambedkarism was constitutionalism, and only educated people like he could understand it. He denigrated the then senior leader 'Dadasaheb' Gaikwad (1902–1971), calling him dhotarya (dhoti-wearer, implying yokel), and accused him of flirting with the communists by foregrounding the struggle over livelihood issues of the dalit masses. Some young leaders early on saw no future for themselves in the RPI, and joined the Congress purely for greener pastures, but without giving up the Ambedkarite label. Later, in 1964, when the RPI under the leadership of Dadasaheb Gaikwad carried out a nationwide land satyagraha, the Congress took warning from this radical turn and schemed to co-opt dalit leaders and blunt their movement. Implemented through Yashwantrao Chavan, the first chief minister of Maharashtra, none other than Dadasaheb Gaikwad, more aware than most of likely counter-tactics, fell prey to the Congress' blandishments. Soon after the expiry of his term as an RPI member in the Lok Sabha (1957–1962) he was made a Rajya Sabha member and honoured with the Padmashri in 1968.

In the late 1960s, when the entire world was in turmoil with various peoples' movements, dalit youth in Maharashtra, who had by now begun to pour out of universities but nonetheless faced bleak prospects, were angered by the continued pathetic state of dalits as well as the intellectual and moral bankruptcy of the RPI. Reacting to the increasing incidence of caste atrocities, the Dalit Panther was formed by Namdeo Dhasal and J.V. Pawar in 1972, emulating the Black Panther Party in the US. Attempting to fill the vacuum in dalit politics left by a hopelessly splintered RPI, they tried to transcend caste by enfolding all the socially oppressed and economically exploited people into the category of dalits, and its manifesto spoke a militant language of transforming society:

> The struggle for the emancipation of the dalits needs a complete revolution. Partial change is impossible. We do not want it either. We want a complete and total revolutionary change ... We will not be satisfied easily now. We do not want a little place in the brahmin alley. We want to rule the whole country ... Our ideas of social revolution and rebellion will be too strong for such paper-made vehicles of protest. They will sprout in the soil, flower in the mind and then will come forward with full force with the help of steel-strong means (in Satyanarayana and Tharu 62).

The sheer change in the idiom of dalit self-expression stunned observers and was perceived as a threat by the establishment. Amid rising violence against the dalit community in Maharashtra, young men and women came out armed with sticks and bicycle chains, to offer resistance. Although no great tangible change occurred, the sign of this wrath of the wretched did give pause to the perpetrators of atrocities.

Sadly, by the 1980s, Dalit Panther was to be struck by the same affliction that had earlier split the RPI. Raja Dhale, one of the leaders, raised the issue of Ambedkarism, accusing others of leaning towards Marxism which, he contended, Ambedkar had opposed. Dhale's idea of true Ambedkarism was Buddhism. The Dalit Panther splintered and practically disappeared before sprouting again in a degenerate form as the Bharatiya Dalit Panther, with the likes of the late Arun Kamble and Ramdas Athawale leading it. Around the early 1980s, when the nostalgia of the dalit masses for Babasaheb Ambedkar grew stronger, Prakash Ambedkar, his grandson, appeared on the scene. The dalits began to respond to him. Supported by some ex-Panthers, he led struggles for getting land to the landless and took on the sugar barons of Maharashtra. Sharad Pawar, then chief minister, was alarmed by the potential re-emergence of an independent and radical dalit movement. He followed the example set by his mentor, Yashvantrao Chavan, who had successfully placated Gaikwad earlier; Pawar duly won over Ramdas Athawale to his side, in order to weaken Prakash Ambedkar. He would henceforth play more such games to decimate the dalit movement in Maharashtra through his stooge Athawale—who has certainly kept up with changing times and is now a minister in Modi's cabinet.

The entire dalit universe revolves around its only sun, Ambedkar. As one Marathi dalit poet—Yamaraj, from Mumbai—stated in his perceptive challenge to these self-seeking leaders: 'vagalun bhimachya nava, tumhi pudhari hovun dawa' (drop the name of Ambedkar, and show us how you become a leader). The leaders know that without demonstrating allegiance to Ambedkar, they cannot exist.

The dalit movement in Maharashtra today is reduced to numerous factions of the RPI and Dalit Panther with a plethora of names and tags, and innumerable billboard and letterhead outfits that come alive on the eve of elections to claim their share of political rent from the ruling classes. They all swear by Ambedkarism; one faction might ally with the Congress, another with the BJP, one with the Shiv Sena and still others with some other party, but they would all style themselves Ambedkarite. The story is more or less the same in other states. The idea of the Dalit Panther inspired youth in many states to form their own Panther parties. Gujarat, the neighbouring state to Maharashtra, saw a vibrant Panther movement but it, too, was stubbed out. In Karnataka, the Dalit Sangharsha Samiti—founded in 1974—lasted longer, carrying out several inspiring campaigns, but could not survive the usual combination of internal ideological fission and enticement from the ruling classes. By far, the only exception in the political arena has been the Bahujan Samaj Party created by the late Kanshi Ram.

As Kanshi Ram averred, he had learnt how not to do politics from the RPI, and kept a tight control over the BSP in his own and his close confidante, Mayawati's, hands. They ensured that there were no leaders of independent standing in the BSP to be wooed by the ruling class parties. Anyone who left the party would soon be reduced to a non-entity. The inherent danger of a split was thus averted by the totalitarian control of the BSP supremo. The party, given the unique advantage of the dalit demography in Uttar Pradesh—21.1 per cent of the total population, according to the 2011 census, i.e. a good 5 per cent higher than the national average, and a huge majority of it comprising a single caste of jatav/chamars—succeeded there and emerged as a formidable political force. Although it never projected itself overtly as an Ambedkarite party, its backbone was constituted by dalits who saw it as one. The BSP was by no means averse to sustaining this image. The prestige of the association, the credibility and votes were a real gain, while the cost involved was minimal—just cosmetic tinkering, with scores of statues, the naming and renaming of roads, colonies, institutions, creating Ambedkar parks and memorials, and so on.

Besides political parties, offshoots of the original Backward and Minority Communities Employees Federation (Bamcef), founded by Kanshi Ram in 1978, exist in factions and carry on with the charter of the original—community service—although with diminished zeal.

They appear to have prospered in one sense, going by the geographical range of their conferences; for the last few years at least one faction has been holding its conferences abroad. They persist with Kanshi Ram's rhetoric that the bahujans would one day vanquish the forces of brahminism. Ambedkar had rejected the racial theory behind varna or caste differentiation. This does not affect their claim to be Ambedkarite, even as many of the Bamcef factions now swear to an autochthonous racial identity of mulniwasi (original inhabitants) for themselves. These factions have not yet begun to operate in the mainstream political arena, but such quibbles do not dampen their political ambition of overthrowing the brahminical order. Their current phase, which has been in progress from at least the early 1970s, is supposed to be the phase of awakening. Once the mulniwasis have fully awakened to the fact that they have a lost kingdom to reclaim, they would come out to wage the concluding battle and fell the fortress of brahminism! This nonsense sells in the name of Ambedkarism.

There are, in addition, many Buddhist organisations, initially confined to Maharashtra but slowly spreading across the country, which are working to realise Ambedkar's supposed dream of making India a Buddhist country. They also claim 'Ambedkarite' as their rightful identity. On the eve of his conversion to Buddhism on 14 October 1956, Ambedkar had formed the Bharatiya Bouddha Mahasabha (BBM, or Buddhist Society of India) to manage the integrity of the neo-Buddhist community and take the conversion movement forward. After his demise, his son Yashwantrao alias Bhaiyyasaheb Ambedkar became the president of this organisation, followed by his widow Mira-tai Ambedkar, in September 1977. The BBM, too, suffered multiple splits and it is difficult to even ascertain how many factions exist today. Almost every town and city in Maharashtra has multiple BBMs but without any connection with one another. There are still more Buddhist organisations under other labels. All of them of course claim to be Ambedkarite.

Then there is the Samata Sainik Dal ('Equality Corps'), founded by Ambedkar with an objective 'to promote the idea of equality as also to keep away the mischievous elements from obstructing the implementation of the constructive ideas by the workers in the movement.' It was birthed by a group of people from the Samaj Samata Sangh ('Corps for Social Equality') who volunteered to counter any possible attacks on dalits during the Mahad satyagraha of 1927. After 1956, one section of opinion upheld Ambedkar's dictum that there was no need for dalits to use agitational methods and insisted that they should instead focus on constitutional methods. Consequently, the SSD suffered an erosion of importance and almost disappeared in the years after Ambedkar's death. It has been resuscitated several times over the years by a variety of interested people and now exists as a shadow of its former self. Like the RPI and the BBM, there exist multiple SSDs of course, all run by 'Ambedkarites'. There are also numerous community organisations (such as youth organisations and mahila mandals) spread across slums, hamlets and villages under various names, which have set up Buddha viharas, erected statues, and opened libraries and boarding houses for students. To the extent that most of them would be connected to some leader or the other, they are also afflicted with the factionalism that pervades dalit politics.

Thanks to the policy of reservation, dalits constitute a sizeable proportion of the employment in the public domain (in central, state, local government bodies; in PSUs, financial institutions and banks). While in the initial years, these employees remained a part of mainstream trade unions and officers' associations, over time they began forming their own outfits. The main reason was that the mainstream union or association would not take up their issues, which were often in conflict with the interests of others. They were also under-represented at the leadership level of these bodies. As the journalist P. Sainath reported of one instance: 'In Tamil Nadu, one of the biggest unions in the country, the BHEL [Bharat Heavy Electricals Limited] union, split on caste lines in 1996. The dalits from all unions complained of discrimination. It was found that barring one national union, none of the eleven unions on campus had a dalit office bearer' (*PUCL Bulletin*, June 1999). Since caste-based associations cannot be recognised as trade unions, they operate as SC/ST employees' welfare associations in each organisation. Needless to say, they all call themselves Ambedkarite.

As government servants are statutorily barred from participating in agitational politics, a quasi-middle class layer of upwardly mobile dalits found their purpose in welfare activities. Some of them came together and created larger entities over an expanded domain of industry, across regions or even countrywide. At least one of their leaders, Udit Raj, has made it big out of such a 'confederation' to become a BJP MP and a member of its national executive. Apart from this, he is the national chairman of the All India Confederation of SC/ST Organisations, an organisation which exists only on paper. Officially, such bodies are meant to take care of the interests of their own members in service matters. However, they tend to extend themselves into the community in the spirit of Ambedkar's call to 'payback to society'. All these associations, it goes without saying, claim to be Ambedkarite. They prove the claim to their own satisfaction by doing 'social service' on the numerous red-letter days of the Ambedkarite calendar: distributing food packets to people, opening eye camps and handing out free spectacles to the needy, or holding free clinics for check-ups and the distribution of commonplace medicines.

In the academia, NGOs and beyond

With the role model of Babasaheb Ambedkar and his mantra 'educate, agitate and organise' before them, dalits made a good deal of progress in education, although they still lag significantly behind other communities. While the number of graduates in the general population rose from 5.7 per cent in 2001 to 8.2 per cent in 2011, for the SCs the figure has nearly doubled from 2.2 per cent to 4.1 per cent. In higher education, there is a high incidence of dalits in the humanities courses. The majority of them try for the Union (or State) Public Service Commission jobs or non-technical jobs in public sector units, particularly banks, or take up the teaching profession. Dalit teachers in universities enjoy academic freedom to critically reflect upon the state of dalits, unlike their counterparts in commercial organisations. While much of their output may be considered routine, catering to academic rituals and requirements, some drift towards critical thinking and become potentially dangerous to the ruling establishment. Perhaps to placate this growing tribe of dalit academicians, several Ambedkar Chairs and Ambedkar Centres have been launched, and a centre for inclusion and exclusion (or some equally catchy theme) in every major university. As part of the eleventh five-year plan (2007–12) the University Grants Commission started Centres for the Study of Social Exclusion and Inclusive Policies at thirty-five central and state government universities. These initiatives are invariably poorly provided for and manned largely by dalits, creating another kind of ghettoisation. They offer regular courses in 'Ambedkar Thought' and social issues, carry out research on these themes, and speed up their further proliferation. It is as if the academic energy of the entire higher educated dalit class were sought to be contained within this newly created framework. There has been a spurt in research activity, and consequently in Ph.D. theses of questionable quality on issues related to Ambedkar. Apart from consolidating an identitarian outlook among dalit academics and exacerbating the pre-existing tendency among dalit groups to splinter, another constant among these bodies is that they all call themselves Ambedkarite.

If literature is a mirror of society, then dalit literature could not escape the marks of the degeneration of the dalit movement. In the second half of the twentieth century, dalit literature shook up the literary establishment hitherto monopolised by the upper castes, and in due course won itself a certain degree of recognition. It was not an organised movement of writers who coordinated their output or directed their efforts by a common manifesto, although something like this effect was perhaps achieved by their inveterate attendance of sahitya sammelans (literary fests), which have proliferated in states like Maharashtra—the birth place of dalit literature. These effects usually show in the obsessive subjectivism of the writer and the stereotyping of dalit life. Barring a few works, there is hardly an authentic reflection of contemporary conditions, still less the angst or anger of the dalit masses. The litterateurs are more usually to be found squandering their energy in sterile debates over whether their literature should be termed dalit, or Ambedkarite, or Phule-Ambedkarite, or Buddhist or something else. Besides literature, there are groups which work for cultural awakening among dalits through the medium of songs, music, street plays and dramas, also without much coordination among themselves. Not having anything objective to relate to, they all revolve around singing paeans to Ambedkar and strengthening the bhakti cult around him. In transports of poetic imagination, they shower superlatives on him that fortify his godhood and make him unavailable to a critical reading.

In addition, there are professional organisations of dalit engineers, doctors, lawyers and various professional groups with their own Ambedkar associations to stress their identity. They extend abroad in the form of the dalit diaspora. Their cultural mainstay is to commemorate the important anniversaries of Ambedkar's life, work to memorialise him abroad, and nowadays, to celebrate their own digital presence on social media. There have been numerous virtual networks of email groups and blogs and communities on Twitter and Facebook, all resolute in labelling themselves 'Ambedkarite' but quite amorphous in terms of what it means—not unlike a fan club.

Finally, with the winding down of the state as a welfare institution—as mandated by the Washington Consensus of the neoliberal order after 1990—and the consequent loss of jobs in the reserved sector, NGOs have proliferated to alleviate the pain of the dalit masses. According to a Home Ministry handout published in the *Hindu* (20 February 2017), the fiscal year of 2015–16 saw a flow of Rs 17,208 crore from foreign donors facilitated by 33,000 NGOs registered under the Foreign Contribution Regulation Act. Of course, much of the funds land up in hindutva's coffers. Perhaps to suppress this fact, the Indian state and rightwing outfits aggressively brand NGOs as supporting Christian missionary activity on the sly, since they work among dalits, adivasis and those other marginalised sections of society whom the state easily abandons. The current dispensation under Modi has, in order to disable resistance in the country, throttled the flow of funds to NGOs except for the hindutva ones. It is not that NGOs are a desirable end, still less is the depoliticisation of public consciousness that attends the work of most of them. Some of them, however, have tried to do some good on the ground and also contributed to internationalising the issue of caste discrimination. Dalits have always been a natural subject of interest to NGOs. As the dalit movement weakened, they rushed in to occupy its vacated space, and the NGO sector duly became a significant employer of dalits with degrees in the humanities, typically capped with a postgraduate degree in social work. With the prospect of public-sector jobs drying up, NGOs became still more promising as potential employers. However, these organisations distract dalits from seeing their woes as systemic by offering them piecemeal solutions. With their professional outlook, and being staffed by youngsters, they have more prestige than dalit political leaders. Needless to say, most of these NGOs also swear by Ambedkarism.

When multiple interests with incompatible ideological proclivities stake a claim to being Ambedkarite, we get a situation of multiple absurdities and a severe identity crisis. In 2011, when the Shiv Sena with its well-known history of denigrating Ambedkar, came up with a new formulation of political algebra, 'Shiv Shakti + Bhim Shakti = Deshbhakti', the erstwhile stormy petrels of the Dalit Panther and some dalit intellectuals upheld the preposterous idea. In the Worli riots of

1974, one of the first battles of the Dalit Panther, the Shiv Sena had brutally martyred Bhagwat Jadhav, a Dalit Panther member. In 1978, the Sena had vehemently protested the renaming of the Marathwada University in Aurangabad after Babasaheb Ambedkar. The old name meant to be jettisoned was a retrograde one, the caste name of the powerful marathas. The Sena chief Bal Keshav Thackeray had poured ridicule on the agitating dalits with an infamous statement, 'Gharaat nahi peeth, magtaay vidyapeeth'—they have no bread to eat but demand a university. A number of dalits were raped and murdered; their properties destroyed by the Sena cadre. In 1988, the Sena rioted in Bombay for the removal of the chapter, "The Riddle of Rama and Krishna" from Ambedkar's posthumously published work, *Riddles in Hinduism.* It has always opposed reservations, which are identified with dalits and particularly with Ambedkarite dalits. On 11 July 1997, during the Sena–BJP rule in Maharashtra, ten dalits were massacred in police firing in Ramabai Nagar. The government doggedly protected the sub inspector, Manohar Kadam, who was responsible for the murders. With such a track record, the Sena still succeeded in getting support from the likes of Namdeo Dhasal and Ramdas Athawale, who no doubt managed to square the betrayal with their 'Ambedkarite' conscience. Athawale's conscience should be hardened to such tests by now (notwithstanding the obligatory noises he made over the brahmin and maratha-led violence in Bhima-Koregaon over the bicentennial celebrations of the imperial obelisk for the last of the Anglo–Maratha wars of 1818).

Meanwhile, upwardly mobile dalits, without discarding the Ambedkarite identity, uphold capitalism or proudly project themselves as dalit capitalists, or worse, suggest that capitalism is the new emancipator of the dalits, quite disregarding Ambedkar's warning against the twin enemies of dalits—brahminism and capitalism. Addressing the G.I.P. Railway Depressed Classes Workmen's Conference held in Manmad in 1938, Ambedkar had said:

> There are, in my view, two enemies which the workers of this country have to deal with. The two enemies are brahmanism and capitalism … By brahminism I do not mean the power, privileges and interests of the brahmins as a community. That is not the sense in which I am using the word. By brahminism I mean the negation of the spirit of liberty, equality and fraternity. In that sense it is rampant in all classes and is not confined to the brahmins alone though they have been the originators of it (in Das 2010, 50–1).

Ambedkar constantly acknowledged identity—in his case the inescapable untouchable identity—as a political, socio-historical and existential fact. Yet, he sought to transcend it with pragmatic logic. Ambedkar had warned that brahminism is not necessarily limited to the upper castes but pervades all communities. Nevertheless, even Buddhism, which Ambedkar embraced as a doctrine of social morality, is reduced by the Ambedkarites to a marker of cultural identity, meant to be displayed by building viharas, learning Pali, singing prayers, practising rituals, and lately, attending vipassana.

The Fabian and Deweyan seams

As suggested earlier, it is not easy to construct an ideological Ambedkar, beyond the broad characterisation that he was a liberal. To acknowledge this still falls short of fixing his location within the broad spectrum of liberalism, one end of which comes close to radicalism and the other to its antithesis. It is likely that he himself did not lose sleep over nugatory issues of nomenclature. Ambedkar's greatness lies not only in foregrounding the caste question but waging a tireless battle against discrimination. (Establishing whether his efforts succeeded, or to what extent, is a secondary matter.) He was dealing with a problem for which he had little reference to go by except the stray instances of some individuals in history. He had no available theorisation he could bank upon and had to create his own theories conversant with the struggle. Theorisation, moreover, was not his objective; it came as the by-product of practical struggles that he waged—evidenced in his voluminous writings, half of which are posthumously published. It is clear enough that he saw dalit emancipation as a project of universal import, an integral part of the emancipation of humankind, though it needed to be worked out from the particular to the universal. Perhaps Buddhism was his path to bridge the distance.

Ambedkar could be seen constantly changing, or to use a better word, evolving. He never hesitated to change his opinion when facts so warranted. Against making a virtue of consistency, he quoted Emerson, who had called consistency the virtue of an ass. One finds multiple strands to his personality. For instance, Upendra Baxi saw many Ambedkars in his persona. In an essay published in 1995, "Emancipation and Justice: Babasaheb Ambedkar's Legacy and Vision", Baxi identified as many as seven Ambedkars from his discourse. The first Ambedkar is an authentic dalit who bore the full brunt of the practice of untouchability. The second is an exemplar of scholarship. The third, an activist journalist. The fourth, a pre-Gandhian activist. The fifth is locked in mortal combat with Gandhi on the issue of legislative reservations for the Depressed Classes. The sixth is the constitutionalist involved in the discourse on transfer of power and the processes of constitution-making. The seventh Ambedkar is a renegade Hindu, not just in the sense of being the man who set aflame a copy of the *Manusmriti* in Mahad in 1927, but in his symbolic statement on conversion in 1935 (that he should not die a Hindu) and his actual conversion to Buddhism in late 1956. And this is not the only way to go about it—one could equally take another approach, using his philosophical coordinates to see different Ambedkars, and perhaps obtain the opposite, a holistic view of him.

A recurring motif in Ambedkar's public life was the deep impact of his professor John Dewey while he was a student at Columbia University. As K.N. Kadam put it in his essay "Dr Ambedkar's Philosophy of Emancipation and the Impact of John Dewey" in *The Meaning of*

Ambedkarite Conversion to Buddhism and Other Essays (1997), 'Unless we understand something of John Dewey ... it would be impossible to understand Dr Ambedkar.' This influence ran through his writings as well as his tactical formulations. His classic tract *Annihilation of Caste* (1936) abounds in passages inspired by Dewey's *Democracy and Education* (1916). Dewey's philosophy of pragmatism or instrumentalism considered all knowledge as tentative. The meaning of reality could only be realised through the interaction of human agents in coping with problems that are thrown up by their environment—practical, rather than theoretical problems. He borrows from the pragmatism of Charles Sanders Peirce and William James, as well as the instrumentalism of the Logical Positivists but differs from each in subtle ways. While Dewey accepts Pierce's postulation that meaning arises from human activity (praxis), he rejects his 'realistic metaphysics' which posits that there is a reality-in-itself which has a definite character independent of what any individual thinks about it. He, likewise, accepts James' pragmatism focused on the real-life problems and difficulties of ordinary human beings but differs from his individualistic orientation. He shared with these figures a reliance on the 'scientific method' or 'verificationism' but differed from their passive 'experimentation' that simply took data from controlled observation and used it to confirm or disconfirm a hypothesis. For him the goal of the 'scientific method' in life was to induce intelligent reflection on our practices in order to enhance them—so as to approach a social order in which poetry and religious feeling may become, as Dewey's aestheticised image has it, 'the unforced flowers of life'. Dewey had maintained that an idea agrees with reality, and is therefore true, if and only if it is successfully employed in human action in pursuit of human goals and interests; in Dewey's terms, if it leads to the resolution of a problematic situation. Ambedkar can be seen *creatively* following this brand of pragmatism all through his life. His reservations about Marx parallel those of Dewey and his interpretation of the Buddha is imbued with Deweyan instrumentalism—to obtain a

Deweyan Buddha as Meera Nanda (2004) characterises it.

A plethora of anecdotal and scholarly evidence can be cited besides Ambedkar's own admission in a letter to Sharda Kabir, from New York, as late as June 1952 (when he was awarded an honorary doctorate by Columbia University), that he owed his 'entire intellectual life' to his professor John Dewey in Columbia. This philosophical approach rules out any overarching thesis or a priori truth or ism regarding historical progression. Dewey's outlook is suspicious of the metanarratives of history and of any mechanistic progression from simpler to more complex socio-economic formations. Thus, the Deweyan position is implicitly non-Marxist. The scholar Arun Prabha Mukherjee studied the influence of Dewey on Ambedkar and showed how Ambedkar was deeply influenced by the Deweyan idea of democracy as 'associated life' which went beyond electing a government at regular intervals. Mukherjee (2009, 356) notes that Ambedkar picks up and develops the Deweyan concept of 'associated life' into a political tool. She says both Dewey and Ambedkar believed that democracy should not be restricted to the political realm, but should also manifest itself in other areas, such as education, industry and the public sphere.

Another scholar, Scott R. Stroud, also charting the influence of John Dewey on Ambedkar, notes Ambedkar's translation of Dewey's pragmatism into an Indian context filled with injustice and underwritten by religion. Arguing how Ambedkar's pragmatist rhetoric focusing on conversion as a solution to the problems of untouchables is to be seen as 'translational activity', he says:

> Instead of merely creating a new *text*, Ambedkar's appeals for religious conversion also promise to create a new *self* in the form of the audience member. This appeared to be Ambedkar's motive in speaking to various audiences around India: he was appropriating Dewey's thought to change the very important mental habits of those listening to him. He created new ways of talking through his pragmatism, as well as new selves in his audience members through conversion. These features of Ambedkar's pragmatist rhetor translating between two

> conceptual schemes for a melioristic purpose can illuminate a potential sense of rhetorical reorientation resident in pragmatist theory. Many have found that Dewey's sense of pragmatism lacks any notion of revolution or immediate significant change; indeed, this criticism seems to undergird Dewey's critique of Marxist revolutionary means (2016, 7, emphasis original).

Dewey was also a prominent American Fabian socialist and the co-author of the "Humanist Manifesto" (1933). In 1884, a small group of English intellectuals formed the Fabian Society with the aim of establishing a classless, socialist society as envisioned by Marx, but differed with him on how the revolution would be accomplished and by whom. In contrast to Marx's revolutionary socialism, this brand of socialism would be brought about gradually through reforms by the enlightened middle classes (and not with the working classes at the vanguard). The Fabians worked for world revolution not through an uprising of the workers, but the indoctrination of young scholars. They believed that these intellectual revolutionaries would eventually acquire power and influence in the official and unofficial opinion-making and power-wielding organs, and gradually transform the world into a socialist society. In practice it meant slow, piecemeal changes in existing concepts of law, morality, government, economics, and education. At the climax of his career in 1950, Dewey became the honorary national chairman of the American counterpart of the British Fabian Society, called the League for Industrial Democracy.

Ambedkar certainly could not have been oblivious of these ideas. After Columbia, he landed at the London School of Economics, founded in 1895 by members of the Fabian Society (Sidney and Beatrice Webb, Graham Wallas and George Bernard Shaw). He creatively used the Deweyan concept of democracy in dissecting caste society and saw that without caste being annihilated, nothing worthwhile could be established. His socialism is a correlate, an essential ingredient of democracy. His idea of socialism was surely Fabian, again adapted from Dewey and Edwin R.A. Seligman (his PhD supervisor in Columbia), and reinforced during his stay at the LSE. Ambedkar's first political party, the Independent Labour Party, founded in 1936, was fashioned after the Fabian-backed party of the same name in England, founded in 1893. It clearly propounded the socialist goal and proudly adopted a red flag. Later, in *States and Minorities* he famously proposed that a model of state socialism be incorporated into the Constitution as its basic feature, not ordinarily alterable by the legislature (*BAWS* Vol. 1, 406). His embrace of Buddhism at the end of his life was a step towards socialism for, according to him, it had the same ends as Marxism but without its deficient means—violence and dictatorship. Whether it is Ambedkar's socialist ideas or his emphasis on higher education over school education, his attraction to as well as reservations about Marxism, his ardent belief in reforms and skepticism about the feasibility of revolution, emulation of the Fabian Independent Labour Party, his model of state socialism in *States and Minorities*, etc.—all are a direct attestation of his Fabian influences.

Re-creation, recreation

Did Ambedkar's writings and career reflect, much less leave behind, a systematic theory that explains or predicts the world or guides action, so as to constitute an ism? Except for the identity-obsessed, the honest and objective answer to this question has to be in the negative. To think otherwise is to negate the core of his work. His life reveals that he tried various strategies and tactics depending on the unfolding situation, caring little for consistency. What informed his inconsistencies was the philosophy of pragmatism.

It was in 1942 while addressing the All-India Depressed Classes Conference at which the formation of the Scheduled Castes Federation was proposed, that Ambedkar concluded his presidential address with these words:

> My final words of advice to you are *educate, organise and agitate*; have faith

> in yourself. With justice on our side I do not see how we can lose our battle. The battle to me is a matter of joy. The battle is in the fullest sense spiritual. There is nothing material or social in it. For ours is a battle not for wealth or for power. It is a battle for freedom. It is a battle for the reclamation of human personality (in Keer 1954, 351).

His methodological direction to his followers comes from this call—*educate, organise and agitate*—the famed mission and slogan of the Fabian society (Pugh 1984), which he had already emblazoned on the mast of his paper *Bahishkrit Bharat* (founded in 1927). Ambedkar stressed the ever changing nature of reality and the need to be enlightened enough to comprehend and confront it. 'Educate' so as to understand the world around you; 'agitate' against evil; and 'organise' in order to gain strength to root it out. He exhorted his followers to be prabuddha (enlightened), with the cognitive capability to analyse their situation, develop abhorrence towards injustice, and unitedly struggle to root it out. He did not impose his methods or conclusions on his followers but rather expected them to devise appropriate means in their own space and time as enlightened people.

Following Ambedkar does not necessitate fabricating the identity of an 'Ambedkarite'. It does not mean that we idolise and worship him. Following him may mean being inspired by his vision of 'liberty, equality and fraternity', critically engaging with the contemporary world and devising strategies to realise changes in it. Following Ambedkar means being enlightened and not willingly blind, hymn-singing devotees. It means not taking anything as a fact just because some great person had held it so. Following Ambedkar means dissecting his ideas and legacy in order to understand why, despite the adulation paid to him, the relative condition of ordinary dalits as remains pathetic as ever. In a speech (later published as a book) called *Ranade, Gandhi and Jinnah* delivered in 1943 in Poona on the 101st birthday celebration of the scholar–reformer Mahadev Govind Ranade, Ambedkar himself warned against hero worship:

> Hero-worship in the sense of expressing our unbounded admiration is one thing. To obey the hero is a totally different kind of hero-worship. There is nothing wrong in the former while the latter is no doubt a most pernicious thing. The former is only man's respect for everything which is noble and of which the great man is only an embodiment. The latter is the villain's fealty to his lord. The former is consistent with respect, but the latter is a sign of debasement. The former does not take away one's intelligence to think and independence to act. The latter makes one a perfect fool (*BAWS* 1, 231).

Quite like the Buddha, who exhorted his disciples not to take his advice uncritically but be a light unto themselves (atta deep bhava), Ambedkar cautioned against uncritically accepting the maxims and conclusions of anyone, however great. Leading by example, he had re-examined the teachings and ideas attributed to the Buddha and made them new. In the same speech he goes on to say:

> What a great man does is not to impose his maxims on his disciples. What he does is to evoke them, to awaken them to a vigorous and various exertion of their faculties. Again the pupil only takes his guidance from his master. He is not bound to accept his master's conclusions (240).

The march of the Ambedkarites in light of this could be seen as anti-Ambedkar. Indeed, they have consistently disrespected him in their acts of commission and omission: ignoring his vision of the annihilation of caste and achievement of socialism to overtly celebrate caste identities instead, and promote slavish devotion to ill-constructed and inert icons of the great iconoclast. They have ghettoised him in their sectarian temples as an infallible god and made him unavailable for future generations to learn from. His words in a parliamentary debate in 1954 make his non-dogmatism clear: 'I am prepared to pick and choose from everyone, socialist, communist or other. I do not claim infallibility, and as Buddha says, there is *nothing* infallible; there is nothing final and everything is liable to examination' (*BAWS* 1, 960, emphasis in original).

Ambedkar was great simply because he genuinely strove to make this world a better place to live in. This is not to be equated with his struggle for the emancipation of dalits as his own caste or to say that he was right in doing all he did. To seek the betterment of one's own folk is a basic tribal instinct. Such collectives could be seen as extended families and truly are an extension of the self, and also a buffer against the external environment. If Ambedkar had taken up cudgels for dalits merely as his own people, he would not qualify for greatness. He took up the cause of dalits because it was crucial to the ideals of human equality and democratisation, and necessary in the immediate sense to extricate Indian society from stagnation and degradation. It was an integral part of the struggle for the liberation of human beings from the structures of exploitation and oppression. His greatness lay in confronting castes in their existing form—to annihilate them—and not trying to shoehorn them into some prefabricated framework as the Indian communists did. His diagnoses and prescriptions may not have fully worked—indeed they did not—but that is a different matter.

Philosophy that grips people becomes a live force. It may be backed by academic construction but more than that it is shaped and communicated through the struggles of people. To be effective in people's hands, any philosophy, in whatever shape it was propounded by its originators, needs to be reshaped through struggle. Certain elements of Ambedkarism may well have been forged out of a dialectical contention between the two processes; however, neither is easy to decode—Ambedkar's thought or the popular experience of struggles—especially in their interface with the state. It is one thing to acquire political power through a people's struggle and quite another to get it by allying with the existing powers. The former is an earning while the latter is alms. By default, such a statist Ambedkarism easily becomes a mutant form of Deweyan pragmatism, one warped by the Indian climate. In the absence of moral anchors, it degenerates into rent-seeking from the state, thereby strengthening the state structure—

the root cause of all oppression in modern times. The state does not come across clearly as the culprit in Ambedkar's schema; he takes it as the sum of the people comprising it. It could be bad if people are bad, but conversely, it can be good if people are good. As for the role of maintaining goodness in people, he assigns it to religion. It is not hard to show that states proclaiming Buddhism as their religion—the best according to him—are not substantively different from the worst states.

Even if we were to arrive at a universally satisfactory definition of Ambedkarism, it would be worth bearing in mind that isms tend to be premised on something that worked in the past. They are of questionable value in an era characterised by rapid change. The caution applies equally to Marxism, for while it is a recognisably integral system of thought based on a scientific approach, in the hands of its adherents it is often reduced to a quasi-religion. Marx endorsed Descartes' exhortation, 'de omnibus dubitandum' (doubt everything), proposing a process of a perpetual search for truth through critical praxis, but this is ignored by zealous disciples who settle for the mentally lazy alternative of pietism, in which Marx's writings are the last word. The results are before us. Static isms are shown to be merely products of human inertia. They are beneficial to the ruling classes as they guide popular attention to the past and deflect focus from the oppressive present. They often raise identitarian passions in people and make their responses predictable. An Ambedkarism channelled into slogans, poetry, flags, banners, Buddha viharas, congregations—the entire arsenal of symbolic displays—is simply an ecstatic mood without ideological content, and can be harnessed to various and conflicting ends. As we have seen, Ambedkarism could be a constitutionalist disapproval of the entire gamut of agitational politics, or an inactive Buddhism that pushes people to look inwards—and cleanse their minds with vipassana—instead of addressing outside reality. It has manifested as anti-communism, keeping dalits antagonistic towards class questions. It is sought to be submerged within Hindu ritualism, as the entire paraphernalia of idol worship is steadily assembled around Ambedkar as the godhead, luring dalits into the reactionary camp of the BJP. It has also been harnessed to the narrative of pushy individuals on the make who happen to be dalit: whether Ambedkarite Hindu nationalists, Ambedkarite capitalists or other such deformities.

For a people with the demographic profile of dalits—a huge mass of predominantly landless labourers, suffering from every conceivable deprivation—the struggle against the power structure is the only way to secure their rights and build up a political presence. Babasaheb Ambedkar's life was a beacon to inspire such a struggle. Ambedkarism should take shape through the processes of practical interpretation of his writings, speeches and critical thought. Moreover, struggle is the best mode for the political education of people, the best fortress to protect ideological resources from plunder. Ambedkarites missed this fundamental logic and ran after the mirage of political power, shunning the hard work that struggle demands.

Ambedkar is dead. The innumerable Ambedkarisms of the Ambedkarites continue to thrive, hurrying past the dalit masses engulfed by misery.

4

Violence as Infrasound

Khairlanji, Kawlewada, Dulina, Bhagana...

On 29 September 2006, just three days before over a million-strong gathering of Ambedkarite dalits would congregate at Deekshabhoomi, Nagpur, to celebrate the fiftieth anniversary of their mukti din (liberation day)—the day Babasaheb Ambedkar had administered them deeksha (initiation) into Buddhism—a gruesome atrocity took place in a village called Khairlanji, just 125 km away. The entire family of a farmer, Bhaiyalal Bhotmange, was lynched to death—including his wife Surekha (40), daughter Priyanka (17), sons Roshan (19) and Sudhir (21). The details of the torture inflicted on them were hardly credible as the act of human beings—a mother and daughter paraded naked in the village centre and gang-raped to death, the genitals of the boys crushed with stones, and the corpses callously thrown into a canal. The Bhotmanges were Ambedkarites and Buddhists. Their ravaged hovel of unplastered brick walls and a thatched roof stood in solitude outside the village, telling the tale of dalits after fifty years of supposed liberation.

The first news of the horror appeared in a Nagpur paper on 31 September, where it was reported as the murder of four members of a family by villagers outraged at the illegitimate relationship Surekha

Bhotmange with a man from the neighbouring village. Without revealing the caste identities of the victims, the story was given the slant of a crime at the hands of villagers whose moral sensibilities were provoked beyond endurance by a woman's adulterous conduct. None took note of it. The Deekshabhoomi celebrations on 2 October 2006 concluded with no inkling of something untoward. Even after news began to pour in and the details became known, there was still no reaction anywhere over the incident. It went unnoticed by a second congregation in Nagpur on 14 October, gathered to commemorate the deeksha ceremony by the Gregorian calendar.

The incident may have been passed over entirely, with the usual rigmarole of arrests, investigations and bail, but for the protest march by dalit women in the district town of Bhandara on 1 November. By this time, before the police cordoned off the village, people from the Vidarbha Jan Andolan Samiti (Vidarbha Organisation for People's Movements) and the Manuski Advocacy Centre had completed fact-finding missions and publicised the gory details of the case. Activists led by dalit women mobilised the community for protests. In Amravati, they made a small poster of the photographs first published by Manuski on its website, with the caption: 'How long are you going to tolerate this?' Soon, protests engulfed all of Maharashtra. Raosaheb Ramchandra Patil, the state home minister, termed them naxalite-induced and gave the police a free hand to unleash terror on protesters in the streets of Nagpur, Kamptee, Amravati, Yavatmal and across the Vidarbha region. The police attacked dalit bastis, thrashing young and old, men and women, abusing them in the filthiest terms. School and college-going boys were tortured in custody. The fact-finding that we of the Committee for Protection of Democratic Rights carried out into police atrocities impelled me to call the aftermath a worse atrocity than Khairlanji. As the protests began to cool off, news of the desecration of an Ambedkar statue in Kanpur once again provoked dalits to take to the streets. They blocked the outbound trains at Kalyan station in

Mumbai. Some people, after clearing out passengers from two bogeys of the air-conditioned Mumbai–Pune Deccan Queen, set the bogeys on fire. Who exactly did it was not ascertained, but the police went berserk in rounding up young dalit boys from their hovels in the Kalyan slums.

The corporate media that had taken no notice of Khairlanji for weeks was prompt in condemning 'dalit rage'. Editorials wondered aloud, disingenuously, if Ambedkar would have approved of such unruly acts by his followers. Hundreds were beaten up and arrested, including dalit lawyers, doctors, businessmen and middle class professionals, and several cases were foisted on them invoking draconian laws. The atrocities unleashed on thousands of dalits who sought justice for the Khairlanji victims had created a saga of terror that I have detailed at length in my book, perhaps the first devoted to caste atrocities, *Khairlanji: A Strange and Bitter Crop* (2009). These tricks to terrorise dalits into submission could not work this time. The government had to task the Central Bureau of Investigation with investigating the crime and designate the sessions court at Bhandara as a 'fast track' court.

The state, however, managed to control the outcome by appointing as its prosecutor the high profile, flamboyant Ujwal Nikam, hyped as the super-lawyer of the state, while ignoring the name of advocate Shashi Bhushan Wahane proposed by the Khairlanji Dalit Hatyakand Sangharsh Samiti (Committee for struggle against the Khairlanji dalit massacre), the organisation that played a big role in exposing the incident. As the legal proceedings ground on, the fast track court—instituted on the premise of applying the PoA Act—reached the conclusion that there was no caste angle to the crime and that the Act did not apply. Furthermore, they found no ground to consider 'outrage to women's modesty' (Victorian legalese for sexual violence) and it was held that the attack was not premeditated. The shattering atrocity was transformed into a simple crime committed in a fit of rage. The prosecution failed its brief on every front, whether in using the available hard evidence, or establishing an order of events that would have confirmed a history of caste abuse preceding the crime, or unearthing the fact that revenge executed in such a ghastly manner for defying the writ of the powerful had a clear caste context. The crime was far from being without precedent, it was merely the latest in a series of similar atrocities, and the neglect of this context could only have been deliberate.

Thanks to statewide agitations led by dalits, without any political party or outfit at their head, the Khairlanji case saw one of the speediest trials in an atrocity case. Within two years, on 24 September 2008, Judge S.S. Das, of the district and sessions court of Bhandara, dramatically pronounced the death sentence on six persons and life terms for two. This was hailed by many dalits and even the media as a historic verdict. For the first time in post-independence India, capital punishment was given to the killers of dalits. It completely overshadowed the fact that the judgement had taken away all the strong points of the case. The motive of the crime was made out to be revenge for the women's having stood witness in an earlier case of assault on Siddharth Gajbhiye, a friend of the Bhotmange family and the police patil of a nearby village. The provisions of the PoA Act, were not invoked. Judge Das also did not invoke Section 354 (assault or criminal force with intent to outrage the modesty of a woman) or Section 375 (that deals with rape) of the Indian Penal Code, although it had been demonstrated by several independent fact-finding reports in October–November 2006 that the mother and daughter, Surekha and Priyanka, had not only been raped repeatedly but tortured in ghastly ways (after being stripped and paraded naked).

Eight people were convicted by the Bhandara court and are in jail. The High Court confirmed the decision, although it commuted the death sentences of six of them to life imprisonment. As Manoj Mitta points out in his book *Modi and Godhra: The Fiction of Fact Finding* (2014), this has become a practiced routine in the judiciary's handling of cases involving civil violence. The lower court first weakens the prosecution's case by diluting the terms of trial—the relevant laws and evidence by which it shall proceed—but concludes by awarding a heavy sentence. When the case moves up on appeal, the terms of trial have already been established and may not be altered; it is the findings and the verdict of the lower court that are in dispute. At this stage the sentence is found to be excessive for the terms of the case as defined, and gets duly reduced. The courts treated the Khairlanji outrage as just another criminal act, stripping the context off of one of the most horrific caste crimes in post-independence India. That the fiendish act was committed by a mob of forty to sixty people was noted by various fact-finding reports, and corroborated by the initial arrest of forty-six persons. During the CBI investigation, many of them were discharged and charges were framed against just eleven, of whom eight were eventually convicted. The question is: are the ones in jail the key culprits, or are they lackeys used as pawns by the powerful men of the village who led the attack? At least some of them do not figure among those named by Bhaiyalal Bhotmange in the First Information Report. Was justice really done? Will justice ever be done? Meanwhile, Bhaiyalal died of a heart attack in January 2017.

The fact of the matter was that the Bhotmanges had attained a certain amount of economic independence coupled with the cultural awakening implicit in their neo-Buddhist and Ambedkarite identification. This, along with the educational progress of the Bhotmange children, and Surekha's assertiveness in confronting upper caste harassment, was taken as a violation of the caste code, an unpardonable crime in the caste culture of this land. The local police station had on record the history of caste persecution experienced by the Bhotmanges, but did nothing to protect them.

Khairlanji broke many myths that prevailed among the dalits and even others. Representational logic was a pivot of the Ambedkarite dalit movement, which held that if a few dalits occupied strategic positions in the administration, they would take care of the interests of the dalit masses. In Khairlanji, every rung of the relevant administrative apparatus, from the lowest (a constable) to the highest (the superintendent of police), included personnel—both men and women—who were dalit. The Bhandara superintendent of police, Suresh Sagar (actually 'Khobragade' before a name change) and deputy superintendent of police, V. Susatkar, were both dalits. So was the constable Baban Meshram; the doctor who performed the first postmortem, Avinash John Shende; the district civil surgeon, K.D. Ramteke who instructed Shende, a junior doctor, to proceed with the postmortem; and even the public prosecutor who advised against invoking the PoA Act in the case, Leena Gajbhiye. Not only were they dalit, all of them belonged to the same mahar community as the Bhotmanges. As I learned later, the Andhalgaon police station inspector, Siddheshwar Bharne, while not a dalit, certainly belonged to a backward caste and was therefore within the span of the category 'bahujan'—that promissory note issued by BSP politics and never realised. Nobody can fault 'brahminical people' or a 'shudra mindset' here for the anti-dalit prejudice of the investigative procedure. The entire chain of the bureaucracy, staffed with dalits, failed not once but repeatedly to ensure justice to the Bhotmanges. The grand myth of the dalit movement was given the lie.

As a matter of fact, Babasaheb Ambedkar who conceived of this scheme had himself experienced its failings but dismissed these as individual instances of betrayal. He did not reach for the theoretical deduction that such privileged individuals experience a shift in class position that distances them from the common dalit folk, and results in the transference of their class loyalties. The outrage over Khairlanji had not yet died down, with scores of people who agitated over it still suffering police harassment, when the Maharashtra government in a bid to prove that Khairlanji was just an unfortunate incident that had nothing to do with caste, declared it a tanta mukt gaon (dispute-free village) in 2010—four years after the torture and lynching of the Bhotmange family, and just a year after the launch of the Mahatma Gandhi Tanta Mukti Gaon Mohim (dispute-free village initiative) by the state's Congress–NCP government. Clearly, the scheme ladles salt over the wounds of dalits by ignoring simmering caste tension, and serves as a warning that they had better peaceably accept the status quo of the caste order. As dalit activist Sudhir Dhawale put it, the scheme works as nothing short of a khap panchayat dominated by the upper caste/class people who develop a nexus with the police, ensuring that atrocities against dalits and the oppressed do not get reported. The substantial prize money that comes with inclusion in the list of tanta mukt gaons is an incentive to the suppression of disputes by the village panchayat, or at least of their reports being lodged with the state apparatus.

Contrary to commonplace understanding, atrocities—particularly the aforementioned kind, committed by a collective of caste Hindus against a few dalits by way of teaching a lesson to the entire dalit community—are a post-independence phenomenon. They are the product of a particular path of political economy charted out by the ruling classes. The postcolonial rulers used popular slogans of the freedom struggle as a cover for their self interest. They implemented land reforms to create a class of rich farmers who would be their agents in the countryside. The Green Revolution—a marriage of capitalism and agriculture—was introduced in the name of redressing the prevailing food crisis, but was in fact to create a vast market for capitalist industries via the marketable surpluses of landowners. The fallout of these twin policies was the erosion of an ethos of economic interdependence in the countryside, thereby reducing the dalits to a rural proletariat working as farm labourers in the fields of these new rich farmers. The emergent class contradiction between dalit labourers and the feudal-capitalist rich farmers would spill out through the familiar faultlines of caste into gory atrocities. Kilvenmani in the erstwhile Thanjavur district of Tamil Nadu inaugurated this new genre of atrocities on 25 December 1968, when forty-four women and children were killed by landlords and their henchmen, as punishment for a strike by landless dalit labourers in the paddy fields, demanding higher wages. Kilvenmani also established the trend of egregious violence followed by impunity for the attackers that has repeated itself ever since.

Much water has flown down the rivers since the dream of a 'democratic republic' was conjured (a republic on whom it dawned only in 1977—when all rights were suspended under the Emergency—that it was also 'secular' and 'socialist'). Reality shows a widening gap between the haves and have-nots. As the 'golden period' of capitalism (1945–1965) faded into a phase of crisis, global capital cooked up the doctrine of neoliberalism and pushed it down the throats of developing economies as a conditionality for the rescue loans they sought to tide over the financial crisis created by the oil price hike of 1973. It was packaged as a programme of macroeconomic stabilisation and structural adjustment. India informally adopted these measures from mid-1980s but formally did so in July 1991. The Soviet model beginning to crumble (1989–91) under its own contradictions did not help matters. The Nehruvian Third Worldist policy of non-alignment also took a beating. Neoliberalism—an extremist version of capitalism, its social Darwinist ethos inherently elitist and hence detrimental to the poor—had come to be embraced. The mounting agrarian crisis that has devoured more than three lakh farmers' lives, the general deprivation of people from the lower strata, marketisation of public services like healthcare and education due to the withdrawal of the state, informalisation of jobs, dollarisation of prices, naked loot of peoples' resources and a fascistic consolidation of state power to suppress the voice of the poor against such anti-people policies—these trends have been on the rise for the past two decades. The ethos of free market competition has legitimised the loot of India by a handful of people who masquerade as entrepreneurs as well as by politicians. Peoples' resources are being squandered to Americanise India for the upwardly mobile middle classes.

Discontent with neoliberalism is borne out by galloping inequality and a sharpening crisis for common people. With the dalits, these factors have played out in several ways. They were certainly affected as part of the general poor, but also additionally, with their identity as socially disadvantaged people. Amid the pro-globalisation din by dalit intellectuals sponsored by the ruling classes, I have laboured to explain how it was injurious to dalit interests on every count (in the chapters "Reservations", "Slumdogs and Millionaires" and "Dalit Protests in Gujarat"). Neoliberalism has even resurrected the use of caste to humiliate dalits.

The crises unleashed by neoliberalism impelled people to seek psychological shelter in their 'faith' which in turn gave rise to religiosity, fundamentalism, and irrationality all over the world. In India, neoliberalism has catalysed the resurgence of hindutva. Its flag-bearing political party, the Bharatiya Janata Party, got catapulted from the fringes to the centre of political power. Its camouflaging of democratic politics notwithstanding, hindutva is the brahminical 'brand' of Hinduism which believes all that existed in India, including the caste system, was glorious and needs to be restored to regain India's imagined past glory.

What a Hindu rashtra is was explicated by the founders of this poisonous creed, but it is equally on display in the prototype presented by Narendra Modi for the last four years in New Delhi and tested for over a decade in Gujarat. It is modelled on the fascist states that arose between the two world wars in Europe, with due adjustment for Indian specificity and the time difference. Neoliberalism is not ideologically inimical to a Hindu rashtra but there is some contradiction in their processes. Neoliberalism serves global capital which harms the BJP's core constituency of small-scale business owners expanding upwards to the middle classes. This bloc has been consolidated with aggressive hindutva as a useful diversion that keeps attention fixed on assertions of cultural triumphalism and away from worsening income inequality, job security, and quality of life under neoliberal economics. While hindutva intoxicates large sections of the Hindus with pride, the turbulence created by it in society is risky and may not be liked by global capital. Together, both hindutva and neoliberalism, however, are detrimental to the dalits. Hindutva seeks to enslave them back into their ghettoised existence and neoliberalism pushes them off the margins into non-existence. Paradoxically, dalits are critically important as an electoral constituency and hence the BJP is going overboard in wooing them with displays of devotion to Ambedkar and by recruiting dalits leaders as its agents. These unctuous efforts cannot fully disguise the ugly face of reality. It keeps resurfacing in the form of prejudicial actions, such as against the students of the Ambedkar Periyar Study Circle, or the death of Rohith Vemula, or the atrocity in Una (as detailed in the chapter "Saffronising Ambedkar").

Criminalising victims

In the early hours of 17 May 2014, within twenty-four hours of the BJP's victory in the Lok Sabha elections, the dominant caste group of powars in Kawlewada village of Gondia district of Maharashtra demonstrated their exultation at the Modi wave by setting on fire fifty-year-old Sanjay Khobragade, a leading dalit activist. This was done in retaliation to his persistent demand for land to build a Buddha vihara in the village that has only forty dalit households, compared to 1,500 powar households (a maratha subcaste that is also used as a surname). This was similar to Khairlanji where four dalit families were outnumbered by 181 OBC families.

Khobragade, who survived with 94 per cent burns for another six days, had named six persons, all powars, in three separate statements to the police, and to newspersons and dalit activists. Video recordings of his statement exist as well, which upon his death should have been treated as his dying declaration, enabling the police to charge the named persons. The police rejected these testimonies instead. On 19 May, inspector Anil Patil suddenly came up with the motive of a 'love affair' behind the murder of Sanjay and arrested the victim's forty-eight-year-old wife Devakabai and their neighbour Raju Gadpayale, with the concocted story that they conspired to kill Khobragade after he had discovered them in a compromising position. The story claimed that Devakabai and Raju were old paramours and had been carrying on an affair for the past thirty years. It was left to the Khobragades' son Pradeep to point out that the story, if true, would imply that the forty-one-year-old Raju Gadpayale was eleven at the start of the illicit relationship! Unsurprisingly, the witnesses who contributed to and corroborated this salacious fiction were all powars. None of the dalit neighbours of the Khobragades and Gadpayale—residents of the dalit toli in this caste-segregated village—had noticed the 'affair' being conducted under their noses.

The bogey of sexual promiscuity is an easy and popular fallback, recognisable to anyone who has been following incidents of caste atrocities. It had been raised against Surekha Bhotmange in Khairlanji as well, where the murders were reported first in the local Marathi newspapers (starting with the Nagpur-based *Deshonnati* and later in the largest selling Marathi paper *Lokmat*) as the consequence of an illicit affair between Surekha and her cousin Siddharth Gajbhiye of the neighbouring village of Dusala; caste was not even mentioned as a factor at first. In Khairlanji, Gajbhiye's actual crime was that as a police patil (an honorary post without much authority) he had been helping Surekha fight her case against encroachments by the marathas on her 4.79 acres of land.

In Kawlewada village, Gadpayale was a fellow activist with the same Ambedkar Justice and Peace Mission as Sanjay Khobragade. He, too, was a keen supporter of the project of the proposed Buddha vihara, for which a no-objection certificate had been sought from the village panchayat samiti (at the block level). The decision on the grant was expected to be favourable as government permission for it had been received as early as 2012, and two Hindu temples built earlier on the neighbouring patch of government land had supplied the precedent. The plot of land granted to the Buddha vihara was, however, coveted by the Bahyababa Trust Sanstha—dedicated to a local saint, with at least three of the six accused among its members—and in early 2014 the Sanstha began building on the land, most likely to foil the panchayat samiti's upcoming decision by presenting its structure as an accomplished fact. Khobragade, who had first approached the police against the Sanstha members and their incursions in 2012, and even had his little provisions shop burnt down in retaliation, was determined to assert himself against this encroachment. He went to the home of the sarpanch, Madhuri Tembre—who, along with her husband, Krushipal Tembre, then block-level general secretary of the BJP and ex-sarpanch, also one among the accused—to demand that a no-objection certificate for the vihara be issued by the gram sabha (village assembly) as a preemptive measure against the Sanstha, but was told the matter would be decided after the Lok Sabha election results on 16 May. The significance of the date becomes clearer when we see that another of the accused, Shivprakash Rahangdale, the deputy sarpanch, was president of the Bahyababa temple trust.

The election results sealed Sanjay Khobragade's fate. When the police did not show up at Kawlewada on 17 May despite being informed of the attempted murder, Devakabai and Pradeep Khobragade had to go to the police station the next day to get their complaint registered. The six accused were taken into custody and released the following day. On 19 May, the police arrested Devakabai and Raju and held them in a single cell. It had now arrived at its preferred explanation of the crime, as a tale of conjugal jealousy and extramarital passion. The entire village and dalit activists were aghast at this police fabrication but that could not save Devakabai and Gadpayale from undergoing police torture and social ignominy even as they learned of Sanjay's death. The police claim that the Khobragades' complaint was duly registered under the PoA Act, is belied by the fact that the six accused were given judicial custody on 18 May and let out the next day, with the Gondia lower court granting them conditional bail on 27 May; PoA Act offences are non-bailable. Meanwhile, an *Indian Express* report of 9 June 2014 stated that the police had not even recorded the family's statement.

In this case as in Khairlanji, it is impossible to draw a line separating the atrocity from the state's response. Violence against the Khobragades began from the day Sanjay filed his complaint against the Sanstha's encroachments upon land granted by the government for a Buddha vihara. It was an assertive dalit's recourse to the law that drew this prolonged assault of lawlessness upon him, as well as his family and their political fellow travellers. The ensuing violations of their rights, dignity and peace involved the connivance of the police, the dominant caste group of the village and the village's self-governing body, and continued undiminished after Sanjay Khobragade's murder. In the circumstances, it becomes difficult to even draw a line around the atrocity—to know quite where it begins or ends. The case before the courts concerns only Sanjay's violent death. Meanwhile, the powars of Kawlewada not only snuffed out his life, but caught his wife, their son, and their neighbour in the snare of a punishing legal battle, one in which the victims made their first appearance as the accused. Accompanied by the grim rhythm of hindutva consolidation, what this story conveys to assertive dalits is not an invitation to hope.

One could list atrocity after unique atrocity—since more than five crimes are committed against dalits every hour—and perhaps still be none the wiser. Dr Ambedkar himself did this in many of his works such as *Untouchables or The Children of India's Ghetto* (published posthumously in 1989 under Volume 5 of *BAWS* series). In this work, found as a 208-page manuscript likely written in the 1940s, he devotes an entire chapter entitled "Unfit for Human Association" to list and analyse various forms of casual crimes committed against untouchables. To cite but two from those times: in 1936 in Kalady, the birthplace of the arch-brahmin monist philosopher Sankara, a man jumps into a well to rescue the child of a young woman but when it is discovered that he is an untouchable he is beaten up for polluting the well; in 1937, an employee of the Madras Holmes Company is stabbed while participating in a funerary ceremony for a colleague where he joins others in ritually throwing rice at the pyre, for it is discovered that he is an untouchable. Ambedkar concludes his chapter thus: 'The tale told by these cases is clear and simple. No comment is necessary. To the average Hindu, the Untouchable is not fit even for human association. He is the carrier of evil. He is not a human being. He must be shunned' (*BAWS* 5, 34). This remains just as true today, but what accounts for the manifold scaling up of violence and the intensity of atrocities? Is the power asymmetry between the dalits and non-dalits an incitement to violence, especially when coupled with cultural assertion by dalits? While Surekha Bhotmange's Ambedkarite spirit ensured she would not take upper caste insolence lying down, Sanjay Khobragade's insistence on land to build a Buddha vihara was equally based on the belief that justice might be accessed beyond the confines of the local order. The justice of the state proved unavailable in both instances.

Violence on the rise

Acts of violence against dalits logged by the National Crime Records Bureau show persistent growth, having gone up by 74 per cent from 27,070 in 2006 to 40,801 in 2016 at the all-India level, which means 111 caste crimes every day or 4.6 caste crimes every hour. The rising atrocities against dalits under the BJP is proven by the fact that the top five states as per the crime rate—Madhya Pradesh, Rajasthan, Goa, Bihar, Gujarat—are all BJP-ruled states, with Uttar Pradesh, Bihar and Rajasthan accounting for the highest number of reported crimes. And these are but police figures; the actual crime rate is anybody's guess. The numbers, as admitted by the NCRB, do not reveal the complete picture of crimes, and are an under-estimate; nor do they convey the intensity of human tragedy behind them.

Take the case of Dulina, near a town called Jhajjar in Haryana where on 15 October 2002, the day of Dussehra, five dalits were lynched to death within the compound of a police check post by a crowd of caste Hindus. Some people on their way back from burning the effigy of Ravan at the Ramlila, spotted these dalits carrying a dead cow in a tempo. They took them to the police post and accused them of slaughtering the cow on the day of Dussehra. The police, as admitted by the official in charge of the post, knew that it was not a case of cow slaughter, but chose not to defend or protect the accused. The crowd soon swelled into a murderous mob. They dragged the five people out after breaking open the door of the police lockup, killed them on the spot and threw the bodies of two into a fire in the presence of senior police officers and officials of the district administration. The police personnel did not fire a single shot to disperse the assailants. This open and shut case, the violence having taken place in front of law-enforcers, should have taken no time to prosecute, but the state government set up a commission, headed by R.R. Banswal, the then commissioner of Rohtak range, to inquire into the circumstances that led to the incident. The exhaustive 383-page commission report, submitted in December 2002, summed up the sequence of events and recommended action against the police officials concerned for dereliction of duty.

The police who had stood by and watched as dalits in their custody were killed, claimed that they were overwhelmed by the number of the attackers, but their actions contradicted this defence when they booked only twenty-eight persons after a month. All of them were released on bail by the court within a couple of months. The case was eventually decided by the district court at Jatoday on 9 August 2010, eight years after the incident, by acquitting nineteen and convicting seven (six jats and one dalit), two others having passed away during the trial. Incidentally, they were held guilty under various sections of the Indian Penal Code but acquitted under the relevant sections of the PoA Act. They all were awarded life imprisonment and a fine of Rs 20,000 as penalty. The order noted inter alia that 'there was no cogent evidence to prove that the crime was motivated by the caste of the victims.' It reiterated the version of the accused that they were not even aware of the caste of the victims, helping them avoid the applicability of the PoA Act. It conveniently ignored the deposition of Rajinder Singh, station house officer, Dulina, that someone from the mob had shouted, 'the victims were dhed (a derogatory term used for dalits), they were doing the job of Muslims and they should not be spared' (*Frontline*, 10 September 2010).

On the day the judgement was pronounced, a huge crowd had gathered outside the Jhajjar court in support of the accused, demanding that no action be taken against the people who had killed the 'cow slaughterers'. The role of the Vishva Hindu Parishad in this crime was quite evident. According to the fact-finding report of the left parties (17 October 2002), the killing had taken place against the background of an ongoing gauraksha campaign in the area, run by the VHP. The VHP was directly involved in mobilising the crowd that gathered at the police chowki and inciting it to violence. Its involvement was further confirmed by the victory procession in Jhajjar on 16 October, conducted by the VHP and Bajrang Dal, in which the people responsible for the killing of the dalits were lauded. The VHP's senior vice-president, Acharya Giriraj Kishore, defended the VHP's position by quoting Hindu scriptures to aver that the life of a cow was more precious than that of a human being. The local units of the VHP and the Bajrang Dal had also submitted a memorandum to the police asking them not to take action against anybody in connection with the killings. By 2015, at least four of the seven convicts who went to jail had managed to get bail from the Supreme Court.

The Dulina atrocity clearly set the template for the Sangh parivar's experiments with a slew of cow-slaughter bans in the BJP-ruled states across the nation since 2014. The easy assumption of moral righteousness by a lynch mob confident of its impunity is a familiar theme today, but these qualities are not spontaneously generated. The self-assurance of such mobs has grown over the years, from watching institutional authority cave in under their assault, from the predominance that certain caste groups have achieved—electorally and in the state apparatus—which emboldens them to appropriate still more of the public space for themselves, and from the passive or active complicity of state institutions that facilitate the mob's violence and protect it from legal consequences. The lynchings that are commonplace today have numerous, if much less remarked, precedents in dalit experience. They are the honed expression of a strategy perfected over many years of experiment and observation.

The zan, zar, zameen syndrome

What better way to teach the dalits a lesson than by using dalit women's bodies as sites of violence? The state of Haryana exemplifies this tendency: ruled by khap panchayats, with an incidence of forced abortion of the female foetus well above the national average, where honour killings happen all too often, where incest is rampant, and where dalits are treated worse than slaves, lynched and raped at will. After separation from Punjab in 1966, Haryana has remained a predominantly Hindu state with jats as the dominant caste, and the distribution of income and wealth is very unequal—the jats have disproportionately cornered the benefits of rapid economic growth, and their leaders seek to keep other communities in thrall.

On account of the worsening female sex ratio (there are just 879 females per 1,000 males, far below the national average of 940 as per the census of 2011), the incidence of incest is high. Given the active persecution of intra-patrilineal clan (sagotra) marriages by the khap panchayats, dalit girls have increasingly become the victims of sexual assault. The NCRB reports show that the number of (reported) rape cases where SC girls or women were the victims went up from 1,346 in 2009 to 2,536 in 2016—an increase of 88.4 per cent nationally, while the increase in Haryana was a whopping 167 per cent. The unabated sexual abuse of women by the jats in villages, the khap panchayats' honour killings, the public justification of such killings by jat spokespersons and politicians, and numerous other acts of this description demonstrate the impunity of the rich jats of Haryana.

While the government's response has been lethargic, the notorious khap panchyats of the dominant caste have justified rape by advising that girls should be married off before they reached the age of puberty to avoid being raped. Big-name politicians unashamedly endorsed this shocking 'solution' in public; some of them even dismissed the rapes as consensual acts turned sour. These are not one-off examples of reckless statements by some discredited individuals; the sexual assaults and the don't-care-a-damn attitude of the political establishment represent an abiding pattern that makes the state a veritable hell for dalits.

On 23 March 2014—incidentally the anniversary of Bhagat Singh's martyrdom along with his comrades, Sukhdeo and Rajguru—the village of Bhagana, 13 km from Hisar and barely a three-hour drive from the national capital, added another horrific incident to the long list of ghastly atrocities on Haryana's dalit women. That evening, four dalit schoolgirls, between thirteen and eighteen years of age, while urinating in a field near their homes, were attacked by five men belonging to the dominant jat caste. They were drugged and gang-raped in the fields and abducted in a car. They were perhaps raped the entire night before being left in the bushes outside the Bhatinda railway station, 170 km away, across the border in Punjab. The sarpanch of the village, Rakesh, was in the know of it. When the families of the missing girls approached him, he nonchalantly said the girls were at Bhatinda and would come back the next day. Only with the threat that they would file an FIR did he, along with his uncle, accompany them to Bhatinda where the girls were found in a miserable condition precisely where he expected. After their return, horrified by the abduction and rape, the families sought to file an FIR but the police would not oblige. Only under pressure from more than two-hundred dalit activists and the confirmation of rape in the medical report did the police at Sadar Hisar police station file the FIR under the PoA Act. Later, it again took an explosion of public protest with over a hundred dalits agitating at Hisar's mini secretariat and ninety dalit families from Bhagana on a sit-in at Delhi's Jantar Mantar from 16 April, for the Haryana police to wake up and arrest the five rapists—Lalit, Sumit, Sandeep, Parimal and Dharamvir—on 29 April. Having decided to pursue justice, the dalits of Bhagana simply could not go back to their homes for fear of being killed by the jats. The Hisar district court, in turn, acquitted all of the accused.

An earlier fact-finding report of the People's Union for Democratic Rights and the Association for Democratic Rights, "This Village Is Mine Too: Dalit Assertion, Land Rights and Social Boycott in Bhagana" (September 2012), suggests that the Bhagana rapes are more than savage sex-crimes. They were committed in order to teach a lesson to dalits who have been protesting against the takeover of their land, water and even burial grounds by jats in the village. Over the years, Haryana's powerful jats benefited hugely from soaring land prices as agricultural land fast turned into booming real estate. Therefore, land sharks in the villages, with the active support of powerful politicians, were grabbing shamlat land, i.e. communal land or the commons of the village. In 2011, the Bhagana panchayat had decided to distribute some 280 acres, including shamlat land, among the resident landless dalits. This was in compliance with an electoral promise made by the Congress party. However, even after a wholly illegal registration fee had been extorted from many of the putative dalit beneficiaries, the ownership of the land was not transferred to their names. The struggle of the Bhagana dalits for shamlat land constitutes a clear backdrop to the atrocity.

Jat landlords feared that once the dalits got land, they would no longer work on their fields or obey their writ. In May 2012, all the 450-odd dalit families of Bhagana were forced to leave their village by the land owning jats. The evicted dalits protested at the mini secretariat at Hisar and at Jantar Mantar, Delhi, demanding land and action against those who wanted to dispossess them. They exhausted all the protocol and remedies of democratic redress meeting leaders, ministers, members of assemblies and parliament; made representations before various commissions, etc. but to no avail. Worn out, some of them went back. Nearly a year later, the incident of rape took place. In fact, Bhagana is not alone; the jats and their khaps of over fifty-eight villages have formally asked the government to not distribute village communal land to dalits.

After the incident of 23 March, the jats imposed an economic and social boycott on the dalits. With their lives under threat, they left the village and made the mini secretariat at Hisar and Jantar Mantar their home as well as stage of protest. It was a standing shame to Indian democracy and all the boasts made in its name. The middle class, actively supported by the media, had carried out a countrywide protest after the rape and murder of an 'upper' caste middle class girl in December 2012, emotively naming her 'Nirbhaya' (the fearless). The protests were presented as the dawn of a new consciousness among citizens who would no longer tolerate sexual violence against women. Both the media and the middle class were conspicuous in their silence over the plight of the Bhagana girls. The indifference continued as the government forcibly evicted them from the protest site which was also their shelter. Driven to their wit's end, ultimately, on 8 August 2015, the Bhagana Kand Dalit Sangharsh Samiti (Committee for dalit struggle against the Bhagana atrocity) called a meeting at Jantar Mantar, and resorted to the historical weapon of last resort: religious conversion. They embraced Islam.

It had all happened under the Congress government headed by a jat chief minister, Bhupinder Singh Hooda. In 2014, when the BJP won elections both in the centre and the state, people felt that the new government would do justice, out of a desire to show the Congress down and woo dalits if for nothing else. Accustomed to calculating the weightage of caste, Bhagana's dalits hoped that Manohar Lal Khattar, the non-jat chief minister, would listen to them, but the hope proved futile. Their desperate rebellion by embracing Islam is all the more interesting in that their choice did not fall on Buddhism which Ambedkar had chosen for them. Their answer was that Buddhism had not been able to protect the dalits. Was this not true? After all, the Bhotmanges of Khairlanji were ardent Buddhists. Instead of protecting them, their Buddhism as a cultural identity had become the cause of their woes. Their murders failed to rouse to action the Buddhists who congregated in their hundreds of thousands at the Deekshabhoomi, Nagpur, to show devotion to Ambedkar. Their stupor was perhaps broken only by concerns over the not-so-devotedly Buddhist (left oriented) elements among them taking the lead in protests against Khairlanji. This is not to say that Islam can protect dalits but at least it stands as an acknowledged symbolic affront to the Hindu forces.

Failure of the system

The track record of the state reassures the perpetrators of caste crimes that they can carry on with their acts of savagery. Structurally speaking, in examining a caste atrocity one has to take cognisance of the existing disequilibria of social relations between caste Hindus and dalits, as also the effectiveness of those protective mechanisms in favour of the dalits mandated by the Constitution should this imbalance precipitate into injustice. Disequilibria in social relations are constitutive of caste society. So long as dalits submit to the humiliating demands of the caste Hindus, it may appear that there is social harmony. The dynamics of social relations, in the normal course of events, are mediated by the perceived strength of each group as independently assessed by both. The state can play an instrumental role in enhancing the perception of dalit strength by its protective measures. But the record of atrocities on dalits reflects the opposite. The state has faithfully served only the ruling classes, whose interests lie in preserving the existing caste divide, even accentuating it. As such, the state has never made a sincere effort to pre-empt impending caste atrocities. On the contrary, it has frequently been complicit with the perpetrators of such crimes.

If the state had performed its role, the menace of caste atrocities would have abated substantially by now. The very process of dalits registering a crime with the police is fraught with hurdles, starting with a fear of reprisal from the dominant castes in their village where they are a minority, or of incurring social prejudice, as in the case of crimes involving women as victims, and thereafter in the reluctance of the police to register the case. The case gets counted in the statistics of crimes only after it gets past these primary hurdles. More often than not, the local police take sides with the perpetrators and against the dalits, and everything possible is done to protect the guilty. Political pressure and money play a significant role. Even if sufficient pressure is brought to bear upon the police to get the crime registered, the process of investigation and the collection of evidence remain in their hands. Shoddy investigation by the police in such cases is virtually a given, as evidenced by the extremely paltry rate of conviction—27.6 per cent in 2015 (and 28.8 per cent in 2014) as projected lately, after hovering in single digits until then. Compare this to cases tried under the IPC where the rate of conviction in 2015 was 46.9 per cent. (In the case of crimes against women, the conviction rate touches a new low at 21.7 per cent for 2015.) There is a tacit assurance to the oppressor castes that the official protectors of the law would not come in the way of their dealings with dalits. Such reassurance plays a key role in sustaining the growth of atrocities year after year. It is the complicity of the police that gives caste Hindus the licence to punish dalits for upholding their dignity and self-respect.

The entire system is designed to not disturb the power imbalance in society. The Constitution, often uncritically cited as providing protection to the dalits, may prove to be the antithesis of that if one critically examined it. Instead of being an instrument of change, it has, in operative terms, fortified the rule of the entrenched classes. The first-past-the-post election system, adopted as a method to effectuate democracy, is the primary mechanism that guarantees the perpetuation of the status quo. The structural absence of the feature of checks and balances between the three wings of the government—the legislature, executive and judiciary—considered most vital for any constitutional democracy, also furthers the same object. In India, the first two, i.e., the legislature and executive, collapse into a single oppressive apparatus that manifests in the nexus of police, bureaucracy and politicians at the ground level, playing a maleficent role in every atrocity case. The only hope for ordinary people has been the judiciary, which for all its infirmities, has evinced a certain independence of mind from time to time. However, if one takes a view from the perspective of the exploited and the oppressed, its record is also pathetic. Barring some honourable exceptions, the courts have always been biased against the poor, tribals, dalits, and Muslims.

The saga of injustice to dalits from the justice delivery system beggars belief. The Khairlanji case was unusual in getting past the high court without acquittal of the criminals for 'want of evidence', as had occurred in a series of infamous preceding instances. In the matter of the Kilvenmani atrocity of 1968, alluded to earlier as the inaugural case of a new genre of atrocities, the Madras High Court had acquitted all twenty-three landlords by simply dismissing the possibility that gentlemanly landlords, some of whom owned cars, could commit such a ghastly crime as killing forty-four dalits. Incidentally, in the same chain of events, eight dalit farm labourers had undergone punishment—one, a life sentence, and others one to five years of imprisonment—for the alleged murder of P. Padaiyacchi, a hitman of the landlords.

In the Tsunduru case (in which eight dalits were slaughtered by caste Hindus on 6 August 1991) the Andhra Pradesh High Court in 2012 quashed the trial court's order sentencing twenty-one persons to life terms and thirty-five others to one-year imprisonment, saying that the prosecution had failed to produce sufficient evidence before the court. In a previous case involving the massacre of six dalits in Karamchedu on 17 July 1987, the Andhra Pradesh High Court had similarly struck down the Ongole trial court's conviction of 159 people to life imprisonment and acquitted the accused. It was only in 2008, after twenty-three long years that the Supreme Court delivered its final verdict—a life sentence to the main accused, Anjaiah, and three years of jail to twenty-nine others.

In the Patna High Court, there has been a series of summary acquittals in cases concerning the massacre of dalits by the dominant castes. In what became a regular pattern, the court acquitted all Ranvir Sena militants arraigned for the mass murder of dalits in different places—Bathani Tola (1996, with twenty-one dalits killed), Laxmanpur Bathe (1997, fifty-eight dalits killed), Miyapur (2000, thirty-four dalits killed), and Nagari Bazaar (1998, ten communist supporters killed). In the Bathani Tola case the court dismissed the evidence of the eyewitnesses with the marvellous deduction that they could not have been present at the scene. Had they really been there, the court noted tautologically, they would have all been killed! The recurring pattern here is of lower courts, under public pressure, awarding harsh punishments that are duly waived in favour of wholesale acquittals by the high courts. Should the victims display unexpected stamina and persist with the case, the Supreme Court upholds and reinstates part of the punishment. One ought not to leap to the inference that the judgement of the courts is always clouded by the caste of the judges—the most pro-dalit judgements having come from privileged caste judges like Krishna Iyer or Chinnappa Reddy, while some dalit judges have delivered judgements that have gone against dalits. Nonetheless, the hegemonic hold on institutions of one single caste does mar the independent perspective desired in democracy; as *Outlook*, citing a study by the Centre for the Study of Developing Societies, reported in its issue of 4 June 2007, 47 per cent of all Supreme Court chief justices between 1950 and 2000 were brahmins. During the same period, 40 per cent of the associate justices in the high courts and lower courts were also brahmin. The Backward Classes Commission, in a 2007 report, said that 37.17 per cent of the Indian bureaucracy was made up of brahmins.

The dismal conviction rate in cases of caste atrocity exposes how these cases, admitted with extreme reluctance by the police, are then deliberately weakened in the investigation or invalidated by non-compliance with rules, mishandled by the prosecution in the courts and at times perversely adjudged by the courts themselves, whether under political pressure or in caste solidarity with the perpetrators. On the other hand, three dalits were awarded the death sentence and six life imprisonment for the killing of thirty-five bhumihar-brahmins in Bara in February 1992, a sentence confirmed by the Supreme Court in 2002, within a year of the case moving on appeal. Three more dalits were given death sentences by the TADA (Terrorist and Disruptive Activities Prevention Act) court as members of the Maoist Communist Centre. At the same time, the Andhra Pradesh High Court released all the accused in the Tsunduru violence, which was one of the worst massacres of dalits in Andhra Pradesh. Along with the victims of Lakshmanpur Bathe and Bathani Tola in Bihar, Kumher in Rajasthan (where thirty jatavs were set ablaze by jat attackers and 254 hutments destroyed in 1992), the caste victims of Dharmapuri district in Tamil Nadu (where over two hundred houses of dalits were torched when a vanniyar girl eloped with a dalit boy in 2012), are among many who have received no justice so far. Is justice merely to be awaited passively, to be received from on high? And if it does not yet exist, should it not be brought into existence by those who seek it?

Such is the disparity in the dispensation of justice when it comes to the caste identity of the accused, or of the victims. It cannot be mere coincidence, yet the state insolently expects us to believe it is so. To complete this picture, consider the high percentage of dalits languishing in prison according to the NCRB: 20 per cent of all prisoners belong to the Scheduled Castes and 11 per cent to Scheduled Tribes. Of the prisoners on death row, as of 2016, 76 per cent (279 prisoners) are from the oppressed castes. In most atrocity cases—even in stark instances as Khairlanji and Jhajjar—the judges did not recognise the caste angle and dismissed the applicability of the PoA Act. One might ask the reverse question: How can anyone prove that a crime is committed because of caste alone? The PoA Act defines it simply: an atrocity is a crime committed by a non-SC/ST on an SC/ST person. Considered as the 'only act with teeth', it is rendered completely ineffective when the courts get into the question of its applicability.

Combating caste violence

It is also significant that dalit politics, whose raison d'être is to safeguard dalit interests from caste discrimination, does not focus on atrocities against dalits, which may be seen as the concentrated and authentic manifestation of caste. However, the dalit politicians will never be spotted seeding or leading any protest against atrocities. The reason is that they cannot afford to embarrass their ruling class political patrons. The anger of dalit protesters—who rallied under the banner of the Khairlanji Dalit Hatyakand Sangharsh Samiti—was as much against the state and the dalit politicians as it was against the perpetrators of caste atrocities. Khairlanji, and for that matter all atrocities, are a reflection of the impairment of the political strength of dalits for which dalit politicians have to take the blame. People from all walks of life—lawyers, doctors, businessmen, middle class professionals and slum-dwellers—took to the streets over Khairlanji without any support system, and were prepared to suffer but did not look to dalit legislators for help. Indeed, repeated instances of violence on dalits have taken this divide between dalit politicians and the dalit masses to a new high.

It is a myth that there exists a significant section of Indian society that is against caste. There is indeed a large section of people who hold progressive ideas on many issues, such as communalism, gender discrimination, the general exploitation of labour and the peasantry, and so on. However, when it comes to caste, which arguably lies at the root of all the above evils, they conveniently leave it to the dalits to deal with. When the Khairlanji protests broke out, they should have come forward to express their support to the dalits, but they didn't. After the Bhagana rapes, the anti-patriarchy or gender discrimination squads were nowhere to be seen, nor the waves of middle class protesters that had created 'Nirbhaya'. The protests that took place after Bhagana did so without party affiliations and were organised by people who in some ways shared middle class ideas of progressivism. Why then was the middle class not present? Why is it that people who fight against the communal oppression of Muslims so zealously are not moved on the issue of caste oppression? Why is the opposition to caste bracketed with casteism, not with human rights? It would appear that progressivism does not necessarily mean anti-casteism in India. Even the communist parties, who claim to have changed their stand on caste issues, do not think that they need go beyond tokenism. Why did they not mobilise their cadres to protest against Khairlanji?

Caste violence is more than just an analogue of caste consciousness which may be taken as primordial. It constitutes a specific temporal environment, reflects a life world that subsumes within it traditions of caste discrimination, untouchability, etc.—of an innately violent character and doubly manifest in acts of caste violence. At the same time, there is a quality to contemporary caste violence which I distinguish from the embedded forms of it, as a new genre of atrocities engendered by the forces of the postcolonial political economy. This violence requires the coincidence of three ingredients as shown by me in *The Persistence of Caste (2010)*. The first is the grudge or resentment against dalits, which of course stems from caste consciousness insofar as they are seen as different people, with a different set of interests. When they appear to be making progress, it is seen to disturb the status quo and creates a more lively resentment in others—evident in the case of reservations and various other protective schemes—the crisis-ridden non-dalit population in the villages views any cultural assertion by the dalit population with acute insecurity, and sees any material improvement in their conditions as undeserved. It sharpens the grudge against them. The second factor is the institutional assurance that no harm would come to those who commit punitive violence against dalits. And the third is the trigger, an immediate spark to set off the violence. This schema also gives us a clue as to how one may combat this menace. If one could isolate or eliminate any one of these factors, caste violence would be eliminated.

Foremost, the uprooting of caste consciousness, which entails the destruction of caste identities associated with the notion of hierarchy—the annihilation of caste—would be the ideal solution as its benefits would extend beyond the limited sphere of caste violence. As castes have been consecrated in the Constitution with a cobweb of social justice measures woven around them, akin to transplanting castes from the wasteland of Hinduism into the modern soil of the Constitution, the project of annihilation of caste does not appear feasible at the moment. A solution exists, however long-drawn and tortuous it may appear to prejudiced minds, if one wants to try it out. It must begin with dalits foregrounding the need to annihilate caste and reorienting themselves to see society in class terms. This is the best way to build bridges to similarly placed non-dalit sections that play foot-soldier to the village hegemons. It may appear impossible to many accustomed to viewing Indian society through caste spectacles, but it need not be. We need to recognise castes as anomalous, not their absence. Given the present circumstances, when Ambedkarites themselves do not believe in the vision of their mentor and think that the annihilation of caste is impossible, while others live under the spell of such poisonous creeds as hindutva and neoliberalism, it is bound to be a slow process. Such class unity is moreover to be achieved only through the mode of struggle, as Ambedkar attempted during the anti-khoti agitation of the late 1930s.

An associated task is to wake up to the subterfuge that has gone into the making of the Constitution. Dalits will have to understand that the postcolonial ruling classes have skilfully preserved caste and religion, the two most potent weapons to divide people in the Constitution. This was done under the pretext of delivering social justice to the oppressed castes and reserving space for the state to institute religious reforms, respectively. Seven decades later, the underhandedness of the ruling classes remains undetected, or even celebrated by its very victims. Unless it is understood and condemned, the project of the annihilation of caste may prove impossible to attempt, let alone accomplish. Castes (and religion too) are a propellant of political appeal which the ruling classes would never voluntarily relinquish. With these enormous reserves of fuel at their disposal, they would keep feeding the fire. The success of their pyromania is attested by the growing identity obsession among middle class dalits, antithetical to Babasaheb Ambedkar's vision of annihilation of caste. Desirable as it is, this approach does not appear feasible in the short term.

The second factor is the impunity that perpetrators of caste violence currently enjoy. They are safe from the law. It has two components: one, the protective backing of a network of power for the perpetrators of atrocities, and two, the weakness of the dalits to resist them. The kingpin behind caste violence is the rich farmer, typically on the shudra bandwidth of the caste spectrum, a product of the postcolonial political economy developed under the presiding influence of the Congress party. Although the actual executors (foot soldiers) of the violence may be as resourceless as the dalit victim, they have the material and moral support of this person who has further backing from the political network and thereby the local administration. This power asymmetry between the dalits and non-dalits in villages has grown alarmingly over the last seven decades. It is this factor Ambedkar had referred to in his speech "Mukti Kon Pathe?" (What path to salvation?) at the Mumbai Elaka Mahar Parishad at Naigaum on 31 May 1936, as the reason dalits suffer atrocities: their numerical weakness, financial backwardness and lack of confidence in facing up to their oppressors. The remedy he proposed was to merge into another existing religious community by means of conversion. His thinking evolved around the rationale for religious conversion over two decades and he eventually converted to Buddhism which did not offer a community in India to merge with.

Can anything be done by dalits about this factor? They probably cannot do much about the first component, i.e., the power of the village hegemon who engineers the atrocity as a means to teach dalits to abide by his code. He is reasonably assured that he would be able to manage the consequences with his money, political connections and influence over the local administration. Dalits most likely are no match for this component. However, this component is activated after the atrocity is committed. And the atrocity is committed because of the intrinsic weakness of the dalits, their inability to offer resistance. They do not have the financial or possibly the numerical strength to create deterrence, just as Ambedkar had spelt out. In addition he also referred to a third strength, moral strength, that is more important than any other. He reasoned that because of their subjugation for centuries, the dalits had lost their moral strength. But should that be so even after their awakening during the last century? Dalits have to invoke this fortitude to resist the perpetrators of atrocities. It also includes avenging the wrong. If the perpetrators learn that dalits can fight and pay them back in their own coin, it would give them pause. Middle class sensibilities cringe at violence but they need to understand that violence as a principle cannot be wished away. Violence characterises the human world. For the dalits, who get murdered at the rate of two a day or raped at more than five a day, pontification against violence is the advocacy of tolerance towards atrocities. Violence—and we are speaking of defensive violence—must be understood as part of the intense form of struggle that engenders and sharpens political consciousness. The wrath of the wretched scares the world. The fair demand is that the world sit up and recognise their wretchedness.

5

Manufacturing Maoists
Dissent in the Age of Neoliberalism

In the film *A Huey P. Newton Story* (2001) on the life of Huey Newton who along with Bobby Seale founded the left-wing Black Panther Party for Self Defense in October 1966, Newton, played by Roger Guenveur Smith, makes a perceptive observation:

> If you read the FBI files you will see that even Mr J. Edgar Hoover himself had to say that it was not the guns that were the greatest threat to the internal security of the United States of America … it was the Free Children's Breakfast Program.

The Free Breakfast for School Children Program, a seemingly ordinary community welfare scheme, was launched by the Black Panther Party in January 1969 to feed a handful of kids at St Augustine's Church in Oakland, California. It became so popular that by the end of the year, the programme had spread to nineteen cities where more than ten thousand children were fed free breakfast (bread, bacon, eggs, grits) every day before going to school. While the programme operated in predominantly black neighbourhoods, children of other communities, including those of partly middle class localities in Seattle, were also fed. It raised public consciousness about hunger and poverty in America, and also brought people closer to the social mission envisioned by the founders of the Black Panther Party. The programme's success spoke volumes about the needs of the black community, and the national reach and capacity of the party. It exposed government inaction towards the problems of the poor, by highlighting the inadequacies of the federal government's lunch programmes in public schools across the country. Despite, or rather on account of, its success, federal authorities attempted to clamp down on the breakfast programme. In a giveaway of the security establishment's mindset, the director of the FBI, J. Edgar Hoover, noted it as an 'infiltration'—an intrusion into the domain of the state even if the state was disregarding its obligation towards the welfare of a certain class of citizens.

This is precisely how the Indian government thinks about the naxalites. It is worried about the prospects laid bare by such an expression of grass-roots level dissent. It is not afraid of the guns of the naxalites; it is afraid of the counterpoint they represent. Naxalite ideology—whatever that may be—holds no terror for the state, but the simple fact of dissent does: be it an uncompromising recognition of or disagreement with the state's anti-people policies. Taking up the cudgels for the poor, speaking against the violation of democratic rights or questioning the constitutionality of government actions do not go down well with the Indian state. In a masterfully designed false equation, it labels as naxalites or Maoists—synonymous with enemies of the state—those who pose the 'greatest threat to national security'. The status of naxalites as enemies of the state ends up being doubly affirmed and shifts beyond the realm of disputation. To choke such dissent, the state has exerted all its might to discredit and eliminate individuals it deems a threat to its apparatus.

Whatever its form, the essence of a working democracy is the protection it extends to citizens against the state's overreach. The space to voice dissent is an essential provision in any such polity. While boasting for decades that it is the world's largest democracy, India has systematically constricted the availability of such spaces to its people. We are now down to small designated areas in each capital city, such as Mumbai's Azad Maidan, where people may shout their complaints out to the indifferent skies if not to a responsive government. Even such limited spaces are not available as a political right any more. In October 2017, Delhi's Jantar Mantar was summarily repossessed by the state, and its rag-tag assemblage of protesters evicted. The wide lane behind the eighteenth century observatory where the charade that India is a democracy was allowed has now become out of bounds for any citizen wronged by the republic. If you are an adivasi woman from Manipur brutalised by provisions of the Armed Forces Special Powers Act that gives uniformed men the license to rape and loot in the name of protection of sovereignty, a farmer from Tamil Nadu desperately seeking relief from drought, a dalit from Bhagana seeking justice for four minor Dalit girls abducted and gang-raped by men of the jat community, or a victim of the 1984 Bhopal gas leak still hoping for justice, you must now pay for the privilege of self-expression. For an adequate daily fee, the treeless expanse of the Ramlila Maidan is yours to occupy—as a pitiful speck in its vast emptiness—far removed from the nerve centre of power, or indeed the notice of the world. Not unlike a jail, with its barbed wire fences and narrow openings guarded by a posse of armed policemen, these designated areas quarantine expressions of dissent and keep them from infecting the population at large. The custodians of India's democracy have not been content with merely a general strangulation of democratic space; the state often goes on the offensive against dissenters by slapping criminal charges on them and conveying them into physical jails.

Despite its mode of expression, the much-maligned naxalite movement is essentially an act of dissent, a public protest, a fact occasionally acknowledged by the government itself, although the actions of the latter never reflect this admission. The state has always preferred to criminalise naxalites, to the extent of waging a full-fledged war upon tribal populations in the guise of fighting naxalism. It extends this attitude to all those who question the government's violations of civil rights. The government labels them as naxalites/Maoists and unleashes its repressive might on them. Many legal luminaries and activists, who have taken it upon themselves to defend the civil rights of citizens as per the Constitution, aver that the ordinary laws available to the government are capable, if operated equitably, of tackling any criminal activity of which the state accuses naxalites. Instead, the government has preferred to create a range of draconian laws expressly to deal with the naxalite 'menace'. There is no empirical evidence that such laws have achieved anything apart from misrepresenting the notion of security: alienating the interests of state security from the security of the population. Invariably, they have operated as oppressive tools against defenceless people and thereby aggravated the very problem that they were supposed to solve.

Sudhir Dhawale, a well-known social activist in Maharashtra, who was arrested by the police for his alleged links with the Maoists, was released from Nagpur's central prison in May 2014 after being acquitted of all charges. Yet, he had had to spend forty months in jail as an undertrial. Eight of his co-accused were also acquitted with him. In 2005, the dalit poet Shantanu Kamble was arrested on similar charges and tortured for over a hundred days before he got bail. He now stands cleared by the court of all charges. The radical political activist, Arun Ferreira, confined in jail for well over four years, was tortured and harassed, repeatedly arrested in fresh cases after being acquitted in earlier ones, before he could finally get bail in January 2012.

The lesser known cases of the arrest of twelve members of the Deshbhakti Yuva Manch of Chandrapur in January 2008 and of Bandu Meshram from Nagpur on very similar charges also come to mind. All these people have been acquitted but not before undergoing mistreatment at the hands of the police and the humiliations of jail life. There are scores of other cases from remote rural areas where young women and men were arrested on the vague charge of being Maoists, many without the charges even being framed, who now face the ruin of their youth and future as they await trial without any support or legal aid.

Warning shots at civil society

As the state opened hostilities against its own people, it came out with the high-pitched propaganda about naxalites building an urban network. It implied the threat that any criticism of government action against the naxalites would be construed as support for them and attract the wrath of the state. In 2007, an example was made of Binayak Sen, a revered doctor with an impeccable record of public service, who was sentenced to life imprisonment. Sen—out on bail currently by order of the Supreme Court—paid a heavy price for exposing the Chhattisgarh state's unconstitutional operations.

As general secretary of the People's Union for Civil Liberties' Chhattisgarh unit and its national vice-president, Sen was involved in the investigation of cases of civil rights violations committed by the state in the name of fighting a Maoist insurgency. He participated in many fact-finding inquiries into the murder of unarmed and demonstrably innocent civilians by the police. For instance, he had exposed the fact that twelve alleged Maoists killed by the police in a supposed gunfight in Santoshpur village, on 31 March 2007, were actually ordinary tribals executed at close range. The Chhattisgarh Human Rights Commission took note of his investigation and ordered the bodies of the victims exhumed. Sen was arrested in Raipur just a few days after this development, on 14 May 2007—under the new-minted Chhattisgarh Special Public Security Act, 2005, which permits detention for up to seven years without recourse to review or appeal, for any expression that the state regards as a disturbance to public order. The arrest occurred when Sen came all the way from Kolkata to present himself to the Raipur police, since he had learnt that they would be coming for him and decided to spare them the trouble. The accusation against him was that he used to carry secret letters from Narayan Sanyal, senior leader of the banned CPI (Maoist), then lodged in the Raipur Central Jail, to his associates. Apart from the CSPSA, Sen was charged under the draconian provisions of the Unlawful Activities (Prevention) Act (1967) as well as an assortment of other charges from the IPC, a cocktail mixed for anyone charged with Maoist-related offences. It was clear to the world that the case against Sen was trumped up because he had dared to expose the evil operations of Salwa Judum, a vigilante organisation in Southern Chhattisgarh that had been armed and supported by the state government and the Ministry of Home Affairs since June 2005, purportedly to combat the Maoist insurgency.

Enlightened opinion represented by as many as twenty-two Nobel laureates among others sought his release, but the haughty state refused to yield. His bail was refused four times—twice by the Raipur court and once each by the Chhattisgarh High Court and the Supreme Court. The police case against Sen pivoted principally on his meetings with Narayan Sanyal, but the fact remains that all his visits took place with the permission of the deputy superintendent of police and under the close supervision of jail authorities. The lies of the state were exposed in the trial, which began on 30 April 2008. As per the original charge sheet, eighty-three witnesses were meant to depose against him. Of these, six were declared hostile and sixteen were dropped, while the remaining sixty-one testified in court. Not one of these witnesses was able to provide any legally admissible evidence to support the accusations in the charge sheet. Even the jail officials, the superintendent and the jailer, who were called as witnesses by the prosecution, ruled out the possibility of Sen carrying out letters from Narayan Sanyal from the high security Raipur jail. Sen was eventually released on bail after spending more than two years in jail, but the state was undaunted. By holding a high-profile prisoner like Sen despite the global clamour for his release, the state had achieved the crisp communication of what lay in store for anyone raising a voice against it.

Arun Ferreira, a member of the Deshbhakti Yuva Manch (Forum for Patriotic Youth), perceived as a 'Maoist front' by the state, spent nearly five years in jail undergoing all the torture that comes with the Maoist label. He was eventually acquitted by the court in all eleven cases slapped against him—new charges having been filed after the collapse of every previous case. Ferreira's case was no exception and the Maharashtra police was acting true to type.

Ferreira was arrested by the Anti-Terrorist Squad in Nagpur on 8 May 2007 along with Ashok Satyam Reddy alias Murli at Deekshabhoomi in Nagpur, armed with such deadly weapons as a pen drive and leftist literature. To justify their action, the police concocted a story that they were plotting to blow up the Ambedkar Memorial there on Dussehra, when Ambedkarites congregate in large numbers to commemorate their liberation from Hinduism. The police were resorting to the most hideous lies to induce hatred among the Ambedkarite youth who had joined the Maoists in significant numbers in the Vidarbha region.

As Ferreira revealed at his press conference in Mumbai on 11 January 2012, the police had used various techniques of causing bodily pain without leaving any visible injuries. He was subjected to narco tests, not once but twice, despite scientific question marks over the value of information derived from such tests. The staff administering the tests in Bangalore were already infamous for producing data tailor-made to suit the police case. The results of his narco-analysis were to prove a trifle inconvenient to his inquisitors. Stupefied with drugs, he revealed inter alia that Maoist activities in Maharashtra were funded by Bal Thackeray, news that made it out and caused a sensation. When the mere mention of a name by an alleged Maoist is sufficient grounds for arresting a person, should not the alleged bankroller of Maoism have been arrested and subjected to investigation, with a little narco-analysis thrown in? Ferreira was charged in nine naxal-related crimes, from murder and sedition to planting bombs, and of course under sundry sections of the UAPA. In over four years of legal battle, the court did not find a shred of evidence against him and he was acquitted in all the cases.

Ferreira's ordeal illustrates the blatant illegality of the actions of the police. With his arrest, they violated his fundamental right to liberty, expression and more importantly, life (which also covers the deprivation of personal liberty), guaranteed by the Constitution. This was followed by a series of unlawful acts: in threatening his friends with dire consequences if they voiced their support, torturing him in custody, forging his signature on the consent form for the narco test, concocting false charges against him, making a series of false representations before courts, kidnapping him after his release from jail, manhandling his lawyers, and much more. No charge against Ferreira could stick but the police still managed to hold him in jail for well over four years. Ferreira gained media attention because he was from Mumbai, from the middle class dream suburb of Bandra, and educated at the elite St Xavier's College. Because he could afford it, Ferreira has sued the state—and rightly so—for infringing his fundamental rights to liberty and freedom of movement, and demanded an apology and compensation of Rs 25 lakh. Dalit and adivasi victims of the state's criminality have no option other than to meekly swallow the injustice of the system.

Mopping up subaltern protest

While the anti-national tag has come to refer to all left-liberal civil rights activists and protestors in urban spaces, another accusation hurled repeatedly, if they dare to protest against the state, is that they are simply subsets in the Venn diagram of naxalites. In Maharashtra most people arrested as Maoists are dalits and adivasis. The Maoist label is compounded by their caste identity which already renders them vulnerable. Although the ruling classes have succeeded in enervating the dalit movement, the Ambedkarite consciousness among dalits remains alive. It occasionally manifests itself in militant outbreak against the system's excesses, as in the wake of the Khairlanji murders and the more recent actions of the Bhim Army in response to the violence against dalit households in Saharanpur, UP. It is this kind of incipient dissent the state wants to nip in the bud by pinning the label of Maoism or naxalism on dalit and adivasi youth in particular. Sudhir Dhawale expressed this idea in clear terms to the *Indian Express* (23 May 2014), following his release from prison:

> Dissenting voices are stifled. We rarely see the oppressed caste fight back. Sustained agitation that we saw post-Khairlanji [against caste atrocities] is no more a common sight. Many of us who participated in protest rallies then (post-Khairlanji) have been booked in cases. We were labelled as 'Naxals'.

With the arrest of Dhawale, the well-known dalit social activist and editor of *Vidrohi*, yet another Binayak Sen emerged. Not an exact copy, as Binayak Sen comes from a bhadralok family, earned his postgraduate degree from a prestigious medical school, has an enviable academic record and certain well-deserved decorations received in the course of his professional life. Sudhir Dhawale comes from a poor dalit family, he is moderately well-educated and has lived without any notable social acclaim so far. What makes their cases similar, apart from their unflinching dedication to the oppressed, is the neurotic behaviour of the state towards them.

Sudhir Dhawale has been a political activist right from his college days in Nagpur when he was part of the Vidyarthi Pragati Sanghatana, a radical students' organisation in the 1980s. He never hid his ideological leanings or association with the mass organisations that professed Marxism-Leninism, loosely identified as naxalism, and now lumped together with Maoism by the state, after the merger of the most militant naxal parties—CPI (ML) (Peoples' War) and the Maoist Communist Centre—into CPI (Maoist). He denied any connection with the

Maoist party or its activities, least of all the violent actions committed by it. Starting in 1995, Dhawale worked actively to resist atrocities against dalits and campaigned for the effective implementation of the PoA Act. After moving to Mumbai, he became active in the cultural movement and took part in organising an alternative Vidrohi Marathi Sahitya Sammelan in 1999 in protest against the mainstream literary gathering which is heavily sponsored by the state government. This initiative took the form of the Vidrohi Sanskrutik Chalwal (Forum for Cultural Resistance), with its own bimonthly organ, *Vidrohi*, of which Dhawale became the editor. Soon *Vidrohi* became a rallying point for radical activists in Maharashtra. He drew on his literary flair to write pamphlets and books propagating revolutionary ideas in support of the ongoing struggles of adivasis and dalits. After the Bombay police gunned down ten dalits and injured several persons protesting the desecration of an Ambedkar statue in Ramabai Nagar on 11 July 1997, Dhawale was among those at the forefront seeking justice. He played a leading role in the foundation of Republican Panther on 6 December 2007—Ambedkar's death anniversary—which identifies itself as 'a movement for the annihilation of caste'. He was active in the state-wide protests that erupted after the gory caste atrocity at Khairlanji, protests perversely attributed to the naxalites by the then home minister of Maharashtra, R.R. Patil. That was when Dhawale came under the police scanner.

Dhawale was arrested by plain-clothed police officials on 2 January 2011 at the Wardha railway station, while returning from a literary conference held in the town. He was charged under Section 124 of the IPC and Sections 17, 20 and 39 of the UAPA, which amounts to sedition and waging a war against the state. When questioned over the arrest, all the police had to say was that they had found incriminating literature in his house and that one Bhimrao Bhoite, an alleged Maoist who was arrested earlier, had mentioned his name. The literature in question was eighty-seven books by Ambedkar, Marx, Lenin and

Arundhati Roy, confiscated by the police in a raid on his house during which they ransacked the place and took away his computer and books, the possession of none of which is remotely illegal. Rather, the illegality lay, as he alleges, in the entry and search of his Mumbai apartment in the presence of only his two children, both minors.

Similar was the case against Binayak Sen, which relied upon the literature he possessed, a line of argument shot down by the Supreme Court: 'If Mahatma Gandhi's autobiography is found in somebody's place, is he a Gandhian? No case of sedition is made out on the basis of materials in possession unless you show that he was actively helping or harbouring them [Maoists].' None of this helped Sen get a simple bail from the same court.

The Gondia Sessions Court acquitted Dhawale on 22 May 2014 trashing the police case, but to what avail? The police's objective of punishing Dhawale and terrorising activists like him was accomplished. The other eight persons—all dalits—acquitted along with Dhawale had also been arrested on trumped up charges and made to undergo torture, harassment and humiliation in the course of their imprisonment. In February 2014, at least 169 undertrials lodged in the Nagpur jail, among them women, had the Maoist tag imposed on them. Their number came to include the relatively recent inmates, Hem Mishra, Prashant Rahi and the Delhi University professor G.N. Saibaba. These cases were flashed in the media and the role of the police was widely condemned. But the remainder are nameless and faceless adivasi youth from the interiors of the Gadchiroli district of Maharashtra, most of them rounded up in the wake of some Maoist action nearby.

Two adivasi youth became the oldest among undertrial inmates with the naxalite label in the Nagpur Central Prison. One is Ramesh Pandhariram Netam, 26 in 2014, an activist of a student organisation, who remained in jail for nearly eight years. He was released on bail in 2016 and now stands acquitted in all cases like most made-up Maoists. His parents were activists in the mass movements identified as

Maoist-inspired. His mother, Bayanabai, active in the Dandakaranya Adivasi Mahila Sanghatan, was arrested by the Gadchiroli police and killed during torture. The villagers had protested the killing but their voice never reached the mainstream media. His father is said to have surrendered in 2012. Whenever he was about to be released, the police would slap fresh charges to detain him in jail. This happened not once but thrice. In May 2014, when he was about to be released upon the dismissal of all the cases against him, the police slapped two more charges to keep him in jail. The other adivasi youth Buddhu Kulle Timma, 33, from an interior village in the Gadchiroli district, was also acquitted in 2011 but remained in jail as the police slapped six fresh cases on him. He was also acquitted in all the cases in 2016.

Most adivasi prisoners are illiterate peasants. One can imagine the magnitude of their helplessness in the human tragedy that is unfolding. Even the trials of some among them are held via video-conferencing. The cases are heard in the Gadchiroli court with local advocates, but since the accused are not taken to court, there is no communication between them and their advocates. They do not know about the contents of depositions by witnesses, what arguments were made or what the judges remarked. Videoconferencing effectively deprives them of all this relevant information. As a result, when they are required to make a final statement, they make it with no sense of what came before, of the context into which they are delivering their words. Many of them are innocent not merely of crimes but even of the knowledge of what they are in for, and have grown increasingly resigned to their fate. Each of the accused has undergone immense personal suffering along with their families' incalculable distress, facing humiliation and disrepute in society, the ruin of relationships, and the loss, on average, of four to five years of their productive lives for no fault of theirs.

It seems to have become the standard operating procedure of the police to hold people in jail as long as they wish. Nowhere in the IPC is Maoism defined as a crime but the police treats it as such. The Supreme

Court has held, in separate judgements delivered on 3 February and 31 May 2011, that mere association with any outfit or adherence to any ideology, or possessing any literature, cannot be an offence unless it is proved that the person concerned has committed a violent act or caused others to do so. If this is the law of the land, surely the police may at the very least be expected to know it. The sad but unsurprising fact of the matter is quite the opposite. In one such case, of Shyam Balakrishnan, son of a former judge of the High Court of Kerala, who had been picked up in 2014 on suspicion of being a Maoist, the Kerala High Court in May 2015 reproached the state for 'disguised aberration of law in the cloth of uniform' where 'protectors become aggressors'. In a rare instance of a court being judicious in recent times, the single-judge ruling by Justice A. Muhamed Mustaque said:

> Being a Maoist is no crime, though the political ideology of Maoists does not synchronise with our constitutional polity. It is a basic human right to think in terms of human aspirations… therefore, police cannot detain a person merely because he or she is a Maoist, unless police forms a reasonable opinion that his activities are unlawful (*Hindu,* 22 May 2015).

He even ordered the state to pay a compensation of one lakh rupees and a legal fee of Rs 10,000 to Balakrishnan. In case after case, the courts have commented adversely on the conduct of the state. As police aggression continues unabated, the force seems legitimized by the direction and protection of the political establishment.

The Kabir Kala Manch was a Pune-based cultural troupe of poets, musicians and singers, mainly comprising young dalits who came together in the wake of the Gujarat carnage in 2002 to spread an anti-caste, anti-communalism and democratic message. They were arrested for their alleged links to Maoists following the April 2011 arrest by the Maharashtra Anti-Terrorism Squad of Angela Sontakke, alleged to be the secretary of the Golden Corridor Committee of the banned CPI-Maoist. When one of the KKM members, Deepak Dengle charged with the UAPA, got bail in 2013, other members—Sheetal Sathe and her husband Sachin Mali—with the help of activists like filmmaker Anand Patwardhan, came out of hiding and staged a 'satyagraha' outside the state assembly, stressing that they were innocent. Their courageous gesture cut no ice with the police who promptly arrested them under the UAPA. Sheetal got bail on humanitarian grounds as she was pregnant, but Sachin had to spend forty-five months in jail before the Supreme Court granted him bail along with Ramesh Ghaichor and Sagar Gorkhe. The incarceration of the KKM team was based solely on the charge of the Anti-Terrorist Squad that they had links to Maoists. This did not constitute a crime under the terms unequivocally stated by the Supreme Court judgement of February 2011 in the *Arup Bhuyan vs. State of Assam* case: 'Mere membership of a banned organisation will not make a person a criminal unless he resorts to violence or incites people to violence or creates public disorder by violence or incitement to violence.' The KKM members taken captive still had to struggle for two to four years before being granted bail.

Although the previous Congress regimes were happy to press for draconian laws that impinge on personal liberties, since the ascent of the Modi government in 2014, charges of sedition have spread out of control. Siddharth Narain and Geeta Seshu in an essay (*Hoot*, 19 August 2016), draw our attention to how in the Shreya Singhal case, decided on 24 March 2015, the Supreme Court, striking down section 66A of the Information Technology Act 'carefully distinguished between "discussion", "advocacy" and "incitement", and reiterated the high threshold that has been laid down in earlier free speech related precedents'. They also cite the Supreme Court's ruling in the 1960 Ram Manohar Lohia case, where 'the state must prove that the connection between what is said and the public disorder that the state claims will result because of the speech, must be proximate, and not remote, hypothetical and farfetched'. However, the courts have often refused to exercise such discretion.

The case of G.N. Saibaba, who is 90 per cent disabled and was a Professor of English at Ram Lal Anand College of Delhi University, reveals how the police and our own justice delivery system can manufacture monumental injustice. The world was aghast at the May 2014 arrest of this disabled person as the mastermind of a crime committed more than a thousand kilometres away. Following the example set by the Chhattisgarh police, who had arrogantly held Binayak Sen in jail for nearly four years to teach a lesson to the so-called urban network of Maoists by ignoring the protests/condemnation/appeals of the entire world, the Maharashtra police wanted to go a step further in its treatment of Saibaba. With great difficulty, he managed to get bail from the Supreme Court in June 2015, against vehement opposition from the Maharashtra state counsel. Even Justice Khehar had to reprimand the counsel opposing bail: 'You have been extremely unfair to the accused, especially given his medical condition. Why do you want him in jail if key witnesses have been examined? You are unnecessarily harassing the petitioner.' This relief proved short lived. In March 2017, the Maharashtra state got back at him with a sessions court verdict from Gadchiroli pronouncing a life term on him along with four others, a judgement that legal luminaries tore apart for its prejudice and irrationality. Perhaps the Maharashtra government wants to see him die in jail so that no one would dare to oppose it in the future.

Justice man-handled

Soni Sori's travails had begun before her arrest by the Delhi Crime Branch on 4 October 2011. An educated woman from a politically-active tribal family (her father was a sarpanch for fifteen years, her uncle a CPI Member of Legislative Assembly, her elder brother a Congressman, and her nephew a journalist), she grew up in Dantewada, South Chhattisgarh. When Sori (35), and her nephew, Lingaram Kodopi (25), who had studied journalism in Delhi, began voicing the concerns of their people, this automatically brought them under the radar of both the Maoists and the police, and also into conflict with some powerful local people. The police tried to co-opt them as informers but when they paid no heed, they became victims of police harassment instead.

On 30 August 2009, the police took Lingaram away and kept him in a police station toilet for forty days. He was released on 10 October only after a habeas corpus petition was filed in the Chhattisgarh High Court. On 9 September 2011, the police picked up Lingaram and one B.K. Lala, a contractor of the Essar group, from their houses but claimed that they were caught red-handed exchanging money in the marketplace. Soni Sori, who had tried to discover the whereabouts of Lingaram, was declared absconding. Both were charged for acting as conduits for extortion money being paid by the Essar group to Maoists in order to safeguard its mining operations in the area. Despite the fact that the entire episode was exposed as a concoction (as reported by *Tehelka*, 15 October 2011), the police persisted with the charge, even after her acquittal in six out of the eight cases.

While in police custody, Soni Sori was brutally tortured and sexually harassed, which caused blisters in her genital area, leading to hospitalisation. She described this torture in her letters—how she was pulled out of her cell at the Dantewada police station at midnight on 8/9 October and taken to the superintendent of police, Ankit Garg, in whose room she was stripped, sexually assaulted, and tortured with electric shocks. After a Supreme Court order, a medical examination was conducted during which two stones were found to have been inserted in her vagina and one in her rectum, which were the primary cause of her abdominal pain. Despite such evidence of police brutality, the Supreme Court declined her plea to be kept in any jail outside Chhattisgarh, gave the state government forty-five days to respond and effectively handed her back to her torturers.

In her letters she specifically levelled accusations against Garg, saying, 'He has taken my all. I have been tortured in ways I can't describe here.' Her husband, Anil Phutane, who ran a restaurant at their native place in Dantewada, was already arrested as a Maoist and tortured so badly that he turned paralytic and eventually succumbed to his injuries in August 2013. She was not allowed interim bail to attend his funeral and make arrangements for her three daughters aged five, eight and thirteen. Her case provoked international outrage and people like Noam Chomsky and Jean Drèze protested against the 'brutal treatment meted out to her' but to no avail. On Republic Day 2012, her tormentor Ankit Garg was awarded a police medal for gallantry by the president of India.

Soni Sori's arrest came barely a year after the arrest of the then twenty-year-old Arati Majhi from Jadingi, an adivasi hamlet in Gajapati district, Odisha. The details are vividly documented in a fact-finding report dated January 2011 by Women against Sexual Violence and State Repression. At about 4 am on 12 February 2010, some forty-odd Special Operations Group personnel and policemen from the Adava police station raided Jadingi seeking two Maoists, Sagar and Azad. They forcibly entered houses, dragged people out, beat them up and threatened to shoot them if they did not reveal the whereabouts of Sagar. One of the houses belonged to Dakasa Majhi, where Arati Majhi, his daughter was doing her usual morning chore of pounding the rice, while her parents, brother and sister-in-law were asleep. The security forces, all male, dragged her outdoors and began thrashing her, accusing her of interacting with the Maoists. Next, they picked up her cousin Lajar Majhi from another house, and Prasanno Majhi, a youth from a neighbouring village, whom they mistook for Sagar. They took Arati Majhi and the two boys with them, while her younger brother, Lalu Majhi, followed. They went on to pick up another Majhi relation, Shyama Majhi, and a boy, Dakua Majhi, from Tangili, the next village. After going some distance, they asked the boys to return but Dakua and Lalu stayed on asking for Arati's release. In the jungle near Baliponka, some security men gang-raped Arati, their crime witnessed by these boys.

On reaching the police station, the boys were threatened with death if they revealed anything. They were not only scared for their lives but for the lives of their family members, most of them already behind bars or being targeted by the police. It is said that one of Arati's brothers and a sister had left home and had probably joined the Maoists, but Arati was not a Maoist. It is clear that she was not arrested for any crime, not even for being the sister of suspected Maoists, as the police would not otherwise have turned her brother away. She was arrested because she could be tortured and raped with impunity. On reaching the police station they foisted eight cases on her, none of these backed by any evidence, but which sufficed to keep her in jail.

In March 2012, Maoists issued a thirteen-point demand under the name of Sabyasachi Panda, alias Sunil, secretary of the Odisha State Organising Committee of the Communist Party of India–Maoist (CPI–M). In exchange for the release of two Italian tourists they had abducted in Daringbadi in Orissa's Kandhamal district the previous week, the letter demanded a range of actions, from the political—by lifting the ban on the CPI–M—to welfare measures such as the provision of potable water to every village. The fourth of these demands was for the arrest and trial of police officials involved in the gang rape of Arati Majhi and in false encounter cases and custodial deaths in the region. Her name was also included in the list of thirty-two adivasis including Maoist sympathisers whose release was demanded by the Maoists. However, she was not released during the hostage exchange.

She was finally acquitted in all the eight cases on 17 July 2013 after spending nearly three and a half years in jail. Arati is back in her home but with her world completely shattered.

Who watches the watchmen?

These cases represent the plight of thousands of tribals and dalits in India. A plethora of constitutional provisions are in place to protect the Scheduled Castes and Scheduled Tribes, and yet, in practice no

SC/ST law comes to their rescue or penalises the culprits. Why? Because they have been given the dreaded label of 'Maoist', an identity inconsequential in law as decreed by the Supreme Court but deemed self-evidently criminal by the police. To be designated a Maoist is to be implicitly considered 'the greatest internal security threat to our country', to use Dr Manmohan Singh's words on naxalism. The facts speak otherwise. The police who abuse and insult the poor, beat and torture them, molest and rape women, indulge in forgery and lies and foist false cases on innocents to cover up their own misdeeds are the main catalysts in manufacturing Maoists. Politicians who tacitly promote police criminality and endanger democracy are the real internal security threat to our country.

A cursory look at the so-called Maoist cases will reveal that the main intention of the police is to harass people by keeping them in jail for as long as possible. Their muddled logic informs them that such heinous treatment of leading activists would terrorise the general public into submission. Empirical evidence goes to show the contrary. Neither are the activists who are subjected to such blatant atrocities and injustice scared into giving up their activism, nor has there been any decline in the incidence of dissent. Rather, these acts of lawlessness by state actors further alienate people from the system and impel at least some of them to become Maoists.

All that is reflected in these episodes is the Indian state's intention to harm its own people, no matter how high the costs to the country. There are thousands languishing for years in Indian jails for the 'crime' of being Maoist. Invariably each one has suffered illegal torture during police custody and humiliating conditions thereafter during judicial custody. Custodial torture and lawlessness of the police are the norm in our democracy. India signed the "United Nations Convention against Torture and Other Cruel, Inhuman or Degrading Treatment or Punishment" in 1997 but is yet to ratify the treaty in domestic law. India does not have any specific law against custodial torture, nor does it have robust procedural safeguards against custodial violence. This directly feeds into the lawless behaviour of the police. One may not quarrel with the professional privilege of the police to arrest people and frame charges based on whatever information they may have, but these charges are subject to judicial scrutiny. When executive privilege is wantonly and grossly misused—as repeatedly established—one expects that some kind of check would be instituted against the lawlessness of the police. As it turns out, there is effectively none. The police can arrest anyone they want as a Maoist, torture and entangle them in a few dozen cases, which would easily mean jail time for a minimum of four to five years irrespective of what the court finally decides. One can see a pattern in Maoism-related cases where police lawlessness emerges as the sole culprit.

In the prevailing confusion, the distinction between the organisation and the ideology is deliberately blurred and people are charged with being Maoists on the ludicrous grounds of possessing literature on or by Marx, Lenin, Mao and even Ambedkar. On 15 October 2004, the Chandrapur police arrested Sunita Narain of Daanish Books, who had put up a book stall at an event to observe Babasaheb Ambedkar's mass conversions to Buddhism on Deeksha Day, in order to sell books on left ideology along with titles on Bhagat Singh and Babasaheb Ambedkar, all bearing the standard author's details as well as those of publication. The police registered an FIR under Section 18 (punishment for conspiracy and knowingly facilitating the commission of terrorist acts, etc.) of the UAPA. It was a charge surpassing every limit of absurdity, to connect the public sale and display of books with acts of violence threatening the sovereignty of India and striking terror in people (the general definition of 'terrorist acts' under the UAPA). The police acted either with wanton illegality or utter foolishness, which warranted that action be taken against them. But nothing happened to the police. Narain, on the other hand had to undergo the travails of defending herself against the onslaught of state machinery.

If at the very basic level of its interface with the people, the state conducts itself in the grossly inhumane and unlawful manner evidenced above (instances that are only a handful of the total), the entire constitutional superstructure simply crumbles, crushing whatever hopes people have of the state. This is the process that makes Maoists out of 'ordinary' people. Even if they were not Maoists to start with, by the time they come out of prison, they are tempted to embrace Maoist ideology. Police repression has thus been the biggest catalyst in manufacturing Maoists. Every unlawful act of state repression has brought windfall gains to the Maoists.

Even if those who were arrested are indeed Maoists, that does not make them criminals. It is not an issue of whether the Maoists are right or wrong, and even less so of justifying or condemning their actions. After all, they are people, who are responding to the deceit and violence of the state in their chosen way. One may disagree with their ideology or methods but one has to admit the horrific conditions which impel them to take a radical path. After six decades of a constitutional regime proclaimed in the name of the people, promising all kinds of lofty ideals, it has only aggravated the inherent injustice, inequality, violence, corruption, and doublespeak in society. While the rich flaunt their opulent lifestyles, the vast majority of people go hungry. The country has the dubious distinction of having the largest number of malnourished, anaemic, hungry people and underfed, underweight, and stunted children in the world. Indeed, the rot has gone much deeper than is usually imagined. Middle class attempts at tweaking the system appear trivial and ill-judged. In contrast, the alleged Maoists stand apart with their agenda of revolution. They are the only ones who appear to have correctly comprehended the dimension of the problem. It is utterly stupid of the state to think that imprisonment, torture, encounter killings, custodial rape and death are going to deter them from their goal. No revolutionary has ever buckled under these methods and shunned revolution.

The Maoists, by any sensible assessment, are neither closer to demolishing the Indian state nor are they progressing in that direction. Physically, they are holed up in the forested tracts of Chhattisgarh, Jharkhand, Orissa and Maharashtra with most of their important leaders already behind bars. Ideologically, of course, their influence extends beyond these areas but certainly not to the extent that the state projects. But for the help they get from the state, the Maoists would not be in a position to attract even the numbers they do. Nevertheless, the state proceeds to alienate vast sections of the people in the name of—to borrow from counter-insurgency argot—'flushing out' Maoists, and exposes the hollowness of its own democratic credentials. It unscrupulously operates its own terror machine in the name of a 'war on terror' or in the name of ensuring 'internal security' in combating Maoism. This, of course, is in addition to the ideological fortification it has constructed, taking advantage of the debacle of the socialist regimes and the resurgence of capitalism in the form of neoliberalism, whose cultural apparatus promotes crass individualism and an ethos of social Darwinism. However, deepening inequalities, the marginalisation of the lower classes, blatant elitist policy biases and the systematic erosion of democracy are kindling resistance.

The highhanded attitude in evidence today towards poor dalits and tribals is the primordial marker of an uncivil caste society that merely feigns civility. It has zealously maintained the divide between the dalit and non-dalit universes within itself. It is unfortunate that the modern constitutional state we created, instead of doing away with this incivility has imbibed it in full measure, promoting and accentuating the divide. The state apparatus favours those who are against dalits and tribals, and opposes those who stand up for them. If you sympathise with dalits and tribals, you become an outcaste, but if you despise them, you are welcomed into the fold. Maoism and nationalism are simply modern day euphemisms for outcaste and caste, respectively.

6

Dalit Protests in Gujarat
A Shifting Paradigm

Gujarat has had a long history of feudal repression, most conspicuously of its dalit community. Compared to their national presence of 16.6 per cent, the dalits of Gujarat are no more than 7.1 per cent of the state's population, and form less than 15 per cent of the electorate even in reserved constituencies. Given this low-key presence, the community has remained politically inert for the most part, tacking itself to the Congress party in M.K. Gandhi's home state, except for a brief flash of strength by the Dalit Panther in the early 1970s. In 1980, the Congress swept to power in the state, bagging 141 out of 182 seats by using the KHAM formula—an instrumental alliance of kshatriya, harijan, adivasi and Muslim voters proposed by the veteran Congressman Jinabhai Darji. The then chief minister Madhav Singh Solanki had introduced reservations for the Socially and Economically Backward Classes, based on recommendations submitted by the Bakshi Commission in 1976. The reservations scheme—particularly its implementation in medical and engineering colleges—incensed the privileged castes. To counter the Congress-engineered social alliance, the Bharatiya Janata Party created one of its own, uniting the angry brahmins, banias and patidars against reservations. The patidars were a valuable addition, as an economically powerful, widespread and populous community that made up a quarter of the state's population. As a new caste formation that emerged formally with the 1931 census, patidars are akin to the small landholding peasant community of kunbis in Maharashtra and the jats of the Northern states. Hitherto a committed vote bank of the Congress, the patidar community was disgruntled at finding itself unrepresented among the ministers in Madhav Singh Solanki's cabinet, in a first since the formation of the state.

In 1981, the BJP mobilised these assets to lead a hundred-day stir against the reservations scheme, and riots ensued in eighteen out of Gujarat's nineteen districts. Although reservations had favoured the SEBC (roughly coterminous with the Other Backward Classes or OBCs), dalits became the choice targets of mob violence, making up the majority of more than forty people who lost their lives. According to the scholar Achyut Yagnik, Muslims had often sheltered dalits during the riots. In reaction to these events, for the first time, a spate of Ambedkar Jayanti celebrations were held all over the state, an awakening that sadly proved to be short-lived.

In 1985, protests against another concession of reservation—this time securing 28 per cent of seats to the OBCs—once again left dalits the principal victims of the violence. However, the BJP had by now realised the electoral importance of the dalits and begun wooing them towards a new social alliance, one comprising dalits, OBCs and Scheduled Tribes, who together account for 75 per cent of the electorate. This required the party to replace its overt focus on caste Hindu interests with one based on hindutva consolidation. As Achyut Yagnik explains in the essay "Search for Dalit Self-Identity in Gujarat":

> After the 1981 agitation the national leadership of the BJP became conscious of the growing anti-BJP feeling among the dalits, and by the mid-1980s they had systematically begun co-opting adivasi and dalit communities. By 1986-87 they had some success with the urban

> dalits, using the VHP's hindutva-based programmes. The party's anti-reservation stance was also corrected, and after 1985, the ABVP started talking in favour of a reservation system for the dalits and the adivasis. The following year, the VHP, in one of its Hindu Yuva Sammelans, asked the youth to dedicate themselves to the abolition of untouchability. They were also asked to work for the all-round development of 'economically and socially backward Hindu brothers'. All this paid dividends (2002, 32).

The dalits succumbed to the new charm offensive, and the second part of the BJP game-plan was realised once Muslims replaced dalits as the objects of collective hatred. This became plain with the 1985 protests over reservations, which had begun as clashes between caste groups among Hindus in Ahmedabad but segued into anti-Muslim riots, with dalits joining the assault. By the following year, dalits were to be found participating in a big way in the Jagannath rath procession at Ahmedabad. They were invaluable as hindutva's foot soldiers, particularly during the 2002 post-Godhra carnage of Muslims. However, nothing has changed for dalits on the ground. The discrimination, exploitation, and atrocities—often going unreported both in the media and in police records—have continued unabated with state complicity to anti-dalit elements in civil society. Even what makes it into the records presents an alarming picture. As per the interim data for 2015 compiled by the National Commission for Scheduled Castes and placed before parliament on 9 March 2017, the BJP-ruled states of Gujarat, Chhattisgarh and Rajasthan reported the highest rates of crime against Scheduled Castes in 2015; these figures being calculated by taking the total incidence of crime against SCs upon the total SC population of a state, and the rate expressed per 100,000 citizens. At a total of 6,655 cases of atrocities, the crime rate worked out to a whopping 163.3 for Gujarat followed by Chhattisgarh with 3,008 cases and a rate of 91.9, and then Rajasthan with 7,144 cases and a crime rate of 58.5. In absolute numbers, Uttar Pradesh ranks highest, with 8,946 cases of atrocities, but its crime rate comes to 21.6. Based on crime rates, the NCSC marked out Rajasthan, UP, Bihar, Gujarat and Chhattisgarh as deserving special attention.

Gujarat has always been one of the worst states in India in terms of atrocities on dalits. While aware of the awakening of dalits in neighbouring Maharashtra, those in Gujarat could not raise their voices on account of the terror of dominant castes and the benumbing influence of Gandhi's harijanism. Ambedkar's influence in terms of the Republican Party, Buddhism, and the later upsurge of dalit literature and the Dalit Panther, was to be seen only in certain pockets of urban Gujarat. As elsewhere, the condition of Gujarat's dalits presents a distinctly worsening trend under BJP rule. The state that earned the epithet of being a laboratory of hindutva for its genocidal experiments on Muslims, bared its fangs with respect to the dalits too. On an average, 1,100 dalits become victims of atrocities every year. In 2012, in Thangadh, a small town in Surendranagar district of Gujarat, three dalit youth were gunned down by the police on two consecutive days (22 and 23 September) and Narendra Modi as chief minister never uttered a word although he was only seventeen kilometres away from the spot leading a Vivekanand Youth Vikas Yatra. On the first day, police opened fire on dalits protesting against the bharwads (a caste group of pastoral origins), who had beaten a dalit youth during a previous clash between the communities. The police firing seriously injured a seventeen-year-old boy, Pankaj Sumra, who later died in a hospital at Rajkot. News of his death sparked outrage among the dalits, who took to the streets demanding that a complaint be filed against the police officials responsible for it. The next day, the police again opened fire on agitating dalits, injuring three dalit youth, two of whom—Mehul Rathod, 17, and Prakash Parmar, 26—died in the Rajkot civil hospital. These killings, just before the state assembly polls in 2012, sent shockwaves across the state and complaints were lodged against four police officials. Investigation was handed over to the Crime

Investigation Department (Crime). However, despite three FIRs filed against policemen, a charge sheet was filed in only one case and one of the accused, B.C. Solanki, was not even arrested. The report of the inquiry committee headed by the principal secretary of the social justice and empowerment department of the government of Gujarat, was never released. In a summary report before the Gujarat High Court in March 2015, the CID investigation presented its finding that in this matter no one was guilty of crime. The near-total absence of political will for justice when it comes to dalits and Muslims in Gujarat now stands institutionalised.

Una: an atrocity and its aftermath

The 2016 agitation over the public flogging of four dalit men in Una brought the darker side of Gujarat to the fore. But many incidents of a similar nature just prior to Una did not make it to the news. For instance, on 22 May 2016, a team of self-styled gaurakshaks—who are basically bloodthirsty goons affiliated to some outfit of the Sangh parivar emboldened since 2014—assaulted dalits in Rajula town of Saurashtra. On 6 July, a dalit, Ramabhai Singarakhiya, was murdered at Sodhaana near Porbandar. Three days after the Una atrocity, on 10 July, a dalit undertrial, Sagar Babubhai Rathod, died due to custodial atrocities by the police. These incidents were never inquired into. A recent study by the Navsarjan Trust has demonstrated that of all the atrocity cases that occurred across four districts in Gujarat, 36.6 per cent were not registered under the PoA Act and, of the cases where the Act was applied, 84.4 per cent were registered under the wrong provisions, thus concealing the intensity of the violence. Interestingly, the Navsarjan Trust, founded by Martin Macwan in 1988, owes its birth to anti-dalit violence. In 1986, the landlord darbar community of Golana village in Anand district had brutally attacked the dalits, gunning down four of Martin's colleagues and badly wounding eighteen others, while many houses were set on fire. After a thirteen-year legal battle, life imprisonment was awarded to ten of the murderers.

Earlier, the Ahmedabad-based Council for Social Justice had studied 400 judgements under this Act, delivered—over the course of ten years since 1 April 1995—in the Special Atrocity Courts of sixteen districts of the state, and found wanton violations of the rules by the police with the aim of weakening the prosecution's case. The judiciary also contributed its own prejudices to render the Act toothless. No wonder the conviction rate in atrocity cases for crimes against SCs and STs, during the ten-year period under study, was six times lower in Gujarat than the Indian average. In 2014 (the latest available data), 3.4 per cent of crimes against SCs in Gujarat ended in convictions, against a national rate of 28.8 per cent—a whopping 88 per cent lower than the national average. Unsurprisingly, a report titled "Understanding Untouchability: A Comprehensive Study of Practices and Conditions in 1,589 villages"—covering the state during 2007–10 and conducted by the Navsarjan Trust in collaboration with the Robert E. Kennedy Centre for Justice and Human Rights—revealed untouchability as widespread, even rampant in rural Gujarat.

Flaunted as a model of 'development' by none other than Narendra Modi, Gujarat ranks fourth among India's states in terms of the incidence of atrocities against dalits. Despite gross violations of the rights of minorities (and as if his complicity in the 2002 riots wasn't evident enough), Modi's image as the 'vikas purush' (development man) catapulted him to the top job of the country. He has continued to apply the Gujarat model largely through a shrewd manipulation of images and symbols, where daily lynchings of dalits and Muslims colligate with a feinting display of love for Ambedkar. The new generation of dalits, faced with a dark future amid the sea of prosperity around them, can no longer tolerate this. The inevitable build-up of resentment and anger, accentuated by sugar-coated anti-dalit policies from the ruling BJP, exploded in the aftermath of the horrific incident in Una.

Una, a small town in the Gir Somnath district of Gujarat, shot to infamy when a video clip of four dalit youths being publicly flogged by upper-caste men went viral on social media. On 11 July 2016, members of a gauraksha samiti entered the house of Balubhai Sarvaiya, a dalit, in the village of Mota Samadhiyala, some twenty-five kilometres away from Una, and assaulted seven people: Sarvaiya, his wife Kuvarben and sons Vasram and Ramesh, two relatives Ashok and Bechar, and a neighbour, Devarshi Banu, who had come to the family's rescue. Later, the mob picked up Ramesh, Vasram, Ashok and Bechar, stripped and tied them to the rear of a car and dragged them half-naked to Una, where they were again flogged in front of a police station. The mob was so confident of its act that the proceedings were captured on video and posted on social media as an inspiration to others of their ilk. The video went viral but not as scripted; before it could click with the hindutva mobs and inspire them to follow its lead, it spread indignation among dalits and gave rise to a spontaneous protest movement.

Violent protests by dalits erupted in Gujarat on Wednesday, 13 July, with incidents of bus burning, clashes and highway blockades being reported from both Saurashtra and North Gujarat. In the town of Kadi in Mehsana district, three public transport buses were torched by mobs, following which the authorities shut down the bus station. In Ahmedabad district, two group clashes were reported and the police had to use tear-gas shells to disperse the crowds that blocked the highway. The culprits in the mob that had attacked the Sarvaiya family were arrested. Given the charged atmosphere, Anandiben Patel, the chief minister of Gujarat at the time, had assured the victims in the Rajkot hospital that a specially designated court would be set up to depose the case within sixty days. That still had not happened till the December 2017 state election. Instead, twelve of the forty-six accused are out on bail, the rest have also applied for bail, while their four dalit victims remain incapacitated by their wounds—physical and mental—even as they face an insecure future. The livelihood of the Sarvaiya family has been heavily affected ever since, and the family leads a threadbare existence on the compensation given to them by the Gujarat government, the BSP leader Mayawati, and the Congress.

Until this point, Una read like any other caste atrocity. However, it was to change the course of future struggles. The ensuing agitation did not follow the usual procedure of lamenting, protesting, or begging for justice from the state—which had become routine after previous atrocities, despite the knowledge that rarely is the perpetrator of a caste atrocity punished in this country. Protests tend to occur within limits which, if exceeded, are followed by much harsher repression by the state, as in Khairlanji (2006) and most other cases. Such repression by upper castes and self-restraint from dalits were premised on the weakness of dalits. Historically, dalits themselves internalised the idea of their weakness and could never imagine that they too had strength. The biggest departure the Una struggle presented was with its tactical approach, realising that the strength of the dalits lay in what appeared to be their weakness—that dirty work of dragging and flaying dead cattle for which Balubhai Sarvaiya's family was flogged. The Una protesters—under the banner of the Una Dalit Atyachar Ladhat Samiti (Una dalit atrocity struggle committee)—decided to use this new found strength and couple it with the demand for land and livelihood, to fire the imagination of the youth that gathered under its banner. Led by a young activist, Jignesh Mevani, people gathered in huge numbers and pledged to stop skinning cattle carcasses and cleaning gutters. Powerful slogans like 'Gaay nu puchdu tame raakho, ame amaari jameen aapo' ('The cow's tail is yours for keeps, just return us our land') were thrown up by this protest. Dalits stopped skinning carcasses and cleaning manholes as a mark of protest against the incident. It is worth recalling that Ambedkar had always urged the dalit community to give up degrading occupations, but in the absence of alternatives for a livelihood, they persist till date. The Una Samiti demanded livelihood options from the government, along with the allotment of five acres land to each dalit family. It would come from the wastelands in possession of the government. (Why dalits should demand wasteland and not good quality land always foxes me. When Ambedkar realised in 1953 that he could not do anything for the rural dalits and asked his followers to launch a satyagraha for government wasteland as an immediate and achievable objective, it turned into a set demand whenever dalits raised the land issue. Why should dalits not ask for radical land reforms to get their due share?) Mevani, along with Valjibhai Patel and Rajesh Solanki, who had been struggling to secure actual possession of 1,63,707 acres of land allotted to dalits three decades ago, used the agitational momentum to pressure the local administration to start measuring and give possession of these lands. An inventive measure followed, as protestors threw cattle carcasses into the compound of a couple of district collectorates, the stench of which shook the administration into compliance. It immediately undertook measures and released 300 acres of land to dalit allottees. Thus, Una strategically linked the issue of land ownership to the atrocities dalits suffered.

Land and dalit liberation

Given the demographic fact that dalits are predominantly rural—their rate of urbanisation being half that of the non-dalits—land plays a very important role in the schema of dalit liberation. Dalit social degradation is inextricably tied up with economic dependence on farmers of the dominant castes. This dependence was part of the hierarchical structure of autonomous village society. Dalits were meant to be the village servants, in exchange for which the village would offer them a bare subsistence. The dominant castes understood that if dalits came to own the means of survival, they would repudiate their servile status and its attendant social bondage. Land spelt such a means of liberation. While it is true that a few dalits in certain parts of the country did possess land and considerable wealth but were nonetheless treated as untouchables, this does not refute the importance of owning land. Economic power does not automatically negate caste but the lack of it certainly accentuates it. Economic independence is an aspect of liberty and its absence, as a corollary, spells slavery. The prolonged neglect of economic factors by the dalit movement is one of the reasons for the pathetic state of dalits today, a neglect all the more surprising when we recall that economic factors brought the movement into being in the first place. While economic advancement is no guarantor of equality, it is nevertheless an indispensable resource for any struggle. If not for a section of dalits migrating to the cities, getting jobs in modern sectors of the economy or the British military, and thereby achieving a certain level of economic independence, one cannot conceive of a beginning of the dalit movement.

The pre-Ambedkar dalit movements were also based upon economic uplift, whereby people began to think beyond the confines of their caste, came to recognise the injustice of the prevailing order, and revolt against it. For instance, Ayyankali (1863–1941), although unlettered—and in that sense different from later dalit leaders—presents a shining instance of the pre-Ambedkar dalit leadership in Kerala's caste-ridden society, and a prototype of dalit self-awareness. His family's modest landholding allowed him a measure of autonomy, which enabled him to challenge the prevailing proscriptions on dress, on the use of public roads and the entry of pulayar children into government schools. Economic independence, as much as leisure, catalyses the germination of political consciousness in people; those who have to slog all the time to meet their basic needs do not have the respite to reflect upon their condition or plan an alternative future. Economic strength gives people the confidence to weather adversity. It also gives them a stake to defend and inspires them to take risks for long-term gain.

The later leaders of the dalits came typically from the educated class. Compared to Ayyankali's localised interventions, they had a sophisticated outlook on the problem of untouchability, but the role played by economic independence in facilitating their work for social reforms is undeniable. This salient feature of their own background impelled them to identify untouchability overwhelmingly as a religio-cultural problem. The religio-cultural sphere drew their focus, and only secondarily the matter of economic uplift—if pressing for recruitment into the British army even counts as an economic plan. Untouchability, in their understanding, was due to the guile of the brahmins and also due to the internalisation of certain customs by the dalits themselves. It followed that they had to battle against the brahmins on the ideological front and simultaneously work to educate the dalit masses to give up their caste specific customs. These leaders struggled on two planes: one, to demonstrate that untouchability did not have the sanction of religion; and two, reforming the dalit community to adopt better ways of living so that others would not consider them a source of defilement.

Harichand Thakur (ca. 1812–78), who pioneered the first recorded movement against untouchability in mid-nineteenth century Bengal (the Gopalganj area, now in Bangladesh), utilised a religio-cultural articulation to preach the importance of education in the uplift of dalits. He was regarded as a god and his teachings became a quasi-religious movement, the Matua movement. Gopalbaba Walangkar (ca. 1840–1900), whom Ambedkar regarded as the pioneer of the dalit movement in Maharashtra, was a retired soldier. Inspired by Mahatma Phule, he also worked primarily for the cultural uplift of the dalits, i.e. their education and inclusion at public events and ceremonies, through organisations that he founded, such as the Anarya Dosh-Parihar Mandali (Association for redress of grievances of non-Aryans), and the journal *Vital-Vidhwansak* (Destroyer of untouchablity). Dalit leaders in the Nagpur area, like Vithoba Raoji Moon-Pande (1864–1924), who was educated in a mission school and became a cotton trader, worked through his Antyaj Samaj (Society for the outcastes), which he later renamed the Loyal Mahar Sabha in 1912. In 1903, when the mahars were not allowed to bathe in Ambalaghat in Ramtek, Moon-Pande secured permission from the temple committee at Shrikshetra Ramtek to allow the mahars entry, with the proviso that they would give up eating beef and renounce 'unhygienic' practices. Four years later, in 1907, he built a Shiva temple for the mahars. Kisan Fagoji Bansode

(1879–1946), who emerged as a prominent dalit leader in the Nagpur region, was a trade union leader at the Empress Mills and also saw his task as one of working primarily for the cultural uplift of dalits. Outside the Marathi speaking West, figures like Achchutanand (1879–1933) in the United Provinces and Mangoo Ram (1886–1980) in Punjab also worked mainly for cultural advancement and securing rights from the colonial government. As the economic betterment of a few did not alter the social status of the community, these leaders did not see economics as the determining factor of advancement. Moreover, instances abounded of poor people belonging to the dominant castes enjoying all the privileges of their caste identity, which reinforced the notion that economics was a subsidiary factor.

Ambedkar was not unaware of the plight of the dalits in villages. He knew the importance of agriculture in the economy of the country. His essay on small holdings—published in Volume 1 of the *Journal of the Indian Economic Society*, 1918, when he was twenty-seven—testifies to his early interest and deep insight into the agrarian economy. After the landmark events around Mahad (1927), the next issue that engaged his attention was the struggle of tenants against the exploitative and horrendously oppressive khoti system—a kind of landlordism, or revenue farming system prevalent in the Konkan region. The khots, or landlords, were mostly chitpawan brahmins, but also included marathas and Muslims, while the tenants were kunbis, mahars, bhandaris and shudra castes such as the agris. The struggle therefore was against a complex mix of class and caste exploitation. It had begun in the early 1920s, supported by the leader Rao Bahadur S.K. Bole of the bhandari caste, who had risked excommunication for his support to the Arya Samajis on communal inter-dining. He had earlier got his Bole resolution passed by the Bombay Legislative Council in 1923, opening public places and public water resources to the untouchables, a resolution that inspired the iconic Chavadar tank satyagraha of Ambedkar in 1927. Bole had also attempted to introduce an anti-khoti legislation on 6 October

1922, pushing for the appointment of a committee to inquire into the conditions of tenant cultivators under the khoti system in Ratnagiri and Kolaba districts.

Ambedkar started the anti-khoti movement in April 1929 with a speech to the Shetkari Parishad (Agricultural Conference) at Chiplun. He had targeted the khoti system in his presidential address to the Ratnagiri District Conference the previous day. The conference was followed by the mobilisation of people by A.V. Chitre. A peasant meeting on this issue was subsequently held at Goregaon in the Mangaon Taluka (of today's Raigad district). The manifesto of Ambedkar's first ever political party, the Independent Labour Party, founded in 1936, had included abolition of the khoti system. On 17 September 1937, Dr Ambedkar introduced a historic bill in the Bombay Legislative Council for the abolition of the khoti system, but the Congress did not let it come up for discussion; therefore, Ambedkar planned a massive march of peasants starting from Konkan. On 12 January 1938, 20,000 peasants—mahars, kunbis and other castes—marched to the Bombay Council Hall. It was the biggest pre-independence mobilisation of peasants and the first ever demonstration of the struggle to achieve caste–class integration. Ambedkar was the first legislator in India to introduce a bill for the abolition of the slavery of agricultural tenants. The bill aimed at securing occupancy rights to the tenants with a provision for payment of reasonable compensation to the khots for the loss of their rights. The bill proposed the substitution of khoti with the ryotwari system, to give poor farmers who were in actual possession of land the status of occupants under the Land Revenue Code of 1879.

Nothing concrete came of this struggle, however. The Congress party that enjoyed a majority in the provincial legislature opposed him tooth and nail. Ultimately, the khoti system would not be abolished till after independence, in 1949. Ambedkar also took up the land question in his memorandum on states and minorities (1946), demanding the nationalisation of land and proposing collective farming. It was part of his plan to hard-code a socialist structure of society into the Constitution of independent India as its unalterable feature. Strangely, even during this period when he was at his radical best—from proposing the abolition of khoti in 1937 till, almost ten years later, when he proposed state socialism in *States and Minorities*—he allowed his liberalism to override socialism. In the Bill (No. XX of 1927) to abolish the khoti system, he outlined how the Khots would be compensated (*BAWS* 2, 96), and in *States and Minorities* he argued for compensation to the landlords for their lands that would be nationalised. In 1953, he raised the land question again, this time as a means of emancipation for rural dalits. But when he proposed that the dalits should struggle for land, it was fallow government land that he had in mind. As a result, the struggles in response to his prompting did not demand the land of landlords. Despite all the dust and noise raised over land reforms, India remains one of most unequal countries in terms of land distribution. Just 9.5 per cent of rural households hold 55.6 per cent of the cultivable land; and if one excludes the land on which their houses stand, 41 per cent households count as landless.

Although Ambedkar fully knew the importance of land in the emancipation of dalits, he also knew it would not be easy to secure it for them. His idea of state socialism presented a mere generalisation that made it still more difficult to achieve. It was one thing to give a vision of socialism to the Constitution, as he claimed having done in the Directive Principles of State Policy, but it was virtually unthinkable that such radical reforms might be instituted through a Constituent Assembly structurally representative of the elites and propertied classes. It would have been so in any constituent assembly however constituted. This could only be achieved through a revolution, which Ambedkar thought impossible in India. He preferred representation as a means of advancement. His choice was informed by the pragmatism and Fabianism he had imbibed from his favourite professor at Columbia University, John Dewey, and again during his time at the London

School of Economics, an institution established by the Fabian Society. The strategy postulated that if educated dalits occupied important positions in the state structure, they would influence state policy and gradually bring about revolutionary changes. This was why he emphasised higher education for the dalits and struggled for their representation in the power structure. Even within his lifetime, he was to witness the failure of this method.

In a remorseful moment during his last years, Ambedkar expressed regret on this score to the Marathwada unit of the Scheduled Castes Federation that visited him at his residence in Delhi. He said that whatever he had done benefited only educated dalits in urban areas, but he could do nothing for the vast majority of his rural brethren. He asked whether they would be able to launch a struggle for land. On his return, B.S. Waghmare, the leader of the unit, undertook the first ever satyagraha to get fallow land transferred to landless dalits in Marathwada in 1953. For this momentous satyagraha in which 1,700 people courted arrest, he received help from Dadasaheb Gaikwad. In deference to Ambedkar's wishes, two more land struggles were undertaken following his death, both under Gaikwad's leadership: the first in 1959 in the Marathwada–Khandesh region of Maharashtra, and the second in 1964–65 all over India. The latter began on 6 December, the death anniversary of Ambedkar, with hundreds of people courting arrest daily over a month in Punjab, Madras, Mysore, Delhi, Gujarat, Uttar Pradesh and Maharashtra. Over 360,000 people were imprisoned by 30 January 1965.

The union government took serious note of this new turn of the dalit movement. So far, the dalit struggle had revolved around either the abstract issue of discrimination or of political representation, matters that could be addressed with token gestures by any ruling party. But if the dalits were to raise material issues demanding their share in resources, it would be difficult to contain without a structural overhaul. The Congress, representing the ruling classes, worked to co-opt dalit leaders, marking the beginning of the end of the dalit movement.

Never thereafter did the dalit leadership raise the land question, save for a flash in March 1983 when Prakash Ambedkar led a long march from Nashik to Mumbai with 'land for landless' as one of its demands. The Dalit Panther claimed its legacy and inspiration from the Maoist Black Panther Party of the United States, but before it could speak of class issues, it split over the issue of what Ambedkarism meant, the very issue which had split the RPI earlier. During the RPI split, Ambedkarism was identified with constitutionalism, and in the Dalit Panther split, with Buddhism. The only commonality between these splits was anti-Marxism, those evicted from either movement being charged with communist leanings. By the 1970s, a new middle class began emerging among dalits, which found that it remained vulnerable to various kinds of discrimination. Contrary to Ambedkar's expectations that this class would provide a protective cover for the dalit masses, it needed to form its own SC/ST employees' associations to protect its interests. Designed to be apolitical and physically detached from the rural masses, it could only work in the cultural field: by building Buddha viharas, vipassana centres, the promotion of congregational activity, etc. which distanced it further from the material issues of the dalit masses.

Land struggles in Gujarat before Una

U.N. Dhebar, the chief minister of the erstwhile state of Saurashtra, had enacted the Saurashtra Land Reforms Act, 1952, giving occupancy rights to 55,000 tenant cultivators over twelve lakh acres of land, out of a total of twenty-nine lakh acres held by girasdars (mainly upper caste kshatriyas, known as darbars, literally meaning rulers), spread over 1,726 villages. The remaining seventeen lakh acres were left with the girasdars as their personal holdings. Tenant cultivators were mainly patels by caste, who gradually became the owners of this land. The patels enriched themselves by undertaking massive cash crop cultivation of groundnut, cotton and cumin, and later graduated to setting up cotton ginning, oil mills, and other industries. This process saw the evolution of the Saurashtra patel lobby, euphemistically known as telia rajas (oil kings), who came to occupy the dominant position in the politics of Gujarat. With their social capital and state backing, they went on acquiring huge tracts of agricultural land all over the state, most notably in the tribal belt of South Gujarat. Laws were suitably amended to facilitate the acquisition. Two of the most helpful of these interventions were—the doing away with the eight-kilometre limit for an agriculturist to own farmland away from his residence, thereby allowing absentee landlordism, and the changing of the order of priority for the right to cultivate government surplus land by giving precedence to the original landlords over the STs, SCs and OBCs.

Through yet another law, the Saurashtra Estate Acquisition Act, 1952, the government acquired 'uncultivable' and cultivable wasteland, gochar land (village grassland for cattle grazing) and other assets by compensating the girasdars. These enormous tracts of land that came in possession of the state became the theatre of a land grab struggle in the early 1960s, by dalit landless peasants and agricultural labourers under the leadership of dalit textile workers of Ahmedabad. In the words of Somchandbhai Makwana, an influential leader of that movement, an estimated two lakh acres of land was grabbed by dalits and OBCs, which still remains in their possession, albeit without regularisation by the government.

In many cases, dalit and OBC peasants and/or their cooperatives tilling lands under the government's ek-sali (one year renewable tenure) scheme for several decades, were evicted and their lands reverted to the ownership of the 'original' dominant caste landlords. Gandhinagar, the capital of Gujarat, was a mute witness for over three years, 2009–12, to a number of dalit families (mostly from Saurashtra) participating in a satyagraha on the footpath near the Assembly against such machinations. The amendments to the Acts referred to above emboldened the upper castes and the state machinery to violently evict dalits from lands they had cultivated for decades. In a gruesome incident, on 27 November 1999 in Pankhan village in Saurashtra, a mob of eight hundred upper caste men attacked dalits with swords, spears, pipes and fire arms and seriously injured sixty men and women in the course of evicting them from 125 acres of land.

Back in 1997, a landmark struggle by dalits went largely unnoticed by the dalit-free corporate media. Santh (title) orders were given for 150 acres to forty dalits of Bharad village in Dhrangadhra taluka of Gujarat's Surendranagar district. Two of these forty, Devjibhai and Kanabhai (a blind agricultural labourer) asked the 'upper' caste patel occupant to vacate the land that had been allotted to them. Dominant caste landlords responded with violence but were met with serious resistance. Violent group clashes ensued and in one such confrontation, six persons suffered serious injuries. Dalits endured severe social boycott by the upper castes. Devjibhai was apprehended and imprisoned under the Prevention of Anti-Social Activities Act 1985, for daring to enter the land of which he was the de jure owner. It was at this stage that the Council for Social Justice led by Valjibhai Patel, a veteran Dalit Panther, stepped in, creatively combining legal and agitational methods to get Devjibhai released. It organised an 'Ambedkar Rath' through 28 villages over seven days to mobilise dalit support, which culminated in a rally of over 10,000 landless dalits on 6 December 1999, the death anniversary of Ambedkar. The struggle encompassed all 12,438 acres of prime agricultural land declared surplus under the Agricultural Land Ceiling Act, for which 2,398 dalit families and fifty tribal families were given the santh, but not actual possession. The land, apart from being fertile, was potentially valuable because the Surendranagar district was to be the biggest beneficiary of the Narmada irrigation scheme.

A parallel struggle took place in another village, Kaundh, where a young textile mill worker Dungarshibhai of Ahmedabad left his job to take up the fight on behalf of his people in the village. In defiance of one of the biggest tyrant darbars in the district who owned nearly 3,000 acres of land, he drove a tractor on the land given to his family in santh but which had remained in possession of the darbar. As the entire group of dalits stood behind Dungarshibhai, the darbar allowed him to cultivate the land, but proceeded to seize the harvest. The CSJ filed a criminal complaint that saw three darbars put behind bars. Dungarshibhai today is revered as an unchallenged dalit leader in Surendranagar district.

These struggles, isolated as they seem, had to be waged by the legal owners of the land for its repossession from illegal holders. While the government had eagerly publicised the distribution of land to SC/ST beneficiaries, it intentionally or otherwise neglected the physical transference; thereby necessitating these struggles. The process for handing over possession involved the village talathi (accountant) preparing the records of rights and the 'farmers' book' along with a rough map of the plot. After receiving these documents from the collector's office, the district inspector of land records had to send surveyors to prepare the final map, physically mark it out and hand over its possession to the beneficiary in the presence of the collector's representative. In most cases, no part of this procedure had been carried out. The beneficiaries were also deprived of the Rs 5,000 per acre due to them under the rules. The officers responsible should have been punished as per a government notification of 1989, but no action was taken.

In 2011, yet again, nobody took note of the little vibrations that occurred literally on the margins of the much-publicised 'Vibrant Gujarat', the annual global investors' summit on 24 January. In the little-known village of Joradiary in Vav taluka of Banaskantha district in North Gujarat, on the Rajasthan–Pakistan border, a procession of around two hundred dalits accompanied by the beating of drums and slogans of 'long live Ambedkar' marched into a farm under the illegal control of a rabari (wealthy landowner) to restore its possession to a dalit. Valjibhai of the CSJ—which led this struggle to its culmination—had invited me to spearhead the physical handing over of the land to the de jure owners. The dominant castes in the belt had a history of violent reprisals, and as he rightly apprehended trouble, he wanted someone from outside to lead it. Such was the terror of the rabari that he feared the beneficiary might not even come forward to take possession of his land from the usurper, his master. The dalit titular owner of the land had actually slaved for the dominant caste usurper for nearly three decades on this very patch of land. Our strategy was to organise a sizeable mobilisation of the dalits of the area at a public meeting before taking out a victory march. Some three to five hundred dalits reached the outskirts of the village for the march to the land. Dominant-caste men had gathered there but did not pose any resistance. We dismantled the structure they had erected on the land and performed a small puja to mark the transfer of possession. More such takeovers followed until the evening to encourage people to take possession of their lands being illegally held by the upper castes. In the Vav taluka alone, thirty-five dalit families benefited by regaining the ownership of over one hundred and fifty acres. The struggle, led by the CSJ, spurred the state machinery into action, enabling other dalits in the taluka to take possession of lands that rightfully belonged to them. But this impressive struggle sadly failed to arouse the enthusiasm of the reservation-obsessed middle class dalits, revealing the blind spot of the 'emerging classes' among dalits—their lack of concern for ground-level movements for self-empowerment in rural India. Unknown even to most dalits, this was a landmark event that could be likened to the one that took place in Mahad on 20 March 1927 when the delegates to the Bahishkrit Conference had marched under the leadership of their newfound leader B.R. Ambedkar to the Chavadar tank and asserted their civil right to use its water.

Towards a new grammar of struggle

When the Una dalits raised the demand for land to replace their humiliating caste vocations, tellingly, middle class dalits began to question the movement's efficacy. The question they should have asked themselves was whether they wanted rural dalits to be doing the dirty work that their forefathers did. The demand for land was logical, particularly since the Gujarat government had on paper distributed 163,808 acres to the dalits in the 1970s and 1980s but had never delivered on the commitment. The land was not even demarcated physically, far from being handed over to the beneficiaries. As a result, in most parts of Gujarat, one can still encounter the weird spectacle of de jure owners of the land working as the bonded labourers of a dominant-caste de facto owner. Activists like Valjibhai Patel, Rajesh Solanki and Jignesh Mevani have been struggling by different methods to restore these lands to their legitimate owners. Their struggles were co-opted by the post-Una movement, along with the decision of giving up the caste vocation. Those who doubt the efficacy of the demand should see it from the viewpoint of those who, in the absence of land, had to continue flaying dead cattle or practice manual scavenging. The post-Una struggle creatively foregrounded the land question in dalit politics.

The ideological apathy among Ambedkarite dalits towards the land question is because they associate land redistribution with a communist programme, and have for decades stigmatised it as such. They insist that land is no more a feasible solution to dalit problems; instead, the formula should be dalits adopting education, urbanisation and secondary and tertiary sector occupations. Some argue that there simply does not exist enough cultivable land to be distributed among dalit farmers. Such arguments are based on ignorance and need not detain us. Another assumption lurking in the backdrop is that dalits have never had success with farming. Given that they have largely been a landless or near landless people, the basis of such an inference is hard to make out. It is natural that people who have been in a particular profession for generations would appear to be better at it. This is a lazy notion which ignores the fact that dalits lack merely the experience of managing their own farms. History has ensured that they do not lack knowledge of agriculture or experience of labour in the fields. Nor is it as if the dwija and shudra landowners had made a resounding success of the farming sector either.

Land ownership is important for the obvious reason that it makes dalits independent and alters the relations of production in the countryside, the very prop of the caste system. The counter-argument to this concerns the negative terms of trade that prevail in agriculture, especially against small and medium-scale farmers—with high risks, small marketable surpluses, poor access to credit from formal sources, and dependency on local markets—together ensuring that the dice are loaded against the producer. Moreover, the sustainability of land ownership remains precarious in the face of crop failure and non-repayment of debt. This argument is largely valid but at stake here is the independent subsistence of dalit farmers, where the question of trade does not necessarily arise. Besides, no enterprise can be launched with a foolproof blueprint for profitability. That is a matter of organisation and technology, which would follow once the land is distributed among people.

Dignity and secure livelihood are the antonyms of brahminism and capitalism in Babasaheb Ambedkar's formulation of the 1930s. He termed the latter pair the dual enemy of dalits. However, amid his contentions with dogmatic communists, the joint struggle of the working class got de-emphasised. Except for the ILP phase in the 1930s, when working class unity was expedient for the 1937 elections, the need for a concerted front encompassing and transcending dalits has not been expedient in the dalit movement. Circumstances impelled Ambedkar to dissolve the ILP and form the SCF, but he always yearned for a broader unity of people and thus, declared his intention to float the RPI. Given the uniqueness of caste, with its propensity to split like amoeba and the deeply ingrained notion of hierarchy, it can never be the basis for any radical struggle of the downtrodden. Jotirao Phule's pioneering effort to conceive a shudra–atishudra category or Ambedkar's lifelong efforts to construct a dalit category including and uniting all the untouchable castes, did not really succeed. The debacle of the dalit movement and the resurgence of caste identities among dalits amply testify to this fact. Hanging on to caste identities serves ruling class interests and hence, benefits the champions of the caste system, not the larger masses who are its victims. The conclusion is inescapable: unless dalits transcend caste and forge a class unity with other marginalised people, their struggle can never reach fruition. Class unity is not necessarily communist—the bête noire of the dalit middle class. Notwithstanding historical mistakes on the part of the early communists, history testifies to the fact that whenever dalits and communists have joined hands, their struggles have threatened the ruling establishment. The post-Una struggle revived this implicit strategy in attempting to build bridges with other movements.

Having set the tone by taking an economic route to dignity, the Una Dalit Atyachar Ladat Samiti organised a dalit mahasammelan (grand assembly of dalits) at Ahmedabad calling for an end to social discrimination, along with oppression and political apathy. The victims of Una, Thangadh and many other atrocities exposed the ugly face of Modi's Gujarat, testifying to the widespread and deep-rooted untouchability and discrimination rampant in the state. Nearly twenty thousand dalits pledged in the name of Ambedkar that they would give up their caste vocations and instead demanded jobs and land for rehabilitation. Their anger was palpable, but this time it was not directed against any abstraction of manuvadi or casteist elements, but the politicians, RSS, BJP and the state. It was followed by a ten-day-long march from Ahmedabad to Una from 5–15 August 2016. (Their march recalled the seven-day 'Ambedkar Rath' of 1999, in the Surendranagar district, to press for the transfer of the actual control of land to the dalits who held formal titles of ownership). Several dalits and progressive people from across the country joined the march and the concluding rally at Una. A series of actions were planned, some of them executed and some thwarted by the state. The changed tone of protests after Una forced the chief minister to resign and the prime minister, not otherwise known for reacting to peoples' woes, to criticise—if softly—the self-appointed gaurakshaks. Modi shed crocodile tears, and speaking from within his multiple rings of security declared, 'If you want to beat someone beat me, but do not beat my dalit brothers.' The Azadi Kooch (Freedom March) held to commemorate one year of the Una struggle touched upon issues that concern all oppressed people: freedom from casteism, mob lynchings, price rise, farmers' suicides, and the exploitation and unemployment of workers. Apart from many noted progressive individuals in the country, Muslims, Backward Castes and even patels joined the march. At the end of the march, dalits took symbolic possession of land from among the 1,63,808 acres allotted to them three decades previously but which remained in the possession of the dominant communities. Una certainly presents a new grammar of the dalit struggle rooted in a well thought out strategy. It has discarded the abstract cultural argument for dignity and linked uplift to the livelihood issues of the vast dalit masses who are being systematically excluded, primarily by the state. It faces many challenges, both internal as well as external, but one hopes it will not deflect from its path.

Ripples beyond Gujarat

The uprising in Una shook the political establishment in Gujarat and spread to other parts of India as well. The first Una-inspired dalit agitation erupted somewhat expectedly in Karnataka. It all began with discussions of Una on social media that led to an impromptu meeting being called at Bengaluru, to which over three hundred youth turned up. They decided to re-enact 'Chalo Una' by leading a march from Bengaluru to Udupi, one of the dens of the hindutva forces, where in

August 2016, Praveen Poojary, belonging to a backward caste, had been beaten to death by eighteen VHP and Bajrang Dal activists camouflaged under the banner of Hindu Jagarana Vedike, after they found him transporting two cows in a vehicle. Interestingly, twenty-nine year-old Poojary was himself a BJP member and pleaded with them that he was merely transporting the calves for a friend. His explanations, of course, did not matter as he became yet another victim of the obnoxious cow vigilantism of the Sangh parivar.

On 4 October 2016, the 'Chalo Udupi' rally, which simultaneously brought together dalits, other minorities, and left activists, began from Freedom Park in Bengaluru and travelled over the next five days to Udupi, holding meetings and performing programmes against the fascist onslaught of the hindutva forces at Nelamangala, Kunigal, Channarayapatna, Hassan, Belur, and Chikmagalur. As it reached Udupi on 9 October, it was welcomed by a thundershower. A small stage with a banner of 'Chalo Udupi' drenched in rains was wiped clean. By the time the meeting began, the crowd in the Ajjarkad ground swelled to ten thousand, overwhelming saffron Udupi with its blue flags. The rally expressed its solidarity with the struggles of Gujarati dalits and the Dalit Mahila Swabhiman Yatra (dalit women's self-respect march) which took place in Rajasthan from 18–28 September.

Jignesh Mevani also attended the meeting at Udupi. Exposing the hollowness of the much-flaunted Gujarat model, he recounted how dalits were the single largest group of victims after the Muslims and also counted among those most commonly arrested for the 2002 riots. The speeches renewed the slogan 'Food of our choice, land is our right.' Mevani promised to return to Udupi with a three-point agenda: to ban all gaurakshak groups; to enter the maths (temples) in Udupi that observed pankti bheda (separate seating arrangements for brahmins during lunch); and to ask the Karnataka government how much revenue land it has given to the dalits and tribals according to the state land grant rules of 1969.

In Gujarat, the plight of dalits at the hands of the state is compounded by the vile resonance hindutva has with neoliberalism in its complete lack of compassion. To express their anger and isolate their degenerate leadership, dalits in various parts of the country have been spontaneously coming out into the streets sans leaders in recent decades. This trend first manifested itself in 1997, in response to the gunning down of ten people in Ramabai Nagar, Mumbai, and then significantly, after Khairlanji (2006). But the protesters could not articulate a long-term direction for themselves. Una for the first time has achieved this by going beyond the atrocity that ignited the protest. It could transform the weakness which led to humiliation into strength. It has already shaken the citadel of Modi, impelling the state administration to initiate measurement and effect the actual handing over of the plots of land. Despite the impending threat of violence, as the Mevani-led Azadi Kooch wound up in July 2017, they reclaimed twelve acres of land that had been allotted to four dalit families fifty years ago in Lavara, a village in the Banaskantha district. This is already a revolutionary outcome.

In the last Gujarat election, the strategy was extended towards participation in electoral contest to strengthen gains secured through struggles on the street. It was a difficult decision. The swamp that is electoral politics has sucked in scores of well-meaning people, turning them into custodians of the very system they were trying to upend. While remaining fully cognisant of this fact, in a move to intensify the peoples' struggle, Mevani contested the assembly election in December 2017 as an independent candidate supported by the Congress. He emerged victorious, once more marking the prowess of the Una strategy, hopefully translating it into political reality.

7

Slumdogs and Millionaires

The Myth of Caste-Free Neoliberalism

Why did the global Occupy movement of 2011 fail to take root in India? Despite widespread income inequality in the country, the Occupy movement didn't provoke many Indians to stand up and say, 'We are the 99 per cent!' All we saw by way of that was a small rally in Kolkata on 19 October 2011, and an attempt to stage an 'Occupy Dalal Street' in Mumbai on 4 November which made no headway because it lacked support, and was also marked by the prompt arrest of a significant section of protestors by the Mumbai police. The middle (caste and) class youth who had excitedly thronged behind the fasting Anna Hazare in April the same year to demand a Jan Lokpal Bill, simply ignored the wide-angle picture of corruption put forward by the Occupy Wall Street movement, linking government to corporations, financial institutions and the media. It is ironic that some commentators mistakenly traced the inspiration of the Occupy movement to the Anna Hazare-led campaign, without accounting for the fact that Hazare's movement sought a surreal solution to the real problem of corruption, and even that within the confines of the status quo, whereas the Occupy movement symbolically challenged the rubric of capitalism itself.

The cue for the OWS movement came from the Arab Spring protests in Tunisia. The mass dissent against feudal regimes in the Arab world spread like wildfire from country to country. Taking inspiration from this collective rage, an artist at the *Adbusters* magazine in Vancouver designed a poster of a ballerina executing a graceful move upon the back of the Wall Street bull, with a legend above her head that asked in red lettering, 'What do we want?' Under the bull, in white, came the tag 'Occupy Wall Street'. The poster appeared in July 2011, and its terse closing line—'Bring tent'—resonated with people. More than 1,500 protest actions took place on 15 October 2011, the 'global day of action', in eighty-two countries. At one such protest, hundreds of police officers in riot gear clamped down on the OWS encampment at Zuccotti Park in Lower Manhattan, New York City, in the predawn darkness of Tuesday, 15 November 2011. They demolished the tent city that had come up there since mid-September as the epicentre of a protest against corporate greed and economic inequality. Around two hundred people were arrested—their tents, sleeping bags and equipment were carted away, and by 4:30 am the park was empty.

The protests the OWS movement fanned soon spread to over a hundred cities in the US. This leaderless movement sprouted across the world from Australia through Asia, Europe, and, of course, the Americas. Although these demonstrations were crushed at various places, their spirit will live on to inspire future struggles. Such forms of spontaneous mass upsurge, indeed, do not have a beginning or an end; they signify the beginning of the end of what they rally against.

Every mode of production in every historical phase provokes its own form of struggle. Previously, the anti-capitalist movements were marked by militant workers' strikes. But things altered fast with changes in the form of capitalism. It has, on the one hand, nearly succeeded in marginalising the proletariat and, on the other, adopted increasingly predatory forms of exploitation. Advances in technology that not only displaced human labour but also set human labourers further apart in the sphere of production have helped blur the exploitative contours of neoliberal globalisation. At the same time, resistance has begun to manifest itself in novel forms. One of the first major protests of this kind was in 1999 during the ministerial conference of the World Trade Organisation in Seattle, Washington. The crowd of protesters numbering no less than forty thousand was mobilised outside the hotels and conference venue through informal networks in the pre-social media days of resistance. They effectively stalled the meeting and shook the citadel of global capital.

The WTO was compelled to devise in 2001 the vent of the World Social Forum with its illusory slogan 'Another world is possible'. After nine annual WSFs by the end of the decade, and scores of regional social fora, the roughshod march of global capital had not only left 'another world' trailing in the dust but also brought the immediate world to the brink of collapse. The massive financialisation of economies enacted to facilitate accumulation—via cheap credit for instance, and mutually reinforcing circles of institutional investment, alongside the deregulation of financial institutions—intensified the multiple resulting crises to unprecedented magnitude. The Asian financial crisis of 1997, the sub-prime lending crisis of 2008 in the US, and the European sovereign debt crisis that began the following year are but flagposts in this continuing process of the concentration of global capital. Each successive crisis was followed by a massive transfer of public funds to save the crumbling banking system. Estimates of public funds harnessed to resuscitate corporations in the wake of the American sub-prime crisis put the figure as high as $16–23 trillion. It serves as a neat illustration of the Marxian dictum that the state is but a committee of the bourgeoisie to advance its own interests at the expense of the public. Such transfers of public funds into private hands provoked mass outrage. The slogan of the OWS movement—'We are the 99 per cent'—pointed to the extreme concentration of wealth in the hands of the top one per cent of income earners, and drove home the message that an overwhelming majority of the people were paying the price for the speculative dealings of a tiny minority.

The Nobel-prize winning economist Paul Krugman said that the 99 per cent slogan was an understatement. Writing in the *New York Times* on 1 November 2011, he pointed out that a large fraction of the top one per cent's gains have actually gone to an even smaller group, the top 0.1 per cent—the richest one-thousandth of the population. In a number of opinion pieces written for the *New York Times* at the time, he noted that the top 0.1 per cent of the population saw the sharpest increase in income share, taking home over 10.4 per cent of the nation's earnings in 2008 as against a share of 1 per cent in 1970 and 2.6 per cent in 1975. During the last two decades of neoliberal globalisation, inequality has been growing all over the globe. Krugman cited a Congressional report which held that between 1979 and 2005, the inflation-adjusted after-tax income of Americans in the middle-income group rose by 21 per cent; the corresponding increase for the richest 0.1 per cent was 400 per cent. Deepening inequality in the so-called emerging economies like Brazil, China and India has been still worse.

In December 2017, the "Report on Global Inequality 2018" coordinated by economists Thomas Piketty, Facundo Alvaredo, Lucas Chancel, Emmanuel Saez and Gabriel Zucman, was released. Among its findings is a damning assessment of income distribution in India. By 2014, the year at which the report's data ends, the top 0.1 per cent of India's earners had captured more growth than the bottom 50 per cent combined. The richest 10 per cent of the adult population shared around 56 per cent of national income, while the bottom 50 per cent had a share of just over 16 per cent. This is in contrast to the first thirty years after independence, when income inequality was actually reduced and the earnings of the bottom 50 per cent grew at a faster rate than the national average. The reversal in the fortunes of the poor coincided exactly with liberalising measures undertaken by the government, and has accelerated with the entrenchment of the neoliberal system.

India's brazen embrace of inequality

If corporate greed and inequality were the targets of the Occupy movement, India should have been fertile ground for such protests. Income inequality, both in rural and urban areas, has gone up since the 1990s. Consider the index of inequality, the Gini coefficient. Its values go from zero to one, with zero signifying perfect equality and one the highest level of inequality. In a society where everybody's earnings are the same, a Gini coefficient of zero would indicate the absence of any difference of income; whereas a Gini coefficient of one would mean that all earnings are monopolised by a single person. Corresponding to this is the Gini index, its span expressed from zero to hundred, with hundred signifying the highest possible inequality. The Gini coefficient of consumption expenditure in India, as measured by the National Sample Survey, reports a rise in consumption inequality from 0.32 in 1993–94 to 0.38 in 2011–12, for urban areas. Corresponding Gini estimates of consumption expenditure in rural areas were 0.26 in 1993–94, and 0.29 in 2011–12. An interesting point to note is that inequality based on consumption expenditure as measured by the Gini index between 1983 and 1993–94 had either declined or remained more or less at the same level (from 27.1 to 25.8 for rural areas, and from 31.4 to 31.9 for urban areas), but thereafter it rose steeply to 28.7 for rural and 37.7 for urban areas.

The consumption expenditure surveys of the National Sample Survey Office have been the primary source to track inequality in India, despite the non-comparability of its data with other countries (whose data tracks income instead). In this half light, India with a Gini index of 34.7 looked better than some of the high-inequality countries, such as Brazil (56.9), China (42.5), Mexico (46.05), Malaysia (37.9), Russia (40.8), United Kingdom (37.6), United States (40.6) and Vietnam (36.8) in 2004–05, or South Africa (67.4 in 2006), despite the visibly stark inequalities of Indian society. This continued until the India Human Development Surveys (the first for 2004–05, and the second 2011–12) made data available to compute income-based Ginis, which exposed India as the second most unequal country in the world, next only to South Africa. As against the consumption-based Gini of 34.7 (which may be expressed alternatively as 0.34), the income-based Gini was 0.53 in 2004–05, while the gap between the two in 2011–12 stood at 0.35 (or 35.9) to 0.55. This inequality is also confirmed by the asset-based Gini, which in 2002 was 0.73 for per capita land holding, for per capita asset holding was 0.65, and per capita holding of financial assets an astounding 0.99 (Jayadev et al, 2007).

If one comprehends the social Darwinist character of neoliberalism, the broad trend of increasing inequality in the world is quite predictable. It favours the strong and condemns the poor as uncompetitive. The world over, the trend of a weakening working class vis-à-vis the capitalist is glaringly visible. In India, the government has systematically fuelled corporate greed by valourising the private sector. In just six years from 2005–06 to 2011, it wrote off corporate income tax worth Rs 3,74,937 crore in successive union budgets. Besides these direct transfers, there have been massive transfers to the private corporate sector through disinvestment, giving away natural resources and opening up business opportunities for public services like healthcare and education. Corporate plunder has provoked people's resistance movements in various parts of the country. But the self-indulgence of the corporate honchos, evident in their billion dollar residences, private planes and so on, knows no end. According to the Union Budget of 2017, the government provided the corporate sector Rs 76,857 crore in tax breaks or exemptions in 2015–16, and a projected tax exemption worth Rs 83,492 crore in 2016–17. Compare this with the 2016–17 allocation for agriculture and farmers' welfare at Rs 35,984 crore, and the Mahatma Gandhi National Rural Employment Guarantee Scheme's Rs 38,500 crore. Bibek Debroy, chairman of the prime minister's Economic Advisory Council, himself admitted on 8 December 2017 that revenue worth 5 per cent of GDP is lost to corporate tax exemptions. In the twelve-year period between 2004–05 and 2015–16, the estimated total tax concessions given to the industry works out to a whopping Rs 50 lakh crore. The rulers of emerging economies such as ours have fooled the people by saying that their free market policies would bring economic growth that would in turn trickle down to the lower strata, making everybody better off in the long run. These policies have instead led to an unprecedented accumulation of wealth in the hands of the elite, even as they simultaneously dispossessed the vast majority. The resultant inequality would not have been a problem so long as people experienced a reasonable degree of improvement in their living standards. However, this has not been the case for the majority of people. The processes of deindustrialisation, jobless growth, devastation of the environment, and commercialisation of public services unleashed by these policies have eroded living standards. The politics shaped by these policies has undermined democratic expression among the working classes and weakened the security of the middle classes, who have also felt the jolts of repeated economic crises.

However, the latter have been jubilant over these policies. After all, they extricated the economy from the five-decade-long syndrome of the 'Hindu rate of growth', brought recognition to the rich immigrant community in the US—their El Dorado—catapulted many of them to the top of the corporate ladder and bolstered a megalomaniacal pride in the nation.

A crucial factor is still missing from this account. The Indian middle class is infused with the ideology of the caste system. The post-1991 economic boom and the recognition of India by the Western world, particularly the USA, boosted the latent consciousness in the middle classes, the majority of whom belong to the upper castes, that they were regaining their past mythical glory. For decades they were made to feel ashamed of their traditions and customs and forced to speak apologetically of their faith but the neoliberal paradigm has restored their self-assurance. It manifests in their speaking proudly about the irrationalities of India's past, justifying everything in its tradition and customs by its great antiquity—including the caste system—and flaunting their Hindu-ness with religious marks on their forehead and coloured strands wrapped around their wrists. Even as they experience erosion in their living standards, pride in their recovered sense of superiority suppresses the articulation of it. This resurgent caste consciousness, this sense of superiority, will never allow them to make common cause with the lower strata of society or persuade them to say, 'We are the 99 per cent!'

What about the dalits, crushed at the bottom of the caste pyramid? Why aren't they speaking out against the neoliberal globalisation that is clearly against the lower strata? The answer to these questions may be attempted in two parts: One, the apathetic response of the dalits towards economic matters is a holdover from the formative days of the movement when they had positioned themselves in rivalry with the communists, and two, the incoherence caused by the movement's subsequent disintegration over a long period. Politically, the dalits are splintered into numerous fragments; socially, they have reverted to their subcaste identities; ideologically, they have lost coherence; and economically, they represent a mixed bag—while the invisible majority suffers from extreme deprivation, a more visible, articulate middle class in urban areas represents an aspirational ideal of prosperity. Some self seekers from this section have stepped forward to sing the praises of neoliberalism and celebrate the rise of a 'dalit bourgeoisie'.

The demographic profile of the dalits reveals that they are a predominantly rural people (at 81 per cent) linked to the soil as landless labourers and marginal farmers. As for the remainder in urban areas, the majority lives in slums and works in the informal sector. Under the new order, they have been found to be 'uncompetitive' and are being pushed off the margins. They are undeniably victims of the new elitist and social Darwinist policies of neoliberalism. Neoliberalism holds that progress accrues through free competition among individuals, the globalisers' free market on a microcosmic scale. It follows that the mightier an individual proves to be the greater would be his gain, and the sum of personal gains is abstracted as economic growth. Needless to say, this economic growth benefits mostly the upper layers, (which neoliberalism accepts as natural). It counsels the poor to wait for the benefits to come trickling down to them. This 'trickle-down' theory, both theoretically untenable and empirically false, was the theme song of the rulers in the early years of globalisation. In the face of reality it has since faded away. Over the last three decades, globalisation has produced an alarming degree of inequality, a crisis of well-being for the world's poor, an upsurge of primordial identities, and the erosion of democracy. Extreme concentration of wealth in the hands of a few can only be celebrated if one deliberately chooses to ignore the marginalisation of the multitude.

The precept that processes of capitalist modernisation automatically undermine the significance of social identities like caste, creed and race and their role in affecting economic outcomes, is not new. One could intuitively agree that social identities restrict market competition, impede institutional change, raise transaction costs and make markets non-competitive, and that market-driven economies would undermine ascription-based social identities. Writing in the *New York Daily Tribune* (5 August 1853), Marx had prophesied that modern industrialisation would destroy the Indian castes:

> The railway-system will therefore become, in India, truly the forerunner of modern industry [...] Modern industry, resulting from the railway system, will dissolve the hereditary divisions of labour, upon which rest the Indian castes, those decisive impediments to Indian progress and Indian power.

India has come to possess the fourth largest railway network in the world, just behind the US, Russia and China, and a large industrial base with many global companies; but the caste system, instead of collapsing, is menacingly alive and kicking. Although many may relish pointing out how Marx was wrong, capitalism did affect the caste system insofar as it largely dissolved the ritualistic aspects of caste among the dwija castes (as discussed in the chapters "Reservations" and "The Caste and Class Dialectic"). It has also benefited dalits immensely in terms of drawing them out of the village and providing opportunities for their economic uplift. Indeed, the making of the dalit movement can be traced to these developments in colonial times. But capitalism also saw the utility of caste as a powerful divider of the working classes and embedded it in the postcolonial state. It has strengthened the traditionally dominant castes and accentuated power asymmetry, as well as generating new points of friction between dalits and non-dalits, making the former more vulnerable than before. Unfortunately, economic considerations were sidelined by the dalit movement in favour of social, political and religious concerns. Paradoxically, this happened under the leadership of Ambedkar who was primarily an economist.

The apathy can be traced to the altercation between Ambedkar and the early communists who had made a dogma out of the Marxian metaphor of base and superstructure and employed it to ridicule the dalit struggle as trivial, lying within the superstructural realm of culture. Although Ambedkar had ignored neither economic factors nor Marxism, he was a political rival of the communists who saw him as a divisive influence on the proletariat. A certain vested interest in the dalit movement skilfully capitalised on his occasional polemics against the communists to reorient the movement away from economic concerns. They devised a crude syllogism: Ambedkar was against the communists, the communists privileged economics, so Ambedkarites who engage with economics are ideologically suspect. The very first split of the Republican Party of India that had been formed in deference to Ambedkar's wishes in 1957, was over this issue. Dadasaheb Gaikwad, close lieutenant of Ambedkar, was castigated by B.C. Kamble who accused him of going over to the communists because of his concern for issues of livelihood of the dalit masses. Even the Dalit Panther split on the same issue, with Raja Dhale accusing Namdeo Dhasal of being influenced by the communists. The anti-communist obsession has only increased with the growing dalit middle class.

The dalit apologists of capitalism

Dalit apathy towards economic issues manifested itself when Mayawati's Bahujan Samaj Party members of parliament first absented themselves from voting in the Lok Sabha on 5 December 2012, and then, two days later, voted in the Rajya Sabha in favour of 51 per cent foreign direct investment in multi-brand retail, with the sole purpose of supporting the United Progressive Alliance government. Of course, the economic merits of the case had nothing to do with it. Ostensibly, it was done 'to keep communal forces at bay', a pious phrase useful for excusing any vagaries of political conduct. In this context, an article in the *Times of India* (5 December 2012)—"To Empower Dalits, Do Away with India's Antiquated Retail Trading System"—written by Chandra Bhan Prasad and Milind Kamble, both evangelists of dalit capitalism, presented a curious economic argument. Expectedly, the duo lauded the government's decision to allow up to 51 per cent FDI in multi-brand retail that would pave the way for the entry of global retail chains like Walmart and Texaco. They argued that FDI in retail would have a favourable effect 'on the fledgling class of dalit entrepreneurs in India'. The main thrust of their case was that FDI, being caste neutral, would be more favourable to dalit entrepreneurship than the existing caste-bound retail sector. In support of their argument, the authors cited two studies.

The first was a study of dalit enterprise by the Centre for the Advanced Study of India at the University of Pennsylvania. The CASI project—that resulted in a book, *Defying the Odds: The Rise of Dalit Entrepreneurs* (2014)—tried to prove how neoliberal reforms have been greatly beneficial to dalits in general and dalit entrepreneurs in particular. A second study, supplementing the first, was conducted by members of the Dalit Indian Chamber of Commerce and Industry, and concerned a search for adhatiyas (middlemen or brokers) from dalit communities in Delhi's Azadpur fruit and vegetable mandi; that expectedly led to none. No one should have been surprised at the findings because it is a truism that caste networks have been central to the conduct of business in India, whether to mobilise capital and investments, collect and conserve information, or secure political patronage, which is why so much of early modern and colonial capital is identifiable by caste. In the post-Independence period, these groups of Marwaris, Gujaratis, Kutchis and so on were joined by others such as nadars, patels, gounders, Sindhis, etc, whose businesses today enjoy the support of global networks of their caste group. Both these studies could be easily faulted for their glaring methodological deficiencies and outlandish inferences but that is besides the point here. The basic premise of the article, that the retail sector was caste bound and FDI would bring casteless retail chains to India, betrays an ignorance of reality. The fact is that the retail sector in India—ranging from pedlars to street vendors to road side kirana shops, large corporate retail chains being just the newest additions (and the only ones to crave FDI)—cannot be termed caste bound, and the intrusion of FDI would only spell the expansion of corporate retail chains that would root out the existing retailers, the majority of whom may be dalits and backward caste people. It is not likely to change the complexion of corporate retail to a caste neutral shade. That such preposterous views not only find space in the corporate media but also get respectability in neoliberal scholarly circles is a testament to their usefulness to global capital.

The protagonists of dalit capital along with their neoliberal backers in University of Pennsylvania spread a deliberate falsehood that dalit entrepreneurship is a post-1991 phenomenon. Among the many castes comprising 'dalit', there are always one or two in every region of the subcontinent who are numerically dominant such as the mahars in Maharashtra, chamars in UP, malas in Andhra Pradesh, holiyas in

Karnataka and parayas in Tamil Nadu. In a closed village system, all castes were bound to their traditional vocations but no single vocation could be assigned to the caste group with a large population. How and why these castes came to possess such large populations is a matter of speculation involving theories either of the collapse of many castes into a single consolidated entity or the disappearance of many traditional vocations in the course of history, but resolving this is not our concern here. What is important to understand is that since most people of these castes were not restricted to a single assigned vocation, in order to survive they adopted any line of work that came their way. It is these people who left the village for the towns and cities when opportunities arose during Mughal and subsequently colonial rule. They took up weaving, peddled their wares, opened kirana and cycle shops, and then graduated to contracting and allied businesses. Even in the villages, although they remained preponderantly farm labourers and general workmen, there were also weavers, masons, carpenters, tailors, pedlars, manufacturers, shopkeepers, moneylenders, contractors and so on from among the dalits. The DICCI, inordinately proud of the success of its entrepreneurs, can be shown examples of such entrepreneurs that would exceed its entire membership, all in existence since long before 1991.

One could easily find hugely wealthy dalit individuals in every part of the country in the decades before 1990. There were extremely rich dalit individuals even in colonial times, although they did not flash their possessions in the self-congratulatory way that some DICCI members strut their Mercs and BMWs. On 4 January 2011, the *Wall Street Journal* reported Chandra Bhan Prasad asking, 'Who is going to buy a helicopter next year?' and almost in answer by 14 April the same year, as if to mark Ambedkar's birth anniversary, the *Washington Post* reported that Ashok Khade, heading a flourishing $32 million construction business in Mumbai and in possession of a BMW, now wished to buy a chopper. Then, as now, their wealth made little difference to their status as dalits, and still less to the well being of their community. During colonial times (and earlier), dalits displayed ample entrepreneurial prowess by accepting new vocations, setting up petty businesses or modernising their caste vocations and making huge progress. The dalit movement was actually the by-product of this process as it is precisely these relatively well-off people, either with some entrepreneurial background or as employees in the organised sector, who constituted the base of the Ambedkar-led dalit movement (as mentioned in the chapter "Dalit Protests in Gujarat"). Therefore, to attribute dalit enterprise or its success to globalisation is misleading. If dalit youth are at all impelled towards entrepreneurship, the reason is the unavailability of job opportunities due to the constriction of public sector jobs. In 1997, employment in the public sector peaked at 19.7 million, consistently declined thereafter and came down to 18 million in 2007, ringing the death knell of reservations as a career prospect. While entrepreneurship among the higher castes is associated with risk-taking towards the multiplication of wealth, it spells a reverse syndrome for dalits—the compulsion of survival. Whereas caste Hindus become entrepreneurs by choice, dalits are entrepreneurs by compulsion. In the absence of jobs, this remains the only available option. The Economic Censuses of 1990, 1998, and 2005 reveal a more truthful picture than that of motivated ad hoc studies. Caste-wise data relating to the ownership of enterprises are available for 1990, 1998 and 2005, and have been put together in a 2011 Harvard Business School study.

As per the study, the average employment per enterprise for 2005 was 2.3, indicating that the vast majority of firms were a single-person enterprise. The incidence of such enterprises was far higher among the SC and ST categories. In the context of dalits, the scale of enterprise ranges from a roadside cobbler to a millionaire member of the DICCI. As the data clearly shows, over the period since liberalisation began, the share of dalit ownership of enterprises remained more or less the same, refuting the claim that globalisation has boosted dalit entrepreneurship. The study observed that the dalit millionaires claimed by the DICCI do not represent the broad swathe of SC/ST entrepreneurship.

While the growth of ancillary industries or outsourcing has surely been accelerated by globalisation, it is presumptuous to assume that dalit entrepreneurs will beat others on price competitiveness to grab a share of outsourced processes or products. Given the social handicap they suffer from, they can only make costs competitive by extra-exploitation of their employees. The dalit capitalists lack faith in the free-market meritocracy of their slogans and in emancipation as a value. This is betrayed by the fact that they not only retain their caste epithet, but also exploit it to the hilt—as a bargaining chip and business opportunity. Their entire effort is to seek reservation in government purchases. The newly launched magazine *Dalit Enterprise* (2017) uses business jargon—'supplier diversity'—to express this overriding aim. To the political parties that constitute governments, the opportunity to oblige wealthy dalits is godsent. On the strength of these gestures, they can project a caring image to the larger dalit masses, while withdrawing support from schemes of social uplift. It is no accident that the same government that did not hesitate to thrash dalit youth demanding scholarship funds owed to them, readily accepted the DICCI's demand and reserved 4 per cent of purchases from Micro Small and Medium Enterprises for businesses belonging to dalits and tribals (who together account 25 per cent of the population), which means a whopping quantum of Rs 25,000 to Rs 94,000 crore worth of business may eventually come to dalit-run units (*Economic Times*, 12 September 2011). Nor does it stop at that. The government that arrests and incarcerates genuine dalit activists as Maoists, turns to shower honours on handpicked dalit capitalists, some of whom, like DICCI's Kamble, have been awarded the Padmashri and are then obliged to meet the RSS chief Mohan Bhagwat.

The difference between rhetoric and reality is a different matter however. At the end of March 2017, government procurement from SC/ST-owned MSME was a mere 0.37 per cent of its purchases from the sector, far short of the 4 per cent quota announced with fanfare in October 2016. A report titled "Modi Government Has Near 'Zero Effect' in Meeting Procurement Quota From Dalit, Adivasi Enterprises" in the *Wire* (9 February 2018) said that according to an estimate by the Organisation for Economic Cooperation and Development, government purchases account for 30 per cent of the GDP.

Prasad and Kamble's arguments make a mess of concepts. For instance, they claim that dalit entrepreneurs tend to succeed in the modern sectors—building bridges, tunnels, machines, etc. In fact, these enterprises are an extension of the traditional (brick and mortar) sector in which dalits have operated for ages. The modern sector in this age of information comprises knowledge-based enterprises in which dalit entrepreneurs still do not exist. The putative success of dalits in the brick and mortar industry may perhaps indicate non-dalits moving up the value chain, leaving the low end for dalits—a replication, not repudiation, of Manu. Next, modernisation is erroneously understood as undermining the caste system. It actually represents a cultural hybridisation which can coexist with tradition, as a change in lifestyle does not necessarily imply a reformed social outlook. The simplest example of such superficial hybridisation can be seen in the matrimonial advertisements of highly educated Indian-Americans working in frontier industries who seek brides from their own subcastes. Let dalit individuals become big bureaucrats, the haute bourgeoisie or make it big elsewhere in the system, this caste conscious society does not relax the stigma associated with their name. As individuals they cannot count for much in the emancipation project of the dalit community, which requires nothing less than a thoroughgoing social transformation. While a few dalit business tycoons are adequate representatives of the winner-takes-all message of globalisation, it is reckless to propose that their wealth makes globalisation an agent of economic justice, or that its logic of increasing concentrations of wealth and of inequality—in a world divided between winners and losers—is working towards a revolution for dalits.

If globalisation has been such a facilitator of dalit enterprise, why should the DICCI seek 'reservation,' the non-market dole, for itself? The protagonists of DICCI are blinded by life under the spotlight and infatuated with the rhetoric of being 'job givers and not job seekers'. They fail to see that they are essentially an SC/ST wing of FICCI—almost like the SC/ST 'cell' in the Congress or the BJP. The very fact that DICCI exists and demands a dalit share in capital—seeking doles/reservation of a kind—punctures their boasts about power as well as refuting their rhetoric of emancipation. The idea of dalit capitalism is analogous to that of black capitalism—and the magazine *Dalit Enterprise* proudly claims inspiration from *Black Enterprise*—which enriched certain black individuals in the US but flopped demonstrably in empowering the black masses. The argument for symbolic representation undergirds policies that rely upon the rise of certain individuals from the disadvantaged communities in the belief that they would ultimately benefit 'their' masses. It is an unsound position. When a black or dalit person transcends class, they cease to identify with their fellow people left behind:

> You know, everybody looks down their noses at poor Black people. They fault them for their own poverty, suffering and even deaths. They 'lie, cheat and steal,' both the smug well-to-do whites and suburban upper class Blacks say about the poor. They, of course, feel themselves every bit superior to 'those people.' If they hear about the mass of Black youth now gone off [or going] to prison, if Black people are homeless and living in the streets, or if they are slain by a racist cop, then good enough for them! 'They deserve it,' say the Black bourgeoisie (Lorenzo Kom'boa Ervin, 2001).

In *The Color of Money: Black Banks and the Racial Wealth Gap* (2017), Mehrsa Baradaran, a professor of law at the University of Georgia, argues how the idea of black capitalism was developed by Nixon as an answer—by way of a détente—to the possible attraction communism had for blacks, since he viewed the Black Power movement as a major 'internal security threat'. Nixon linked discrimination-free employment, specifically with regard to black people, as part of battling communism and aiding national security. It received the backing of corporate America. The entire idea of black capitalism, Baradaran says, was 'more a way to mollify black activists and assure white voters that racial tension and upheaval would soon end than they were an actual effort to erase racial economic inequality.' The African American sociologist Robert L. Allen, who along with the Black Panther was an outspoken critic of black capitalism, writes in *Black Awakening in Capitalist America* (1969) that 'the urban uprisings of 1967 made it painfully obvious to American corporate leaders that the 'race problem' was out of control and posed a threat to the continued existence of the present society'. Allen says institutions like the Danforth Foundation (now defunct) and later the Ford Foundation worked towards ensuring that urban centres remained riot-free so that the interest of business was not affected. And so it came to be that 'law and order', or more specifically riot control, was one of motives behind state support to black capitalism initiatives.

It must also be remembered that the blacks in the US could call for and effect boycotts (starting with the iconic year-long Montgomery bus boycott of 1955–56 sparked by Rosa Parks refusing to give up her seat for a white person). In contrast, India's dalits, lacking in any economic power, are often themselves the object of various kinds of social boycott, and pose no such threat to law and order. However, the state had begun to sense a looming discontent with globalisation in general and with its adverse impact on reservations in particular. In a pre-emptive move, the Congress government of Madhya Pradesh initiated the Bhopal conference (12–13 January 2002), helmed by dalit activists and intellectuals, and came out with a Bhopal Declaration, announcing proposals to promote dalit enterprise and seeding an inchoate idea of reservations in the private sector. It served its purpose by diverting public attention from the legitimate target of globalisation, and towards the moonshine of reservations in the private sector and the promotion of entrepreneurship. Terms borrowed from the American discourse—such as supplier diversity—were used liberally in the document.

The move reversed an incipient discourse of discontent into affirmation, creating propaganda through the claims of some dalit intellectuals that neoliberal policies promoted dalit mobility and enterprise. Quite like dalit capitalism, the term black capitalism disregards a long history of black entrepreneurship that preceded the immediate phenomenon. Such entrepreneurship, even in the form of significantly large establishments, existed among the blacks as early as the dawn of the last century. For example, after the 1905 oil boom, the black Greenwood section of Tulsa, Oklahoma, housed a variety of commercial establishments, including nine hotels, thirty-one groceries and meat shops, and two theatres. The community's boom ended in 1923 when spurious reports of a black man's attempted rape of a white woman touched off a violent white invasion in which fifty people died, a thousand homes were destroyed and the business district was left in ruins. Such islands did exist at many places in the US, at the mercy of the surrounding elements. The coinage 'black capitalism' is different merely in signifying the addition of state patronage or political brokerage.

Since DICCI and other votaries of dalit capitalism hark back to the imagined success of black capitalism, it is worth a fact check. The Nixon administration meant nothing by creating the Office of Minority Business Enterprise in the Commerce Department in 1969. As Gillian B. White says in her review (*Atlantic*, 21 September 2017) of Baradaran's book, no funds were allocated to it; these programs and others that followed were set up to fail.

> The board that oversaw the OMBE was largely white… and indifferent to the outcome. The head of the black-capitalism program, Maurice Stans, derided an early proposal by one of the highest-ranking black members at OMBE, Abe Venable, to invest $8.6 billion in the creation of 400,000 minority businesses, and then promptly shut it [OMBE]

down. In 1979, the OMBE was rebranded as the Minority Business Development Agency by the Carter administration, and still exists with the mission of advancing minority-owned business operations. By 1971, a Small Business Administration program had doled out $66 million to minority firms, but that accounted for one-tenth of 1 per cent of the government contracts granted that year.

As a matter of fact, the theory behind developing a separate black economy had been that economic power would lead to political power, but as Baradaran argues, the opposite happened. Dalits enamoured of such ideas ought to understand this. At the beginning of the twentieth century, Booker T. Washington and W.E.B. DuBois represented mutually distinct visions of an emancipatory programme for African Americans. DuBois called for a class politics of the blacks that would integrate them into the nation's political, social and economic fabric, whereas Washington called for identity politics orienting black development via the building of basic skills and a strong economic base for the black community. The latter push culminates in such ideas as black capitalism, the kind of tokenism that allows a handful of privileged blacks like Colin Powell, Condoleezza Rice and Barack Obama to figure prominently on the stage, while the position of the great majority of working class and poor black people has not substantially improved, indeed continues to generate shocking data in terms of the concentrated prevalence of poverty, unemployment, poor access to healthcare, high rates of incarceration, or any other axis along which discrimination may be assessed.

The capitalists and the entire neoliberal camp rushed in to celebrate the phenomenon of dalit millionaires. The who's who of the corporate world marked their presence at the conferences and fairs organised by DICCI. Influential economic journalists like Swaminathan Anklesaria Aiyar showered praise on the idea through media columns especially since DICCI spokespersons glibly announced dalits no longer needed reservation (deemed a foul word) but merely the opportunity to prove their merit. Some people came out with suggestions on how instead of targeting castes, the dalits should use them in building social capital. The success stories of certain castes like the Marwaris, Kutchhis, khojas, patels and others who built industrial empires using their caste network and, in recent times, those of the gounders and nadars in Tamil Nadu were hitched to this narrative. The gounders are known to have established a global knitwear industry in Tiruppur, and the nadars the matches and printing industries in and around the Sivakasi district. The idea coheres well with the identity-obsessed among dalits. However, a simple fact eludes them—what is possible for the resourceful castes and communities is not an available option for resource-starved people like dalits. A proletarian cannot become bourgeois for his emancipation, first because it is not within his means to do so, and more importantly it would not count as emancipation if he did. It is akin to selling the dream of exploitation to the exploited. The logic could be extended to politics, that dalits cannot institute an organisation like the RSS and still claim a coherent identity or progressive political programme for themselves.

As the popular online magazine *Madame Noire* expressed in February 2016, the reality is that all the money in the world could not keep Oprah Winfrey from being racially profiled at an upscale boutique in 2013. And all the graciousness in the world did not protect President Obama and his family from racist jeers and jibes. Likewise, not all the combined wealth of black millionaires has brought about 'the political force needed to ensure that clean and drinkable water gets to the most disenfranchised among us in Flint, Michigan.'

Poster boys and whipping boys

Notwithstanding the airy dismissals of our burgeoning neoliberal middle class that caste is of no consequence in modern India, it remains as pervasive as ever. It requires only an ordinary degree of sensitivity to feel its presence. A section of the middle class haughtily claims that caste is the excuse of the non-meritorious and the staple food of politicians. Maybe, but for dalits—not all of whom are on the way to securing the good things in life—caste still is the biggest bane. This difference of perspective on the caste question between dalits and non-dalits itself proves the existence of the problem. The vast majority of dalits, those who slog in the countryside and urban slums to eke out an existence, are hardly in a position to compete with anyone. They do not lack merit in their domain. Yet this mass of dalits suffers humiliation and is the victim of atrocities on account of its caste. The market, contrary to middle class notions, is not caste neutral. Thorat et al (2012) provided empirical evidence on how in the neoliberal economy, caste discrimination in job applications is rampant and unceasing.

That dalits continue to be discounted or objectified is evident from the breezy manner in which they have been utilised as propaganda figures for the neoliberal economy; and still more evident in light of the deprivations suffered by the majority under these new economic arrangements and the concomitant withdrawal of the government from employment and public services. Now, just as the objectification of dalits underlies their celebration as lions of entrepreneurship—Milind Kamble, founder of the DICCI, is flashed on prime minister Modi's website—it is also made obvious by the old uses to which dalits are put in this supposedly new story: as objects of stigmatisation.

A sidelight of the post-liberalisation period has been the number and scale of corruption scandals in quick succession that have arrested public attention and fuelled protests. As noted before, the protesters in India have been fixated upon miracle cures, whether in Anna Hazare's 'India Against Corruption' movement which sought remedy in the institution of a Jan Lokpal, or in the yoga tycoon Ramdev's attempt to steal Hazare's thunder by launching his own anti-corruption movement the same year, telling the public mouth-watering stories about the quantities of cash in Swiss accounts that could be repatriated to change the fortunes of every family in this country. (His own enterprise,

Patanjali Ayurved, run with his friend Acharya Balakrishna, ended the 2017 fiscal year with an overall turnover of Rs 10,561 crores amidst accusations of nepotism and misdemeanours.) Another curious and telling aspect of the corruption scandals, however, is the light they throw on casteism in the public discourse and institutional arrangements of this globalising economy.

Corruption cannot be the monopoly of any caste, creed, race or nationality. Broadly, corruption is the product of a market transaction between those who have discretionary power and those who have the resources to swing decisions their way; in India, the domain of the upper castes is the locus classicus of corruption as they enjoy both privileges. The entry of dalits into the precincts of power is a relatively recent phenomenon. So, it becomes essential to ask: what is the part of caste in the play of corruption? When corruption is traced to a dalit, it gets amplified; when non-dalits engage in it, corruption appears muted or is simply dismissed as being of little consequence. In a society where reservation (and not caste) is seen as the root of all its ills, at a literary festival held in Jaipur (January 2013), political psychologist Ashis Nandy claimed: 'It is *a fact* that most of the corrupt come from the OBCs, and the Scheduled Castes and now increasingly Scheduled Tribes.' It caused an uproar, and someone was affronted enough to file an FIR against him under the PoA Act. A rattled Nandy subsequently tried to disown his statement by saying he had been misunderstood.

Of course, caste does not play out as neatly as this might suggest. Those dalit individuals who become part of the power web—and their number is ever increasing—get disproportionate rewards because they serve not only the web but the entire institutional structure. They prove more reliable—because of their subservience—compared to others; and, more importantly, they provide legitimacy to the system to claim non-discrimination. Although dalits become highly visible in this location against the backdrop of social prejudice, they still lack the clout to counter upper-caste hegemony and seldom rise to the highest positions. Given their prudently limited ambition and restricted scope for corruption, they generally find their opportunities in petty misdemeanours, instances like small bribes or pilferages. But when they are caught, all hell breaks loose.

Over the course of 2012, a spate of exposés of the corrupt deals of Robert Vadra, Salman Khurshid and Nitin Gadkari by Arvind Kejriwal and other activists of IAC confirmed what was already known to Indians—how depraved our political class is. When Vadra, a nondescript trader, emerged as a notable business tycoon—thanks to his 1997 entry by marriage into the Nehru–Gandhi family—with a series of shady land-grab deals, and duly received a clean chit from a Haryana government panel in 2013, nobody was surprised. When the senior Congress leader Salman Khurshid could not stomach allegations of financial irregularities against a non-governmental organisation—the Dr Zakir Hussain Memorial Trust, meant to serve the physically handicapped—being run by his wife and chaired by his mother, his behaviour was no different from a mafia don's. He was captured by television channels indulging in crass falsifications and issuing an unbecoming threat of death to Kejriwal, who had made the accusations. Yet, soon thereafter, he got a promotion in the UPA-II cabinet reshuffle of October 2012, being shifted from the ministry of law to external affairs, and again no one was surprised.

On the other side of the aisle, the exposé against Nitin Gadkari, where it was alleged that he was lobbying for certain contractors in the building of a dam in Vidarbha—obviously intended as a balancing act to demonstrate that Kejriwal and his fellow activists were targeting both the Congress and the BJP—did not have much of an initial sting. However, upon further probing by the media, it snowballed into a mega malfeasance. Those who were surprised expected him at least to tender his resignation as president of the BJP, in keeping with the precedent set by Bangaru Laxman, a madiga dalit from Andhra Pradesh, who had also been president of the BJP before he was forced to resign upon being implicated in corruption in a dramatic 2001 sting operation by *Tehelka.com.* But Gadkari would not follow in Laxman's footsteps, and thus the part of caste in the play of corruption came to the fore.

Bangaru Laxman joined the Rashtriya Swayamsevak Sangh, a brahminical organisation, at the age of 12 in 1953, and in 1969 became a member of the Jana Sangh, precursor to the BJP. He went on to become one of the showpieces of its window display, useful for the saffron brigade to camouflage its brahminical core. The party further embellished its credentials in the perpetual one-upmanship game with the Congress by making him its fifth president in August 2000. But the man was careless enough to be caught in a sting operation, ostensibly to facilitate an arms deal, taking a bribe of Rs 1 lakh. Foolish on several counts, but how could he have fallen so far beneath his stature as the president of the main opposition party for such a paltry sum of money? Recall the faux pas of another dalit leader, Beni Prasad Varma, a ministerial colleague of Salman Khurshid, who defended him against the charge of embezzling Rs 71 lakh via his NGO, by saying it was too small an amount for a cabinet minister to take such trouble over. Laxman found no such champions and was forced to resign his post by the BJP. He underwent a criminal trial, was convicted by a Special Central Bureau of Investigation court on 27 April 2012 at the age of 72, under the Prevention of Corruption Act, and was sentenced to four years in jail. The only person who defended Laxman and deposed in his favour in court, it turns out, was Ram Nath Kovind, the BJP's new dalit face and now the president of India. Out on bail on an alibi of old age and poor health, Laxman died on 1 March 2014.

No citizen, leave alone a dalit, should ever follow in the footsteps of Laxman. That said, even self-seeking, unscrupulous dalits do not succeed in escaping their caste, as is revealed in this case. Laxman was no scapegoat, nor a victim of the system. At the same time, we have to recognise that the system does not pursue all malefactors alike. The National Crime Records Bureau's data on prison statistics for

2015 make this case pithily. The data show that Muslims, dalits and tribals—who together constitute 39 per cent of India's population, and the most disempowered sections of it—make up over 55 per cent of all undertrials and 50.4 per cent of the country's convict population. What is their crime? It is not just theft, murder, rape, arson, or corruption; many of them are labelled as terrorist and Maoist. Government propaganda has made these labels up to be self-fulfilling, not requiring further explanation. The bearers of these tags are demonised, not deserving of access to the law. They are to be killed, if not summarily via 'encounters', then by having their lives waste away in the recesses of the jail and judicial systems. It is for the expediencies of governance that they are held within jails worse than the proverbial hell. Let us not forget that most of them are there for a notional crime without any evidence, as the data on numerous concluded cases would reveal.

And those who get away

Now contrast this picture with some of the blatant crimes committed by so-called respectable people. The rule of law, said to be the back bone of democracy, is conspicuous only in its absence when self-styled 'Art of Living' guru Sri Sri Ravi Shankar, who—iconised by the nationalist middle class—gets away with multiple infringements of the law in full public view, and indeed with a very public defiance. On the other hand, a Ramesh Pandhariram Netam of Gadchiroli is left to rot in the Nagpur jail for eight years for no crime, just because he is a tribal. (On this as well as other instances of the witch-hunt of Maoists, see the chapter "Manufacturing Maoists".)

In April 2017, the expert committee formed by the National Green Tribunal submitted its report on the damage done by Ravi Shankar's Art of Living Foundation to the Yamuna floodplains of Delhi in the course of a three-day international jamboree of self promotion (11–13 March 2016) attended by prime minister Narendra Modi and virtually all BJP members of parliament. The report pegs the cost of restoration at Rs 42 crore and states that it may take up to ten years to undo the environmental damage.

The extravaganza began as a blatant violation of law in defiance of the constitutional authority of the NGT. Once the controversy erupted, many acts of omission came out into the open, showing how authorities had erred in acceding to the organisers' demands. The Delhi Development Authority under the Union Ministry of Urban Development had granted organisers of the event permission based on an application that had suppressed facts. The NGT that was against any event on the ecologically fragile Yamuna floodplains—based on an understanding derived from a February 2016 report of a committee headed by Shashi Shekhar and including A.K. Gosain of the Indian Institute of Technology, Delhi—had wanted the Art of Living Foundation to deposit Rs 120 crore as reparations for damage. The organisers simply ignored the demand. The NGT stepped back and lowered the reparations to Rs 5 crore. But Ravi Shankar denied causing any damage to the banks, alleging that the Art of Living 'has neither polluted air or water or earth. We have left the World Culture Festival site in a better condition than what we had got' and that it was the victim of a 'conspiracy.' Although the god-man eventually paid up Rs 5 crore, resolving to get it back through the Supreme Court, this was more of a face-saver for the NGT than an embarrassment for the Sri Sri, who, unlike Bangaru Laxman, needed no 'sting' to expose him as he could flout the law openly and, what is more, stare down the forces of law.

Let us consider the case of Vijay Mallya, serial defaulter on loans and famed hedonist, who revels in merrymaking at the public's expense. Mallya's loans turned non-performing assets way back in 2011, and in 2014 the Kolkata-based United Bank of India declared him a wilful defaulter. This stricture was, however, short-lived as the Kolkata High Court invalidated it. Deepak Narang, the upright executive director of the bank who had initiated the move against Mallya, was hounded by various authorities with a litany of charges, and his pension was stopped after he retired in March 2015. Later, the State Bank of India and the Punjab National Bank also declared Mallya a wilful defaulter. Mallya, who not only defaulted on bank loans and the payment of employees' salaries, but also on statutory dues like income tax, service tax and provident fund monies, could easily have been arrested. Instead, he was able to retain his membership of the Rajya Sabha till he resigned on 2 May 2016, exactly three months after he had fled the country, owing money to his countless employees and seventeen banks.

There was much outrage after he left the country, a large part of which was over irrelevant details and suppressed the basic fact of the government's complicity in letting Mallya go free in spite of his many financial crimes. Mallya, however, is neither the only such defaulter nor is he the biggest of them. Gautam Adani, a friend of Modi's, who is seen everywhere he goes, owes the banks in excess of Rs 72,000 crore, more than eighteen times what Mallya does. In the teeth of the Mallya crisis, the SBI, allegedly at Modi's behest, was made to sign a memorandum of understanding to lend Adani $1 billion for his Carmichael coal mine project in the Galilee Basin in Queensland, Australia. In 2017, a spate of newspaper reports in Australia exposed this project for cases of alleged bribery, corruption and potential environmental danger to the Great Barrier Reef, provoking nationwide rallies against Adani in all major Australian cities like Sydney, Brisbane, Melbourne, the Gold Coast and Port Douglas in North Queensland.

In all, corporate India owes PSU banks more than Rs 5 lakh crore. The Mallya episode, and high-end diamond merchant Nirav Modi's defrauding of banks merrily to the tune of Rs 14,500 crore and going undiscovered by government watchdogs till February 2018, are merely symptomatic of the ills of crony capitalism, now coming out into the open. In India, capitalists do not invest in productive capital; they invest in the networks of complicity that allow them to loot public money. According to a report by ICICI Securities issued on 16 March 2015, the total problematic assets of banks stood at a whopping Rs 10.31 lakh crore, the public-sector banks accounting for most of the amount. The State Bank of India, the strongest of them, has 60 per cent of its net worth as stressed assets and the Indian Overseas Bank, 221 per cent. It is this profligacy and stealing of public money by corporations against which the Occupy movement was ignited by *Adbusters*. India had almost become a textbook case for the issues raised there but they did not evoke much response from the public.

Middle class outrage at individual instances of corruption has a wilful blind spot built into it, in choosing not to view them as a systemic failing and in not recognising the real victims of the banditry facilitated by the system—the poor of India. This again is the reason we do not and probably will not see Occupy-style protests in India. An illustration of this would be the contrast between the public indignation over the Commonwealth Games scam of 2010 and the accompanying silence over India's failure to meet its Millennium Development Goals commitments in the same period. On 22 September, barely a fortnight before the CWG, the MDG Summit had concluded in New York with the adoption of a joint resolution by the General Assembly of the United Nations. This event received little attention in India as, the previous day, a footbridge under construction had collapsed at the principal stadium for the then-upcoming games. Media and public fury was directed towards the prospective loss of face for India and the expression of nationwide disgust over stories of corruption among the officials tasked with organising the large-scale sporting event. The news about India's dismal progress in meeting its millennium development goals, flashed briefly by the print media on the eve of the MDG Summit in New York, now went totally ignored.

Back at the Millennium Summit in September 2000, 192 UN member-states and some twenty-three international organisations had unanimously adopted the Millennium Declaration, which was elaborated upon at the fifty-sixth session of the UN General Assembly in 2001 by the Secretary-General's report entitled "Road Map towards the Implementation of the UN Millennium Declaration". This report spelt out eight development goals with eighteen targets and forty-eight indicators, commonly known as the MDG. The first seven goals focus on the following: eradicating poverty and hunger, universalising primary education, promoting gender equality, reducing child mortality, improving maternal health, combatting diseases like malaria and AIDS, reducing the proportion of people without access to safe drinking water, and ensuring environmental sustainability. The final goal outlines measures to build a global partnership for development.

The UN succeeded in motivating most countries to take these goals seriously. It carried out its first comprehensive review of the MDG in 2005, which considered further efforts required to achieve the goals. Over $50 billion per year was promised by 2010 to fight poverty and to support education, healthcare and anti-malaria efforts. This UN initiative has indeed significantly improved the human development situation in many countries. In 2010, a working paper for the Centre for Global Development, "Who Are the MDG Trailblazers? A New MDG Progress Index" by Benjamin Leo and Julia Barmeier noted dramatic achievements by many poor countries such as Honduras, Laos, Ethiopia, Uganda, Burkina Faso, Nepal, Cambodia, and Ghana. Incidentally, Sub-Saharan Africa accounted for many star performers. The list of laggards largely consisted of countries devastated by conflict, such as Afghanistan, Burundi, the Democratic Republic of Congo, and Guinea-Bissau. In contrast to this, based on the "India Country Report 2009" it was inferred that India 'as a whole will not be on track for a majority of the targets related to poverty, hunger, health, gender equality and environmental sustainability'.

Although India had incorporated MDG targets into the national Tenth Five-Year Plan (2002–7) in the form of National Development Goals, despite its much hyped economic advances in the two decades since liberalisation the human development indicators have barely improved. In 2015, India remained the world leader in child mortality, accounting for 20 per cent of the 5.9 million deaths of children under the age of five. Of the 26 million children born in India each year, nearly two million die before the age of five, half of them within a month of birth, from preventable causes like malnutrition, diarrhoea and pneumonia. On eliminating hunger, India's record is just as dismal. In 2015, it topped global charts in the number of people living with chronic hunger. The Food and Agriculture Organisation of the UN put the number at 194.6 million, or over 15 per cent of the country's population. The global average is 10.9 per cent of the world's population. On the Global Hunger Index compiled by the International Food Policy Research Institute, India's ranking in 1992 was 76 out of a total of 96 countries for which data was available; in 2017 India stood at 100 out of a total of 119 countries, behind even North Korea (93), Bangladesh (88) and Nepal (72). The report claimed that India's GHI score 'brings to the fore the disturbing reality of the country's stubbornly high proportions of malnourished children'. It lies at 'the high end of the 'serious' category, and is one of the main factors pushing South Asia to the category of worst performing region on the GHI this year'. On the sanitation front, its record is much worse. Only 15 per cent of the rural and 61 per cent of urban population had access to a toilet. It is said that some 21 million people will need to gain access to basic sanitation every year if the MDG of just halving the proportion of people without sanitation is to be met. For a country that had committed to fully meet the MDG by 2015, even meeting the 2020 deadline of the Swachh Bharat Mission seems like a distant dream. (For a progress report on this, see the chapter "Swachh Bharat").

The poor and their needs are no more visible than before; and still less remarked is the social composition of the poor—the overwhelming proportion of dalits, tribals and Muslims it contains. Meanwhile, new vanity projects involving bullet trains and colossal statuary exercise the imagination of the middle class. The myth of a caste-free new economy devoid of such vast inequalities is as powerful as ever. The neoliberal obsession of the rulers for GDP growth is enriching a few and pauperising the vast masses for whom the crisis of living has intensified through galloping unemployment, insecurity, inflation, the neo-fascist turn of the polity, and pervasive corruption. The stench of the rotting system comes into the open each time with the exposure of a scam or corruption scandal, but given the disturbing frequency with which such incidents occur, our nostrils have gotten used to the odour by now. Nothing ever happens in the country to those who have pelf and power, even as millions get pushed to the margins to be finally enveloped in the peace of the dead.

8

Saffronising Ambedkar

The RSS Inversion of the Idea of India

'We built a temple for god to come in... but before the god could be installed...the devil had taken possession of it.' These words uttered by Babasaheb Ambedkar in the Rajya Sabha on 19 March 1955, in explanation of an earlier outburst of 2 September 1953, where he had denounced those who called him the architect of the Constitution. By this time, Ambedkar, who once exhorted his followers to shun agitational methods and follow only the Constitution to undo the injustice meted out to them, had not only disowned what he had previously called a 'wonderful document', but also condemned it as useless, accusing the Congress of having used him as a hack. The fact that it took him only three years to be disillusioned shows that matters were bad enough soon after independence. India's new rulers adopted the hardware of colonial governance and embellished it with high-sounding constitutional parlance, but replaced the software of Western liberalism with brahminical cunning. In doing so, they effectively reversed the meaning of democracy, freedom, socialism, secularism, and other 'isms' that democratic institutions hold dear to their functioning.

In the first four decades after independence, brahminical assertion was somewhat muted. With the rise of the Bharatiya Janata Party—the political child of the self-proclaimed cultural organisation, the Rashtriya Swayamsevak Sangh—and its coming to power with a clear majority at the centre in 2014, the masks and gloves are off. Brahminism is now brazen like never before.

The plans for a brahminical takeover of modern Indian politics had commenced with the establishment of colonial rule. The brahmins who felt suppressed during centuries of Muslim rule tried to regain their hegemony by organising Hindus and launched reform movements such as the Brahmo Samaj, Arya Samaj and Prarthana Samaj in various regions. Among them, the Arya Samaj, floated in 1875 in Lahore by Dayananda Saraswati (1824–1883), a brahmin from the Kathiawad region of Gujarat, had extensive influence. When Dayanand died in 1883, the Punjabi Hindus decided to launch Hindu Sabhas which within a few years spread across the province. British administrators and intellectuals created the ideological basis of communalism through their organisation of Indian history and social analysis. In 1906, the Muslim League was formed in Dhaka, followed by the foundation of the Hindu Mahasabha (as the Sarvadeshak Hindu Sabha) in 1915. Meanwhile, with the Morley–Minto Reforms (or Indian Councils Act) in 1909, the colonial plan to seed Indian politics with communalism was realised. Political representation was divided between the Hindus and Muslims represented by the Congress and the Muslim League, respectively. During the negotiations preceding the Act, the Muslim League had challenged the Congress, asserting that dalits and adivasis were not part of Hinduism. The incipient dalit movement, which was still focused on the fundamental right of dalits to be treated as human, had not yet taken the form of independent political articulation. They were not ready to exploit this development. Both the Congress and the Muslim League, eager to see further devolution of power take place soon, decided to work together towards an agreement to pressure the British government into adopting a more liberal approach to India and give Indians more authority to run their country. Both the parties held a joint conference at Lucknow in December 1916 and signed what is known as the Lucknow Pact. One of the points of the Pact was to provide for 'separate electorates for all communities until they ask for a joint electorate'. By then, political awakening among the dalits had begun to manifest itself. The Congress apprehended the risk of losing dalits into a separate community unless they were taken into confidence. It decided to mobilise its forces to secure the approval of dalits for the Lucknow Pact, so as to avoid any communal aberration in the Montagu–Chelmsford Reforms towards the promulgation of the Government of India Act, 1919. The Montagu–Chelmsford Reforms for the first time secured a token nominated (unelected) representation for the Depressed Classes in provincial governing bodies, and this was the first time in history that the Hindus took political note of the dalits. Incidentally, it was M.K. Gandhi, returned from South Africa in 1915 with the new-minted halo of a warrior against British rule, who for the first time spoke against the evil practice of untouchability in June 1916 in Ahmedabad. In that year, the Congress organised at least four conferences in the Bombay province alone, to seek the support of the dalits.

Even at these pre-Ambedkar conferences, the dalits voiced their disapproval of the Congress–Muslim League Pact and insisted that the Congress pass a resolution for the removal of disabilities of the Depressed Classes and for their right to elect their own representatives to the Legislative Councils in proportion to their numbers—which was carried more or less verbatim by the Congress resolution of December 1917. At another conference, under the leadership of Bapuji Namdeo Bagade in November 1917, they urged the British to hold still—i.e. not proceed towards provincial autonomy—until all classes and specifically the Depressed Classes rose to the level where they could effectively participate in the administration. Also, they said that if the government had decided to give political concessions to the Indians, the untouchables should be granted their own representation in the legislative bodies to ensure their civil and political rights. At yet another event, held in 1918 under the leadership of Subhedar Ganpatrao Govind Rokde, they appealed to the government to protect the interests of the untouchables by granting them separate electorates.

When Ambedkar took over leadership in the 1920s, he articulated these popular demands with scholarship and erudition. At this stage, he reared a hope that with the dalits agitating for civil rights, advanced sections among the Hindus would be roused to take up reforms in Hindu society. But when the Mahad struggle in 1927 belied this hope, he switched to creating an independent political identity for the dalits. His attacks on the Hindus (he called them 'the sick men of India … [whose] sickness is causing danger to the health and happiness of other Indians') and their religion, which culminated in his renouncing Hinduism and embracing Buddhism barely two months before his death, permanently stamped a separate religio–cultural identity on dalits. Before that, he had won them a separate political identity through separate electorates with reserved seats in 1932, but this gain was neutralised by the Poona Pact that he was blackmailed into signing by Gandhi. Ambedkar's remains the bitterest critique of Hinduism; it pervades hundreds of pages of his writings. It was not just criticism, his actions spoke the ultimate abhorrence for Hinduism. This history now comes in the way of the Sangh parivar in accomplishing its goal of making India a Hindu rashtra—a euphemism for restoring the old brahminic hierarchical paradigm of the totalitarian rule of high-bred elites under the unitary command of a supreme leader, comparable to the ein Volk, ein Reich, ein Führer (one people, one nation, one leader) ideal of Nazism.

Dalits constitute an important part of the Sangh parivar's game plan. Its strategic apple cart—meant to polarise the Indian population into Hindus versus others: Muslims, Christians and communists (i.e. those who do not agree with it)—could be toppled by the dalits. It cannot be taken for granted that dalits would identify themselves as Hindus anymore. With their historical, social, ideological and cultural profile, they have the potential to play spoiler for the BJP's agenda for the nation. It is for this reason that Ambedkar assumes critical importance in the Sangh parivar's strategy. Unless Ambedkar were adequately saffronised, the rejection of Hinduism by the dalit masses under his leadership would continue to plague its efforts. The new-found love for Ambedkar stems from this political expediency. The parivar's project is helped along by the ideological weakness of the dalit movement, the bankruptcy and venality of its leadership, the self-centred dalit middle class, and the deification of Ambedkar in place of Hindu gods who had been discarded at his instance; so that what might have seemed a fool's errand—saffronising Ambedkar—begins to look practicable.

Despoiled legacy, burgled icon

It was during the tenure of Madhukar Dattatraya alias Balasaheb Deoras, perhaps the most low-profile sarsanghchalak of the RSS, from 1973 to 1994, that active work among dalits was initiated under Seva Bharati, the Sangh's non-governmental organisation devoted to the purpose. The ensuing shifts of stance included placing Ambedkar among the Sangh's pratahsmaraniya (literally, one who is venerated in the morning prayer), and floating—on Ambedkar's birth anniversary in 1983—a purpose-built vehicle, the Samrasata Manch, to woo middle class dalits who yearned for social recognition from the upper castes. Until then, Ambedkar had been anathema to the Sangh parivar, for his vitriolic attacks on everything they held sacred. Once the shift was accomplished, the parivar began projecting him as the friend of its founder, K.B. Hedgewar—'the two doctors' was how this outlandish pairing was styled, as if the two had held learned confabulations together. It may be worth recalling here that Hedgewar was a mere licentiate practitioner with a diploma, not a medical degree holder, while Ambedkar held two doctoral degrees from world-renowned universities; but registering the gaps between fact and fantasy was never the parivar's strong suit. In the same vein, Ambedkar came to be projected as the greatest benefactor of Hindus, an admirer of the RSS, one opposed to Muslims and communists, a supporter of ghar wapsi, an advocate of the saffron flag as the national flag, a hyper-nationalist, and so on. These were clever misrepresentations, with at best a tenuous link to the facts of the case, and often none at all, but they were projected as truths with unflinching zeal.

However easily one may recognize the gimmickry, it cannot be ignored or dismissed. It created the specious grounds for co-opting dalit leaders into the saffron fold. The BJP has made steady gains in the reserved constituencies over the years and, in the general elections of 2014, won more reserved seats than any other party. However, just winning reserved seats are not enough. The BJP's polarisation strategy is contingent on de-radicalising dalits and winning them over. Since this formula turns on the deliberate alienation of religious minorities—who, along with dalits, constitute up to 30 per cent of the electorate—not having the dalits on their side would seriously impede their plans for a Hindu rashtra.

All the preceding factors have left hindutva-vadis desperate to co-opt Ambedkar as a saffron icon. Yet, Ambedkar, who was committed to evolving his views until his last days, wrote in *Pakistan or Partition of India* (1945):

> If Hindu Raj does become a fact, it will, no doubt, be the greatest calamity for this country. No matter what the Hindus say, Hinduism is a menace to liberty, equality and fraternity. On that account it is incompatible with democracy. Hindu Raj must be prevented at any cost. (*BAWS* 8, 358)

Another tract of Ambedkar, *Philosophy of Hinduism* (published posthumously in *BAWS* 3), analyses the worth of Hinduism 'as a way of life' and lambasts it as antithetical to 'liberty, equality, fraternity', failing on the front of justice as well as utility and moral and practical worth. Of course, this may not deter the saffron followers in persisting with the lie that Ambedkar was a great Hindu. Turning a deaf ear to facts is a practised art with them, and is essential to their survival.

The problem for the RSS, as evident from the above, is that Ambedkar happens to be studied intensively by an increasing number of dalit and other student groups around the country. Wresting him from scholarly engagement is an imperative if right-wing groups are to get away with their spurious treatment of his life and works. In the wake of the controversy around the 'derecognition' of the Ambedkar–Periyar Study Circle in May 2015 by the authorities at the Indian Institute of Technology, Madras, which provoked protests all over the country and even beyond, the *Organiser*, the mouthpiece of the RSS, wrote an exasperatingly muddled editorial against the protesters: "Unmasking Pseudo Ambedkarites" (June 2015). It accused them of 'caste-based identity politics', and of not knowing that Ambedkar was pro-Hindu and against communists, and, of course, justifying the derecognition of the APSC. To buttress its point with the appearance of erudition, the editorial began with a quote from Ambedkar's *Annihilation of Caste*, lifted, lazily enough, from *ambedkar.org* and not the original text. The editor's quotation of choice was set out in bold typeface: 'Brahminism is the poison which has spoiled Hinduism. You will succeed in saving Hinduism if you will kill Brahminism.' Conveniently lost to view is the fact that Ambedkar goes on to argue in the next two paragraphs how the Hindus 'must give a new doctrinal basis to [your] religion—a basis that will be in consonance with liberty, equality and fraternity; in short, with democracy', and to effect this 'complete change in the values of life,' he says, 'you have got to apply the dynamite to the Vedas and the shastras, which deny any part to reason' (*BAWS* 1, 74–5).

A preposterous and cynical ploy of the editorial was the claim that protesters against the ban on the APSC were 'reds.' Were the well-known scientists of the country, the ones who wrote to the IIT-M director against his undemocratic action, 'reds'? Just as 'liberal' in the United States gets construed to mean communist, the RSS takes 'rational and democratic' to be 'red'. While Ambedkar did have a difficult relationship with the Indian communists, he did not disagree with the ideals of Marxism (especially the goal of revolution). He was also more than clear in his denunciation of Hinduism. It is patently false of the RSS to claim that Ambedkar was an anti-red and pro-saffron personality, or that his critiques of the communists left him proportionately pro-Hindu. The question arising here is: Can brahminism be isolated from Hinduism, as the editorial line of the *Organiser* tried in its slippery way to achieve? While addressing reformist Hindus in 1936, Ambedkar tried to explain what ailed Hinduism and said that brahminism was the disease. The two terms were synonyms, he explained. Historically speaking, there is nothing called Hinduism; it is a medieval term, heteronomously applied to brahminism, the religion that was predominant beyond the Sindhu river. One is left wondering why a quote that implied no eulogy or sympathy for Hinduism was used by the RSS mouthpiece at all.

It is important to note that while the Sangh parivar and its BJP government wax eloquent over Ambedkar, they are slyly and systematically engaged in eroding his secular legacy. Ambedkar's vitriolic comments on Hinduism and hindutva should have made him the greatest enemy of the parivar. Tragically, with the ideological disorientation of the dalits and some nimble footwork from the parivar, this threat was transformed into a golden opportunity. By inducting Ambedkar into its pantheon, the parivar has been disfiguring Ambedkar even as it appropriates him. The NDA government's Pancha Tirtha project, setting up a pilgrims' circuit between five places of significance in Ambedkar's life—his birthplace in Mhow, the house in London where he stayed while studying in the UK, Deekshabhoomi in Nagpur where he converted, 'Mahaparinirvan Sthal', or the house where he died in Delhi, and Chaityabhoomi in Mumbai where his mortal remains were cremated—is another attempt to control the terms on which people engage with him, replacing the uncompromising thinker with a deified object of rituals, a saffron Ambedkar, a handy Trojan horse for ghar wapsi.

How does casteism synchronise with the right-wing government's new-found love for Babasaheb Ambedkar? This is not difficult to fathom. The BJP is desperate to woo dalits and needs them to accomplish its hindutva agenda. For that, Ambedkar is shamelessly projected as having been in favour of ghar wapsi. They declare that he is the greatest benefactor of the Hindus. Why? Because, rather than a semitic religion, he accepted Buddhism which they claim is just a sect of Hinduism. A staggering lie. They proclaim that he was against Muslims. They boast of his 'friendship' with Hedgewar as well as that other guru of poisonous ideology, Golwalkar, and claim that he was all praise for the Sangh and so on. Yes, it is true that Hedgewar, Golwalkar, Savarkar and others in the RSS went and met Ambedkar—not vice versa, it must be noted—but that scarcely amounts to his being friends with them. He never praised their creed. It is true that B.S. Moonje, along with his friends, met Ambedkar at the Bombay airport, when he was a member of the flag committee, and handed over a saffron flag to him with a plea to make it the national flag. This cannot be construed to mean that Ambedkar supported their cause, or that he proposed Sanskrit as the national language. If he can be accused of being partisan, it is in imbuing the new republic with many Buddhist symbols between 1947 and 1950. As Christophe Jaffrelot notes in *Dr Ambedkar and Untouchability: Analysing and Fighting Caste* (2005, 132), these include 'the chakra (the wheel of dhamma) on the Indian flag, the lions of Ashoka—the Buddhist emperor of ancient India—as the national emblem, and the inscription of a Buddhist aphorism on the pediment of Rashtrapati Bhavan.' By weaving enormous cobwebs of lies around tiny particles of truth, the parivar obscures Ambedkar, dwarfing him to their own stature as a petty communalist, all in the hope of bringing the dalit community into their fold.

Such appropriation is a direct insult to Ambedkar. But the many varieties of Ambedkarites strewn across the political landscape are too inebriated with memorials and identitarian concerns to notice this.

Hindu, Hinduism, Hindutva, Hindustan

The fall of the peshwai in 1818—the peshwas being the brahmin administrators of the kingdom of Shivaji (d.1680), who became the de facto rulers from circa 1713 onwards—deeply hurt the chitpawan brahmins of Pune. This impelled many of them to take up arms against the British, a development that has been shoe-horned into an anti-imperialist and revolutionary narrative, which was in reality imperialist and reactionary. The peshwas were simply trying to regain their lost kingdom. If they were truly anti-imperialist, they would have noticed the ubiquitous caste oppression of two-thirds of their own people. Vinayak Damodar Savarkar, the founding father of hindutva, was the inheritor of this tradition of 'brave revolutionaries'. He provided the ideological basis for his people to organise and work for their revanchist dream. Muslims and Christians, having come largely from the lower castes, were to be the 'other'. The potential threat from the incipient social movements of dalits in Maharashtra by the early 1920s also spurred these revivalist Hindus to group into the jingoistic nationalist organisation, the RSS.

Fascism and Nazism in Europe have been the RSS's inspiration. One has only to glimpse at Golwalkar's gems of thought to recognise how insidious they are, and how shot through with fascist influence. Realising that they could not progress with their takeover of society without brahminising the larger masses, the sanghis created a number of organisations, constituting a continuum, to reach out to and further their agenda with most social groups. Over the years, they succeeded in indoctrinating large sections of tribals, dalits, and 'backward castes' into their own subjugation. While the other minor dalit castes were easily trapped, the followers of Ambedkar—who was by far the bitterest critic of brahminism—were also meant to be netted by the Samajik Samrasata Manch. The Sangh parivar has seen great success with its subterfuge, but its internal contradictions have also grown alongside and may well limit its rise and sustainability. These contradictions stem from its muddled ideological content. The fondly conceived quartet of Hindu, Hinduism, Hindutva, Hindustan may appear real but is a piece of plagiarism, or pseudo-indigenous identity-making: factitious and foggy. These particular H-words existed neither in this land's ancient past which the Sangh noisily claims to represent and restore, nor in any other tradition of homegrown antecedents. In the same way that the 'divine' figure of Bharat Mata is an unacknowledged borrowing from Britannia and Germania, and the revered map of 'akhand Bharat' is a product of Western cartography, the very nationalism of flag and anthem which the Sangh promotes with such zeal is entirely lifted from modern European traditions. So, for that matter, are the RSS uniforms, salute and penchant for marching. The strident rhetoric of the RSS is calculated to keep public attention diverted from its sheer absurdity. In a truly Goebbelsian touch, it claims its agenda is to 'decolonise the Indian mind'. Ahead of a three-day colloquium called Lokmanthan in Bhopal in November 2016, RSS ideologue Rakesh Sinha who also heads the think-tank India Policy Foundation, said, 'Marxist dominance has defined and seen India from the Western prism... Indian intellectuals have never challenged the Western concept of conflict and caste. This is something we would set out to do through such colloquiums' (reported by *news18.com* on 11 November 2016). Participants included C.K. Janu, one-time leader of the Adivasi Gothra Maha Sabha who, after having waged a just and admirable struggle for land against the communist government there in 2001 and 2003, saw fit to contest the Kerala assembly election with the BJP's support in 2016.

Mohan Bhagwat, the reigning RSS supremo, has a syllogism that India is Hindu-sthan, the land of the Hindus; the autochthonous people of this country are Hindu, so that India is ipso facto already a Hindu rashtra. Typically, he appears not to realise that this is both an ignorant proposition and a self-defeating one, since it implies that the RSS's mission has been accomplished and the enterprise may as well pack up. Ancient Persian cuneiform inscriptions and the *Zend Avesta* employ the word 'Hindu' as a geographic name rather than a religious one. When the Persian King Darius I extended his empire to the (indefinite) borders of the Indian subcontinent in 517 BCE, the ancient Persians referred to the people from the latter region as 'Hindu'. The ancient Greeks and Armenians followed the same pronunciation, and thus, gradually the name stuck. The word Hindu, like its cognate 'India', is found neither in Sanskrit nor in any of the native dialects and languages of India. This is typical of the entire mental baggage of the Sangh. When it comes to the meaning of Hinduism, explicators like Bal Gangadhar Tilak (1856–1920) and the first vice president of India, S. Radhakrishnan (1888–1975) provided its non-definition, which included practically anything and everything. Ultimately it became a matter for the Supreme Court to decide what it is, which it did in 1966 and again in 1995. In the case filed by the followers of Swaminarayan (1780–1830) claiming to be non-Hindus in order to challenge the applicability of the 1948 Bombay Harijan (Temple Entry) Act, which guaranteed dalits access to all temples, the Supreme Court, in 1966, defined Hinduism by its tolerance and inclusivity, citing the definitions of Radhakrishnan and some Europeans. It is ironic that this observation of the court was provoked by the desire of certain Hindus to *exclude* other 'Hindus' (dalits) from their temples. Contrary to the contentions of the Sangh parivar, its claim that everyone in India is a Hindu was never true, least of all in the ancient period on which they base this claim.

The real object of the Sangh's efforts, its raison d'être, is not theorising (however foolishly) an ersatz Indian identity into existence, but the practical business of manufacturing a consolidated Hindu vote-bank. If one part of this effort involves drowning Ambedkar's voice by raising a noisy cult of adulation around him, the other part is about driving a permanent wedge between the dalit and the Muslim communities. They are feared as potential allies against hindutva. As the most numerous religious minority group in India, Muslims are in one sense convenient to the majoritarian politics of hindutva-vadis: they form a target large enough to focus Hindu wrath against. But they are also an inconvenient presence. The very size of the community in the subcontinent is evidence of the fissiparous tendencies of the brahminical social order; further, their numbers make Muslims potential spoilers of the best-laid electoral plans.

The Sangh parivar's animosity towards the Muslims may be explained by their non-Hindu status. In terms of Savarkar's ethno-nationalistic definition of true Indians as necessarily Hindu, the pitrabhoomi (land of birth) and punyabhoomi (holy land) of Muslims being outside India, they are permanent outsiders who supposedly live in a parallel society. The salience of their population (14.2 per cent as against the small populations of other non-Hindu communities), their past as 'tormentors' of the Hindu faith and of Hindus as presented by colonial historiography, and their alleged villainy in dismembering an 'akhand Bharat' (although many RSS leaders such as Syama Prasad Mookerjee were vehement in their demand for Partition), are all grist to the mill of scaremongering and stigmatisation. These strenuous efforts avoid confronting one crucial factor, that the majority of Muslims (along with Christians) converted from the dalit and 'lower' castes, which is the real grudge against them embedded deep in the 'upper' caste psyche. From both sides, Hindu as well as Muslim, this grudge spills out. In the wake of Curzon's partition of Bengal in 1905, Syama Prasad Mookerjee—credited with founding the Jan Sangh in 1951—had grimly predicted that the bhadralok in East Bengal would now have to live under the chandals (a derogatory term for dalits in Bengal who had begun to call themselves namashudra). Sir Syed Ahmed Khan blamed the 'jahil' (ignorant riff-raff) element for Muslim participation in the Revolt of 1857, in an attempt to persuade British authorities that the 'ashraf' and 'raees' ('well-born' gentry) were loyal subjects. In "The Causes of the Revolt", a pamphlet he rushed into print in 1858, he noted the lack of breeding displayed by the mutineers—their drinking, rapine and debauchery, their disloyalty to their patron's 'salt'—and pronounced that they were not real Muslims at all. The stereotype of the immoral inferior he invokes here provides an unmistakable lead to the sub-text: precisely which kind of people, according to Khan, were not true Muslims. The distinction retained its force him. Addressing a gathering of zamindars at Lucknow in 1887, he was still making the same point: 'And tell me how many years ago [the] Government suffered such grievous troubles [which] arose from the ignorant and not from the gentlemen?'

None other than Swami Vivekananda (1863–1902), whom the hindutva-vadis idolise, had this to say in 1894: 'Why among the poor of India so many are Mohammedans? It is nonsense to say that they were converted by the sword. It was to gain liberty from zamindars and priests....' (*The Complete Works of Swami Vivekananda*, 2127).

Largely, people of the oppressed castes became Muslims and that really lies at the root of Bhagwat's brahminical hatred. These castes willingly embraced Islam because of its relative egalitarianism, experienced through the Sufis, Islam's mystics, who preached love and compassion in an idiom that appealed to them. They were forbidden from entering Hindu temples but were embraced when they entered Sufi dargahs. Members of these castes also became Christians, not because they were forced by the Christian rulers or missionaries, but of their own volition. As the argument of coercion is empirically indefensible, the Sangh parivar prefers to speak of tribal and dalit peoples being 'bribed' by the missionaries. What constitutes the bribe? The promise of human dignity, social status, education, occupational mobility and equality under law. These universal markers of progress acquire a pernicious character in the eyes of the hindutva-vadis, simply when applied to dalits—for whom the major reason behind becoming Muslim or Christian was the exclusionary and oppressive caste system of Hinduism.

This lie that the Muslim rulers and Christian missionaries converted the Hindus either by force or with bribes constituted the basis of the shuddhi movement of the Arya Samaj which was particularly active in the 1920s, and was re-launched by the Sangh parivar as ghar wapsi after Modi came to power. Parivar outfits claimed to have successfully shepherded people back into the Hindu fold in Andhra Pradesh, Kerala and Goa, which investigations revealed to be cases of bribery and coercion. Such bribery is not limited to the efforts of vigilante groups. No less an institution than the Supreme Court held on 26 February 2015 that 'reconversion' to Hinduism will not prevent a person from accessing quota benefits once the convert adopts the caste of their forefathers. This was in response to a question regarding which caste the 'returning' converts—the victims/beneficiaries of ghar wapsi—would land up in. The court's answer legitimated 'reconversion', not least by using the term, and also incentivised ghar wapsi by holding out the cookie jar of the SC quota as allurement. What is also striking about the court's response is how closely it echoes Vivekananda's answer in an April 1989 interview to the journal *Prabuddha Bharata* (that he had founded in 1896): 'Returning converts will gain their own castes, of course. And new people will make theirs.' This is exactly the line peddled by Yogi Adityanath, current chief minister of Uttar Pradesh and a hindutva hardliner beyond even the standards that prevail in the BJP. He illuminated the matter thus: 'those being subjected to ghar wapsi will be given the gotra and caste from which they converted.' That means most converts to Islam and Christianity, being from the oppressed castes and having converted to escape the yoke of caste bondage in Hinduism, would be incarcerated again within the hellhole of Hinduism which their forefathers strove to escape. A fine prospect for the Muslims and Christians of India!

Ideas of India?

Ambedkar's ideal of liberty, equality and fraternity seems light years away, and gets more distant with each passing day. Liberty has been a chimera for a vast majority of people, gripped by basic livelihood concerns and additionally fettered by the police state that has effectively stifled their voice. Equality no more survives even in public discourse; its place has been usurped by the World Bank's formulations on inclusion and the hindutva brigade's notion of samrasata, with the result that India today ranks among the most unequal societies in the world. Fraternity was always inconceivable in a caste society. There is not an iota of improvement in terms of these keystones of Ambedkar's political vision; on the contrary, things have worsened rapidly in neoliberal India and the proto-fascist India of post-2014.

The outcome of the 2014 elections stunned the nation. The BJP won 282 seats out of 543—53 per cent of the total number of seats, with a mere 31 per cent of the vote share—and broke the spell of the coalition era which many people thought had come to stay. Adding the seats won by its allies, the tally rises to 334. The scale of the BJP's victory—rapidly painting the map saffron in successive state elections—has put the government in a position where it can do what it wants.

In the long list of outrages since the BJP came to power—such as the attacks on churches, coercion in the ghar wapsi campaign, exhortations to Hindu women to produce at least four children in order to 'preserve' Hinduism, moral policing against girls, anti-Romeo squads against 'love jihad' in UP, cow vigilantism, or the repeated assaults on campus democracy—the running theme has been the ritual humiliation of Muslims and dalits. While the brutal killing of Mohammad Akhlaq in Dadri on September 2015, on suspicion of possessing cow meat, or the June 2016 murder of Junaid, a fifteen-year-old Muslim youth, and the stabbing of his companions in a minor dispute over seats in a Mathura-bound train from New Delhi, may exemplify the oppression of the Muslims, the institutional murder of Rohith Vemula, a promising PhD scholar in Hyderabad Central University in January 2016, and the flogging of the Sarvaiya family in Mota Samdhiala and Una town of Gujarat in July 2016, exemplify the repression of dalits under the Modi government. (On the Sarvaiya case, see "Dalit Protests in Gujarat".)

The ban on cattle slaughter threatens the livelihoods and ways of life of a vast number of people—mostly belonging to the so-called lower castes and Muslims—engaged in the production, distribution and consumption of beef, and in the leather industry. The beef ban is politics of the foulest kind being used to splinter India by targeting Muslims and dalits under the garb of cow protection. If we identified the people affected—dalits, adivasis, the non-farming OBC castes, Muslims, Christians, the entire North East and much of Kerala—altogether, perhaps half of India's population would turn out to be beef-eaters. Contrary to the projection of India as a vegetarian country, over 71 per cent of Indians over the age of fifteen are non-vegetarian (according to the Sample Registration System Baseline Survey 2014 of the Census of 2011). This is a giveaway of the logic of caste rather than democracy that underpins the decisions of the government. Even if the number had been smaller, to ban beef is a gross violation of the fundamental rights to life, freedom and livelihood. The hindutva brigade is sheltering under Article 48 of the Constitution, the Directive Principles of State Policy, that says:

> The State shall endeavour to organise agriculture and animal husbandry on modern and scientific lines and shall, in particular, take steps for preserving and improving the breeds, and prohibiting the slaughter of cows and other milch and draught cattle.

It is a testament to the anti-people character of the ruling classes that they have systematically ignored all directive principles, including the one about completing the provision of free and universal education of all children up to the age of fourteen within ten years, and singularly focused all state machinery on gauraksha. The cow has become more important than the future of the country; rather, it appears the cow has become the future of the country—a position espoused by every brahminical source and ratified by none other. In point of fact, the constitutional article in question does not imply the unqualified prohibition of cow slaughter, but it has been twisted to mean that and even the courts have accepted this unquestioningly. It talks of banning the slaughter of cows, not the eating of cow meat; and least of all the meat of non-milch cattle. Sadly, it has now come to mean all that.

Even after the gruesome killing on 28 September 2015 of Mohammad Akhlaq in Dadri, which also left his twenty-two-year-old son severely injured, the police filed an FIR against the victims for the consumption of beef. The meat in the refrigerator was subjected to forensic tests (although the consumption of beef is not banned in the state).The BJP MP Sakshi Maharaj criticised Akhilesh Yadav, chief minister of UP at the time, for announcing an ex-gratia compensation to the victim's family, claiming that 'when a Muslim dies they will give 20 lakhs and when a Hindu dies he won't even get 20,000.' The RSS in fact justified the Dadri mob lynching of Mohammad Akhlaq in its mouthpiece *Panchjanya*. An article carried as the cover story said, 'Vedas order killing of the sinner who kills a cow.' It slammed writers who returned their Sahitya Akademi awards in protest over the murder and called them insensitive to Hindu sentiments, while an editorial—"Selective Amnesia" (20 October 2015)—in its English counterpart, *Organiser*, carried the justification that 'riots and lynchings had happened earlier too'. It accused the award renouncers of seeking fame through political manoeuvring and inducing a 'fear psychosis' in the populace since they 'cannot imagine coming of age of home grown wisdom based on ancient Bharateeya culture and heritage'. But the culture and heritage of the nation that the BJP intends to preserve is precisely the cause of fear among the people, since it—let it be plainly said—amounts to slaughtering people; not just some five dalits in Jhajjar or a Muslim in Dadri or a Kashmiri trucker in Udhampur, but millions of farmers with cattle to sell, who are already distressed because of the negative terms of trade in agriculture, and the policies of the ruling government.

In the University of Hyderabad, Rohith Vemula's suicide on 17 January 2016 exposed the criminality stemming from the casteist mindset of the saffron establishment. His dream of becoming a science writer like his idol, Carl Sagan, ended abruptly at the altar of caste. But the public reaction to his death raised hopes of a peoples' movement to prevent a recurrence of the circumstances that led to the young scholar's dreams being crushed. Rohith Vemula's death is not a stray case of a life claimed by caste prejudice. Atrocities against dalits have intensified with the rise of hindutva forces. While the persecution of dalit scholars in the recent past has gone relatively unnoticed, the spontaneous outburst at Rohith's death became a new movement against communal forces, particularly sparked off by the stirring suicide note he left behind that defied the prevailing contempt towards students in reserved seats:

> The value of a man was reduced to his immediate identity and nearest possibility. To a vote. To a number. To a thing. Never was a man treated as a mind. As a glorious thing made up of stardust. In every field, in studies, in streets, in politics, and in dying and living.

On campuses all over the country, the entire student community spontaneously condemned the hindutva hooliganism of the BJP's student wing, Akhil Bharatiya Vidyarthi Parishad, which had led to the suicide. The agitation by Rohith's fellow students, the resolute support of their teachers (some of whom were suspended), and national and international outrage brought exposure to the conceited administration. Students, who had greatly contributed to the BJP's win in the 2014 elections, now came together to say an emphatic no to its casteist and communal agenda.

The prime minister, speaking at Lucknow University, described Rohith's death as the loss of a son to a mother—the same son his minister Bandaru Dattatreya had earlier called anti-national—and shed a showman's tears. But he kept mum over the misdeeds of his own ministers that abetted Rohith's suicide. Human Resource Development minister Smriti Irani's histrionics in Parliament in the aftermath of this incident stirred more controversy as she was accused of lying about the sequence of events only to preserve her cabinet post. Rohith's claim that 'never was a man treated as a mind' was proved right in the ensuing controversy that revolved around his caste identity—proof was sought of his 'dalit-ness', with district authorities scrambling to ascertain if indeed Rohith's family belongs to a Scheduled Caste. It registered with a few that he had enrolled for a PhD in Science, Technology and Society Studies on 'merit', without availing quota. The magnitude of the mishap proved that the BJP's brahminical pride continues to blind the party, as it failed to see Rohith's noose tightening around its own neck.

The deaths of Mohammad Akhlaq and Rohith Vemula stem from the same source, the brahminical order that the BJP and its parivar outfits are at pains to restore. Theirs is an ideology of elitism based on the systematic persecution of the downtrodden. The cynical appropriation of Ambedkar by hindutva is an attempt to veil this connection, but the BJP's actions reinforce the link between its casteism and anti-Muslim ideology. Let us take the case of Gujarat under Narendra Modi. As Christophe Jaffrelot has revealed (at a talk in Princeton University on 12 November 2015), Modi's much-touted Gujarat model of development is marked by systematic underspending on the social sector. The results show on indices of both education and healthcare, as well as along social faultlines. In 2011, after ten years of Modi's governance, the percentage of children with normal weight (for their age group) in Gujarat was 43.13 per cent, the lowest in the country. Who are all these undernourished children in a state that regularly ranks second, third or fourth nationally by per-capita income? They are the children of the poor, of the dalits, adivasis and Muslims. The 'Gujarat model' is already notorious as a byword for religious polarisation; Jaffrelot shows us that it stands for socio-economic polarisation as well. The proportion of Gujarat's SCs who were below the poverty line in 1994 was 31 per cent. By 2005, 34 per cent of the state's SC population was BPL. This emphatic jump in poverty is a rare phenomenon in demographics, because the regular trend is for any community to shrink its BPL figures, however marginally. Between 2001 and 2010, Gujarat's spending on public education was 3 per cent below the national average, and the only state in the country to commit a lower share was Madhya Pradesh, also under a BJP government. This is not a matter of policy oversight but of deliberate neglect, as deliberate as an architect's plans. It becomes clear when we consider the fate of a central government scheme initiated after the Sachar Committee's recommendations (2006), designating 5,500 scholarships per state for deserving Muslim students. Under the modest budgetary allocation for the scheme, the centre would contribute Rs 3.75 crore per annum and each state government Rs 1.25 crore. Gujarat was the only state that refused to implement the scheme and, what's more, took the central government to the Supreme Court, claiming the policy was discriminatory. Why would any state discriminate so blatantly against the downtrodden? Who benefits? In Gujarat, it is the middle class.

It is important to unravel the 'Gujarat model' since the RSS plan is to convert India into Gujarat. As Jaffrelot points out, up to 70 per cent of the state government's taxation revenues during Modi's tenure came from indirect taxes such as the Value Added Tax; not from sources that have their catchment in the middle class: property and land tax, vehicle, stamps and registration taxes—which comprised the bulk of any other state government's earnings before the implementation of the Goods and Services Tax in 2017. The hand that withholds investment from the social sector lavishes it on big corporations instead, such as Ambani, Essar, Tata and Adani, who receive land at throwaway prices and tax breaks running to decades. Writing in the *Indian Express* (20 November 2017), Jaffrelot says while the Gujarat Industrial Corporation had acquired 4,620 hectares in the period 1990–2001, the figure rose to 21,308 ha in the 2001–11 period. This included land acquired for the creation of Special Economic Zones given to industrial units on ninety-nine-year leases, and sold to industrialists at less than the market price. (See "Dalit Protests in Gujarat" for a sense of the treatment dalits staking a claim to land receive.) At this point the question of how such a government can win elections begins to answer itself: by outspending its competitors on a crushing scale.

Conjuring a false reality

To avert the prospect of dalits and Muslims joining forces is a priority for the Sangh parivar. Its intellectuals have been saying that Ambedkar was against Muslims, quoting stray sentences from his *Thoughts on Pakistan*. This book was written in a polemical style in 1941 (and revised in 1945), Ambedkar donning the robes as an advocate for Hindus as well as for Muslims. Unless one reads it with diligence, one could miss many of the arguments. But again, going by Ambedkar's liberal outlook and a multitude of references where he praised the Muslim community to the extent that Islam appeared to be his preference for conversion ("Mukti Kon Pathe?" 1936), he cannot be portrayed as a petty-minded, anti-Muslim person. To give an idea of the quality of research behind the parivar's lies about Ambedkar—from calling him a partisan of Hindu cultural nationalism to his purported view of Muslims as vandals and anti-reformist—I need only mention here that it took me a mere four days to collate a refutation of them from Ambedkar's writings, which I published as *Ambedkar on Muslims: Myths and Facts* (2003).

The votaries of the Sangh parivar need to come out of their delusions and note certain hard facts of history. This country they feign pride in and devotion to is the gift of the colonialists; it never existed before in this shape and size. The Muslims that they love to hate have been part of this land since that seventeen-year-old lad called Muhammad bin Qasim captured Sindh in the eighth century and paved the way for Islamic expansion, not by the sword as they believe, but by Islam's egalitarian appeal to the lower castes, who were oppressed by brahminism. This great subcontinent, so richly endowed, was given a history of slavery by their own brahminical traditions. These, coupled with the supremacist obsession of hindutva eventually led to the Partition. And yet India remains one of the most populous Muslim nations in the world—with 177 million Muslim peoples, it accounts for 10 per cent of the world's Muslim population and ranks next only to Indonesia and Pakistan in sheer numbers. The contribution of Islam and Muslims to the palimpsest of Indian culture is far more extensive than their numbers would imply. It was European colonialists who, albeit driven by their own interests, gave India its modernity and infrastructure, whereas it is its native successors who are running it into the ground.

The more the BJP drives its supremacist project, the more it will alienate people. It is better Modi and Shah (and Bhagwat) heed the words of Babasaheb Ambedkar, whom they consider to be their pratahsmaraniya:

> Hindu society as such does not exist. It is only a collection of castes. ...There is an utter lack among the Hindus of what the sociologists call 'consciousness of kind'. There is no Hindu consciousness of kind. In every Hindu the consciousness that exists is the consciousness of his caste. That is the reason why the Hindus cannot be said to form a society or a nation (*BAWS* 1, 50).

The idea of India is based on the plurality and diversity of its people. It is on these terms alone that this nation made up essentially of caste-based, religious, regional, ethnic and linguistic minorities—what Ambedkar termed a 'congeries of communities'—can survive.

For now, the BJP seems to be riding a wave. Whether the wave holds steady, time will tell. It is unlikely, however, that any component of the Sangh parivar will be much exercised by the questions raised here. Their attitude to the interests of this country, like their attitude towards facts, has always been reckless. Rather, it is for voters to recognise the stratagems at work behind catchy slogans. 'Sabka saath, sabka vikas' has turned out an attractively worded proposition with nothing to substantiate it; least of all Modi's record of leadership in Gujarat. Modi's style of one-way communication avoiding debate and deliberation, the essence of democracy, came in handy time and again to deliver the mandate of capital. With Amit Shah, a longstanding confidant of Modi as the BJP head, the control of this deadly pair over Gujarat gives us a detailed picture of their vision and methods. They provided a prototype of what fascism, in its Indian version of a Hindu rashtra, would be like. Since 2014, they have gone on a winning spree in state after state, notably in Uttar Pradesh, which would bolster their support in the Rajya Sabha. 'Achhe din' or good times was as much of a phantasm as Modi's concern for the poor or his commitment to the rule of law, as much a phantasm as the good that was expected to follow from demonetisation, or the employment that Modi was going to generate at the rate of one crore per year. It is clear why Modi needs to make a saffron phantasm out of Ambedkar. To have the true Ambedkar known would put paid to the parivar's conjuring tricks.

9

The Education Mantra and the Exclusion Sutra

Through much of the subcontinent's history, till the Constitution of India was formally enacted on 26 January 1950, the template of Hindu law and social organisation was supplied by the *Manusmriti* and ideologically kindred shastraic texts. It banned almost 85 per cent of all people from access to education, even literacy—all except men of the dwija castes. This regime had been previously disturbed only with the advent of Christian missionaries who arrived along with European traders and colonisers. The subcontinent came in contact with Christian missionaries as early as the first century of the common era, and Thomas—one of the apostles of Christ—is believed to have established a church in Kerala in 52 CE. Sustained and widespread missionary activity began from the time of Fr. Pedro de Kovilham, who landed on the Malabar Coast along with the Portuguese sailor Vasco da Gama, on 20 May 1498. Since the colonisers were meticulous record keepers and data gatherers, we know that by the year 1534, 1503 Dominicans, 1542 Jesuits, and 1572 Augustinians were working in India (Hillerbrand 2004). Colonial rule and its 'civilising' mission, despite being steeped in arrogance and power, brought numerous opportunities to the oppressed castes. It was Christian missionaries who first opened the doors of modern education to them despite the initially unsupportive attitude of the colonial rulers. In Christianity, education occupies an important place because Christians are supposed to read the 'Word of God' (Neill 1986, 195). Soon enough, various colonial enterprises—Portuguese, French, Dutch and predominantly British—laid the foundation of modern English education in the country. In principle, access to this education was open to all. Nevertheless, education remained a complex negotiation with norms established by the brahminical order that has cast a long shadow up to our times.

Most of the Christian missionaries sent to India were educated men and zealous educationists. Beyond the direct propagation of doctrine, education and healthcare were used by them as instruments of evangelism (Mayhew 1998, 161). Jesuit missionaries established the first college on the Western model in Goa in 1575, becoming the pioneers of the modern system of higher education. Through the eighteenth and nineteenth centuries, as British rule was consolidated, more Protestant missionaries entered the field. Among the initial doubts and hiccups that attended the spread of Western education was the question of whose support it should seek on the ground. So divided was Hindu society that if the oppressed castes attended missionary schools, the dominant castes would not. Converts from the dominant castes would establish the social prestige of the religion in its new habitat. On the other hand, missionaries were enjoined by their faith to serve the weak and disempowered. Much of the literary activity of the early mission—projects of translation, dictionary-making, devising modern scripts for Indian languages, and publishing books and pamphlets—called for partnership with the native elites. The goals of service and maximising conversion oriented them towards the poor.

Amid these contrary pressures, it took longer to begin the dissemination of education among the dalits and for it to convert itself into the kind of modern cultural capital that would germinate unease about the caste system. Mahatma Jotirao Phule (1827–90) who pioneered the anti-caste revolt in Western India was himself a product of missionary education. When he launched his 'non-brahmin' movement and established schools for the untouchables between 1848 and 1852, the Free Church of Scotland and the American Marathi Mission (in Ahmednagar) lent financial support to his efforts, incurring the displeasure of the colonial government which maintained a policy of non-interference in the social customs of the natives. Phule was all praise for the missionaries' work and saw them as emancipators of the subordinate castes. Invoking the metaphor of Bali raja—the mythological king celebrated in popular memory for his generosity and mourned as a victim of brahmin deceit and betrayal by the gods—he wrote: '…missionaries, followers of Baliraja in the West, that is Jesus Christ, came to this country…preached the true teachings of Jesus among the shudras (low-caste) and freed them from the deceit and slavery of [caste]' (translation in Deshpande 2002, 75).

Deposing before the Simon Commission on behalf of the Bahishkrut Hitkarini Sabha on 29 May 1928, Ambedkar would also state how the missionaries had been the only source of education for the dalits:

> The only agency which could take charge of the education of the depressed classes was that of Christian missionaries. In the words of Mountstuart Elphinstone they 'found the lowest classes the best people'. But the government was pledged to religious neutrality and could not see its way to support missionary schools, so much so that no pecuniary grant was made in this Presidency [Bombay] to any missionary school in the early part of this period although the Educational Despatch of 1854 had not prohibited the giving of grants to missionary schools (*BAWS* 2, 419).

Colonial power vs. brahminic impulse

As for the role of the colonial government in the education of Indians, the East India Company's officials had pursued a policy of conciliation towards the native elites. The Company supported vernacular learning—purveyed by native priests and religious scholars with an inherent bias towards traditionalism, privileging 'classical' languages and texts—by founding institutions like the Madarsa Aliya in Calcutta in 1780, for the study of Arabic and Persian languages and Islamic Law, the Benares Sanskrit College in Varanasi in 1791, the College of Fort William in Calcutta in 1800, the Poona Sanskrit College in Pune in 1821, and the Calcutta Sanskrit College in 1824. After 1813, when the Company's territories were opened to Christian missionaries, this policy came in conflict with the views of the evangelists whose orientation towards the propagation of Western knowledge had the support of Charles Grant, Chairman of the East India Company, which led to the establishment of many reputed colleges by missionaries like the Scottish Church College in Calcutta in 1830, Wilson College in Bombay in 1832, Madras Christian College in 1837, and Elphinstone College in Bombay in 1856. By the early 1830s, the debate within the government over what kind of education to support had been settled. The Orientalist camp, which advocated the vernaculars of India as the medium of instruction, was eclipsed by the Anglicists who now gained the upper hand in devising an education policy. This led to Thomas Babington Macaulay's "Memorandum on Indian Education" being passed as the English Education Act 1835, firmly declaring government support for the transmission of Western knowledge and placing the English language at the centre of the education programme of India. Lord Macaulay, the first Law Member of the Governor General's executive council, had submitted his minute to William Bentinck and the ideas he outlined in it were to shape British educational policy in this country 'to form a class who may be interpreters between [us] and the millions whom [we] govern—a class of persons Indian in blood and colour, but English in tastes, in opinions, in morals and in intellect'.

The policy was principally guided by the practical administrative needs of the colonialists. At the time of passing the 1833 Charter Act—which ended the monopoly of the English East India Company over trade in India—the Company was in serious financial difficulties and needed to cut its governance costs in India. One of the methods suggested was to replace expensive European employees with Indians at much lower salaries. It was imperative to educate Indians in English in order to replace European clerks. Second, an English education was also seen as an important basis for expanding the market for British goods in India by propagating English values, habits and tastes. As Macaulay noted, '...but wearing our broad cloth and working with our cutlery, they should not be too ignorant or too poor to value and buy English manufactures...' Macaulay's note, Bentinck's ruling, and the establishment and growth of English education expressed the direct needs of colonial power. The Company's patronage of modern education was a transactional arrangement that was meant neither to equalise Indians vis-à-vis the British, nor to encourage egalitarian campaigns within Indian society. That it eventually did both was a paradoxical outcome.

In 1837, English replaced Persian as the official and court language, and in 1844 Governor General Hardinge announced a preference for English-educated Indians in the civil service. These two steps effectively sealed the prospects of any education other than in English. In 1852–53, some citizens of Bombay petitioned the British Parliament to establish and fund university education in India. In response to this and the general demand for English education came the "Wood's Despatch" in 1854. This despatch of Sir Charles Wood, then president of the Board of Control of the East India Company, became the basis of the education policy of the Company's government. It marked the beginning of a new era in the growth of Western education in India. The despatch recommended the institution of a department of public instruction in each province under the charge of an officer to supervise educational institutions. It assigned the government with the task of creating a properly articulated scheme of education from primary school to university. These proposals led to the founding of the universities of

Bombay, Calcutta and Madras in 1857. The recommendations reflected the needs of the ruling colonial powers to train a section of the upper classes in higher education and set up an administrative structure for education in the country, one which has broadly endured—with its elitist bias—till date.

Tellingly, even after Wood's Despatch, the attitude of the Company towards the inclusion of dalits was not favourable. The general approach was still one of conciliation towards the native elites, which meant a virtual ban on dalits in schools. The issue was forced into the open by the case of a mahar boy from Dharwad (in present-day Karnataka) who petitioned the government in June 1856 against the denial of admission to him in a government school on account of his caste. The case was hotly debated and the British government—which took over the administration of India from the now-defunct Company—had to declare in 1858 that schools receiving government grants should henceforth be open to all students irrespective of their caste or creed (see Mishra 2001). This promise, however, did not deliver a flood of dalit entrants into the schooling system. Dr Ambedkar observes how the government, contrary to its own proclamation, had practiced the exclusion of dalit students from education:

> Under these circumstances mass education as contemplated by the Despatch of 1854 was in practice available to all except the depressed classes. The lifting of the ban on the education of the depressed classes in 1854 was a nominal affair only. For, although the principle of non-exclusion was affirmed by the government its practical operation was very carefully avoided, so that we can say that the ban was continued in practice as before (*BAWS* 2, 419).

Thus, even through the colonial period, the brahminical hegemony over Hindu society continued. Ambedkar argued with evidence in his 1948 work *The Untouchables: Who were they and why they became Untouchables?* (*BAWS* 9) that Manu's law was not a thing of the past and still held sway over society.

Another notable source of education for the dalits during colonial times was the military schools. The Bombay army of the East India Company recruited a large number of mahar soldiers. The British had a policy to educate their soldiers and ran military schools for the purpose (White 1994). Mahars from the Konkan and Western Ghats who joined the army in large numbers and got educated in military schools later played a major role in organising the dalit movement. Zelliot writes that Ambedkar's experiences were 'free from the traditional village role, his early life was spent among educated ex-army men, imbued with the pride of soldiers and acquainted with a more sophisticated Hinduism than that found in the village' (2013, 16). Ambedkar himself gave much of the credit for the dalit movement in Maharashtra to the recruitment of mahars in the British Army. He wrote:

> Until the advent of the British, the untouchables were content to remain untouchables ... In the army of the East India Company there prevailed the system of compulsory education for Indian soldiers and their children, both male and female. The education received by the untouchables in the army gave them a new vision and a new value. They became conscious that the low esteem in which they had been held was not an inescapable destiny but was a stigma imposed on their personality by the cunning contrivances of the priest. They felt the shame of it as they never did before and were determined to get rid of it (*BAWS* 2, 189).

Similar narratives abound from the Madras Presidency area where men of the paraiyar caste benefited from their association with the military:

> The Paraiyans since the 1760s and 1770s had constituted the bulk of the foot soldiers in the [East India] Company's army... The Paraiyans were exclusively recruited for one of the regiments of the Indian army, more popularly known as the 'Queens Own Sappers and Miners' till about the middle of the nineteenth century. But after the Great Rebellion of 1857, there was a shift in the British Government's military recruitment policy. At this time, the British military superiors

felt that the recruitment policy needed to be based on the 'martial race' theory (Dutta 2013, 48).

Access to education during the colonial period was perhaps the definitive revolutionary development in dalit history. Education opened up the world to them; made them question their status vis-à-vis others; helped develop the consciousness of being wronged and imbued them with the psychological strength to resist it. This is exactly the process one finds underway in various agitations articulated by the dalits before Ambedkar.

Postcolonial management of education

From the days when the Congress party had not yet taken the form of a mass movement, its leaders had voiced demands for free education. Indeed, from before the Congress was founded, its future leaders were already doing so. When Viceroy Lord Ripon, in order to address complaints regarding the non-implementation of the Wood's Despatch of 1854, appointed the Hunter Education Commission in 1882—three years before the Congress came into existence—a patrician figure like Dadabhai Naoroji would express the same opinion as Jotiba Phule in demanding that free education for all children be the onus of the state. The Hunter Commission acknowledged the neglect of primary and secondary education in the country and, inter alia, recommended the encouragement of primary education by making the local and municipal boards responsible for it, along with a progressive handing over of secondary schooling to private enterprises with grants-in-aid schemes and an emphasis on moral and physical education.

With regard to education, many promises were made later in the heat of the freedom struggle, promises that would need to be incorporated into the Constitution but turned out too inconvenient to keep. In 1947, a ways and means committee was set up under the then prime minister of the Bombay Province, B.G. Kher, to explore how universal elementary education could be achieved within ten years at an affordable cost. Later the same year, a sub-committee of the Constituent Assembly placed free and compulsory education on the list of Fundamental Rights. Clause 23 read thus: 'Every citizen is entitled as of right to free primary education and it shall be the duty of the State to provide within a period of ten years from the commencement of this Constitution for free and compulsory primary education for all children until they complete the age of fourteen years.' However, the Advisory Committee of the CA rejected this commitment in April 1947 citing the costs involved, and placed education on the list of 'non-justiciable fundamental rights', an oxymoron that later became the Directive Principles of State Policy. In the 1949 debates, the CA removed the first line of Article 36, 'Every citizen is entitled as of right to free primary education and it shall be the duty of the State [etc.]' and replaced it with with the watery promise of Article 45 of Directive Principles—anyway non-justiciable: 'The State shall endeavour to provide, within a period of ten years from the commencement of this Constitution, for free and compulsory education for all children until they complete the age of fourteen years.' This non-binding promise freed successive governments from paying it any heed.

Recognising the need to restructure the education system of postcolonial India, the Central Advisory Board of Education decided to set up two commissions, one to deal with university education and the other with secondary education. The first commission to be appointed was the University Education Commission in 1948 under the chairmanship of the then vice president Dr S. Radhakrishnan, to suggest improvements and extensions that would be desirable to suit the present and future requirements of the country. Among the commission's recommendations was the setting up of occupational institutes that would train technicians in large numbers towards the goal of a self-sufficient economy. Radhakrishnan's recommendations were reinforced by the Secondary Education Commission appointed in September 1952 with Dr A.L. Swami Mudaliar as chairman. Its report, submitted in 1953 to the first elected parliament of the free country, recommended creating infrastructure comprising technical schools, polytechnics, strengthening multi-purpose education, and central technical institutions. The convenient abdication of responsibility towards ensuring universal access to literacy ran parallel to the elaborate plans to skill the elites.

Thereafter, the Indian Education Commission under the chairmanship of D.S. Kothari was appointed in 1964 to advise the government on the 'national pattern of education and on the general principles and policies for the development of education at all stages and in all aspects'. The Kothari Commission observed that realising the country's aspirations would involve changes in the knowledge, skills, interests and values of the people as a whole. It made a profound observation: 'If this change on a grand scale is to be achieved without violent revolution (and even then it would still be necessary), there is one instrument, and one instrument only that can be used, Education'. Based on this commission's report, the National Policy on Education, 1968, was formulated. The Kothari Commission concluded that Indian education needed a radical revamp to meet constitutional goals and to address the various problems facing the country in different sectors. The Education Policy Resolution of 1968 picked up the following six recommendations of the Commission: (1) Use of regional language as the medium of instruction at the primary stage, (2) The incorporation of opportunities of non-formal education, (3) Education for the people, i.e., elementary and adult education, (4) The introduction of a common public schooling system, (5) The standardisation of the educational system on a 10+2+3 pattern, and (6) The standardisation of teachers' salaries.

With the excuse that the Kothari Commission's report lacked in terms of administrative detail, the government next appointed the Banaras Hindu University Commission in 1969. The recommendations of this commission regarding the appointment of vice-chancellors, the structure and composition of university grants, etc., gave the state greater control over the administration of higher education and corresponded with the interests of the ruling classes; hence, they were swiftly implemented. The increasing trend towards authoritarianism in the country penetrated even the field of education. Subsequently, recognising the need to effectively control education and educational institutions, the Constitution was amended during the Emergency to remove education from the state list of subjects, and place it in the concurrent list—with jurisdiction shared by the centre and the state. The formation of the Janata Party government after the 1977 elections saw another attempt at tailoring the educational system, with the Draft Education Policy of 1979. This emphasised, among other things, non-formal education with ideological support from the Gandhian model. The premature fall of the Janata government meant that this education policy fell through.

Just as the policies of the colonial government were based on the needs of the British capitalist economy and its ruling class, it needs to be understood that the policies of the postcolonial government were primarily based on the interests of the Indian capitalist class. The Bombay Plan, produced by a group of Indian industrialists and technocrats in 1944–45, provided a clue to their intentions. The capitalist class being incapable as yet of making the requisite investments on its own, the plan proposed the investment of state resources for a period of fifteen years, so as to reserve an emerging option for itself. While the Bombay Plan was not officially adopted, the strategy of the government's five-year plans after independence was suspiciously similar to the proposals put forward by this plan's signatories—Jamshedji Ratanji Dadabhoy Tata, Ghanshyam Das Birla, Ardeshir Dalal, Sri Ram, Kasturbhai Lalbhai, Ardeshir Darabshaw Shroff, Sir Purshottamdas Thakurdas and John Mathai. The first three five-year plans had almost the same sectoral outlay pattern and appear to be scaled down versions of the fifteen-year Bombay Plan. The only difference is that the government could implement it in the name of the people and under the garb of socialism. As a matter of fact, the postcolonial state was essentially a continuation of the colonial state, and worse to the extent that the native ruling classes had dexterously combined native brahminism with Western imperialism. In the same way as much of the benefit to the dalits during colonial rule was accidental or unintended, such development as accrued to Indian people in the postcolonial period also turns out to be an accidental gain.

At the time of the transfer of power, only 12 per cent of the population was literate. If we consider higher education, particularly scientific and technological education that was expressly required by capitalists, the picture was all the more dismal. The spectacular progress that India made during the early decades may be framed within this perspective. The number of children going to secondary classes increased from 2.4 million in 1947 to 34 million in 1983, and the number of schools from 13,000 in 1947 to 175,000 in 1985. The number of girls and boys successfully completing the higher secondary stage rose from 237,000 in 1960–61 to 840,000 in 1981–82. At the time of independence there were only 700 colleges and twenty universities with an enrolment of 400,000; in 1985 the number had risen to 5,246 colleges and 140 universities with an enrolment of 3.36 million that included 976,000 girls. In 1947, the situation of higher education in India was bleaker but the period after the 1950s saw exponential growth. Between 1950–51 and 1990–91, the number of colleges for general education, colleges for professional education and universities/deemed universities went up from 370 to 4,862, 308 to 886, and 27 to 184, respectively. The total institutions of higher learning thus went up from 605 to 5,932 in this period (Ministry of Human Resource Development 2011, 21).

This progress in the sphere of education helped all sections of society but not equally. Rather, it accentuated the inequality between them. It is clear that had the government implemented the recommendations of the Kothari Commission, it could have laid a sound foundation ensuring free and universal education through a common school system. Instead, it allowed and even encouraged the multi-layered education system, with its multiple providers that had existed since colonial times to grow further to its vulgar form after 1991.

The era of privatisation

The new National Policy on Education that was announced in 1986 made an ideological departure from the earlier approach to education. Instead of strengthening the common school system under the government, it introduced the elitist Navodaya schools, spending huge amounts on select schools and starving the general school system. Thus, it directly reinforced privatisation and elitism in school education and cleared the way in exposing the citadels of higher education to market forces. The central government gradually increased its contribution to the funding of elementary education, all the while decreasing its share in overall education expenditure from 80 per cent in 1983 to 67 per cent in 1999. As a result, the share of higher education in the total expenditure on education declined during 1982–92 from 12.2 per cent to 11.4 per cent for the states, and more dramatically, from 36.2 to 23.3 per cent for the centre. In effect, the government created space for private investment in higher education, leading to the mushrooming of private shops—that would grow into veritable empires—in the garb of educational institutes vending the much-in-demand professional courses. In 1970, India had a total of 139 engineering institutes, and only four of them were private. By the end of 2000, the number of engineering institutes rose to nearly 1,400 out of which only 200 or so belonged to the government. In 2011–12, their number reached 3,393 with a student intake of 1,485,894. Since then, every year, the All India Council for Technical Education has ordered progressive closure (no further admissions allowed) of around 600 private engineering colleges across the country, because of the low quality of teaching and less than 30 per cent intake. Confirming this trend, the *Indian Express* featured a series of reports in December 2017 on India's comatose engineering colleges, and concluded: 'Of the 15.5 lakh BE/BTech seats in 3,291 engineering colleges across the country, over half—51 per cent—were vacant in 2016–17, according to data obtained from the AICTE' (13 December 2017). It also reported that 153 engineering colleges have had over 70 per cent vacant seats in the last five years. Seen against the lack of subsidised higher education opportunities for India's poorest students, the wastefulness in pursuit of profit is of a criminal scale.

The globalisation of the economy has, in terms of its impact on education, matched the recurring pattern of social exclusion highlighted so far. After India formally embraced these neoliberal economic reforms in 1991, the entire conceptual framework of education, particularly higher education, underwent changes with the influx of a market ethos. Higher education became a service to be bought by students as consumers in order to become employable by the corporate sector. A university was no more a formative experience but a service provider, like a shopping mall. There have been concerted attempts towards making higher education self-financing—i.e. non-subsidised, ergo profitable—to increase its attraction as a private investment. For instance, the government appointed two significant committees, the Punnayya Committee (1992–93) that looked into the funding of central universities to recommend how education—especially higher education—should be financed, and the Swaminathan Committee (1994) which looked into possibilities of resource mobilisation in technical education essentially through 'cost recovery' from students. Further down the slippery slope came the Ambani–Birla Report on the Policy Framework for Reforms in Education (April 2000) which, while placing the obligation to provide primary education solely on the government, advocated the privatisation and total marketisation of higher education. It also recommended permitting foreign direct investment to supplement indigenous private resources. Under the alibi of providing financial assistance to the poor strata, it proposed access to private credit in the form of student loans. It is striking how the recommendations of this report conform to the content of the World Bank document, "Higher Education: The Lessons of Experience" (1994). The paper argued, 'higher education should not have the highest priority claim on incremental public resources available for education in many developing countries … because the social rates of return on investments in primary and secondary education usually exceeds the returns on higher education' (World Bank 1994, 3). Although the government has since scaled up self-financing through substantial hikes in fees, it was not politically feasible to completely dismantle the state financing of higher education. These moves, however, did prepare the ground for offering up higher education to the World Trade Organisation under the General Agreement on Trade in Services in 2005. Once the current Doha round is concluded, this will automatically turn into an irreversible commitment.

In preparation, the UPA government in its second term (2009–14) put up various bills—(i) The foreign Educational Institutions (Regulation of Entry and Operations) Bill, 2010, (ii) The Educational Tribunals Bill, 2010, (iii) The Prohibition of Unfair Practices in Technical Educational Institutions, Medical Educational Institution and Universities Bill, 2010, (iv) The National Accreditation Regulatory Authority for Higher Educational Institutions Bill, 2010 and (v) the Higher Education and Research Bill, 2011. The intent of all these bills was to transform higher education into a free market with a regulator, not very dissimilar to the capital market regulator, Securities and Exchange Board of India (SEBI), or any of the other regulatory authorities instituted for various industries. The government, however, failed to get these bills passed in the Rajya Sabha and hence resorted to its pet ploy of bypassing the parliament to launch a Rashtriya Uchchatar Shiksha Abhiyan in September 2013, undermining the University Grants Commission (UGC) and promoting public–private partnership. A choice-based credit system and common syllabus were some of the initiatives to facilitate the entry of prospective foreign players. It envisaged the creation of new infrastructure through corporate investment in higher education. Right from the adoption of neoliberal reforms, the drive of the government towards privatising higher education has been clear.

The eternal argument for the participation of private capital in higher education—coming down from colonial times through the postcolonial decades—has been that there were not enough public resources. The government, that as per the admission of Bibek Debroy, chairman of the prime minister's Economic Advisory Council, that gave away Rs 50 lakh crores to corporations over a the twelve-year period between 2004–05 and 2015–16 as tax concessions (in excess of $100 billion by the exchange rate of the time) now pleads a lack of resources for education! Right from the colonial period, what the government needed was always political will and not resources. To this lame excuse was added the more spurious argument that publicly-funded higher education was of poor quality. As a matter of fact, it could be empirically established that whatever islands of excellence (Indian Institutes of Technology, Indian Institutes of Management, National Institutes of Technology, All India Institute of Medical Sciences, Jawaharlal Nehru University and so on) existed in the sphere of higher education in India belonged to the public sector, not the private one. This lie was propagated assiduously, and taken as true. The state and its princes of capital have worked in tandem to promote this view. A dead giveaway is that the framework of educational reforms should be proposed by two czars of private capital—Ambani and Birla. In 2008, a High Level Group of the Planning Commission on the Services Sector headed by Anwarul Hoda (then member of the Planning Commission), recommended expansion through the growth of for-profit educational institutes, in clear contravention of the constitutional position. In this series also appeared the Planning Commission-appointed Narayana Murthy Committee (headed by the founder of Infosys), to develop a framework which will bring corporate funding into the domestic higher education sector. Expectedly, the committee, while showing concern for the poor quality of higher education, tended to treat higher educational institutions as an investment magnet or Special Economic Zone. For instance, one of its recommendations to the government was: 'Path-breaking measures like free land for 999 years, 300 per cent deduction in taxable income to companies for contributions towards boosting higher education and 10-year multiple entry visas for foreign research scholars.' As Binay Kumar Pathak wrote in the *Economic and Political Weekly*: 'The Narayana Murthy Committee on Corporate Sector Participation in Higher Education (2012) presents a blossomed tree whose saplings were planted by the Ambani–Birla Report and watered by the National Knowledge Commission (GoI 2007) and HLGSS (GoI 2008)' (18 January 2014, 72). No wonder, in such a pro-capital environment, the private sector has grown to cater to 59 per cent of total enrolments in higher education and is expected to contribute significantly in achieving the target gross enrolment ratio of 30 per cent by 2020–21.

India holds an important place in the global education industry. From just thirty universities and 695 colleges in 1950–51, it had 789 universities and over 37,204 colleges and 11,443 stand-alone institutions in 2014 (as per the All-India Survey on Higher Education, or AISHE, first launched by the Ministry of Human Resource Development in 2010). With more than 260 million students enrolled, it is the third largest higher education system in the world, just after the USA and China. Naturally, the Indian higher education sector has been one of the prime attractions for global capital. Since the adoption of neoliberal policies, successive governments have fabricated justifications through a spate of reports and commissions to leave education to the markets. With over 234 million individuals in the 15–24 age group—equal to the US population (FICCI 2011), this segment, worth over $65 billion a year, and growing at a compound annual growth rate of over 18 per cent, comprises 59.7 per cent of the largely price-inelastic education market. It is rightly considered a 'sunrise sector' for investment—with all the ominous implications of that phrase for the poor.

Knowledge as a public good

The entire neoliberal argument for the privatisation of higher education is built upon the assumption that it is not a public good. A public good is quite narrowly defined in economics as non-rivalrous (this being established through the criterion that one person's use of it does not diminish that of another) and non-exclusionary (not based on keeping people out). Typical textbook examples of public goods are lighthouses and national defence. Wholly public goods like these are scarce; often goods fulfil one of the two criteria, or are public goods in certain cases and not in others, depending upon the mode of usage. For example, a painting in an art gallery is a public good unless restrictions are placed on access to the gallery. This means that while free healthcare is a public good, an exorbitantly expensive private hospital is not.

Is not higher education a public good? Higher education, it is broadly accepted, fulfils four major functions: (1) The development of new knowledge (the research function), (2) The training or the teaching function, (3) The function of providing services to society, and (4) The ethical function, which implies social criticism. The development of new knowledge is non-rivalrous; knowledge is not reduced by being shared. Pythagoras' theorem has been used for over two millennia with no noticeable degradation in its ability to produce accurate answers to trigonometric problems. Is it exclusionary? The confusion on this score may be on account of recent practices. It is well known that private research institutes do not share their research. They ask their researchers to sign confidentiality agreements. Similarly, research commissioned by military agencies is closely guarded by the states concerned. These practices make knowledge appear exclusionary. In the WTO, Part 2.7 of the Trade Related Aspects of Intellectual Property

Rights Agreement deals with the protection of undisclosed information enforced through the dispute settlement panel of the body. So, there are legal means in both domestic and international law for excluding access to knowledge and it is also possible to restrict access by not publishing new research. However, there are simultaneous trends such as the open source movement, proving that knowledge grows rapidly when it is freed. The fact is, even the knowledge that is artificially restricted has grown out of knowledge that was public. All the taught content of higher education courses are the fruit of previous research. If research is a private good in the sense of exclusivity, what would happen to the generation of new knowledge in the future? That the knowledge base is so adversely affected by exclusivity suggests that higher education must be envisaged as a public good in the long term.

As regards the teaching function of higher education, due to the diverse methods of teaching currently in use, and innovations such as distance learning methods, it is difficult to make the case that teaching in higher education is purely rivalrous or exclusionary. The student's contact with the teacher does not degrade the teacher's ability to teach, it is indeed necessary to the teacher's existence, so the cooperative aspect of a public good certainly holds for teaching. Exclusivity has, however, been practiced by the ruling classes in every society. In India, until colonial times, shudras and dalits were excluded from accessing education on the principle that knowledge itself, along with its traditional providers and recipients, would be defiled by contact with the 'lower' castes. The Greeks had similarly excluded the sons of slaves and madmen from education. And both societies excluded women. However, in recent times, the idea that education is a right has come to be widely held and is inscribed in the Universal Declaration of Human Rights. There is a strong link between treating higher education as a public good and its status as a human right, a link that will be compromised if market based or other discriminatory mechanisms are allowed to operate unimpeded, under the impact of the GATS and cost sharing initiatives.

The function of higher education in providing services to society is realised in terms of increased vibrancy of economic activity, enhanced communication skills, increased tolerance, increasing literacy rates, improved health outcomes, broader participation in democratic processes, reduced crime and poverty rates, environmental sustainability, and social equality. In a recent report, Unesco outlined how education performs much more than an economic function by enabling individuals, especially women, to live and aspire to healthy, meaningful, creative and resilient lives. It strengthens their voices in community, national and global affairs. It opens up new work opportunities and sources of social mobility. As it is not possible to exclude an individual from the benefits of increased participation in democratic processes, these benefits, logically speaking, are non-exclusionary. Non-rivalry is also a property of these 'soft' benefits. In fact, these goods often self-propagate as they are transferred between people interacting in social environments. This aspect of higher education is a mechanism for the provision of the public good.

Higher education performs a very important function of social criticism, which again meets both criteria to be defined as a public good. Social criticism is generated as part of the effects of higher education: a democratisation that is inferred from the self-critical method of analysis used in academic discourse and learning methods. Where higher education becomes the preserve of limited agents and is localised in nepotistic centres, the resultant mode of social criticism serves the interests of those who have access to higher education; its ideology is status quo-ist—to perpetuate and reinforce inequalities. This is what happened in India when education was confined to the brahminical castes. No sooner was it opened up to the subordinated castes than the anti-caste movements began. Social criticism expressed in a democracy is not an exclusionary practice: it adds a voice to the debate or a vote to the mass. The benefits may be limited in impact but are widely diffused in effect, which is something that the government needs to take cognisance of. Where every member of a democracy has an equal vote, criticism cannot be invidious. Social criticism in liberal democracies is generally recognised as conducive to the shared good and ought to be treated as such.

Exclusion from access to higher education or mechanisms that create a bottleneck to free access—such as entry requirements, tuition fees and intellectual property protection—are examples of the kind of failure evidenced when public goods are provided through market mechanisms. The current commercialisation of higher education is therefore unacceptable. It is akin to a for-profit provision of lighthouses that emit light outside of the visible frequency, and charge subscriptions to certain ships that can afford expensive detectors. Recent policy developments in international organisations such as the World Bank (cost sharing) the alphabet soup of the WTO (GATS and TRIPS), and the policies of governments under their spell to make higher education something to be bought for a price, are a method of propagating inequality and creating exclusive power centres. Understanding higher education as a public good is not an act of rhetoric or posturing but is part of a deeper social movement. This movement is concerned with promoting equality of opportunity and social mobility rather than merely equity and parity of treatment.

Education as business

The worldwide spending on education was estimated in 2004 by the Portuguese sociologist, Boaventura de Sousa Santos, at around 2,000 billion dollars, more than the global automotive sales. Santos also observed an exponential growth in capital investment in education, attracted by one of the highest rates of return. Santos furnished figures: £1,000 invested in 1996 generated £3,405 four years later; yielding a return of 240.5 per cent as against the average rate of just 65 per cent in the London Stock Exchange over the same period.

In the world education market, India holds the greatest potential.

With an expected median age of 29 years for the entire population by 2020—compared to a projected 37 for China—India has today over 550 million people below the age of 25 years. Further, over 32 per cent of India's population is in the age group of 0–14 years. This means that the number of people in India needing primary and secondary education alone exceeds the entire population of the USA. Since these students will be seeking higher education over the next decade, it illustrates the sheer potential of the Indian education market. Presently, about eleven million students are in the higher education system. This represents just 11 per cent of the 17–23 year old population. If this is to increase to 30 per cent by 2020, as the government optimistically hopes it will, huge investment would be needed in the higher education sector. According to the UGC's annual report of 2014–15, the Indian education market is expected to reach a worth of US $144 billion by 2020 from US $97.8 billion in 2016. Already the second largest market for e-learning after the US (pegged at US $2 billion in 2016 and expected to reach US $5.7 billion by 2020), the distance education market in India is expected to grow at a CAGR of around 11 per cent in the period 2016–20. The total amount of FDI inflow into the education sector from April 2000 to March 2017 stood at US $1.42 billion, according to data released by the Department of Industrial Policy and Promotion. A study conducted by the Association of Indian Universities revealed an upswing in the number of foreign education providers in India, from 144 in 2000 to 631 in 2010. Of these, 440 did so from their home campuses, 186 were operating mostly with a concept of 'twinning' (joint ventures and academic collaboration with Indian universities). Many of these twinning arrangements did not have the required approvals according to UGC Regulations.

The much-touted Yash Pal Committee, constituted in February 2008 to suggest ways of rejuvenating and reorienting higher education, provided sought after legitimacy to the agenda of neoliberal capital. Because its argument for encouraging the role of private capital in higher education is studded with progressive-sounding pronouncements about autonomy and features the latest jargon—beloved of pedagogy—the document has drawn compliments from many sectors—for instance the left-leaning *Social Scientist* in an editorial (Vol. 38, No. 9/12, September–December 2010), while taking a critical view of the overall neoliberal trend in education, said the 'only exception is the Yash Pal Committee'. The report of the former chairman of the UGC deliberates on the character of universities, defines their role as centres of knowledge creation, calls for ending the divide across disciplines and asserts the need for interdisciplinarity. The committee expresses deep concern over the 'cubicalisation' of knowledge, sees the intention of profit making through education as problematic, but also believes that 'it will be necessary to encourage participation of the private sector' and argues that foreign universities should be allowed to set up shop here in India. The report talks about the need to (1) constantly update knowledge, (2) allow some autonomy to teachers, (3) make courses job oriented and university education relevant to the needs of the market, (4) consider the market as a significant determinant of what to teach and what not to teach, and (5) centralise the functioning of the university system. It discusses autonomy for teachers and researchers to create knowledge, while in the same breath proposing an increased role for the market—as if these were not contradictory in spirit. While the government claims to follow the report when it comes to privatisation of higher education and imposing a centralised and highly structured body of regulation and management (through the pending Bill for the National Commission for Higher Education and Research), it would define autonomy solely in terms of asking institutions to manage their own finances and be less reliant on the state.

The care after the abuse

Curiously, the neoliberal establishment resolved that the government should take on the responsibility of providing elementary education to its populace. The logic is to endow all with a certain minimum level of education so as to ensure their participation in the market. 135 countries have provided for this minimal education by enshrining the right to education in their statutes. The Constitution of India too had envisaged it but, as noted, relegated it to a non-justiciable category. The National Policy on Education, 1968, had stressed education's 'unique significance for national development' but the first official recommendation for the inclusion of education into the fundamental rights was made in 1990 by the Acharya Ramamurti Committee. Thereafter, several political as well as policy level changes influenced the course of free and compulsory education. The country witnessed an increased international focus on its initiatives after its participation in the World Conference on Education for All in 1990. India also ratified the United Nations Convention on the Rights of the Child in 1992. The Supreme Court first recognised the right to education as a fundamental right in *Mohini Jain vs. State of Karnataka* (1992). It was observed in this judgement that:

> 'Right to life' is the compendious expression for all those rights which the courts must enforce because they are basic to the dignified enjoyment of life. It extends to the full range of conduct which the individual is free to pursue. The right to education flows directly from the right to life. The right to life under Article 21 and the dignity of an individual cannot be assured unless it is accompanied by the right to education.

In another case a year later, *J.P. Unni Krishnan vs. State of Andhra Pradesh*, the Supreme Court narrowed the ambit of the fundamental right to education as propounded in the Mohini Jain case. The court observed that Article 45 in Part IV of the Constitution must be read in 'harmonious construction' with Article 21 (Right to Life) in Part III, and concluded that the state was indeed duty bound to provide every citizen free education up to the age of fourteen, and only thereafter could its finances constrain the availability of further education.

This judicial interpretation shook up the government and it appointed the Saikia Committee in 1997 to advise a course of compliance. The committee recommended that the 'Constitution of India should be amended to make the right to free elementary education up to fourteen years of age, a fundamental right.' Finally, in December 2002, the eighty-sixth amendment to the Constitution was passed with the BJP-led National Democratic Alliance government inserting a new article, 21A, which made education a fundamental right. For the first time since the promulgation of the Constitution, a fundamental right had been added to it. Unlike other fundamental rights, however, the right to education required an enabling legislation to make it effective. Restricting it to children in the age group of 6–14 years effectively denied the right to education to 170 million children under the age of six. They were left with the misty promise of Article 45: 'The State shall endeavour to provide early childhood care and education for all children until they complete the age of six years.' The upper limit of 14 years for coverage under the right can also be questioned. As a signatory to the UN Child Rights Convention, India has accepted the international definition of a child, which is any person below the age of 18. By covering only children from age 6 to 14, India clearly violates the rights of the 0–6 and 14–18 year olds. The wording of this purported fundamental right, viz. Article 21A, is also intriguing as it provides enough leeway to the state to slip out of any obligation whatsoever. It says: 'the State shall provide free and compulsory education to all children of the age of 6 to 14 years in such manner as the State may, by law, determine.' It took another seven years after the eighty-sixth amendment and sixteen years from the passing of the Unni Krishnan judgement before the Right to Education Act was passed in 2009 by the Congress-led UPA government.

While neoliberalism appeared to spare the elementary sector from the claws of the market, unaddressed fiscal constraints regularly force state schools to make way for private capital. Ever since the 1990s, when the World Bank-sponsored District Primary Education Programme deployed the cost-cutting strategy of providing schooling through education guarantee centres and untrained para-teachers, the quality of government schools began to collapse. The dilution of standards was taken further in many states of the country by the Sarva Shiksha Abhiyan. It variegated the government schooling system with a multi-layered range extending from rundown rural or basti schools to the Kendriya, Sarvodaya, or Navodaya schools, thus replicating social inequalities at the very foundational stage of education. Obviously, access to these differently provisioned schools is determined by the social and class background of children, segregating them further.

In addition to establishing these unequal layers of government schools, private schools were left untouched. The RTE Act provided for a minimum of 25 per cent free seats for children belonging to disadvantaged groups—or economically weaker sections in officialese—in all private unaided primary schools. In India, the term 'reservations' has attained a magical power to beguile those for whom it is supposedly meant and annoy those for whom it is not. The provision is just eyewash. According to the District Information System for Education statistics for 2010–11, 75.51 per cent of all schools are government schools with a 61.32 per cent share in total enrolment, making the government the major provider of education. 78.76 per cent of the private schools are unaided schools with an estimated enrolment share of 27.22 per cent. A large number of these unaided schools is minority institutions and therefore exempt from the application of the RTE as per Articles 29 and 30 of the Constitution. Only the balance of non-minority unaided schools are subject to this reservation. The enrolment in the age group of 6–14 years is about 200 million, whereas even if we neglect to exclude the minority schools, the entire unaided school enrolment works out to 54 million. Assuming these unaided private schools have the capacity to absorb an extra 25 per cent enrolment under reservations (an utterly wishful assumption), it works out to 14 million, which is just 7 per cent of the total student population. What is to become of the balance 93 per cent or 186 million students? They will continue to receive education through an unequally provisioned, multi-layered school system with each social segment in a separate layer, the much-acclaimed norms and standards of the bill's schedule notwithstanding. Anil Sadgopal (2008) indicates a hidden political agenda in this 25 per cent provision. 'Whenever the government sets up high profile elite schools—the centrally sponsored Kendriya or Navodaya Vidyalayas and the Eleventh Plan's 6,000 model schools, or the state governments' Pratibha Vidyalayas (Delhi), Utkrishta Vidyalayas (Madhya Pradesh) or residential schools (Andhra Pradesh)—the regular schools are deprived of funds and good teachers alike.' It was a sop, as he termed it, meant to divert political attention away from the ongoing struggle for education of equitable quality through a common school system.

The Act can be faulted on many other operational counts—it does not touch upon the stratified and discriminatory educational system that has evolved in the country. It pays no attention to poor quality education. It tolerates the replacement of a permanent cadre of trained teachers by unqualified, ill-trained and ill-paid para-teachers working on a contractual basis. It legitimises the discriminatory practice of burdening teachers in government schools with election/census/disaster duties, unlike teachers in private schools. It legitimises the freedom of private schools to charge any fee they please. (The bill seems to provide safeguards against a capitation fee but this can well be made up in other fees without being identified as such.) The provision against the screening of parents by schools, provided by the Act, is a rhetorical gesture since the financial ability to pay fees becomes a proxy to screen parents. Pre-primary education is recognised as a crucial aspect of a child's development, while being structurally deleted from the government's obligations. This sector, arguably the most lucrative, thus surrendered to private players. The Act provides that no child will be evaluated as 'failed' up till the eighth standard. Without guaranteeing the quality of education, all it accomplishes is deferring a mass drop out till the eighth standard. The Act is completely silent on the things that really matter: teacher effort, teacher accountability and student learning outcomes. If the RTE Act showcases anything, it is how the government could expertly transform the crisis created by the Supreme Court judgement into an opportunity to push its neoliberal agenda.

Over the years, falling standards in government schools led to the mushrooming of budget (low fee) private schools not only in urban areas but also in rural settings. According to the Annual Status of Education Reports, the enrolment in private schools in rural India has increased from about 19 per cent in 2006 to approximately 31 per cent in 2014. At the national level, in a five year period from 2007 to 2012, the enrolment in private elementary schools has increased from around 28 per cent to nearly 35 per cent. Thus, the RTE Act has become another expression of the government's reliance on private schools to deliver elementary education to about 50 per cent of children in the country (31 per cent of rural and up to 80 per cent of urban children). If private schools did not exist, the entire financial burden of providing elementary education would fall on the government, in whose schools the per-pupil cost is up to 20 times higher than low-fee private schools. The majority of these schools, though poorly resourced, claim better learning outcomes. With the increasing presence of affordable private schools, gullible parents in low-income communities prefer them for their sons and daughters, reducing many government schools to low enrolment. This exodus provides a fig leaf to the government's retrenchment from the sector. As of 2015–16, at least 187,006 primary schools (Class I–V) and 62,988 upper primary (Class VI–VIII) schools were running with fewer than thirty students. Besides, 7,166 schools had zero enrolment. Some 87,000 schools have a single teacher each.

Overall, the numbers indicate the poor state of small schools in India and the proposed 'rationalisation' targets all these schools.

India lacks 1.2 million teachers—including regular, trained and qualified tutors—in government schools across the country. With the RTE Act, instead of improving the standards of these schools, the government began closing them down under the pretext of rationalisation. We are in the absurd situation of seeing school facilities withdrawn in the aftermath of the universalisation of education as a right: more than 100,000 schools across the country were closed in the first five years after the implementation of the RTE Act. The entire school system is being pushed towards the public–private partnership model. The PPP model serves the objective of securing privatisation without public resistance. It allows the state to feign concern for the development of the downtrodden but plead lack of resources. The main selling proposition beyond the paucity of resources is the claim that the private sector is intrinsically efficient. PPP has been popular with rulers all over the world as a quid pro quo arrangement facilitating the transfer of huge volumes of public resources into private hands with contractual sieves that leak significant benefits back to officialdom. Naturally then, PPP has become the default vehicle for most infrastructural projects in recent years. In India, PPP first appeared in the election manifesto of the BJP/NDA in 1999. The following year, the NDA government formed a committee in the office of prime minister Atal Bihari Vajpayee (but later moved to the Planning Commission) to apply the PPP model in various fields. In 2004, when the Congress-led UPA came to power, the same committee continued to function and submitted its report to prime minister Manmohan Singh. In September 2007, Manmohan Singh, while presiding over a meeting of the Planning Commission, declared that initiatives at all levels of education shall be made through PPP. Since then, in the Eleventh and Twelfth Five-Year Plans (2007–17), there has been a rush among corporate houses, NGOs and religious organisations to grab public assets in the educational system.

At the beginning of 2013, the Brihanmumbai Municipal Corporation decided to hand over its schools to private parties, this within the framework of the much-flaunted PPP scheme of 'School Adoption'. On 23 January, it was announced that the schools would be auctioned to well-established corporate houses that would enter into memoranda of understanding (MoUs) with entities recognised for their work in the 'technical or educational field.' The process would be managed under the existing MoU between the United Nations Children's Fund and the BMC for conducting the 'School Enhancement Programme' (initiated by Unicef and McKinsey & Company since 2009, and having NGOs such as Akanksha, Aseema and Nandi Foundation on board). Neither did the BMC provide any reasons for its failure to impart quality education, nor any justification for its assumption that a private partner would be able to accomplish what it could not despite its experience of more than 125 years. It did not even take into account the evidence available through its own experience of having one of its schools run by an NGO. In the Cotton Green area of Mumbai, a school run by Akanksha—an NGO important enough to be on the Board of the School Enhancement Programme—was found to have only one qualified teacher to teach classes one to eight. It basically drew teachers from its Teach India Project, under which employees of companies took a sabbatical to teach in schools. Perhaps it was not politically convenient to pursue this matter; it was dropped.

The BMC, the richest municipal corporation in India, provides free education in eight languages—Marathi, Hindi, English, Urdu, Gujarati, Kannada, Telugu, and Tamil—to nearly 400,000 children enrolled in around 1,174 schools with 11,500 teachers, and spends around 8 to 9 per cent of its income on education, a figure that has increased steadily over the years. In 2011–12, its annual per capita spending of Rs 36,750 was among the highest in the country. However, the number of students attending BMC schools has been falling. It fell from 439,153 in 2011–12 to 383,485 in 2015–16—a steep drop of around 13 per cent. This is the trend in government/municipal schools all over the country: one that favours English-medium schools under the misapprehension that neoliberalism fosters free competition and private schooling is better than public to make a child competitive. It is not as if these private schools offered pedagogical practices designed to help the poor fare better in a higher education market driven by entrance exams. The focus of such exams is on rote-learning anyway. The desire to be a part of an idealised image of Western-style modernity makes the poor spend way beyond their means on institutions whose efficacy they cannot judge, just to ensure their children have a chance at a better life than their own. Ambarish Rai, national convener of the RTE forum, claimed in October 2014 that the government is surrendering assets to private players. He said that the unregulated mushrooming of low-budget private schools and PPP model-based schools are other mechanisms diluting the spirit of the legal mandate. After analysing the proposal to set up 2,500 model schools in the PPP mode under the Eleventh Plan, J.B.G. Tilak of the National University of Educational Planning and Administration, New Delhi, concluded that notwithstanding the claim that PPP is not privatisation or promotion of the profit motive, the plan is sure to promote exactly that—privatisation and a high degree of commercialisation, albeit with one difference, the utilization of public funds (*Hindu*, 24 May 2010).

Then there is the perennial dissembling plea—since Macaulay's days—of the lack of resources for education. The postcolonial government also used it to deny education as a fundamental right. Today, India flexes its economic muscle and finds billions to lavish on its military, but continues to be among the countries that figure at the bottom with regard to public expenditure on education. According to the World Bank, the world on average spent 4.9 per cent of its GDP on education in 2012, but India's share was just 3.3 per cent. It is the lowest spender on education among the BRICS countries (Brazil, 5.8 per cent, Russia, 4.1 per cent, China, 4 per cent, and South Africa,

6 per cent). While India apologetically carries on with the excuse of lacking resources, during the neoliberal period the state has used it to justify opening the sector to global capital in conformity with the Washington Consensus. The National Knowledge Commission (final report 2006–09) estimated that India needed an investment of about $190 billion to achieve the target of a 30 per cent gross enrolment ratio in higher education by 2020 and expectedly advised that it be met through foreign direct investment as the government lacks resources.

Health and education must command top priority in any democratic country. They are the basic ingredients for the development of the demos—the people—and in turn, the prime determinants of democracy itself. The ignorance of the masses has been the greatest insurance for the ruling classes of all times. India's ruling classes had devised the intricate contrivance of a caste system to shut the doors of education to the majority of its population, and it held until the colonial period. It is only during the last two centuries that these doors were opened. However, the alibi of scarce resources meant that the majority of people were still locked out. India flaunts an abundance of social justice schemes for its disadvantaged strata which disguise the fact that the primary ingredients of healthcare and education are missing. While the injustices done to past generations can in no way be corrected or recompensed, the chain of continuing injustice can be effectively snapped if India ensures its entire population gets equal quality education. There may not be any need, then, for the elaborate structure of so-called social justice measures that merely sustain the humiliation of the present generation.

The way out of the mess of education created over millennia lies in simply nationalising the entire school system—to convert it to a common school system based on neighbourhood schools. Make education completely free and compulsory up to the age of 18, when a student is expected to have acquired the basic wherewithal for transiting to responsible citizenship. These are not at all outlandish measures.

In fact, they are in some ways embedded in India's constitutional vision or agreed to by the country through international covenants. Further, ensure that every child that comes into the world is healthy, which means providing pre-natal care to all pregnant women. If all children are provided with the same educational inputs right from the beginning, irrespective of their parents' background, many of the chronic problems (like caste) that afflict India may be halfway overcome right there. It may sound simplistic to many, especially to those who have developed a vested interest in amplifying problems, but all potent solutions to vexatious problems have a tinge of simplicity. If equality is to be meaningfully pursued as a constitutional commitment, we cannot lose sight of the fact that the least unequal societies of the world today, such as Denmark and Norway, are those where education and healthcare are almost entirely the province and responsibility of the state. With this foundation in place, higher education can also be suitably rationalised and restructured to abolish the elitism associated with it. India has all the resources to do this, what it has lacked so far is the political will.

10

No Swachh Bharat
without Annihilation of Caste

On 13 April 2016, the 125-day all-India Bhim Yatra ended on the eve of the 125th birth celebrations of Dr B.R. Ambedkar. The yatra highlighted the pitiable conditions of the most crushed among the dalits—the manual scavengers, whose caste vocation is the removal of 'night soil'. Using a broom, a tin plate and a drum, they clear and carry human excreta from toilets, often on their heads, to dumping grounds and disposal sites. They are exposed to the most virulent forms of viral and bacterial infections that affect the skin, eyes, limbs, respiratory and gastrointestinal systems. Dalits who work as manual scavengers marched 3,500 km across 500 districts in 29 states, under the banner of the Safai Karamchari Andolan—starting from Dibrugarh in Assam on International Human Rights Day, 10 December 2015, travelling to Jammu and Kashmir, and then all the way to Kanyakumari—to conclude their yatra at the Jantar Mantar in New Delhi. Their slogan, "Stop Killing Us", referred to the deaths of more than 22,000 sanitation workers every year caused by their lethal work environment. Studiously ignored all the way by the corporate media, the yatra began with a whimper and ended with another. With tears flowing down their cheeks and in choking voices, several children narrated horrific tales of loved ones dying from the noxious hazards their job exposed them to. Their stories reveal a terrible paradox—while Ambedkar is lionised as a super icon by the state, the people he lived and fought for have to implore the state for the recognition of their humanity and dignity.

There is little doubt that India stands out in the world as a uniquely unclean country. A 2014 report jointly prepared by the WHO and the Unicef says 597 million people practice open defecation in India (reported in the *Hindu*, 9 May 2014). There is no official index of uncleanliness to compare countries. There are rankings for cleanliness but they seem to be based on the cleanliness of the environment, which may not reflect the culture of uncleanliness that afflicts India. Nevertheless, few may dispute the ubiquity of filth that is unique to India. This state of affairs is uncritically attributed to poverty, as if the link between poverty and filth were self-evident. The correlation is untenable. While poverty—individual or collective—does result in the lack of basic sanitation infrastructure and operational wherewithal to maintain cleanliness, whether at the level of the household or the country, there are countries poorer than India that do not look as filthy. Of the fifty-three countries with a lower per capita GDP than India, forty-six have lower levels of open defecation. Even among the South Asian countries, India ranks the worst in cleanliness in terms of the percentage of people who defecate in the open.[1] By 2006, 96 per cent of Bangladeshis were using latrines. To compare their economic status with that of Indians, the same year saw 52 per cent of the poorest Bangladeshi households had dirt floors and no electricity, whereas the figure was 21 per cent for India. However, to this day, with half the world's open defecation takes place in rural India. According to

[1] Unless otherwise stated, the data on toilet use cited in this chapter is drawn from Diane Coffey and Dean Spears' *Where India Goes: Abandoned Toilets, Stunted Development and the Costs of Caste* (2017).

the 2011 census, 70 per cent of rural households in this country lack a latrine.

There is no denying that the poor have to labour in conditions of filth. As landless labourers, they work in muddy fields, and as non-farm workers in the construction or extraction industries, they live and work in a still more unsanitary environment. Yet, they attempt to maintain a functional cleanliness. The poor obviously cannot have the kind of cleanliness identified with the rich, but there exists an awareness of the importance of hygiene and cleanliness. One can easily see this in the homesteads of the poorest of the poor in the villages and tribal hamlets. Even in urban slums, this is largely true. The reason behind this is innate economic sense: they simply cannot afford falling ill from a lack of hygiene and cleanliness. Filth is produced in the civic realm due to the lack of civic sense, a function of culture. And it is the rich who disproportionately contribute to it, quite like how rich countries are the worst offenders in the emission of greenhouse gases.

It is nothing but caste-culture—which is inimical to having in-house toilets—that explains the uniquely enduring practices of uncleanliness in India. A culture based so strongly on ideas of ritual purity that it resists both, access to toilets and the evidence of disease as backed by research. This means the solution is not a simple matter of constructing toilets. A nation-wide rapid survey conducted during May–June 2015 concurrently with the seventy-second round of the National Sample Survey, estimated that 52.1 per cent of people in rural India choose open defecation compared to 7.5 per cent in urban India (*Hindu*, 21 April 2016). The India Human Development Survey of 2012 found that 32 per cent of rural households in which the education of at least one member ran to a graduate degree, continued to practice open defecation. In Bangladesh, this obtains among only 1 per cent of households with an equivalent level of education. Why this enormous gap? The answer surely lies in the concept of ritual purity, with its locus in the household kitchen and shrine to the gods—sites of heightened purity in the ritualistic if not germological sense—and culturally ingrained values that recoil against 'unclean' functions sharing a roof with those deemed pure. Within India, the North-East with its relatively low income levels and the Muslim community with its widespread poverty evince lower levels of open defecation than that across the Hindi heartland. Further, the 2014 SQUAT (Sanitation Quality, Use, Access and Trends) survey analysed data from rural areas in thirteen districts of Bihar, Uttar Pradesh, Rajasthan, Haryana and Madhya Pradesh—the five states that account for 30 per cent of the world's open defecation—and revealed that over 40 per cent of households equipped with a functional latrine had members who continued to defecate in the open.

Indian culture assigns the responsibility of maintaining cleanliness to a particular caste. It stigmatises sanitation work as unclean and sanitation workers as untouchables. More than untouchability, a caste ethos is pervasively reflected in the behaviour of Indians. This ethos, which effectively 'casteises' and genders various tasks, persists despite the spread of education, urbanisation and globalisation.

In respect to cleanliness, the caste culture manifests itself in several ways. Cleanliness in this culture is personal and ritual in character; it does not have a civic component. Therefore, even people who are sticklers for personal hygiene would not mind making their surroundings unclean. This mindset shows in the commonplace behaviour in offices that people would wait for their tables to be cleaned by a peon. They would not clean them lest it lower their status. The world over, people have imbibed a 'civic sense' and bear the primary responsibility to maintain cleanliness, only secondarily relying upon sanitation workers. In India, people of the privileged castes evince a sense of superiority and entitlement in littering the place, knowing that there's always some untouchable scavenger to whom caste offers no privilege but only disabilities, who would clean up after them. Hence, the very function of clearing away filth has acquired an associative stigma that would attach to anyone performing it. So long as this small community of scavengers—treated worse than shit and exploited to the hilt—is charged with the responsibility of clearing the filth generated with impunity by 1,250 million people, the country is destined to remain unclean.

Another section of society that contributes to the cleanliness of the country in an equally thankless way is that of the ragpickers, whose population is estimated at between 1.5 million and four million. Collecting, sorting and segregating waste, they trade their daily collection for small sums of money that barely sustain their livelihood. In doing so, they help clean up a significant proportion of the 62 million tonnes of waste generated annually in India, according to an estimate of the union environment ministry. Of this, plastic waste accounts for 5.6 million tonnes, hazardous waste another 7.9 million tonnes and e-waste 1.5 million tonnes. The per capita waste generation in Indian cities ranges from 200 grams to 600 grams per day. The ministry estimates waste generation will increase from 62 million tonnes to about 165 million tonnes in 2030. Unlike scavengers of excreta—to whom alone the term 'manual scavengers' is applied in India—the ragpickers are not necessarily from any particular caste; but given the economic structure of society, most of them come from migrant communities of dalits, OBCs or the religious minorities. Many countries have recognised the socially beneficial service of this occupation and granted rights to ragpickers. For instance, in Bogota, Colombia, every ragpicker is paid $2 per day by the municipality. In Brazil, the government has made sure that only the ragpicker can collect waste (at source). In India, although their contribution is relatively more than in any other country, they do not have any rights or protection. In 2015, the government announced that they would give three best ragpickers and three associations following best practices, a national award worth Rs 150,000 for their efforts to keep India clean. Even this bizarre proposition has seen no action since. Meanwhile, just like the sewer workers, this section of the workforce continues to make its invaluable contribution to public sanitation and goes about its hazardous occupation without legal or physical protection.

The national ragpicker awards and their fate bespeak more than mere callousness. The government's profound ignorance in the matter of solid waste management is simply the exercise of a trademark 'upper' caste prerogative: its supercilious disregard for a low-prestige occupation like physical sanitation which pervades state and society alike. On 6 February 2018, the Supreme Court caught the government napping when it emerged that the centre was in no position to inform the court of the composition of state-level advisory boards as mandated by the provisions of the Solid Waste Management Rules, 2016. An 845-page affidavit on the subject submitted by the centre was found to be incomplete—lacking data from several states—and was summarily rejected when the government's counsel could not answer the court's questions on it. Then came some stinging censure of the executive, from a bench comprising Justices Madan B. Lokur and Deepak Gupta: 'Whatever junk you have, you dump it before us. We are not garbage collectors. Be absolutely clear about this' (*Times of India*, 7 February 2018). When the government's indifference to waste management and the Supreme Court's rebuke to it both hold the workforce in similar contempt, it is probably safe to say that the difference between the institutions is not one of mindset.

Pervasive hypocrisy

The Constitution abolished untouchability but did nothing to change the conditions that produce it. The safai karamcharis, accounting for about 10 per cent of the total dalit population, suffer untouchability of the worst kind. The minuscule community of scavengers is hopelessly fragmented, ghettoised at every locale, detached not only from the larger society but even the dalit community. They are untouchables to caste Hindus and other dalits alike. Gandhi, notwithstanding his regressive views on the institution of caste, had identified bhangi (the caste that is associated with manual scavenging) as the representative of dalits and posed as one himself—a self-annointed bhangi—to make his point. He set up the Harijan Sevak Sangh in 1932 (which, incidentally, excluded untouchables) and began the publication of *Harijan* to propagate his patronising views on the matter, which included: 'A bhangi does for society what a mother does for her baby. A mother washes her baby of the dirt and ensures his health. Even so the bhangi protects and safeguards the health of the entire community by maintaining sanitation for it.' Ambedkar was critical of the hollow symbolism of Gandhi's actions, arguing that it merely encouraged the perpetuation of a dehumanising practice—he considered Gandhi's exploits to be 'killing untouchables with kindness'. While it was imperative that a secular state give priority to outlawing this dehumanising work and to rehabilitating the people engaged in it, Gandhi's rhetorical pieties made it possible for the state to dodge the issue with its pet strategy of establishing committees and commissions which, while exhibiting concern about manual scavenging, also deferred banning the practice with a stringent law till forty-six years after independence.

Political games on this issue had begun as early as 1949 and continue till date. In 1949, the then government of Bombay appointed a committee, the Scavengers' Living Conditions Enquiry Committee headed by V.N. Barve, to inquire into the living conditions of the scavengers and suggest ways to ameliorate them. The committee submitted its report in 1952. In 1955, the Ministry of Home Affairs circulated a copy of the major recommendations of this committee to all the state governments and asked that they adopt them. However, nothing concrete happened (pun intended), since the committee had not asked for the abolition of dry toilets.

In 1957, the MHA set up a committee headed by N.R. Malkani to prepare a scheme to put an end to the practice of scavenging. The committee submitted its report in 1960; it asked the central and state governments to jointly draw up a phased programme for implementing its recommendations so as to end manual scavenging within the Third

Five Year Plan. Nothing came of these recommendations either.

In 1965, the government appointed another committee under Malkani to look into the matter. The committee recommended the dismantling of the hereditary task structure under which the non-municipal cleaning of private latrines was passed on from generation to generation of scavengers. This report also went into cold storage. In 1968–69, the National Commission on Labour recommended a comprehensive legislation to regulate the working, service and living conditions of scavengers. Predictably, the snarl of committees failed to effectuate any significant reform as they largely recommended ameliorative measures for succeeding committees to assess, and not the abolition of manual scavenging.

During the Gandhi birth centenary year (1969), a special programme for converting dry latrines to flush latrines was undertaken, but it failed at the pilot stage itself. In 1980, the MHA introduced a scheme for the conversion of dry latrines into sanitary latrines and the rehabilitation of liberated scavengers and their dependants in selected towns by employing them in dignified occupations. In 1985, the scheme was transferred from the MHA to the Ministry of Welfare. In 1991, the Planning Commission bifurcated the scheme—the Ministries of Urban Development and Rural Development were made responsible for the conversion of dry latrines and the Ministry of Welfare (renamed Ministry of Social Justice and Empowerment in May 1999) was given the task of rehabilitating scavengers. In 1992, the Ministry of Welfare introduced the National Scheme for Liberation and Rehabilitation of Scavengers and their dependants. Reporting on this issue for the magazine *Frontline* (22 September 2006), Annie Zaidi wrote that an audit of the NSLRS between 1992 and 2002 by the Comptroller and Auditor General said that the Rs 600 crore granted by the centre to the states had 'gone, literally, down the latrine.'

Articles 14 (right to equality), 17 (abolition of untouchability), 21 (protection of life and personal liberty), 23 (prohibition of traffic in human beings and forced labour) and 47 (duty of the state to raise the level of nutrition and the standard of living and to improve public health) of the Constitution can all be seen as predicated upon the abolition of manual scavenging. For instance, Section 7A and 15A of the Protection of Civil Rights Act, 1955, formerly known as the Untouchability (Offences) Act, 1955—enacted to implement Article 17—provided for the liberation of scavengers as well as stipulating punishment for those continuing to engage scavengers. As such, one could argue that there was no need for the Employment of Manual Scavengers and Construction of Dry Latrines (Prohibition) Act, 1993, to abolish manual scavenging. This law was to prove redundant in quite another sense as well. It had received presidential assent on 5 June 1993, but remained unpublished in the Gazette of India until 1997. Furthermore, no state promulgated it until 2000. Irked by the persistent inaction of the government, the Safai Karamchari Andolan—founded by Bezwada Wilson, S.R. Sankaran and Paul Divakar in 1994—along with eighteen other civil society organisations and several persons belonging to the community of manual scavengers, filed a public interest litigation in the Supreme Court in December 2003. Their reason being, as Wilson told *Frontline* (22 September, 2006):

> The law is more like a scheme; it has no teeth. The powers rest with the sanitary inspector or the District Collector, while the worker himself cannot file a case… Workers who clean open gutters, manholes and septic tanks, who are exposed to great risks, are not covered by the Act. Also, though the states have adopted the Act, most have not adopted the rules and regulations along with it.

The PIL called for contempt proceedings against the central and state governments for violation of the Act. Years after its supposed enactment that stipulates 'imprisonment up to a year and fines up to Rs 2,000 or both' for employers of manual scavengers, there has not been a single prosecution. The denial mode of various state governments had to be countered by the SKA with voluminous data during a twelve-year battle that culminated in what may be called a 'sympathetic judgment' on 27 March 2014. The Court inter alia directed the government to give compensation of Rs 10 lakh to the next of kin of each manual scavenger who had died on the job (including sewer cleaning) since 1993. The Bhim Yatra of 2015–16 documented 1,268 such deaths, but only eighteen of the deceased had received compensation.

Meanwhile, away from the unhurried deliberations of committees and court proceedings, an incident that took place on 20 July 2010 illustrates the desperate plight of manual scavengers as well as what neoliberal development has done to worsen it. At Savanur, a small town in Haveri district of North Karnataka, protestors undertook novel action against their helplessness—by demonstrating it. They smeared themselves with human excreta in public before the municipal council office. A trivial stunt for attention, or so the members of the municipal council of Savanur thought and ignored it. However, it was a matter of life and death to the dalit protestors. They had been suddenly served with a notice of eviction by the municipal council to clear them out of a patch of land they had lived on for generations, so that a commercial complex could be built there. The order was illegal but who among them could challenge the authorities on a point of law? As for the dalits' pleas, they went unheeded. Far from showing them any sympathy, the municipal authorities ramped up the pressure by cutting off their water connection. For poor dalits of the bhangi subcaste, this was tantamount to physical eviction. Forbidden to draw water from any other source because of their untouchability, and buying it being out of the question when they could barely subsist on the pittance thrown at them for cleaning dry latrines, what may seem a mere municipal pressure tactic to others was a death knell for them. It drove them to the desperate act of daubing themselves with human excreta.

Although their method of protest was novel, it was so only to the extent of being a protest—a deliberate gesture carried out en masse with the intent of seeking public attention. There was otherwise nothing out of the ordinary in the spectacle of latrine and sewage cleaners caked in shit. The protestors were showing no more than their abjectness and routine sufferings to the public, that was quite inured to the sight and expert at pretending not to notice. When it comes to dalits, the Indian state as well as civil society lapse reflexively into denial. The hypocritical attitude of the government is clearly on view at international fora, where India has long fancied itself a moral leader of the world. The country's overweening pride in its record of opposition to racism, colonialism and apartheid in foreign parts has to be seen against its refusal to countenance even the mention of caste abroad. When the UN's World Conference against Racism at Durban (2001) sought to include caste in its agenda, the Indian government responded with angry bluster and denials. Its arguments ranged from pedantry to standing on national pride to outright lying: now insisting that caste is technically not the same as race, or that caste is its internal matter, or worse, that there is no caste discrimination in India. It was the contention of activists at the Durban conference that as far as descent-based discrimination goes, there is no functional difference between caste and race; this renders any technical distinction between them void. To sustain the act of moral grandstanding abroad alongside ruthless caste exploitation at home, the Indian elite needs its cocoon of make-believe. Part of the act is pretending that caste is a thing of the past. The hypocrisy, as we have seen, is nowhere better exposed than in the case of manual scavenging.

Within days of staging their dramatic protest, the oppressed dalits of Savanur were awash with visitors of every stripe, from holy men to right-wing leaders, mouthing words of shock, hurt, horror, condolence, compassion and compensation. They were brought there not by the workaday reality of manual scavenging across the country but the impact of bad publicity for the district administration for Karnataka, for caste society, and for the Indian government. The chairman of the State Human Rights Commission, S.R. Nayak, put in an appearance on 28 July 2010 and assured the press that he would be receiving a detailed report on the incident from the deputy commissioner. Asked why the commission had failed to act when the bhangi families of Savanur had sent a memorandum to the commission, the disarmingly frank Mr Nayak said that he hadn't noticed the memorandum sent by them. 'If I had noticed it, then I would have definitely taken steps to help them' (*Hindu*, 29 July 2010).

Another disquieting aspect of the protest by the bhangis of Savanur is that it goes against the grain of dalit political tradition, historically characterised by a renunciation of the markers of humiliating social status. Dr Ambedkar had exhorted his followers to give up dragging dead animals and eating their meat, discard caste-indicative ornaments and practices, and had even launched a famous struggle against mahar watans—the fixed amount of land granted to a mahar servant of the village and considered a special right, even a privilege given to dalits by others. The dalit protest at Savanur foregrounded the very marker of their dehumanisation. While it sought to forcefully project the plight of the community of manual scavengers, it also revealed their distance from the idiom of the mainstream dalit movement. Bhangis have been a minuscule minority among dalits and are considered untouchable even by other dalits. As a result, they have always lived in their own ghettoes. The protest exposed the cocooned existence of not just the elites but other dalit communities as well. If such a protest makes it impossible for caste society to sustain its pretence that the continued horrors of manual scavenging can be wished away, it is also an implicit indictment of an emancipatory rhetoric that overlooks the constraints of sweepers—to whom simply walking out of a hateful occupation is an inconceivable luxury. It reveals a blind spot of the dalit movement: if, with the purported goal of annihilation of caste, the movement does not build solidarity across the dalit fold, it will end up cementing distinctions of caste.

The immediate cause of the protest was the Savanur municipal council's plan to construct a commercial complex in their locality. As such, the protestors' outcry was not even against the age-old outrages they are forced to endure but the new squeeze put on them by the local authorities. The 'development plans' at Savanur exemplify the pressure the neoliberal economy has brought to bear on dalits, worsening their plight. Most municipalities and corporations have contracted out sanitation services, turning a majority of manual scavengers into contract workers. They work for a pittance, without any protective gear or job security. As and when modern technology replaces old toilets, the workers are simply junked, like obsolete bathroom fittings. This process was underway at Savanur. Increasingly, at metropolitan establishments like airports, malls and public institutions, the people on the job are called janitors, as in the Western world. They are provided with modern gadgets, uniforms and safety gear. Since the work does not involve any contact with filth, and requires some degree of interface with an upper class public, the dalit manual scavengers would find themselves automatically excluded from these relatively better paying sectors.

Persistence of the problem

The Socio-Economic Caste Census 2015 notes that there are 180,000 households engaged in manual scavenging across India, and some 2.6 million insanitary latrines. The parliament had passed the Prohibition of Employment as Manual Scavengers and Their Rehabilitation Act, 2013; the three-judge Supreme Court bench headed by the then chief justice, P. Sathasivam issued directions to the state, the railways, and several organisations to implement the provisions, but nothing has moved on the ground. The biggest violators of this law are the government's own departments. Take the Indian Railways for instance. Its 14,300 trains transport twenty-five million passengers across 65,000 kilometres every day. Their excreta falls straight onto the railway tracks through 172,000 open-discharge toilets. Given that people habitually take a shit when the train stops at a station, unmindful of who has to clean up after them, a visit to any railway station on a bustling morning would tell its own story. The prime minister who declared India would be scavenger-free by 2019 under his Swachh Bharat Abhiyan, and is eager to get a bullet train in India, could not even set a deadline by which the railways would replace all current toilets with bio-toilets.

As part of the stipulations of the 2013 Act that required surveys of manual scavenging, merely 12,737 manual scavengers were identified in only thirteen states; 86 per cent of them in Uttar Pradesh alone, it would have us believe. The official data is far from accurate. At a July 2016 meeting of the National Commission for Scheduled Castes, minister for social justice and empowerment, Thawar Chand Gehlot, admitted to the absurdity of the numbers, saying they were 'unrealistic, as so many insanitary latrines will not clean themselves'. The mismatch between the compiled numbers of dry latrines and that of manual scavengers points to the failure of state governments in surveying the data, and/or their lack of seriousness in dealing with the issue. The utter lack of political will is evident in the statement made by the BJP government on 19 April 2016, apparently in response to the SKA's Bhim Yatra, saying that it had not received data from all the states. (It still hadn't at the time of its outing in the Supreme Court in 2018.) It promised that the government would directly survey the incidence of manual scavenging in the country. It does not require much intelligence to surmise that this buys the government another decade to wear out the struggling safai karamcharis.

In their recent book *Where India Goes* (2017), Diane Coffey and Dean Spears have shown how even the government's methodology in collecting data on open defecation lacks rigour and reliability. Coffey and Spears cite the Swachh Sarvekshan Report released by the Ministry of Drinking Water and Sanitation in the second half of 2016, and point out that the survey's methods of data collection would conduce to over-reporting latrine use. Quite apart from the flawed methodology of its questionnaire—not addressing its queries to individuals but households, not asking questions to establish the frequency of toilet use compared to open defecation—the report drew its data from seventy-five 'high performing districts' and no village from the states of Uttar Pradesh, Bihar, Andhra Pradesh or Jharkhand. Here's a factoid to illustrate the scale of this omission: out of every eight people on this planet who defecate in the open, one lives in Uttar Pradesh.

While understanding the attitude of the ruling class to the problem is simple, more intriguing is the apathy of the dalit movement towards manual scavengers. The mainstream dalit movement has never really taken up the issue of manual scavenging with any seriousness. The pivot of the dalit movement has been representation. Ambedkar struggled to guarantee reservation in politics and thereafter instituted it in public employment. He expected dalit politicians to protect the political interests of the community and hoped that educated dalits entering the bureaucracy would provide a protective cover to the labouring classes. Reservation, and its brazen non-implementation in several sectors (except in electoral politics), then became the sole focus of the dalit movement. The movement came to distance itself from issues that affect the everyday lives of labouring dalits. The small but resourceful middle class that has come to be nurtured among dalits over the last seven decades—census data says only 4.1 per cent of the 200 million dalits become graduates while for the total population it is 8.2 per cent—virtually got detached from the labouring dalits who do not earn even the minimum wage in several parts of the country. It is revealing that during the 125-day Bhim Yatra, while Ambedkar was an imposing presence as an icon of inspiration, the 'Ambedkarites' were nowhere to be seen. It had become a manual scavengers' issue. A few notable progressive individuals from among non-dalits, however, did register their solidarity with the struggle of the scavengers.

High on rhetoric, low on results

This being the story of seven decades of apathy towards a community that Gandhi claimed was tasked with the 'the most honorable occupation', Narendra Modi, the self-described bhakt of Babasaheb, made people wield brooms on Gandhi Jayanti in 2014 to launch his ambitious Swachh Bharat Abhiyan, declaring that he would make India scavenger-free by 2019. While most of his theatrics have evoked mild controversy, this one, potentially the most controversial and problematic, seems to have gone down well with most people—partly because Modi was doing a Gandhi here, and because the image of India as a 'great nation' was at stake. Beyond all this, the main reason for the silence was collective ignorance of the principal cause of India's uncleanliness—its caste-culture—and the refusal to admit that manual scavenging cannot be eradicated unless caste is annihilated.

Surprisingly, there is no mention of the c-word in Modi's mission, which smacks of the usual protestations of the elite that castes no longer exist—they are a non-issue—while, as far as Modi's party is concerned, only Hindu consolidation matters. It will never occur to Modi that his act of beginning the cleanliness drive from the Valmiki Colony in New Delhi actually reinforced the association between balmikis and scavenging. Gandhi had paternalistically done the same; without speaking against castes, he displayed his mahatmahood by living among the bhangis of Delhi in 1946. Modi borrows snippets of wisdom from Gandhi in speaking about balmikis with a casual disdain that passes for compassion:

> I do not believe that they [the balmikis] have been doing this job just to sustain their livelihood ... At some point of time, somebody must have got the enlightenment that it is their duty to work for the happiness of the entire society and the Gods; that they have to do this job bestowed upon them by Gods; and that this job of cleaning up should continue as an internal spiritual activity for centuries (in *Karmayog*, a collection of speeches by Modi published in 2007 that was withdrawn two years after publication, 48–49).

What Modi iterates is basically the RSS samrasata solution to castes. Samrasata, meaning social harmony, aims at strengthening

Hindu identity by proclaiming that various castes should coexist without conflict; it promotes 'harmony' between the castes and does not call for the abolition of caste. Among the many RSS front outfits is one Samajik Samrasata Manch started in the 1980s (for more on the circumstances of its creation see "Saffronising Ambedkar"); in 2012, Modi, as Gujarat chief minister, even published a book called *Samajik Samrasata* in Gujarati and Hindi. This worldview believes in the greatness of Hindus, their religion and culture. Naturally, it does not see anything wrong with the varna or caste system—the components that define 'Hinduism'. In justifying it, proponents of hindutva indulge in rhetorical acrobatics to confuse the public. On caste, a typical gem of wisdom in its repertoire is taken from Golwalkar who gave the slogan 'Sab jaati mahaan, sab jaati samaan' (All castes are great and all castes are equal), which informs the samrasata project. This is of a piece with the orthodox brahminical formulation that all castes derive from the body of the same viratpurush—the primordial object of sacrifice in the purushasukta hymn of the Rig Veda—and are therefore equal in the cosmic sense. What it truly means is that all castes should uncomplainingly perform their assigned tasks as an article of dharma. This is why the existence of manual scavenging elicits no moral horror from the adherents of this outlook. It simply cannot scandalise their morality.

The SSM has also undertaken the project to saffronise Ambedkar, just as it paints the RSS gurus in improbably radical hues with regard to their intellectual attainments, literary output, anti-colonial record, etc. It has found some opportunistic dalit intellectuals to work with—such as Kishore Macwana (editor of the RSS journal *Sadhana* in Gujarati and compiler of the above-mentioned volume that bears Modi's name as author), Ramesh Patange, and Madan Dilawar—but these efforts have not made much headway among the people.

Modi's remarks about scavenging being a 'spiritual experience' expectedly met with harsh condemnation from dalits—in Tamil Nadu, his effigies were burnt. Two years after this, he repeated the same remark while addressing a conference of about nine thousand safai karamcharis, saying, 'A priest cleans a temple every day before prayers; you also clean the city like a temple. You and the temple priest work alike.' In mimicking Gandhi, Modi betrayed his own monumental ignorance. Ambedkar's attack on Gandhi's packaging of the ugly reality of caste with religio-spiritual humbug has clearly made no impression on Modi. In some ways, such Modi-speak represents the thinking of most dominant-caste people. Not many realise that such a display of seeming magnanimity is the worst expression of casteism rooted in the ideology of brahminism. For how can castes engaged in exploitative relations with others coexist in harmony except by internalising Manu's ideology?

The main motivation behind the Swachh Bharat campaign is the supremacist obsession of the BJP—the same as led to the premature declaration that India was shining in 2004 when more than 60 per cent of its population was defecating in the open. It may be said to the credit of Modi that he has foregrounded this standing shame and decided to construct twelve crore toilets at an estimated cost of Rs 1.96 lakh crore during his current tenure. But here comes his sleight of hand, the government that claims all the credit will rely heavily on Corporate Social Responsibility on the ground—all such contributions to the mission are exempt from taxation. It is not surprising that the pioneer of corporate charity, Bill Gates, endorsed the Swachh Bharat Abhiyan. Gates wrote in his blog on 25 April 2017, 'So far, the progress is impressive. In 2014, when Clean India began, just 42 per cent of Indians had access to proper sanitation. Today 63 per cent do. And the government has a detailed plan to finish the job by October 2, 2019, the 150th anniversary of Mahatma Gandhi's birth.'

Since November 2015, until Modi's 'Good and Simple Tax' came into being in July 2017, a Swachh Bharat Cess of 0.5 per cent was levied on all services liable for service tax. The ostensible aim was to facilitate the construction of toilets nationwide, with the government claiming that 16 million had been constructed in two years. The question of who shall clean these toilets and their sewage pits remains unaddressed, there being no public interest in getting the backstage aspect of the performance right. How the castes traditionally associated with scavenging will be able to rid themselves of this occupation is not part of policy thinking, and this worries neither Gates nor Modi nor India's upper classes. It did worry the UN's special rapporteur Léo Heller who, on 10 November 2017, presented his preliminary findings after a visit to India. His 'end of mission' statement, featured on the website of the Office of the United Nations High Commissioner for Human Rights, warned against the consequences of rapidly building a vast number of toilets without adequate planning and towards concomitant issues of drainage, sanitation and human rights. As he stated, a water-stressed country such as India which recorded 40 per cent of all diarrhoea-related deaths among low to middle income countries in 2012, and moreover, one where sanitation is an area rife with human rights abuse, would be well advised not to treat the issue as one of raising physical infrastructure alone. An environment and human rights based approach would serve better to bring about requisite changes in behaviour and a sustainable solution.

Heller's sober words were delivered on a Friday, and rejected by the Indian government at the start of the week's business the following Monday. Within three days, Reuters reported that the government found Heller's 'sweeping judgments [...] either factually incorrect, based on incomplete information, or grossly misrepresent[ing] the situation'. Clearly, corporate cheerleaders are more to the government's taste than the UN expert on water and sanitation. A grim indication of the future is already in place. It comes from the Sulabh Shauchalayas across the country that are almost completely staffed by members of the scavenging community who earn a far poorer wage than the safai karamcharis on the state's payroll. Even this seemingly reformist endeavour has not been able to break the stranglehold of the caste division of labour and labourers; it has only perpetuated it.

As Modi skilfully sidestepped government responsibility in creating sanitation infrastructure, he has also avoided creating operational jobs by invoking Gandhian spirituality in asking people to put in voluntary labour of minimum two hours a week. If that is what is needed for a swachh Bharat, the estimated voluntary labour will be the equivalent of 40 million jobs as against the less than 18 million currently in the entire public sector. Looking at its feasibility, the idea smacks of the usual governmental assertion—high on rhetoric and low on results.

The government's concern for this section of the population is evidenced by the drop in the allocation for the Self Employment Scheme for Rehabilitation of Manual Scavengers from Rs 557 crore in the 2013–14 UPA budget to 439.04 crore and 470.19 crore in the NDA budgets of the two succeeding years, while the actual expenditure was 'nil'. Unsurprisingly, the allocation was then slashed to a token entry of Rs 10 crore in 2016–17. The allocation under the scheme of pre-matric scholarships to the children of those engaged in 'unclean' occupations shows an even more dismal picture: while the budget allocation was marginally raised to Rs 10 crore in 2014–15 from the earlier Rs 9.5 crore, it was slashed to Rs 2 crore in 2016–17.

As with his image manipulation success in other sectors, Modi is walking away with the credit yet again for highlighting the issue of toilets and cleanliness, given that those who governed India for the last sixty-seven years did not ever formulate policies to end defecation in the open. Although Bill Gates rightly tweeted that Modi 'put a spotlight on a subject that most of us would rather not even think about', he inspires little confidence in the accomplishment of this mission—as proposed, it is going to be one more mega opportunity for corporate investment. The World Bank, in its November 2015 appraisal report of the Swachh Bharat Abhiyan called the campaign 'technically sound' but raised concerns about the various states' lack of 'institutional frameworks and strategies for achieving the goals of rural sanitation', calling them 'ambitious'.

The goals set for the Swachh Bharat Mission are indeed wildly unrealistic, as Coffey and Spears have demonstrated. To achieve its target by 2019, the Mission must construct 67,000 toilets a day, at the rate of nearly one per second. In precise terms, the government has committed itself to bringing down the prevalence of open defecation from roughly fifty per cent of the population—where it stands today—to zero in five years. The fastest such drop in history was in Ethiopia, where open defecation fell by sixteen percentage points in a period of five years. Nothing in the record of the Indian government shows that it is about to outpace Ethiopia—its total population 6 per cent that of India—and what's more, at a rate three times faster. Even if the sums of money committed to the task were sufficient, and leakages from rural development funds were to cease by magic so that the toilets paid for did appear on the ground and were of a satisfactory quality, there is no guarantee that the prospective individual users would obligingly change their toilet habits within this period.

Expectedly, Modi's pet Swachh Bharat campaign is proving hollow like any of his other schemes. As chief minister of Gujarat, Modi had launched a similar campaign, 'Nirmal Gujarat' in 2007, and made tall claims. His record, however, on waste management and pollution in Gujarat has been appalling. The CAG in its report on socio-economic conditions in Gujarat found that despite the state government's claims of significant progress in managing waste, merely 3 per cent of Gujarat's municipalities have any segregation systems in place. Further, none of the state's municipalities have working sewage-treatment facilities, and only one has any semblance of a sewer coverage system.

A nationwide survey of two years of the Swachh Bharat Abhiyan yielded no surprising results. Conducted by the citizen engagement platform LocalCircles, it went to the heart of the fifty-six-inch chest that adorns the mission's hoardings across the country. Only a fifth of the respondents affirmed that local municipalities had improved garbage collection or cleanliness. The study found that hygiene and sanitation facilities have visibly improved in only four states—three of them ruled by the BJP—while the rest of India reported marginal or no change. More than half of all survey respondents said there was no improvement in civic sense. Only a fifth thought availability of public toilets had improved since Swachh Bharat kicked off in 2014. This obviously does not gel with the government's claims. Modi had declared that India would be free of open defecation by 2019. What he means by it is building the targeted number of toilets. Given the record of his administration in fudging figures, he may achieve it without affecting open defecation.

Nonetheless, Gates notes, 'If you don't set ambitious targets and chart your progress, you end up settling for business as usual.' Little does he know that for our prime minister, the Swachh Bharat Abhiyan is indeed business as usual. Unless the culture of caste is eradicated and people internalise the responsibility towards cleanliness, no amount of campaigns and advertising is going to succeed. We need to understand that India cannot be swachh without the system of castes being completely annihilated.

11

Assertion not annihilation

The BSP enigma

Kanshi Ram, who died on 9 October 2006 after a long spell of illness that began in 1995, has been an enigma in contemporary Indian politics. What else would one call a person with no backing or resources, coming from nowhere, and still mounting a challenge to the mightiest in a land that historically despised his antecedents; a politician who abjured all principles and every norm, made a virtue of what is normally considered a vice, but was sought after by political bigwigs; a leader who never revealed his vision of emancipation and was nevertheless followed and revered by people as their messiah? Some people think of a parallel with B.R. Ambedkar and make comparisons. That could be misleading, but it may be surely said that Kanshi Ram emerged as the strongest and most creative leader in the post-Ambedkar dalit movement.

Born on 15 March 1934 into a humble Raidasi Sikh family in Khawaspur village of Ropar district in Punjab, Kanshi Ram earned his BSc degree and took a job as research assistant in 1957 in the Explosive Research and Development Laboratory, a munitions factory in Pune. This was where he was initiated into Ambedkarism by the likes of the late D.K. Khaparde, his co-worker, with whom he would go on to found Bamcef in 1978. With the weakening of dalit organisations through the 1960s, the cultural assertion of converting to Buddhism in Maharashtra was met with brute reaction from other castes, resulting in rising atrocities against dalits. These shocking developments apparently did not affect Kanshi Ram. As Badri Narayan documents in his biography of the leader (*Kanshiram: Leader of the Dalits*, 2014), five years into his job, Kanshi Ram was awakened by a small but symbolic incident at his workplace in which a class IV employee, Dinabhana, was fired for protesting against the scrapping of holidays on Buddha Jayanti and Ambedkar Jayanti. The high caste officers of ERDL had cancelled the holidays to commemorate the Buddha and Ambedkar's birth anniversaries and had wanted them replaced by Bal Gangadhar Tilak and Gopal Krishna Gokhale's jayantis. Several dalit officers fumed at this but were afraid of asserting their protest. Dinabhana was the only one who refused to turn up to work on Ambedkar Jayanti; he even registered his protest formally with a letter.

When Dinabhana—who belonged to the bhangi community from Jaisalmer, Rajasthan—was fired, he decided to fight the battle legally and Kanshi Ram raised the money to support him. The issue soon gathered momentum and Kanshi Ram even got to meet the then Defence Minister Yashwantrao Chavan in this regard. Finally, both Dinabhana and the holidays for Ambedkar and Buddha Jayanti were reinstated. This episode propelled Kanshi Ram into social activism, from which he was never to turn back. By 1971, at a meeting attended by sixty government employees including Khaparde, he had formed the Scheduled Caste, Scheduled Tribe, Other Backward Class, Minorities Communities Employees Association, the precursor to Bamcef.

Mainstream dalit politics was then represented by a faction-ridden Republican Party of India in Maharashtra, which came into being in 1957 as a political party of the non-Congress, non-communist opposition, but proved to be just a new label for the Scheduled Castes Federation that B.R. Ambedkar had founded. Kanshi Ram considered working with the RPI but was soon disillusioned by its runaway factionalism. Curiously, an alternative in the form of Dalit Panther had emerged in the 1970s, offering a radical Marxist interpretation of Ambedkar, but it did not attract him. It is noteworthy that situated not too far from the epicentre of the Panther movement, he spoke about the RPI but never the Dalit Panther. His early comrades even claim he was against the movement. Instead, he discerned potential in an unlikely class of government employees belonging to dalits, backward classes and religious minorities who had accessed their jobs through reservation and now found themselves discriminated against by higher-ranking privileged-caste administrators. These people needed organisational protection, and thus was formed the All India Backward and Minorities Communities Employees Federation—known as Bamcef—on Ambedkar's death anniversary, 6 December 1978.

What distinguished Bamcef from many other dalit outfits was the perseverance and hard work of Kanshi Ram. Of course, he was actively helped by local Ambedkarite dalits, most of them from the Nagpur region. Since Bamcef's apolitical format suited these government employees who yearned to 'give back to society', many people plunged into it and contributed their time and money with a missionary spirit. These members in secure government jobs constituted not just the brain bank but also the money bank of the SC, ST, OBC, and minority communities. Bamcef soon spread across the country, though it remained unnoticed by the mainstream media. To counter this media bias, it launched its own organ *Oppressed Indian* and later scores of daily/weekly newspapers in most Indian languages.

Although Bamcef was confined to government employees who were constrained by service rules from taking part in political activities, its emergence as a strong nationwide organisation played a role in catalysing the entry of many youths into politics. More importantly, it provided funds for Kanshi Ram's political activities. After nurturing it for a decade, Kanshi Ram took a qualitative leap by stepping into the political arena, by launching the Dalit Shoshit Samaj Sangharsh Samiti, known as DS4, on 6 December 1981. It unnerved some people in Bamcef who naïvely believed that they should continue working as a social club. Kanshi Ram, however, went ahead using the DS4 platform to contest the Haryana assembly polls a year later. The manner in which he organised this 'intermediate' outfit (it was divided into ten wings, each with a different role and responsibility); used bicycle rallies as the campaign mode; came up with creative and catchy slogans in a language provocative to the upper castes; and set himself up as a model for young activists, all served to raise his profile. Its theme slogan 'Brahmin, bania, thakur chor, baki sab hum DS4' (brahmins, banias, thakurs are thieves for sure, the rest of us are DS4) aggressively excluded the minority 'upper' castes and attempted to consolidate all others, the 'bahujan' majority. Within a span of three years, Kanshi Ram transformed the DS4 into a full-fledged political party, the Bahujan Samaj Party, launched on Ambedkar's birthday in 1984 with a slogan 'vote hamara, raj tumhara; nahi chalega, nahi chalega' (our votes for your rule; no way). The goal was based on a dictum attributed to Ambedkar by Kanshi Ram, that political power was the gurukilli (master key) to all problems.

Building a constituency, flexing muscle

The trajectory of the dalit movement under Ambedkar was conditioned by the expediencies of the politics of his time. Although firmly moored to universalist values, it appeared tactical, often contradictory and was informed by pure pragmatism. Those after Ambedkar failed to comprehend its intricacies, and constructed Ambedkars and 'Ambedkarisms' of their convenience, splintering the movement into numerous factions. Even the Republican Party of India could not hold itself together, and its members joined the Congress—the party Ambedkar had fought all his life and termed a burning house. The deserters, however, continued to style themselves as Ambedkarites. Later, the Congress consciously carried out a co-option strategy through

Yashwantrao Chavan, reducing dalit politics to the art of brokering dalit interests (as discussed in the chapter "Ambedkar, Ambedkarites, Ambedkarism").

Kanshi Ram was to revolutionise dalit politics through his manoeuvres. His creative genius is reflected in the coinage of names he gave to his organisations, such as Bamcef and DS4, or the catchy slogans with which he mobilised people. By declaring 'jiski jitni sankhya bhari, uski utni bhagidari' (participation must equal vote share), he re-emphasised the rights of people to share political power and revived a strong Ambedkarite sense of dignity and self-respect in the masses who had been reduced to a vote bank of the 'upper' caste leadership of the ruling class parties. He set an example of selflessness, sacrifice, simplicity and devotion in public life. He remained a bachelor and cut off his relationship with his family. He inspired confidence in people by demonstrating seemingly impossible feats, such as launching his own newspapers and declaring his intention to launch a TV channel. He always talked in big terms, never grumbling about resources, which further drew people towards him.

Kanshi Ram's most significant contribution was his conception of the bahujan as a viable political constituency and an approach to controlling the balance of power. Bahujanvad was meant to enlarge the potential constituency to claim 85 per cent of the population. Kanshi Ram's 'bahujan' assimilated all castes and communities, except for the privileged castes, glossing over their different histories, cultures and more importantly, their material contradictions. They were supposed to snatch political power from the 15 per cent–strong 'upper' castes. This would be a winning constituency in any future contest for political power. The idea of bahujan may well be traced to a formulation attributed to Gautama Buddha, 'bahujana hitaya bahujana sukhaya', that emphasised the welfare of the majority or that of everyone. But it was Mahatma Phule who used it with the valency it has today, and Ambedkar invoked it on occasion with his knack for making use of fault lines among the ruling classes. The effective fusion of the term with a political constituency and its operationalisation is to be credited to Kanshi Ram.

Kanshi Ram's choice of Uttar Pradesh as the site to launch his political experiment was planned keeping both history and demography in mind. The region has had a significant history of dalit movements with leaders like Swami Acchutanand (1879–1933) who pioneered the Adi-Hindu movement in the 1920s and 1930s. When Ambedkar shifted his base to Delhi in 1942, neighbouring UP came under his influence. After his death, the Ambedkarite movement in UP was nurtured by leaders such as Buddha Priya Maurya and Sangh Priya Gautam, and the state outperformed Maharashtra in terms of electoral gains. The movement suffered a setback for a decade or so after these leaders left the RPI. Another, perhaps more significant, factor behind the BSP's success was the timing of its foray, when the national mainstream parties were on a weaker footing than before. The trend of fragmentation of politics through the assertion of the regional bourgeoisie in the 1970s had accelerated during the Emergency and, in its aftermath, a wide coalition was ushered into power at the centre. This provided a congenial political climate for the BSP's strategy of exercising a lever in the balance of power by effecting its social construction of the bahujan electorate.

Uttar Pradesh has a unique demography with the SCs accounting for 21.1 per cent of the state's population. This is the third largest proportion of SCs in an Indian state, and the largest population, in numerical terms, accounting for 20.5 per cent of the national population of SCs followed by West Bengal with 10.7 per cent, Bihar with 8.2 per cent, and Tamil Nadu with 7.2 per cent. It has, moreover, a single caste, jatav, accounting for 57 per cent of the total SC population, unrivalled by any other state. The next caste, pasi, accounting for 16 per cent of the SC population, has no traditional rivalry with the jatavs, unlike in many other states where mistrust prevails between whichever groups constitute the two largest segments of the SC population. If dhobi, kori and balmiki are added the jatavs and pasis, this block totals to 87.5 per cent of the SC population, or 18.9 per cent of the state's total population.

In the assembly elections, when even the mainstream parties could not muster the courage to contest all the seats, Kanshi Ram decided to do so, not in order to win them but to cause the defeat of and weaken the mainstream parties. This resulted in the rout of the Congress party in various elections in Uttar Pradesh in the post-Mandal 1990s. The concept of a majboor sarkar (dependent government) in place of everybody's claim to provide a majboot sarkar (strong government) proved a stroke of genius in forcing the mainstream parties to beg the support of the BSP. This gave the party the requisite bargaining power to form and pull down governments in UP repeatedly.

Kanshi Ram used election after election to consolidate his constituency, with its core in the jatavs and chamars. Having their support was a sufficient draw to attract unaffiliated dalits, Muslims, and others who were not particularly enamoured of the Bharatiya Janata Party, Congress or Samajwadi Party. When this strategy began paying off, reflected in a consistent rise in the BSP's vote share, Kanshi Ram could negotiate with various political parties from a position of strength. In the mid-term assembly poll in 1993, which came right after the demolition in Ayodhya, rendering the BJP politically ostracised, Kanshi Ram ran the campaign with an antagonistic slogan that echoed the anti-hindutva sentiment of the secular forces, 'tilak, taraju aur talwar, maaro inko joote char' (Priest, merchant and soldier—boot them out forever). After the election, the BSP joined a coalition government with Samajwadi Party supremo Mulayam Singh Yadav as chief minister. What Kanshi Ram had accomplished in less than a decade was remarkable. As part of a pre-poll alliance, the SP and BSP contested 256 and 164 seats to the 425-member house and won 109 and 67 seats respectively. In a hung assembly, the BJP had emerged as the single largest party (with 177 seats) but to keep it at bay, the left parties, Congress, and Janata Dal backed the SP–BSP alliance with the arrangement that Mulayam Yadav and Mayawati would helm the state for two and a half years each. But cracks developed in the alliance, defections were attempted, and Mayawati was infamously roughed up by SP MLAs in the state guest house. Kanshi Ram withdrew support to the SP after a year and a half, and the BSP then formed the government with the support of the BJP. Kanshi Ram's protégée became the first ever dalit woman chief minister of India with the support of a party of manuvadis. Though the Mayawati-led government lasted less than five months, it was a dream come true for dalits.

Kanshi Ram and Mayawati knew that the bonhomie with the BJP would not last long, and they planned to exploit it to the hilt. The government went on a spending spree, building memorials to dalit icons and naming various institutions after saints from the dalit pantheon. Fifteen thousand Ambedkar statues were installed all over the state, dalit officers were placed in a number of top positions, and festivals to honour dalit and backward class heroes were introduced. What the social historian Christophe Jaffrelot called 'the acme of the symbolic conquest of public space' (2003, 415) was the Periyar Mela that the BSP-led government organised on Periyar's birth anniversary (18–19 September 1995). The Tamil radical leader 'Periyar' E.V. Ramsamy Naicker's *Ramayana: A True Reading* had been banned in Uttar Pradesh since 1969 for it offered a reading of the Ramayana considered blasphemous by believers. In post–Babri Uttar Pradesh, the BSP promoted both Periyar's name and his ideas with a vengeance, annoying its hindutva ally in every way possible. During her short regime, Mayawati appointed dalit magistrates to half of the state's districts; effected transfers of over fiteen hundred officers; reserved 20 per cent of posts of inspectors of police for SCs and eight per cent for Muslims (as part of her move to divide the 27 per cent OBC quota); and as part of the Ambedkar Villages Scheme she ensured that bijli–sadak–paani (electricity–roads–water that helpfully stood in for the party's acronym) and other civic amenities reached the segregated dalit quarters of villages.

As expected, the BJP withdrew its support to the government after 136 days and president's rule was imposed. In the election held in 1996, the BSP failed to secure a majority despite support from the Congress—it won the same 67 seats as it did in 1993, but its vote share increased from 11.2 to 19.64 per cent. Kanshi Ram's dexterity saw him make another deal with the BJP to make Mayawati the chief minister, this time for 184 days. She feverishly continued renaming institutions and unveiling monuments, distributing largesse to her dalit supporters, before making way for the BJP nominee Kalyan Singh. Then, at the centre, the BSP played a key role in defeating the Vajpayee-led National Democratic Alliance government in a no-confidence motion in March 1999—which the thirteen-month-old government famously lost by a solitary vote. None of this prevented the BSP from forming the government in UP with the BJP's support for the third time in 2002. After grabbing power, Mayawati stooped so low as to give a clean chit to and campaign in July for Narendra Modi who was condemned by the entire world for his role in the genocide of Muslims in Gujarat in February the same year. Ahead of the campaign, addressing a press conference, with the then PM Atal Bihari Vajpayee and Modi flanking her, she had said, 'The charges against Modi are baseless. A chief minister will never do anything which will bring bad name to his own government.' The PTI report in *Indian Express* (8 December 2002) also quoted her as saying it was her party's 'moral responsibility' to support the BJP in Gujarat as it was supporting the BSP in UP. Consequently, the BSP supported the BJP in 151 constituencies and contested 31 seats on its own in Gujarat—in effect, positively influencing the dalit vote.

The BSP's volte face on its origins was complete with the 2002 UP elections. The BSP, whose election meetings used to begin by asking upper caste people to leave the audience, now began to woo brahmins by replacing its bahujanvad with sarvajanvad—the spokesperson of the oppressed majority was now championing the cause of all communities, as those the BSP had once denounced as manuvadi were gathered into the soft embrace of sarvajanvad. As for the BSP's electoral symbol, the blue elephant, a new slogan said: 'Hathi nahin Ganesh hai, Brahma, Vishnu, Mahesh hai!' (It's not just an elephant but Ganesh; come stand by the Hindu triumvirate). Further, the BSP that had at one time withdrawn support to the BJP on the charge that the latter was soft-pedalling the PoA Act, now sought to render the Act ineffective by saying that it was being misused. This somersault had the blessings of Kanshi Ram. In July 2002, the BSP government issued a directive signed by chief secretary D.S. Bagga and special secretary Anil Kumar with regard to the PoA Act, instructing the administrative machinery to prevent 'misuse' of the Act and asking them to direct the state's penal and executive bodies to be 'extra careful' about registering cases under the Act. Such crass political behaviour would unsurprisingly lead Mayawati to perform another unblinking flip ahead of the 2014 Lok Sabha election, where she was reported by the *Hindu* (21 February 2014) as saying, 'We will put our entire strength to prevent Narendra Modi from becoming prime minister. It is in interest of the country to prevent the BJP from coming to power. If Modi wins, it will give a boost to the communal forces in the country.'

The virtues of jerry building

Kanshi Ram had a peculiar way of responding to criticism of such expedient behaviour. Before anyone else could accuse him of opportunism, he would rationalise it as his strategy. To be fair, all political parties did the same but they feigned decency and decorum (including the Communist Party of India and the Communist Party of India–Marxist that have often welcomed the All India Anna Dravida Munnetra Kazhagam, Dravida Munnetra Kazhagam or Pattali Makkal Katchi of Tamil Nadu or the many varieties of the Janata party in the North into the 'secular fold' despite their having once shared power in alliance with the BJP). What others did surreptitiously, Kanshi Ram did openly, and thus exposed the prevailing double standards in politics. It is interesting to note that the people who accused him of unprincipled politics, opportunism and unreliability repeatedly sought alliances with him even after his practised misdemeanours. Kanshi Ram had often characterised the Congress and the BJP as two sides of the same coin, calling one 'sapnath' and the other 'nagnath' (loosely, the serpent and the cobra). If, after such indictment, the BJP or the Congress continued to seek alliances with the BSP, it was their opportunism that got exposed in the bargain. Kanshi Ram barely occupied any formal position of political power, except as an MP from Etawah in UP and Hoshiarpur in Punjab. The man considered the greatest dalit leader after Ambedkar never made a mark as a parliamentarian either. However, there may not be any other politician who was feared as much as Kanshi Ram. People believed that this shrewd leader could come up with calculations to catapult himself into the prime minister's seat at any time.

Indeed, Kanshi Ram proved himself a strategist par excellence not only in political matters but also in organisational terms. He never let any stereotypical dictums or opinions from others affect his style of exerting absolute and singular control over the organisational apparatus. Be it his Bamcef, DS4, or BSP, none had any operative organisational structure to speak of; none had any specified chains of command. In other words, everyone's authority was subject to the whims of the supremo. This safeguarded the BSP from internal splits and insulated it from the horse-trading suffered by all other parties, particularly those of its ilk like the RPI. Anyone defying the writ of the supremo invited their individual political demise without denting the party in any manner. Kanshi Ram was accused of being unscrupulous in disposing of people after using them. This is largely evidenced by the fact that none of the prominent people who supported him during his Bamcef days at Pune and Delhi were to be found in the BSP, except for the lone Mayawati. It is the same underlying organisational principle that had sent them into political oblivion. Outsiders may term this organisational approach feudal and autocratic, but in the prevailing political milieu, it proved an effective way of safeguarding the integrity of the party. Unilateral control was ensured not only in structural matters but in every aspect. Kanshi Ram never promised anything or spoke in terms of concrete plans or programmes, nor did he ever issue an election manifesto. He was acutely aware that any such thing would constrict the room for manoeuvre. When pushed for an answer, Kanshi Ram cleverly argued that the Constitution was the BSP's manifesto. Following in his footsteps, Mayawati too issues an 'appeal' ahead of each election in the place of a manifesto. One such appeal, issued ahead of the 2009 Lok Sabha poll, explains this credo:

> As is known to all, Bahujan Samaj Party is the only party in the country, which believes in 'deeds and not in words'. That is why our party, unlike other parties does not release an election 'Manifesto', rather the BSP only makes an 'APPEAL' to people for votes, enabling it to complete the unfinished works of the Sants, Gurus and great men born in the Bahujan Samaj from time to time, especially Mahatma Jotiba Phule, Chhatrapati Shahuji Maharaj, Narayana Guru, Parampujya Baba Saheb Dr Bhimraro Ambedkar and Manyavar Shri Kanshi Ram Ji by following the path shown by them so that it can produce good results in the elections to gain power, and then, with the 'master key' of political power, can make the lives of the suffering and oppressed people prosperous in every respect. (Patil 2011)

Purely in terms of electoral politics, Kanshi Ram's game-plan, or rather the seeming lack of one, proved quite effective, albeit in only certain parts of the country. He gave a fresh impetus to a moribund dalit politics by locating it in the wider space peopled by the downtrodden. He identified these people in terms of their castes and communities, not in terms of class. Many people came to believe in the bahujan identity even if they couldn't see how it might be geared into action. At least at the level of symbolism, Kanshi Ram had succeeded in winning them over. Careful analysis may, however, reveal that a combination of certain historical developments and situational factors made much of this success possible. Such gains are bound to be short-lived and illusory—and limited to a state like UP—unless they are built upon to implement a radical programme to forge a class identity among the constituents. In the absence of such a class agenda, the party was bound to degenerate into manipulative politics to grab political power. The BSP's unprincipled pursuit of power was driven by this exigency. It is futile to see in this manipulative game a process of empowerment of the subject people. Imperatives of this kind necessarily catapult a significant part of the dalit movement into the camp of the ruling classes, as has happened with the BSP. The BSP's electoral parleys with all and sundry of the ruling classes reflect this process of degeneration and expose its own class character.

It is not easy to assess Kanshi Ram, either as a leader or a legacy. The unprincipled pursuit of governmental power that he represented was certainly a great negative. He falsely projected this pursuit as bestowing political power on dalits, whereas it worked to the detriment of every other aspect of the dalit movement. Whether in the long run his model of politics furthers the dalit cause or hampers it is a question that can be posed but not easily answered.

Post-Kanshi Ram: A mayawi revolution

Realising his health was failing, Kanshi Ram bequeathed the BSP mantle to Mayawati in 2001. She took over as national president of the BSP in September 2003, and thereafter an ailing Kanshi Ram hardly ever made public appearances until his death. Mayawati proved a true disciple in matters of strategy and political dexterity, but lacked Kanshi Ram's austerity, sacrifice, dedication, and foresight. Her aggressiveness made the dalits feel empowered, and at the same time rendered them vulnerable, which, in turn, helped the BSP stay in power. They voted zealously for the BSP election after election, even after Mayawati migrated to the sarvajan plank, embracing brahmins on the eve of the 2007 election.

The BSP's victory of 2007 in UP was the culmination of Mayawati's clever game of crafting an alliance between the dalits and brahmins and every jati in between. To label it a 'social revolution' contradicts the very framework of this alliance as a politically convenient arrangement. One forgets that this was in fact the policy followed by the Congress that projected itself as an umbrella party, enabling it to rule the country for more than four decades after independence. Nobody would call that rule a revolution, social or otherwise. Why then Mayawati's? In the post-Mandal phase, she was open about her use of caste arithmetic (keeping winnability in mind) while other parties applied the same logic in a sly fashion. The justification on offer was that during Congress rule, the reins of power were in the hands of the upper caste/class people whereas in the BSP's case, these would be in the hands of dalits. Strictly speaking, the latter is not true. If it means just a dalit chief minister, even the Congress had propped up dalit mascots to such positions. An example of Damodaram Sanjivayya, who briefly became the chief minister of Andhra Pradesh in 1960–62 (to replace Neelam Sanjeeva Reddy who had been forced to resign), may be an apt reminder. Besides the error of equating an individual with the party or her caste, it is also a conceptually erroneous assumption that the BSP is a dalit party. At no time did the BSP, or even its precursor movements such as the Bamcef and the DS4, ever claim to be a dalit organisation. As the BSP's name itself suggests, it is a bahujan party. But having traded the bahujan for sarvajan, it is no longer even what it set out to be. The bahujans certainly no longer hold the reins of power. Just because Kanshi Ram and Mayawati happen to be dalit, the power accrued to the BSP does not become dalit power; it belongs to the sarvajan, literally everyone, privileged castes included.

What does this party of sarvajan mean? Political analysts have not seriously considered this question. This term, indicative of collaboration between castes and classes, should be fundamentally inimical to the caste or class struggle of the oppressed and exploited. It wishes away any contradictions in society. If so, what would be the premise, one may ask, for the existence of the BSP? How could there be a dalit struggle without the definition of friends and foes? Sweeping such issues under the carpet negates the dalit struggle itself. Such slippery terms and nomenclature suit the ruling class interests well, for they seek to paper over existing contradictions in society. Such terms cannot be useful to the lower classes that must target these contradictions in their struggle. Sarvajan, moreover, smacks of the samrasata concept of the Sangh parivar that believes in harmonsing all castes and communities ensuring that the system of castes is sustained and strengthened, not annihilated. As such, when the BSP began claiming that it has become a party of the sarvajan, it was admitting that it had not only become a ruling *class* party, but the ruling *caste* party.

For all the adroit manoeuvres behind installing a dalit's 'beti' as UP's chief minister, it did mean the realisation of a long cherished dream for the dalits. They felt as though they had become the rulers of the state. With this unshakeable dalit base as their support, the BSP could try any kind of stunt with impunity. When the party realised that it had reached the limits of its constituency and that a little increment could win far more seats for the party, it decided to befriend the upper castes. Mayawati's 'social engineering'—as it came to be called by the corporate media—to get the much-wanted increment to bahujan votes, worked perfectly in the congenial electoral climate of UP. The political alliance with the upper castes did not, of course, translate into social relations or what Ambedkar was fond of characterising as 'social endosmosis'—in conventional terms, 'roti–beti ka vyavahaar', the exchange of food and daughters in marriage. This was never BSP's agenda anyway. However, brahmins and thakurs/rajputs were assigned disproportionately more seats than their numbers deserved in the 2007 poll to the 403-member assembly, making a mockery of the early Kanshi Ram ideal of equalising participation and vote share. Of the 139 tickets given to upper caste candidates, eighty-six went to brahmins (whereas the thakurs make up eight and brahmins an estimated 10 per cent of the population). The OBCs (accounting for 40 per cent) were given 110, and dalits (at 21.6 per cent) contested in ninety-three (of which eighty-nine were anyway constituencies reserved for them), and Muslims (18 per cent) were fielded in sixty-one constituencies. Overall, the BSP won a handsome 206 seats. This caste calculus, that panders to rather than upsets social realities, brought the BSP its crucial fillip to wrest power. Its desire to share power without effecting a serious shift in social arrangements made the sarvajan model work a while at the political level. Save for not sharing an overt hostility to Muslims, the resonance with the samrasata philosophy charted by the RSS shows clearly.

If elections are a sport, there is no doubting that Mayawati grounded all the veteran players. If elections are a medium of securing personal power, then there is again no doubt that she left everybody far behind in the race. But if elections are seen as a vehicle to bring about a change in caste/class relations to the benefit of the oppressed and poor people, then Mayawati's unscrupulous manoeuvring throws up a series of suspicions.

The 2007 election offered Mayawati an unprecedented opportunity to demonstrate how political power in the hands of a dalit can make the state look different from others. Never before had a dalit risen to head the state, independently. Dalits had been chief ministers before but only as mascots of the ruling class parties. The rise of the BSP with its aggressive projection of itself as the party of the 85 per cent against the traditional ruling classes, albeit basing itself on and reaffirming caste all the while, was inspiring enough for the dalit masses, particularly in the context of the collapsed RPI experiment. Mayawati's previous stints had been brief, the first in 1995, the second in 1997, both of less than six months each, and the third lasting a little longer, about 16 months (2002–03). But all these stints in power required support from others and she could not, therefore, be expected to fully flex the dalit muscles of her agenda. These spells in power were used merely to fortify her constituency. As she had declared during her first stint, 'consolidation of the dalit vote bank [was her] biggest achievement' (*Pioneer*, 23 October 1995). Renaming public institutions and places after bahujan icons, particularly B.R. Ambedkar, erecting their statues across the state, creating new districts after them—all these moves worked well to assert a dalit presence in the public sphere.

Some of the schemes she launched significantly benefited dalits. For example, the Ambedkar Village Scheme she launched during her very first stint as chief minister allotted special funds for socio-economic development to villages which had a 50 per cent SC population. In June 1995, during her second stint, she extended this scheme to villages which had a 22–30 per cent SC population. All told, 25,434 villages were included in the Ambedkar Village Scheme. The dalits of these villages received special treatment—there were roads, handpumps, houses built in their neighbourhoods. It is due to these material benefits that dalits enthusiastically called her government as their own. There were visible symbolic gains too. Whereas earlier, putting up an Ambedkar statue even within the dalit ghetto, could lead to caste tensions and often brutal violence across India, here was a government that made it its official business to erect thousands of Ambedkar statues. People were generally untroubled by her autocratic style as it promised decisive authority and improved law and order. Unfortunately, the imperatives of power misled her to commit excesses in fortifying her core constituency with huge investments in building memorials to Ambedkar and Kanshi Ram (not to forget monumental statues of herself) and organising lavish birthday bashes.

Surely, she could have used her administrative prowess to curb atrocities on dalits with a heavy hand; she could have improved basic public services such as education, health, and transport, made her administration people-friendly and possibly tried to create village fora that would lead to a weakening of caste identity. Instead, she adopted an ultra-feudal model with regal pomp and darbari culture—including the installation of faux nawabi-style street lighting in the capital Lucknow—distancing herself from the masses. She distributed largesse to those who were loyal to her and extracted rent from others in exchange of political favour. In a country where corruption is a way of life, she earned the dubious reputation of being among the most corrupt. While these traits could be considered as stemming from the political compulsions of her earlier stints, her fourth time in office—with the surprising distinction of being the first CM of the state to have completed a full five-year term—confirmed that these attributes were of her own making.

In 2009, Mayawati was embroiled in allegations around the murder of a public works department engineer Manoj Kumar Gupta, who was brutally lynched in Auraiya by a BSP MLA, for not fulfilling the demand for contributions to Mayawati's birthday fund. Embarrassed, she declared that there should be no collection of funds in the future for her birthdays. The following year, it was not her own birthday that supplied the occasion but the twenty-fifth birthday of her party and the seventy-sixth birth anniversary of her mentor, Kanshi Ram. Once again, she pushed herself into the eye of a storm over a mega rally organised at Ramabai Ambedkar Nagar in Lucknow for the occasion on 15 March, which is estimated to have cost over Rs 200 crore.

The arrangements were of a mindboggling scale that would have made even the extravagant nawabs of Lucknow turn in their graves in disbelief. She was likened by the Congress to Nero playing the fiddle, as the previous week's communal riot in Bareilly had not yet subsided when the revelry occurred. The usual bias of the media also contributed, painting her in a bad light. What stunned everyone on the day of the rally, however, was the giant garland made up of currency notes of Rs 1,000 presented to her on stage. The Congress leader Digvijay Singh had offered this analysis then: 'Each ring of this garland has 45 notes of 1000 denomination, i.e. 45,000 rupees. Each centimeter has got five such rings. 5 x 45,000 is Rs 2,25,000. This garland is 10 meters long i.e. 1000 cm. So 2.25 lakh x 1000 becomes Rs 22 crore and 50 lakh. So there is a reason why I came to this figure.' Her confidant and cabinet minister Naseemuddin Siddiqui expectedly declared that it was just Rs 21 lakh, not Rs 22.5 crore as alleged by Digvijay Singh, and that the money was collected by party functionaries in Lucknow.

Television channels beamed the pictures with characteristic relish and sought to create revulsion in people by conducting motivated debates. They hinted at an imminent income tax investigation and possible action by the Reserve Bank of India for the misuse of currency notes. As middle class indignation peaked, Mayawati responded in her characteristic style the following day by publicly accepting another currency garland, this time valued at Rs 18 lakh, from her party workers and smiling her approval as they declared that she would be gifted only currency garlands in the future. It was reiterated that the BSP collected its funds exclusively through such small donations from ordinary people unlike other parties who got theirs from big industrialists.

The democratisation of hypocrisy

Every move of Mayawati has shattered the sanitised sensibility of the middle class and left it gasping for expression. Invariably, the utterance ends with 'Oh, it is too much!'—whether it is her mega memorials or her rallies, her style evokes stunned responses of this kind. The point to ponder is whether, beyond her deliberately designed-for-dalit demeanour, there is anything essentially novel or unique on offer. The answer would definitely be in the negative. Mayawati is basically a product of the system and she represents it in full measure, albeit in her own inimitable way. It is simply absurd to accuse one person in Indian politics of autocracy and undemocratic behaviour because our entire political culture has been undemocratic (leader-centric) and hypocritical. The precedence and prevalence of feudal practices among other individuals and parties however cannot be a justification for the BSP's leader-centric politics. For someone who started as a dalit grassroots worker, such bizarre behaviour could not have come naturally to her. However, the feudal dictatorial model served to defend her party against ruling class marauders. She, and her mentor Kanshi Ram before her, knew the risk of inner-party democracy in a party of have-nots. They had seen it in the destruction of the RPI whose leaders were co-opted, bought outright, or bribed by the ruling class parties. Even the more radical Dalit Panther had been tamed and silenced during the Emergency period. For this reason, both the leaders avoided having even a formal organisational structure for the BSP. This shrewd mechanism saved the BSP from going the RPI way.

As regards the charge of squandering public money, there are numerous public institutions, roads, structures, statues, parks, and places dotting the entire country, which are named after Gandhi or some scion of the Nehru family. Did anybody ever raise a question of propriety about them? In what way is the 'Tughlaqesque' decision of the Congress government in Maharashtra, the most indebted state in the country, to erect a 309 feet tall statue of Shivaji in the Arabian Sea, at the cost of Rs 500 crore, any different from Mayawati's Ambedkar memorial? The corporate media does not insinuate ridicule towards the monstrous made-in-China 'statue of unity' for Sardar Patel, at a cost of Rs 2,063 crore (US $320 million) to taxpayers, being erected near Vadodara, Gujarat. Nobody can deny that building these memorials is a waste of public money. The question is, ruling parties have been doing it all the time with impunity. Why, then, should Mayawati's projects to commemorate dalit icons be singled out for criticism? The mega memorials that Mayawati constructed were an important element in her scheme of insuring her core constituency. In this, she has clearly not set a precedent but is following several.

Blaming a particular leader for corruption when most of them exponentially multiply their 'declared' wealth, already in crores, is an awkward proposition. There is never a question raised by the vigilant media as to how these worthy figures in social service accomplish such financial wizardry that might put the most adept money managers to shame. A progressive norm like declaration of wealth by people's representatives and public servants has only served to legitimise their corruption. Mayawati is no exception. While there is scope for suspicion that the declaration, as in the case of the traditional elites, may constitute a fraction of their actual wealth, the newer additions to their club, like Mayawati, may be relatively closer to declaring the actual figure. Mayawati paid over Rs 26 crore as income tax in 2009 and became one of the top twenty income-taxpayers in the country, far ahead of the richest billionaires like Mukesh Ambani and Anil Ambani, and certainly the topmost among politicians.

True, there is a case of disproportionate assets, covering the period 1995–2003, pending against her in the courts. This was when her declared income was 'paltry'—Rs 88.7 lakh. By 2010, it had gone up to over Rs 80 crore, almost one hundred times in less than seven years. This massive wealth is claimed to originate from the donations ordinary dalits make on her birthday. The thousand-rupee currency notes in the garlands certainly did not come from ordinary people, most of whom may not have even seen them except in pictures. It is unbelievable that institutions like the income tax department or the banking system are not able to trace the source of these high-value currency notes or for that matter, this business of gifts. Can corruption be pervasive without institutions winking at it? When more than half of the gross domestic product is stolen every year from under the watch of these institutions, corruption itself stands completely institutionalised. If society permits its traditional elites to behave immorally, it loses the right to question victims when they follow suit.

There is nothing novel in the accusations made against Mayawati by the elitist media. Whether it is misusing caste for electoral gains, manipulating people along identities, the feudal arrogance of power, corruption, vulgar display of money and muscle power, gross neglect of people, extraction of political rent, or flagrant misuse of public funds for self-promotion—this has been the standard practice of our political class over the past several decades. Mayawati is a product of the system and she represents it in full measure. Insofar as her moves appear excessive, they only help us to see the system in its naked form.

It is a different matter how soon the people of this country would recognise the rot in the system. Whenever they do, they will realise Mayawati's contribution in exposing it, in a perverse sense, by stretching things that are taken for granted to their limits. No pontificating or punditry by the elitist media could have explained what ails the system as effectively as her actions have done—Mayawati has done the greatest service to the people of this country. Paradoxically, if she has done a disservice, it is only to the dalits.

The question could legitimately be raised by the dalits that just because others have been exploiting them variously, are not their own leaders entitled to cheat them for self-aggrandisement. Political power, as a key to all problems, should have been used by Mayawati to lessen the woes of the dalit masses at least to the extent the system permits. However, she adopted the easier path of intoxicating her voters with the liquor of identity. Intoxication, trance and mesmerisation do not last long; when they end and dalits wake up to their reality, the entire mayawi castle of Mayawati begins to crumble.

While the sarvajan platform paid her rich dividends, it exacted a disproportionate political price—the importance of dalits declined in the BSP's scheme of things. Many castes and communities that had thronged to her in 2007, giving her government an absolute majority, were soon disillusioned. It showed in the 2009 general elections when the BSP's vote share fell from its peak of 30.46 per cent in 2007 to 27.42 per cent, though it increased its tally in the Lok Sabha from two seats to 21. In the 2012 assembly elections, it dropped by another 1.52 per cent to 25.9 per cent, and she was out of power. The immediate comment Mayawati made about the election result of 2012 was that her core constituency of dalits was still intact and that she would come back to power in 2017. But the 2017 assembly elections delivered the BSP its worst drubbing, a mere 19 seats with a vote share of just over 22 per cent, almost 4 per cent lower than in 2012. This shows that other castes and minorities are fast deserting the BSP and the party would be well-advised not to take its dalit votebank for granted.

This does not mean that the BSP is finished. In our first-past-the-post system, where caste–community equations and money–muscle power play a decisive role, it will carry on. It does however seem to be past its zenith, having wandered too far from its pretence of emancipatory politics for dalits. Look at the paradoxes of this system. The Shiromani Akali Dal in Punjab got 56 seats in 2012 with 34.75 per cent of the vote as against Congress' 46 seats with 40.11 per cent vote share. In 2017, ironically, the Congress stormed to power in Punjab with 77 seats albeit with a decreased vote share of 38.5 per cent. Meanwhile, the BSP's share of the vote in UP declined by only 4.52 per cent but this cost it 126 seats, i.e., 31.04 per cent of the total number of seats.

Mayawati could surely have gone further to empower the people, but the question is whether she would then have survived in mainstream politics. Do the people really matter in our so-called democracy? They do figure once in five years at the polling booth to decide who should govern them. But behind this appearance is the reality of intricate brokering networks of castes and communities, and huge, competitive, upfront investment to keep the machinery oiled. We live in times when candidates literally buy their candidature. An idea of the magnitude of the return on these investments can be had from the asset declarations of the candidates who contested two consecutive elections. The Association for Democratic Reforms and Uttar Pradesh Election Watch revealed that the average individual assets of the 285 re-contesting MLAs for the 2012 UP assembly elections increased from Rs 1.21 crore (2007) to Rs 3.56 crore (2012), registering a growth of 194 per cent. Paradoxically, as these returns soared over the years, the voice of the people, the metric of democracy, has suffered a contraction.

Can Mayawati escape this inexorable logic of mainstream politics? Certainly not. As the facts reveal, she has not just played the game but also outdone her competitors. Her party fielded the maximum number of candidates who re-contested elections (120), and their assets grew by a whopping 226 per cent—from an average of Rs 1.22 crore in 2007 to one of Rs 3.97 crore in 2012. The average BSP legislator seeking re-election exceeded her/his counterpart in the pacesetter Congress (27) by 244 per cent, Rashtriya Lok Dal (6) by 421 per cent, Qaumi Ekta Dal (2) by 343 per cent, and Ittehad-e-Millat Council (1) by 523 per cent. Not only that, the number of candidates re-contesting from the other parties is relatively insignificant, as indicated within the brackets against each of these parties. Of the top ten re-contesting candidates ranked by quantum growth in assets, the BSP topped the list. The BSP also dominated the list of the top ten wealthy candidates, with five compared to the Congress' two and Samajwadi Party's one. Even in 2017, the BSP outshone all rivals in the personal wealth of its candidates—84 per cent of its candidates being crorepatis, followed by the BJP at 79 per cent.

Money and criminality are not essentially disconnected. But insofar as the latter is measured by the number of registered criminal cases, it is dependent upon which political party is in power. When the BSP is in power, the criminality of the SP, its arch rival, may be amplified in police records and that of the BSP dampened. Notwithstanding this fact, the ADR/UPEW data reveals that the BSP is not far behind in putting up candidates with criminal charges. In 2012, the SP had the maximum of 199 out of 401, i.e. 50 per cent candidates with ongoing criminal cases against them. The BJP, the self-proclaimed 'party with a difference' stood next with 144 out of 397 (36 per cent) and the Congress came third with 120 out of 354 (34 per cent). The BSP stood fourth with 131 out of 403 (33 per cent). Look at the BSP from any other angle: it appears no different from any other ruling class party, fully sucked into the foul marsh of electoral politics.

Symbolic wins and real defeats

Social revolution, or the transformation of basic caste or class relations, cannot come through the first-past-the-post type of elections we have adopted. While election victories in India do not need even the passive affirmation of a majority, a social revolution needs their active participation. With the growing fragmentation of the polity into interest groups associated with the process of uneven development and expressed through existing fault lines such as caste, the vote share required to rule has already gone down to absurd levels (in 2014, the Modi-led BJP won a mere 31 per cent of the vote to secure its 282 seats, the lowest vote share of any party to win a clear majority in the Lok Sabha). Mayawati's rainbow politics merely represents shrewd electoral arithmetic and hence should never have been confused with social revolution. As the experience in UP amply demonstrates, her kind of caste-based coalition ends up deepening casteism—in ways antithetical to any social revolution.

It is interesting to speculate what Kanshi Ram would have done at this juncture. One expects he would have somehow stemmed the decline and reconfigured political equations to stay in power for longer. If he was around, he would have perhaps catapulted the BSP to power at the centre and given it a new shine. That would have been his ultimate goal, where he would have received the master key to political power. It certainly goes to his credit that the goalpost was within sight. As for whether political power has been the master key to the problems of dalits, Mayawati's four terms as chief minister of UP can be examined in relation to the state's dalits. The fact is that their condition, on most developmental parameters, is worse than that of dalits in other states. Statues and memorials intoxicate people with identity pride, which the ruling classes always relish. It is beneficial to them that the dalits remain in a stupor, oblivious to reality. That is what happened in Mayawati's UP. If she had even thought of altering the structure of society in any manner, she would have realised what it took. Neither she nor her mentor spoke the language of radical transformation.

It might help to conclude with where we began—the Kanshi Ram story. What had first annoyed Kanshi Ram and prompted his entry into public life was the emotional issue of celebrating jayantis, not the spate of caste atrocities in Maharashtra. His political outlook continued to reflect his point of entry into politics. While his choices made great strategic sense, they make proportionately poor sense when seen in terms of comprehending the core problem. Kanshi Ram saw that if dalits had political power, issues like demanding holidays on Ambedkar or Buddha Jayanti or naming universities or stadiums after Ambedkar and raising statues for a new bahujan pantheon would not arise. This crude understanding informed his entire mission. But what constitutes political power and for whom? If Ambedkar had seen politics the way Kanshi Ram did, he would not have warned the nation that equality in politics but inequality in economics and society would be an explosive contradiction that shall continue to haunt India. The oft-cited words of his last speech to the Constituent Assembly, delivered on 25 November 1949, must ring in our ears:

> In politics we will have equality and in social and economic life we will have inequality. In politics we will be recognising the principle of one man one vote and one vote one value. In our social and economic life, we shall, by reason of our social and economic structure, continue to deny the principle of one man one value. How long shall we continue to live this life of contradictions? How long shall we continue to deny equality in our social and economic life? If we continue to deny it for long, we will do so only by putting our political democracy in peril. We must remove this contradiction at the earliest possible moment or else those who suffer from inequality will blow up the structure of political democracy which this Assembly has so laboriously built up (*BAWS 13*, 1216).

Kanshi Ram excelled at taking identity politics to new heights. While everyone played caste politics, he beat them hollow at this game. Identity politics can massage your ego, make you feel good, but it cannot feed your hunger, or liberate you from bondage. It can give you statues and memorials, but not what these icons lived for. Kanshi Ram never agitated on any real issue, but harped on an abstraction of political power. The BSP's accomplishments are painted by its proponents as the empowerment of dalits, even a silent revolution, but all this was confined to the realm of notions.

Kanshi Ram's conception of bahujan glosses over the material disparities between various castes and communities. There is a class divide between rich shudra farmers and dalit farm labourers. Caste atrocities are a manifestation of these contradictions, and the perpetrators are invariably people belonging to the shudra castes, assumed to be constituent of the bahujan category. There is plenty of evidence, right from Jotirao Phule's attempt to bring shudras and ati-shudras (dalits) together, to indicate that the much-desired unity of the working castes has never yet materialised. In the wake of the Mandal reservations, dalits supported reservations, thinking that it would bind them together. There is not the slightest evidence that such a bond was formed anywhere. On the contrary, it can be easily seen, if statistics on atrocities are taken as proxy, that the gaps between the caste factions of haves and have-nots are wider than ever. Not even SCs and STs, who are taken as a conjoint constitutional category, could be homogenised in the last seven decades. The castes demanding reservations, such as gujjars in Rajasthan in 2008 and the herding caste of dhangars in Maharashtra in 2016–17 seek recognition as STs, and pointedly not as SCs.

Castes are inherently divisive, they can never integrate. Nor can they be equalised. It could be said of Kanshi Ram's bahujan blueprint that it rested primarily on the jatavs/chamars. It was never replicated anywhere outside UP despite his monumental efforts. The success of Kanshi Ram or the BSP could be explained, like I have tried to do, only by a unique combination of factors that obtained in UP, rather than by the idea of a bahujan, which has not worked anywhere else and now appears to have become ephemeral even in the state.

12

The Aerocasteics of the Congress, the Acrobatics of Ambedkarites

To say that Rahul Gandhi is great may be redundant, for it follows from the axiom that all Gandhis are great. In 2008, while on a tour of Vidarbha, Maharashtra, he met with Kalawati, the widow of Parshuram Bandurkar of Jalka village in my district—Yavatmal. Bandurkar had committed suicide in 2005, becoming one of over 200,000 farmers to take their own lives in the first decade of the millennium. Politics over this harrowing phenomenon has blurred its analysis. While eminent economists like Utsa Patnaik, Jayati Ghosh and Prabhat Patnaik have been arguing for years that structural changes in the macro-economic policy of the Indian government—favouring privatisation, liberalisation and globalisation—have been at the root of farmer suicides, their views are regularly dismissed as the rants of left-leaning intellectuals. In 2012, a survey was conducted in the Vidarbha region, which involved a qualitative ranking of the ascribed causes for suicide among the farming families who had lost someone. The reasons that emerged in order of salience were as follows: debt, alcohol addiction, environment, low prices for produce, stress and family responsibilities, apathy, poor irrigation, increased cost of cultivation, private money lenders, use of chemical fertilizers, and crop failure (Amol Dongre and Pradeep Deshmukh 2012).

Taken individually these may appear unsurprising, even abiding features of the agricultural landscape, but their concentration into a sociological catastrophe and an epidemic of suicide can be explained only in terms of the effects of the neoliberal policies introduced by Rahul Gandhi's party since the 1980s, and accorded pre-eminence from 1991 onwards. Rahul's visit made Kalawati a household name because of his opportunistic use of her plight during his 2009 speech in Parliament to justify the Indo–US nuclear deal, as though electricity shortages were causing farmers to lose the will to live. On 16 January of the same year, he made headlines when he spent a night, along with the British foreign secretary David Miliband, in a dalit's hut in Simra village in his constituency Amethi, in Uttar Pradesh. He repeated the feat on 23 September 2009—on the eve of the anniversary of the Poona Pact of 1932, whether he was aware of the fact or not—and took the BSP-ruled state police by surprise. He landed unannounced in Lucknow and spent the night at Cheddi Pasi's hut in the Rampur–Deogan village in Shravasti district. The next morning, he bathed in the open by drawing water from a hand pump.

Such stories of his dalitophilia are legion. Do they not remind us of the original Gandhi—the man whom the world regards as the 'Mahatma'? In terms of stage-managed spectacles of solidarity, M.K. Gandhi still has the edge on Rahul. Leah Renold's paper "Gandhi: Patron Saint of the Industrialist" describes the arrangements for his 1946 stay in a 'bhangi colony':

> Half the residents were moved out before his visit and the shacks of the residents torn down and neat little huts constructed in their place. The entrances and windows of the huts were screened with matting, and during the length of Gandhi's visit, were kept sprinkled with water to provide a cooling effect. The local temple was white-washed and new brick paths were laid (1994, 19).

Getting the choreography of political greatness right can be demanding work, but Gandhi's visits to the so-named Balmiki Basti in Delhi played well to the public and are today bathed in the aura of his saintliness. The Marxist historian, Vijay Prashad, in his pioneering study *Untouchable Freedom: A Social History of a Dalit Community*, writes: 'In text and guide books, in fiction and documentaries, the tale of Gandhi and the Bhangi Colony celebrates his compassion' (2001, 140). Prashad goes on to adduce some crucial historical information from the time Gandhi stayed among the sweepers in Delhi in April 1946, a trademark stunt that did nothing but prove his mastery of visual rhetoric:

> The most apparent barrier was inter-dining, for when some Balmikis invited Gandhi to eat with them on 3 April, he demurred…'You can offer me goat's milk,' he said, 'but I will pay for it. If you are keen that I should take food prepared by you, you can come here and cook my food for me.' … When a dalit gave Gandhi nuts, he fed them to his goat, saying that he would eat them later, in the goat's milk. Most of Gandhi's food, nuts and grains, came from Birla House; he did not take these from the dalits (140–41).

The self-dramatising visit, the assumption of benign patronage, the authority to dispense wisdom—Rahul both wittingly and unwittingly follows in these footsteps. In October 2013, with the 2014 general elections in mind, he reached out to the dalits again while addressing a function at the National Awareness Camp for Scheduled Castes' Empowerment at Vigyan Bhawan in Lucknow. His use of an astronomical metaphor—escape velocity—was particularly cringe-inducing. He said:

> The escape velocity for Earth is 11.2 km per second while that of Jupiter is 60 km per second. In India, we have a concept of caste. If one belongs to a backward caste and wants to attain success, then one needs an escape velocity to attain that success. Dalits in this country need the escape velocity of Jupiter to attain success. … We are proud of Dr Ambedkar, he was the first person to use escape velocity.

To a prince aloft since birth in the stratosphere of political power, a metaphor like 'escape velocity' may come naturally. But to the dalits, who are victims of the doublespeak of priests and princes, such words are grating. Not that the jargon of aeronautics is unfamiliar; on the contrary, it evokes an uncanny sense of déjà vu. The metaphor has been familiar to dalits since the days when astronomy was astrology; they have been indoctrinated for centuries with the vedic dictum that their caste can be escaped only in the next birth with karmic points earned by diligent performance of caste duties in the present life.

Rahul's 'escape velocity' is but a savvy translation of the original astrological dictum. He seems to imply that at this velocity, one escapes into an orbit of castelessness. The success of the mission rests on individual capability, intrinsic worth and initiative, and does not concern itself with the system of castes that stays in place. This is precisely what the vedic tenet also meant—you could work and escape your given caste, albeit in another birth, but there was no escaping the caste system. To be fair, Rahul may not have meant to validate the ancient vedic schema. If one wishes to see his remarks in a positive light, he is correct to the extent that dalits have to exert far more effort (Jupiter's escape velocity) than the others (who can manage with Earth's escape velocity) to achieve their life goals. But would doing so begin to facilitate an escape from caste? He spoke of Ambedkar and Kanshi Ram having achieved the desired escape velocity. Did they really escape caste? Can he be so ignorant as not to know that whatever the achievements of dalits, even successful individuals among them remain tagged by caste and are far from accessing anything like unmarked secular citizenship?

It is possible Rahul meant that dalits need the force of external propulsion to escape their stigmatised and miserable existence, implying that the Congress party would motor them upwards. When his party took over the reins of power from the British, it had ample opportunity to think of empowering dalits, indeed, all Indians. It is universally accepted today that human empowerment requires three essential ingredients: education, healthcare and security of livelihood. A look at the Congress administration's record in this regard would be instructive. In free India, education ought to have meant providing all children free, equal-quality education up to the age of 18 years through a common schooling system based on neighbourhood schools, a policy advocated by the first education commission—the Kothari Commission. Education, given its critical importance, should have been the fundamental right of all children, as it is in around 135 countries (according to Unesco's "Education for All: Global Monitoring Report", 2010). It should have had the first claim on the revenues of the state. Instead, the Congress party followed the colonial pretext of the lack of resources and refused to make education a fundamental right (discussed in "The Education Mantra").

Public healthcare remains among the most neglected obligations of the government today. According to the National Family Health Survey–3 (2005–06), the private medical sector remains the primary source of health care for 70 per cent of households in urban areas and 63 per cent of households in rural areas. The study conducted by the IMS Institute for Healthcare Informatics in 2013 stretched to 14,000 households across 12 states and indicated a steady increase in the use of private healthcare facilities in the last 25 years, whether for outpatient or inpatient services across rural and urban areas (*Hindu*, 30 July 2013). The high out-of-pocket cost of private healthcare is found to be a major cause of poverty. While several governments and researchers have talked about the need to spend at least 2.5 per cent of the GDP on health, the Indian government spent only about 1.4 per cent in 2014, according to a PricewaterhouseCoopers report. The report adds that India's total expenditure (public and private) on health is 4.7 per cent of its GDP as against the world average of around 10 per cent.

Livelihood security in rural areas may be conceptualised in terms of land-ownership via radical land reforms, and in urban areas as productive employment through industrialisation. The government of independent India made a show of land reforms but the result speaks for itself. Even today, 9.5 per cent of households own 56.5 per cent of the land, making it among the most unequal land distributions in the world. The Socio-Economic and Caste Census Report released by the government in 2015 reveals that 56 per cent of rural households have no land apart from their homes. The country did make progress in industrialisation but this failed to generate enough job opportunities for people. Ambedkar had provided a valuable insight into these problems with his essay "Small Holdings in India and their Remedies" (*Journal of the Indian Economic Society* Vol. 1, 1918), where he proposed expanding industry to connect the 'crystallised surplus' of idle capital to the vast rural mass of idle labour (at risk of turning 'predatory' in the absence of economic opportunity). Capital investment in productive enterprise would secure its own increase, leading to a virtuous cycle wherein expanding industry would attract more labour and—eventually, as unprofitable holdings in the countryside were abandoned for secondary sector employment—this would make possible an increase in the size of landholdings in the countryside. In the last decade of his life Ambedkar also saw the urgency of altering economic relations in the countryside via land distribution among dalits (as detailed in the chapter "Dalit Protests in Gujarat"). If the Congress party had engaged with this blueprint, five decades of lacklustre economic growth and the continual shrinkage of landholdings might have been avoided. Not only would the livelihood security of people have been addressed but Indian society as a whole may have acquired the escape velocity to transcend its miserable state of underdevelopment. In a word, escape velocity is a product of empowerment and Rahul Gandhi needs to ask himself why such fundamental change was never effected.

Rahul credited Kanshi Ram with being the second person after Ambedkar to advance dalits towards a gravity-free existence. However, he criticised Kanshi Ram's successor, Mayawati, for having stalled the project of empowerment by building a cult around herself. He thundered, 'One or two dalit leaders cannot galvanise a movement; we need lakhs of dalit leaders for it to progress,' not forgetting to add, 'The Congress party is the voice of India. We want people from the dalit community as MPs and MLAs; we want everyone to participate.' Didn't he recognise that Mayawati, or for that matter any Indian politician, was faithfully emulating a pattern of conduct set by the Congress? Didn't he see that there has been no lack of dalit MPs and MLAs all these years? Thanks to his party, and a certain M.K. Gandhi in particular, the independent representation granted to dalits by the colonial government was snuffed out before it could be realised. Such representation through separate electorates had been granted to Muslims, Buddhists, Sikhs, Indian Christians, Anglo-Indians, Europeans and the untouchables. Gandhi did not oppose the grant to any other category but declared that he would oppose it for the untouchables. He justified his opposition as a defence of Hindu unity, as if that was what the caste system had accomplished over the centuries. He went on fast and compelled Ambedkar to give up the hard-won separate electorates for the Depressed Classes, under the terms of the Poona Pact of September 1932 (discussed in the chapter "Reservations"). The entire scheme of political empowerment of dalits conceived by Ambedkar was thus reversed to become its opposite, political enslavement. The so-called dalit leaders who get elected from the reserved seats work slavishly for the ruling class parties that sustain them in positions of power. Rahul Gandhi needs to refresh his knowledge of the fraught history of political reservation in order to understand how his party cunningly re-enslaved dalits under secular pretexts. A good place to begin would be with Ambedkar and Kanshi Ram, since both of them already excite his admiration. He will be interested to learn that they were both bitter about this deceit and had called its offspring, the mercenary dalit leadership elected on reserved seats, stooges.

The pitfalls of this system become evident when political stooges with ruling-class support easily defeat dalit candidates fighting for the cause of their community from outside the patronage networks of mainstream parties. Even Ambedkar lost the first Lok Sabha election in 1952 to the Congress candidate Narayan Kajrolkar, a former personal assistant of his. (Kajrolkar's valuable service to the Congress was repaid with a Padma Bhushan in 1970.) In the 1954 by-election for the reserved (Lok Sabha) seat of Bhandara, Ambedkar was again defeated by a political non-entity, Bhaurao Borkar, fielded by the Congress. The scheme of joint electorates has led to the co-option of dalits under different banners and the fragmentation of their movement, severely limiting the possibility of independent representation or alliance.

Under a joint electorate, since the dalit voters are a minority and count for little in bringing dalit politicians to power, the latter are not likely to care for them, leave alone safeguarding their interests. Rather, since their election depends entirely on the ruling class parties for resources and guaranteed vote banks, dalit leaders are obsequious towards their patrons in those parties. Furthermore, major parties almost never field SC/ST candidates in the 'general' constituencies (and rarely nominate them to the Rajya Sabha, the house of elders, with a total membership of 250). The reserved seats in the Lok Sabha ordained by Article 330 of the Constitution—eighty-four for the SCs and forty-seven for the STs out of its total strength of 543—serve as politically inert additions to the tally of contesting parties and as air suction vents to manage an unwieldy, 'inflammable' section of the populace that has, in the past, known a history of politicisation. Ambedkar realised that this system of political reservation had become a way to perpetuate slavery and demanded its end in 1955, but in vain. Political reservation and the leaders it has produced lend infinite mass to the existing planet of caste; they make escape velocity impossible to achieve.

In the post-Ambedkar period, dalit activists have constantly demanded an end to political reservations, but it has become much too useful to the ruling classes to be relinquished. In 1974, the Dalit Panther of Gujarat symbolically set fire to Article 330 and demanded its revocation. To mourn fifty years of the Poona Pact, Kanshi Ram launched a countrywide movement on 24 September 1982, with sixty simultaneous denunciation programmes from Poona to Jalandhar, stating that such reservations had created a tribe of chamchas (stooges) and demanded an end to 'chamcha raj'. Finally the penny had dropped: the Poona Pact became an awkward landmark in the Congress record rather than an event to celebrate, and prime minister Indira Gandhi was forced to abandon her plans to commemorate the occasion.

Self-proclaimed Ambedkarites

The track record of the Congress vis-à-vis dalits inspires nothing but doubt and dismay. From the days of the 'benign' Mahatma, dalits have endured antipathy from a Congress that harijanised them, while they continued to support it for a lack of alternatives. Ambedkar exposed it all in an exasperated account, *What Congress and Gandhi Have Done to the Untouchables* (1945), and indicted Gandhi for projecting himself as a saviour of the untouchables along with the Congress party, while doing nothing more than practice insincere symbolism (*BAWS* 9, 259). Despite this, in the following year, Ambedkar set aside his pride and misgivings about the Congress party and agreed to cooperate with it. Rather, it was a case of mutual need. After Ambedkar lost his membership of the Constituent Assembly on account of his constituency going over to East Pakistan under the Mountbatten Plan of June 1946, he was elected by the Congress to the CA, a position that he believed would enable him to protect the safeguards for dalits secured under British rule. Later, the Congress made him chairman of the most important committee of the CA—the drafting committee. The following year, he accepted the berth of law minister in Nehru's cabinet. The Congress and its court historians would later make the claim that the party generously chose to overlook Ambedkar's antagonism in offering him these opportunities—without adding that it had its own interests in mind. With Ambedkar as the chairman of the drafting committee—soon to be projected as the writer of the Constitution—the entire lower strata of Indian society would come to emotionally identify with the document, however ineffective it might prove in doing them any good. In the Nehru cabinet, however, they had not much use for him apart from placating the dalits. Ambedkar realised this and resigned from the cabinet in 1951 over the stalling of the Hindu Code Bill—through which he had attempted to bring about essential reforms in Hindu personal law by permitting divorce and expanding the property rights of widows and daughters—which drew widespread opposition from orthodox Hindus. In his resignation letter, he argued that to pass legislation relating to economic problems without addressing inequalities of class, caste and sex is to 'make a farce of our Constitution and to build a palace on a dung heap'.

In the post-Ambedkar movement, dalit leaders pursue their self-interest in the name of 'Ambedkarism' to garner support. Ambedkar had in fact warned dalit leaders against joining the Congress in a speech at Lucknow on 25 April 1948: 'The Scheduled Castes cannot capture political power by joining the Congress. It is a big organisation and if we enter the Congress we will be a mere drop in the ocean ... the Congress is a burning house and we cannot be prosperous by entering it' (*BAWS* 17, Part 3, 389) Both his followers and detractors are given to citing Ambedkar opportunistically. While waiting for better offers to come their way, these Ambedkarites might invoke 'dalit interests'—a tack taken by a few in Ambedkar's times too—but can do little to effect change upon being voted to power. When the Congress spread its net of co-option under the leadership of Yashwantrao Chavan in Maharashtra, Ambedkarite leaders—representing various factions of the RPI—fell into it willingly, proclaiming all the while that they would be able to serve dalit interests better. They justified their barefaced lust for power by arguing that even Ambedkar had joined the Nehru government. While reserved seats under a joint electorate effectively neutralised the dalit vote and precluded dalit aspirations from being reflected in electoral outcomes, co-option—or buying off prominent dalit leaders—took care of any loose threads. What are these 'dalit interests' that the Ambedkarite leaders cry themselves hoarse about?

Don't they know that about 90 per cent of dalits lead crisis-ridden lives as landless labourers, small-scale farmers, artisans in villages, slum-dwelling casual workers and pedlars in the informal sector of the urban economy? Ambedkar had seen this at the end of his life and lamented that he could not do much for the rural dalit population. Have the leaders in the Congress and BJP achieved anything for these people over the last six decades?

The Congress may be identified as the original beneficiary of this arrangement, but it is the BJP that today commands the largest number of reserved seats. It has taken over seamlessly from where the Congress left off. In the 2014 general elections, out of the eighty-four Lok Sabha constituencies reserved for SCs, the BJP won a total of forty-two seats, a significant rise from the twelve it had won in 2009 and still more impressive against the paltry six that remain with the Congress. The BSP drew a blank in the 503 seats it had contested, and after its 2017 assembly election drubbing, Mayawati had to forfeit her Rajya Sabha seat as well—after all no reservations are mandated for the House of Elders where only rank and influence matter. Just a select number of exceptionally pliant dalits from the mainstream parties may hope for a membership.

For the demoralising impact of this legacy on dalit politics and leadership, the case of the three dalit Rams now playing Hanuman to the BJP makes for an instructive example. Ramdas Athavale has been able to amass assets worth crores of rupees and at the same time claim the legacy of Ambedkar, who symbolised extraordinary commitment to the cause of the disadvantaged. A one-time Dalit Panther, Athavale first joined hands with the NCP–Congress coalition government in Maharashtra, before accusing his mentors in the Congress—who had plucked him from a dingy room in Mumbai's Siddharth Vihar and installed him in an air-conditioned suite at Sahyadri as a cabinet minister of Maharashtra—of 'humiliation', and allying promptly thereafter with the BJP. Today he is minister of state for social justice and empowerment. The other Rams—Ram Vilas Paswan (union minister of food and public distribution in the 2014 Modi cabinet and long-term BJP ally), Ram Shankar Katheria (the BJP's in-house RSS-trained dalit leader and minister in the cabinet), and Udit Raj (whose original name was Ram Raj), today the BJP member of parliament from Delhi and chairman of the All India Confederation of SC/ST Organisations—as well as numerous other political pedlars of their ilk, all run enterprising careers in the name of Ambedkar and the advancement of dalit interests. Paswan arguably leads the field, having been a union minister in four successive governments, drawn from either side of the aisle, from 1996 to 2009, and now enjoying his fifth term in executive office.

Communalism qua caste

Seen against the lows to which Indian democracy has stooped, the careerist acrobatics of dalit leaders should surprise nobody. After all, everyone has been guilty of it. Why grudge the dalit leaders their chance? While the difference between the BJP and the Congress is often negligible, the reason for alarm stems from what the RSS–BJP combine has professed so far, and consequently, the public perception of the two parties. Unlike the Congress, which has no doubt behaved as a communal party whenever such behaviour could be turned to advantage, while pandering above all to the bourgeoisie, the BJP is an ideology-driven party committed to the realisation of a Hindu rashtra. Having realised that what appears as the Hindu majority of the country is really a collective of caste minorities, the RSS has in recent years resorted to the ploy of samrasata—harmony between castes—to woo other communities. It may have managed to accommodate token representatives from other communities, including Muslims, but it cannot escape the communal tag. The sight of the BJP's Karnataka president B.S. Yeddyurappa visiting the homes of dalits in May 2017 but preferring to eat food ordered from a hotel, around the same time the Uttar Pradesh chief minister Yogi Adityanath offered soap and shampoo to dalits to clean themselves before attending a public meeting, should compel us to probe the difference between the Congress and the BJP. Is it one of degree or of kind?

This first leads to the question: to what degree can the Congress be called secular, i.e., not communal? The Congress is mistakenly taken as secular, socialist, democratic—words picked up from the Preamble of the Constitution, and which have served to camouflage the party's real character no less than that of the Constitution. The Congress certainly identified itself with the idea that India should develop into a modern nation, but it chose a transactional approach supporting capitalist growth. This approach does not pride itself on coherence or consistency, hence the Congress also faltered. Transactional behaviour takes place in management mode: for instance, according to the capitalist calculus, some amount of socialist rhetoric and give-aways are always beneficial to growth, as exercises in public relations if nothing else. The Congress' appropriation of secularism was equally lacking in conviction. Careful analysis would reveal that the doings and misdoings of the Congress paved the way for hindutva forces at every stage of their resurgence. The beginning of this process may be seen right at the adoption of the distorted secularism—dharmanirpekshata—of the Constitution, which was not the state disavowing religion and instituting a firewall between religion and politics, but holding the door open for religious sentiments to come flooding in, turning passive usher to a majoritarian takeover of the public space. The main contrast between the Congress and the BJP is that between the improvisatory character of capitalism and the unyielding one of fascism.

Casteism and communalism are erroneously viewed as disconnected problems. They are not. As I have argued in my book, *Hindutva and Dalits* (2005), the roots of communalism are to be found in casteism. The hatred of the hindutva forces for Muslims and Christians is not because they follow some alien faith—or because their punyabhoomi (holy land) is different from their pitrubhoomi (land of birth) in Savarkar's language—but because a vast majority of these communities come from the stock of the oppressed castes, people who had defied Hinduism and dared to convert. They still resent these converts, disparaging them as unclean, uncultured, and backward—just as they do dalits. It is a sad comment on the understanding of the left-liberal secularists that they do not acknowledge this connection. While quick to protest against any communal outrage identified exclusively with Hindus and Muslims, they maintain an unholy silence over daily incidents of caste violence. Concern over communal conflict is regarded as progressive but any concern for caste atrocities is taken to be retrograde or irrelevant.

Caste venom is embedded in the body politic of this country. The BJP occasionally spews it; the Congress attempts to conceal it. If one takes a hard look at the Congress party's history, one must acknowledge the condemnable role it played in bringing about the present political configuration. It was the failure of the Congress to accommodate Muslim aspirations that germinated Muslim separatist politics. There is no hiding the fact that the Congress projected itself as a Hindu party in contrast to the Muslim League, a relationship that shaped communal politics to culminate in Partition three decades later. The large number of leaders the Congress shared during this period with the Hindu Mahasabha, and those who transitioned smoothly from the Congress into the Jana Sangh after independence, gives away this proximity. Gandhi, in transforming the Congress into a mass movement, used all manner of Hindu symbols such as an ideal called Ram rajya, hymns like vaishnav janato or raghupati raghav, the concept of sanatan dharma, the exegesis of the Bhagavad Gita, in order to appeal to the masses. Congress governments let Hindu cultural hegemony spread itself over the state as its default culture.

A perfect illustration of the Congress' role in leading the country towards Hindu majoritarianism is L.K. Advani's choice of location for the launch of his 1990 rath yatra. With its revanchist mission to build a Ram temple at Ayodhya, Advani's yatra began from the temple of Somnath in Gujarat, which Congress leaders like Vallabhbhai Patel and K.M. Munshi had been instrumental in rebuilding after independence—as a gesture of 'cultural resurgence' that proved an ominous pre-echo of the Ramjanmabhoomi movement. Patel and Munshi had imperiously overridden the recommendations of both the Department of Archaeology and the Department of Education, which cautioned that the ruins of Somnath should be preserved and the new temple built elsewhere. Patel's response, as documented in Hilal Ahmed's *Muslim Political Discourse in Post-Colonial India*, was:

> The Hindu sentiment in regard to this temple is both strong and widespread. In the present conditions, it is unlikely that that sentiment will be satisfied by mere restoration of the temple or by prolonging its life. The restoration of the idol would be a point of honour and sentiment with the Hindu public (2014, 113).

The ruins were duly cannibalised and built over to raise the new temple, its foundation stone laid on 11 May 1951 by Rajendra Prasad, the president (and veteran Congress figure) who washed the feet of some two hundred brahmins in Banaras the following year, making evident the inseparability of Hindu revivalism and casteism. That K.M. Munshi ended his days with the Bharatiya Jana Sangh rounds off the story to perfection.

The Congress remained unrivalled during the early decades after independence, but did nothing to spread secular consciousness. Ambedkar's exit from the government over the Hindu Code Bill was portentous of the decades to come. The only religious reforms mandated in the last 70 years are the passing of an anti-sati law after nationwide uproar over the burning of the eighteen-year-old Roop Kanwar on her husband's pyre in Rajasthan in 1987, and the recent ruling against the practice of triple talaq. In operational terms, the state's much-flaunted dharmanirpekshata came to mean the hegemony of the majority religion which has blatantly assumed the status of a national tradition. If the chief minister of Uttar Pradesh, Yogi Adityanath, orders grand

Janmashtami celebrations all over his state (*Indian Express*, 14 August 2017), it is not to be taken as an exception but rather the culmination of this default tradition of majoritarianism.

Moreover, the hindutva parties—the Jan Sangh and later the BJP—were a fringe force until the communal intrigues of the Congress bolstered them. History stands witness that it all started with Rajiv Gandhi's unwarranted intervention in the Shah Bano case in 1985. He used his large parliamentary majority to overturn a just, landmark Supreme Court verdict, in order to appease Muslim traditionalists. It provided the requisite spark for hindutva forces to light a communal fire. In a clumsy balancing act, this time to appease the Hindus, Rajiv Gandhi ordered the opening of the locks of the Babri masjid in Ayodhya and let the fire turn into an inferno. The demolition of the Babri mosque and the rioting that followed claimed the lives of hundreds of people and catapulted the BJP to the helm of power. Even in the actual demolition of the mosque, the tacit role of the then prime minister, Narasimha Rao, is variously documented. Instances of such collusion—through the deliberate omission to act—are indeed aplenty. Secularism is not confined in its application only to Islam or Muslims; it encompasses all communities and must necessarily include castes—the bedrock of Indian society. Unsurprisingly, caste never figures even remotely in discussions of secularism and progressive politics, which is why those who live under its multiple impositions are told their only way out is via escape velocity.

Anatomy, physics, and the sorcerer's apprentice

Some dismiss Rahul Gandhi's curious dalitophilia as publicity antics, but I tend to sympathise with him. While his expression may have aimed at image building, there is an element of sincerity in it that cannot be denied. After all, it takes effort to live like an ordinary dalit in a village even for a night, without a camera around, as he did in Rampur–Deogan. We may even provocatively suggest that he went one up on the Mahatma—in that Rahul did not demand goat's milk or nuts, nor did he summon dinner from an industrialist's house. Let his fleeting visit not be cynically dismissed as the adventure tourism of a prince. He is also correct in describing dalits as the reedh ki haddi (spinal column) of the Congress. It is true that dalits have supported the Congress electorally for way too long. However, when he speaks of the need to do more for them, the question that arises is that why the Congress in its long and eventful history has so little progress to report on that front. In more than one sense, the party's neglected spine is in no state to continue supporting the weight of its swollen head.

Going by his illustrious party's track record, Rahul's invocation of frontier science for a solution to the caste problem shows as what it is—opportunistic political rhetoric. Unfortunately, he does not seem to be versed well enough in either the history of caste or the fundamentals of science for the metaphor to work. To say that dalits need escape velocity in order to succeed is a primary-level blunder committed by most analysts in explaining the vexatious problem of caste, which he simply repeats. It should be clear why it is not the dalits but the Indian social structure that needs escape velocity to overcome caste. The logic behind positive discrimination in the form of reservations simply belittles dalits anew, always taking them as subservient beneficiaries, lacking in something, suffering from some disability and therefore to be helped along by a charitable society.

Such logic needs to be turned on its head: it is society that is sick with the disease of casteism and it is dalits who most want to cure it. It is society that needs escape velocity to overcome its disorder and accept the dalits as its own. The disease, particularly when it is of a metastasising cancerous variety like casteism, needs to be treated comprehensively; localised interventions and surgical procedures are a waste of time. This was Ambedkar's diagnosis, and his preferred remedy—expressed in *Annihilation of Caste*—was 'dynamiting the dharmashastras' to achieve this escape velocity. Perhaps Rahul Gandhi should apply himself to a study of this text before issuing his next pronouncement on the situation of dalits.Rahul's application of astrophysics to a social context is similarly misjudged. Escape velocity assumes the absence of atmospheric friction, the force of the latter being negligible compared to the pressure exerted by gravity. In a society, the opposite holds true. Apart from the force field of cultural stasis commanded by the caste system, its rejuvenation under modern institutional structures constitutes an additional frictional force that resists the annihilation project. It may well overwhelm the intrinsic mass of the projectile. Although the onslaught of colonial and postcolonial modernity has somewhat eroded the classical caste system along the purity–pollution axis, caste has made a place for itself at the heart of the post-liberalisation superstructure (further discussed in "Slumdogs and Millionaires"). It is apparent that there is going to be formidable resistance to any propulsion seeking to take the societal vessel out of the orbit of the caste system. While the magnitude of the force impelling us towards annihilation of caste is modest, looking to enhance it with escape velocity is akin to sorcery or faith healing; exactly the kind of snake oil that has been sold to dalits for too long already.

The veteran Congressman P.V. Narasimha Rao candidly wrote in his memoirs that our political culture has always been feudal at the core, where the leader assumes absolute power. Intra-party democracy has never existed in any party. This country, proclaiming itself a republic and vesting sovereignty in its people, condones the concentration of power in a supreme leader. It began at the dawn of self-rule: Mahatma Gandhi, the supreme leader of the Congress anointed Nehru king and simply asked other contenders like Sardar Patel and Maulana Azad to endorse his choice. Barring a few short interludes, when, for instance, Lal Bahadur Shastri became prime minister (albeit not through a general election), for the greatest part of our post-independence history, the Nehru–Gandhi dynasty has ruled. The Congress established the political culture of the country, which others have followed in varying degrees. Who else but a prince ready for coronation would think that empowerment constitutes doling out food, shelter and life lessons to the poor? Such an approach to social problems smacks of feudal vanity—no less than the vanity of Narendra Modi who draws inspiration from the Mahatma's spiritual casteism and repackages it as a Swachh Bharat Abhiyan.

Rahul has a lot of homework to do, not in astrophysics so much as in political strategy. To fight Modi's hindutva with soft hindtuva is to accept defeat. It is pitiful to see Rahul frantically visiting Hindu temples to establish his Hindu-ness, and annoying to see his party's contortions to avoid taking a clear side on issues involving Hindus or Hinduism. It was abhorrent to see it at pains to establish Rahul as a janeudhari brahmin no less. He must know that all efforts at establishing dalitophile credentials for himself stand annulled by this single declaration. If Rahul Gandhi sincerely wishes to restore the Congress party's reedh ki haddi, he should think of how India may attain the escape velocity required to break free from the grip of caste.

13

Aam Aadmi Party

A Political App for the Neoliberal Era

The Aam Aadmi Party was born on 26 November 2012 out of a rift in the nationwide movement, India against Corruption, that aimed to bring about a Jan Lokpal—people's ombudsman—to deal with corruption in high places. Despite the birthmark of a schism, it held out hope to a people disgusted with politicians, in large part because AAP was formed by young people outside of politics, with voices like well-known lawyer Prashant Bhushan and political analyst Yogendra Yadav as its elder counsel and political midwives. Arvind Kejriwal came into the limelight as a man of ready wit, with a plausible manner and a mission to cleanse politics of corruption, and many activists in the left-of-centre movements responded to his call to arms by joining the party. The new outfit appeared to pose a real challenge to the mainstream parties as it caught the fancy of young people with an entrenched hatred for politicians, who still believed that the present system could be cleansed if good people entered politics. Here were those proverbial good people at last, like the answer to a prayer.

AAP entered the electoral fray with the Delhi assembly elections of 2013 and emerged as the single largest party, slightly short of a majority on its own. It formed government with unsolicited outside support from the Congress. The party fulfilled its twin promises of providing subsidised electricity and free water to the citizens of Delhi immediately after being sworn in. It hugely impressed Delhi voters and generated a favourable wave across the country. At the same time, it showed political immaturity in various acts of omission and commission and with signs of intra-party factionalism. Facing a logjam on the issue of the Lokpal, Kejriwal resigned from office and recommended the dissolution of the state assembly. After its misadventure in contesting the 2014 elections for the Lok Sabha, AAP turned to Delhi with mass voter contact initiatives towards the 2015 state elections which were pitched as a prestige battle between Arvind Kejriwal and prime minister Narendra Modi, with both AAP and the BJP using all their resources to win.

AAP created electoral history by bagging 95.7 per cent of the total number of seats (67 out of 70) and 54.3 per cent of the total number of votes cast in the National Capital Territory of Delhi in February 2015. This is a record of sorts, exceeded by only three electoral performances in the past, all in Sikkim, where the Nar Bahadur Bhandari-led Sikkim Sangram Parishad had won all thirty-two seats in the assembly election of 1989. The same performance was achieved by the five-time chief minister Pawan Kumar Chamling's Sikkim Democratic Front in 2009, after narrowly missing out in 2004 when they had won all but one of the 32 seats. Though these records are important as history, the victory of AAP is unique in many ways. First, no party in India has ever won legislative assembly elections—even in a union territory that is at best a quasi-state—on a plank composed solely of the promise of clean governance, transparency and accountability. Second, better or comparable electoral performances have all come from electoral battles among regional parties on regional issues; none of these parties had taken on a mainstream ruling party and threatened the established mode of politics.

It followed naturally that AAP's success in 2015 was widely

celebrated by a vast majority of the population. After all, in the 2014 general election, the BJP had the lowest vote share, 31 per cent, for any party winning a majority in the Lok Sabha. It meant that the 69 per cent who did not vote for the BJP in that election would have reason to celebrate AAP's win. The initial euphoria created by AAP's victory subsided with a series of setbacks to the fledgling party, and yet it remains important to understand the circumstances that caused its rise and even gave some people the hope of it being a bulwark against the Congress and the resurgent right-wing.

The context of AAP's electoral feat makes it unique in many ways. The virtual ashwamedh launched by the Narendra Modi–Amit Shah combine all over the country after the 2014 general election had netted them a series of victories and made the BJP appear invincible. Given the love for anything vedic and ancient among the BJP and its Sangh parivar affiliates, the grisly machismo of the ashwamedh best captures the right-wing's triumphal progress. A vedic yagna, the ashwamedh is conducted by a king wanting to expand his empire. To this end, he sets a white stallion loose for a year, to be followed in its wanderings by his army in full regalia. Wherever the stallion should venture becomes the king's territory. Anyone who challenges this claim—say, AAP challenging the BJP—must offer battle.[1] The arrogance that accrued from each successive win led the BJP and its control centre, the RSS, to bare ever more of their fascist plans for the nation. The ominous maxim that fascists come to power through elections but cannot be dislodged by elections began to appear frighteningly real. This is the context in which the victory of AAP assumes importance.

---

[1] When the horse successfully returns to the capital after a year's tour, it is asphyxiated, the chief queen is made to lie next to it, and a brahmin priest guides its penis against her vagina. It is meant to symbolically herald the birth of a new king. The horse is then dismembered in conclusion of the sacrifice. See Jamison (1996, 68), and Knipe (2015, 236).

BJP's loss, Modi's defeat

The May 2014 general election saw the ascent of Narendra Modi, riding a storm of media-fuelled adulation. The February 2015 Delhi assembly elections might have begun as a routine poll, but were perceived as a referendum on Modi's rule at the centre. The BJP had staked its entire strategic prowess on the capture of Delhi. In the process, it committed one blunder after another. AAP, too, was in complete disarray after a series of miscalculations in its previous, short-lived forty-nine-day tryst with Delhi's governance. As noted, AAP's minority government during its first stint in office had chosen to resign prematurely in 2014 on failing to pass the Jan Lokpal bill in the assembly. Thereafter, it made the foolhardy decision to contest the 2014 Lok Sabha elections all over the country without any organisational or resource support, while its supremo Arvind Kejriwal—attempting a repeat of his earlier humiliation of Delhi's chief minister, Sheila Dikshit, in her own constituency—brashly took on Modi in Varanasi. Kejriwal was clearly trying to catapult himself onto the national stage as the alternative candidate for the highest office. The BJP-led government at the centre could have manoeuvred the electoral calendar to have Delhi's polls take place directly after its sweep of the Lok Sabha, having bagged a whopping 282 seats in the general election. AAP's petulant resignation had lowered it in people's esteem, while the BJP was riding a high. But Amit Shah's hubris and Modi's narcissism led them to believe they would easily dazzle Delhi's voters, all in good time, as the BJP's triumphs came to be widely publicised. Successive victories in Jharkhand, Jammu and Kashmir, and Maharashtra, albeit with a declining vote share compared to the Lok Sabha elections, had gone to their heads and they imagined they were invincible.

After the announcement of the date of elections—7 February 2015—the BJP unleashed its well-oiled propaganda machinery, backed by thousands of RSS cadres. As though to underscore his ashwamedh run, Modi thundered, 'Jo desh ka mood hai, wahi Dilli ka mood hai'

(The mood of the nation is the mood of Delhi), without the slightest inkling that the claim might boomerang on him. The arsenal of the BJP, comprising Modi, money, mudslinging and majoritarianism, got the party nowhere with Delhi's voters who handed it a crushing defeat. It won a paltry three seats in a house of 70—a 95 per cent plummet from the 60 assembly segments it had taken in the Lok Sabha elections, with a fall of 13 percentage points in its vote share.

The BJP tried everything. It fielded a political novice like Kiran Bedi as its chief ministerial candidate. Bedi, in her police service days in Delhi, had earned kudos from the middle classes, and had participated in the IAC movement, rubbing shoulders with Kejriwal. The gambit was to fail with Delhi's voters who now saw her as a betrayer of the movement, for having joined a mainstream party to undermine her erstwhile comrade. Though there may be many reasons for AAP's victory, there was an element of disapproval of Modi's eight-month rule at the centre by the people of Delhi. It was the first wave of disillusionment with Modi's doublespeak and anti-people, pro-corporate policies. His complicity-by-silence with the book burners, film vandals and religious hate-mongers who have had an unbridled run ever since he came to power, and habit of bypassing parliament with recourse to ordinances—as many as eight in a span of seven months—added fuel to the fire. Modi's hollow rhetoric would win the BJP elections in other states but with the voters in Delhi, it proved counterproductive. The people saw AAP, which had delivered on a series of promises from its manifesto within 49 days, as a far superior option.

Contrasted with slogans and hyperbole from the BJP, AAP provided a long and impressive list of accomplishments from its debut tenure of 49 days. The tangible results included the halving of electricity bills for consumption of up to 400 units, instituting an audit of power distribution companies by the Comptroller and Auditor General, making twenty kilo-litres of water free every month, reining in the water mafia, cracking down on corruption in the Delhi Jal Board and other government departments, making the schedule of water tanker operations publicly available, rolling back foreign direct investment in retail, ordering a special investigation team to secure justice to victims of the 1984 anti-Sikh killings, issuing 5,500 new autorickshaw permits to members of the Scheduled Castes and Tribes, setting up an anti-corruption helpline, and disbursing Rs 21 crore in the form of education scholarships. What gained more notice than all of these was the abolition of a much-resented VIP culture in Delhi. Legislators, ministers and leaders of AAP were lauded for doing away with beacons on official cars, elaborate security protocol, and other displays of self-importance that had become habitual to power.

Having apologised for the error of resigning office impulsively early in 2014, AAP set about rebuilding its bridges with the people. The apology was a canny move as it cleared the air. Voters were once more disposed to attribute a positive spin to the party's motives and functioning. Kejriwal's resignation on the issue of the Lokpal reinforced his image as an uncompromising crusader against corruption and brought him the halo of a martyr. The BJP was seen, in contrast, as a party of hypocrites who postured against corruption but did not support the Lokpal bill that AAP wanted passed. The Congress already bore the burden of anti-incumbency after fifteen years in power. AAP was perceived as a party of upright youngsters ready to sacrifice power rather than compromise their principles, unlike seasoned politicians who did not walk the talk.

The media failed to comprehend many of AAP's acts but the party had caught the fancy of the people. In January 2014, Kejriwal and party members staged a street protest against the union home ministry and the Delhi police. In point of law, AAP was in the wrong. It had all started with the union ministry of home affairs, then headed by Sushil Kumar Shinde, refusing to suspend four police officers who, citing the lack of a warrant, did not buckle to the Delhi law minister Somnath Bharti's shrill demand that they search and arrest certain foreign nationals—

Africans, to be precise—suspected of 'immorality'. The ensuing face-off between state and centre saw the chief minister of Delhi spending the night on the road outside the parliament, like a homeless person. The state government now demanded that the Delhi police come under its executive authority, not that of the centre. While the media denounced Kejriwal's agitational conduct in office as anarchist (he responded by cheerfully admitting he was an anarchist), and headlines lampooned him as the state's 'chief protester', it was a feast for the eyes of ordinary people to see a chief minister along with his cabinet colleagues sleeping on the road in the biting cold of Delhi, seemingly for the greater good of the state and its people. The party's conduct was consistent with the disruptive idea it represented as an upstart in politics. The party had come out bruised from the 2014 general election, winning a paltry four seats of the 434 it had contested. Political analysts discounted its capacity to recoup. But with the agility of a neo-liberal start-up geared to press reboot, it organised itself anew, apologised to 'customers' for its follies, listened attentively to their feedback, and tweaked the product it was offering, wrapped in the moral fabric of good and clean governance. The updated AAP 2.0 impressed the people once again.

The new AAP downloads

People, especially the young to middle-aged educated in apolitical campuses since the 1980s and 1990s, and the middle classes who supported the IAC movement in large numbers, welcomed the emergence of AAP as an alternative. They were sick of an established politics that thrived on vote banks based on castes and communities, and politicians who were seen as a bunch of incompetent, corrupt self seekers. AAP's non-identitarian character and urban mien also contrasted with the stereotype of the rural semi-educated leader belonging, as often as not, to the 'lower' castes. The middle class believed in the innate capacity of India to be a global superpower but thought it was being blocked by a politics that thrived on 'appeasing' the lower castes with freebies like reservations. After all, they could see Indians shining abroad in a meritocratic environment.

When India adopted neoliberal reforms, these classes welcomed the new meritocratic (social Darwinist) ethos. The upper castes/classes have an abiding self image of being meritorious, believing that the social and economic positions they enjoy are due to their competence. The reforms associated with globalisation opened the flood gates of opportunity to them, and the benefits that flowed to this small section were construed as being good for India. Indian IT companies had made a mark for themselves by completing the Y2K project (that involved correcting and testing the code of millions of systems whose software was unprepared for transition into the new millennium) before the dawn of the year 2000, which created enough goodwill for them to scale up software services for their global clients. Because of these developments, India began to be seen as an IT hub and its middle classes basked in their new reputation as a technology savvy people. Around the same time, Indian professionals rose to occupy top management positions in US corporations and universities, which proved that given the environment Indians could outcompete others. The lingering sense of inferiority that remained from the colonial period was now dispelled, and replaced with a new found self-assurance: a combative one that maintained there was nothing wrong with India's past—its customs, traditions, culture—including the caste culture. It gave a fillip to the hindutva forces that proclaimed the glory of ancient India and promised to regain it. People who, until the eighties had fought shy of admitting that they believed in god or religion, now began displaying religious markers on their forehead and wearing yellow-red threads on their wrist signifying faith in the occult. Such practices were consonant with the BJP's outlook, but not everyone shared its aggressive communal stance or opportunism in politics. Many people who retained social democratic leanings imbibed in the past, and who might not necessarily share the rancour embodied by the BJP, saw

AAP as a viable alternative and thronged to it. AAP also appealed to people working in NGOs. Its difference from the established political parties and their culture was what clicked with people. This difference was marked by four factors: one, its leadership comprised apolitical individuals from diverse walks of life—with a strong component of urban professionals—who shared a vague idea of Gandhi's vision; two, the party did not dwell on matters of doctrine and ideology but focused on removing corruption from public life, which gave it a results-oriented practical character; its leadership culture seemed relatively free of hierarchy, reflecting collective decision-making based on consensus; four, and most importantly, its claim of transparency in money matters, relying on crowd funding for its own finances.

It is hard not to be impressed by Arvind Kejriwal as a strategist. He is an IIT-ian who has spoken on anti-reservationist platforms such as Youth for Equality and is also adorned with the halo of the anti-communist Magsaysay award—ingredients sure to appeal to the burgeoning middle classes. The manner in which he galvanised people for whom politics was merely a matter of gossip, into a real political force, was an inspired move. There were abundant promises to entice the poor as well. He made his supporters wield broomsticks (long before Modi), thus dignifying a symbol that had hitherto signified the unmeritorious standing of the 'untouchable' underdog. It is hard not to admire the stratagem of deploying the accumulated anger of the majority against the political class, and the gumption of carrying out protests—with exemplary zeal and élan—in the face of an entrenched political establishment's combined opposition. Kejriwal's choice of Anna Hazare from Ralegan Siddhi to be a Gandhi in his campaign for a Jan Lokpal, and instantly cobbling together a like-minded team under the banner of India Against Corruption, all generated nationwide moralistic fervour against the establishment of the time—the Congress-led UPA government.

The way this crusade enthused young people across the country was not just inspiring, but reminiscent of the 1970s when the newly-established opposition Janata Party had made the mighty Indira Gandhi bite the dust. Astutely sensing the mood of the people, Kejriwal made a vivid technicolour production out of his selfless plunge into the 'gutter of politics' to cleanse it from within. In this era of flash memory and media-made news, the timing was uncanny—a spate of scandals as 'breaking news' came in quick succession and took public disgust for the political class to a new level. In addition, Kejriwal has a proven talent for timing his provocations well. In the book *2014: The Election that Changed India*, journalist Rajdeep Sardesai shakes his head in wonder at AAP's expert grasp of the 24x7 news cycle and recounts the numerous occasions Kejriwal's gestures arrived just when they were sure to upstage all other news and dominate prime time coverage. Speed and surprise have been of the essence all along. In 2013, AAP fought the Delhi assembly elections within a year of its founding, stunned everyone by bagging 40 per cent of the seats and put together a government with unsolicited support from a hapless Congress party. These were moves of undeniable tactical brilliance and masterly execution, if laced with a strong hint of opportunism (given that Kejriwal was utterly opposed to the Congress, his coalition partner).

Indeed, AAP is quite like a technology start-up that gives established giants a run for their money with its agile business model, nimbleness and ability to innovate. The self-confident neo-liberal generation in our metros, believing that India's infinite prowess to be a superpower is shackled only by its outmoded, corrupt and incompetent politicians, had longed for such a development. AAP embodies both their mood and their abilities. Receiving its call, they enthusiastically jumped into agitational mode to rid the country of corruption with an instant solution: the Jan Lokpal.

With the success of its test marketing, AAP was launched as an 'anti-politics' political enterprise. It instantly became a hit with all idealists sans ideology. Discarding ideological baggage for new ideas that work may sound like a good rule of thumb in these supposedly post-ideological times, but there remains the risk of slipping down the (political) slope into old ways. After all, beyond feigning it, none of the old political players had any ideology either; what had always worked were the proverbial freebies and majoritarian appeal. Unfortunately, AAP seems little insulated against or averse to using them. The biggest challenge before a fledgling entity is to scale up or be gobbled by the bigger sharks. Remember what Microsoft did to Netscape or what Amazon is doing to Flipkart. In the absence of practical ideas about how to upsize, start-ups end by swelling the coffers of venture capitalists and promoters.

In its manifesto, AAP promised a seventy-point action plan for Delhi, supposedly drawn in consultation with the people. Many of the points entail a huge financial outlay besides depending upon political cooperation from adversaries at the centre and in the state. Ashok K. Lahiri, an economist, conservatively estimated the required financial outlay for implementing AAP's proposed policies at Rs 69,000 crore over five years, or Rs 13,800 crore per year, a third of Delhi's budget—half of which is already consumed by salaries and maintenance—and hence an impossible proposition. The resource gap showed that AAP would not be able to fulfil all that it had promised. In addition, there were jurisdictional hurdles involved because of the peculiar governance structure of the Delhi capital region vis-à-vis the centre—and the AAP–BJP tussle has done nothing to simplify matters. The party had promised that it would be accountable for its manifesto unlike other parties; the least that AAP could have done was to display on its website the scorecard against this action plan, for people to view. It did nothing of the kind. Expectedly, its performance is a mixed bag.

On looking carefully at these seventy points, one finds that twelve are too generic to assess and some others are just a wish list, non-implementable due to the state government's lack of jurisdiction. Much government energy was wasted in the battle with the lieutenant governor, Najeeb Jung, and in accusing the centre of creating obstacles in governance. Nevertheless, the AAP government has done some pioneering work, especially in the field of healthcare and school education. Although the actual achievements fall short of declared targets, they are not a mean showing by any standard.

Speaking of targets, the government had a plan to establish one thousand mohalla (neighbourhood) clinics that would provide certain health care services for free by the end of December 2016, a deadline that got extended to March 2017. As of June 2017, fewer than 150 such clinics were functional. The scheme has developed and deployed appropriate technology in the swasthya slate, a device that roughly costs Rs 40,000 and performs thirty-three common medical tests, collating data from several medical devices like ECG, pulse oximeter, glucometer, BP monitor, etc., cutting down manpower costs and increasing efficiency. The consultations are paper-free, making the entire exercise environment friendly. The medical details of every patient are available on the cloud, and can be recalled at the touch of a button. It is said to have reduced the cost to 5 per cent that of a typical clinic. An associated scheme is the government pharmacy, which distributed nearly 1,400 medicines free as against the 376 medicines on the national list. It is said that not all clinics provide all the services claimed—such as the promised range of 212 tests—which have only been implemented in a couple of model clinics. On the education front, the Delhi government has revived most of its schools with new infrastructure and created an atmosphere conducive to education. It has made Sarvodaya Bal Vidyalaya on Deendayal Upadhyaya Marg the national capital's first 'model' government school with state-of-the-art facilities and infrastructure: audio-visual teaching aids, projectors in classrooms, besides a well-appointed swanky new building. Some 8,000 school rooms had been built by February 2017, two years into the government's term, equivalent to two hundred new schools, and it planned to add an equal number within a year and a half. It has plans to add a hundred new schools in the coming years. In terms of cleanliness, discipline, and teaching in government schools, reports indicate significant progress.

Any implementation may be faulted for imperfections but AAP deserves commendation for emphasising health and education as priority areas. It would do well to push forward with the good work in its remaining term instead of trumpeting achievements—which it has been overdoing. There has been little or no progress on other specific promises such as CCTV cameras to be installed on all buses, the regularisation of unauthorised colonies, twenty new colleges to be set up and making Delhi a free-Wi-Fi city. The last one was too ambitious to be feasible, given the fact that there is no example in the world where five million users, or even one million, have access to a public Wi-Fi system. The government may do better to modify its plan and create Wi-Fi zones in select public spaces such as metro stations, shopping plazas and public access areas in universities. Moreover, in the absence of a viable monetisation plan, the capital investment and thereafter revenue expenditure would be quite a strain on the government budget.

The App Proved Buggy

The main plank of AAP's appeal was a corruption-free administration, and it promptly set up a helpline for people to inform the government about encounters with state corruption. Although such a mechanism is not expected to curb big ticket corruption, the petty corruption that constitutes the experience of ordinary people could certainly be dented. The findings of at least one survey in March 2017, by LocalCircles, a community social media platform, show that Delhi citizens believed corruption in government offices had somewhat abated. Even the Central Vigilance Commission report tabled in parliament in April 2017 noted that complaints of corruption in departments of the government had come down dramatically compared to the previous year.

However, AAP has little cause for cheer when the charge of

corruption—in the procurement of medical supplies and vehicles—is being levelled against none other than Kejriwal himself, by his former colleague Kapil Sharma, who since his expulsion from AAP has joined the BJP. It may be easily dismissed as the BJP's ploy to denigrate and demoralise AAP but for the lack of a clear explanation from Kejriwal. Kejriwal's history and conduct have not been as reassuring as he would have us believe. His claim of simple living, judicious usage of public funds and accountability also is not quite borne out by the facts. He started out by proclaiming that he would live in a simple house but coolly moved into two duplex flats with a sprawling private lounge on Civil Lines, and eventually installed himself in Lutyens' Delhi like any other politician.

Perhaps the most antithetical phenomenon to an ideal democracy is the personality cult, the source of all undemocratic conventions and customs. Kejriwal abhorred the cult around Modi, but built one around himself. As chief minister, his propaganda about his own achievements rivalled all others in the country. Any AAP leader who questioned Kejriwal found themself out of the party. Coming just after the massive win in the Delhi election, the summary expulsion of Yogendra Yadav and Prashant Bhushan along with a few other leaders, allegedly on charges of 'gross indiscipline', had a strong flavour of intolerance towards debate, dissent and power-sharing. Their 'indiscipline' had basically amounted to questioning Kejriwal's autocratic style.

Other promises on AAP's agenda, such as the eradication of VIP culture and the decentralisation of power to mohalla committees, have also not been kept. They had the potential to distinguish AAP from any other party in terms of showcasing its democratic credentials. The essence of democracy lies in negating the differential valorisation of people, which has unfortunately been part of the culture of India. The VIP/VVIP syndrome—humiliating to citizens—has grown to the extent that the country resembles an unreconstructed monarchy more than any existing democracy. In the name of security, politicians have become a menace to the everyday life and routines of people. How do the lives of a prime minister or president, not to speak of numerous other politicians, become more important than that of an ordinary sanitation worker or a village schoolteacher? And get officially acknowledged as such, at public expense?

In the face of such anti-people norms of extant politics, what is the nature of the change that AAP is likely to produce? The established political format which evolved in line with the Keynesian model of a mixed economy was one where the state donned 'welfarist' robes and presented itself as committed to populist ideologies such as socialism, secularism and democracy. Over the years, there have been momentous changes in the economy culminating in the contemporary neo-liberal economic paradigm, which stands in direct opposition to the Keynesian welfare state. The formal rhetoric of contemporary politics did not fluctuate with these changes but maintained the pretence of adhering to the same set of ideologies as before. The resulting dissonance was perceived as the hypocrisy of the political class, creating a space for new political movements. Such movements are emerging all over the world. In the absence of a revolutionary discourse, this space is producing a politics that accords well with contemporary neo-liberalism.

This new genre of politics typically casts itself as post-ideological and discrete—focused on issues—and professes a managerial orientation to social problems. The emergence of AAP exemplifies this process. Its politics is not only in tune with this ethos, it poses no alternative to the prevailing bankruptcy of conviction-driven politics. While the old liberal politics valued a holistic perspective, neoliberal politics deals in topical solutions. The long term is reduced to the here and now, and the quest for the root cause is replaced by attention to discrete manifestations. Its problem-specific approach to situations, without recourse to an overarching political narrative that recognises patterns in human affairs, has given it a powerful appeal among the middle class as well as the working class.

It is said that like China's Deng Xiaoping, Kejriwal too is not interested in knowing the colour of the cat, whether it is black or white, so long as it catches mice. One finds confirmation of this on AAP's website. Kejriwal writes:

> Our goal is to remain solution-focused. If the solution to a problem lies on the left we are happy to consider it. Likewise if it is on the right (or in the centre) we are equally happy to consider it. Ideology is one for the pundits and the media to pontificate about.

Such an approach appeals not only to the new generation, which has grown up hearing about 'the death of ideology' and 'the end of history', but also to the people who have only experienced deception in the name of ideology. It is the premise on which non-governmental organisations come into existence and continue to thrive. Not unexpectedly, NGOs rushed in to support AAP—after all, Kejriwal began his public service career in the NGO or 'development' sector (as the peculiar appellation has it). Even if AAP chooses to speak about rising inequality, social injustice, corruption, and exploitation, its approach to these endemic issues remains superficial and shallow, limited to specific manifestations. AAP's outlook derives from such facile distinctions as 'good' men and 'bad' men; if politics and administration are cleansed of corrupt people, everything will be fine. Those who voice support of the party's campaign join the ranks of the good. Numerous figures of note in public life had stood with IAC whilst the entire tenor of the discourse ran as though corruption was confined to bureaucrats and politicians. The capitalists, who oiled the greed of these people to secure ends of their own, celebrities from Bollywood (which is sustained by black money), babas who have amassed wealth camouflaging it as donations by ordinary people, and even a few politicians were seen among the supporters of the movement. On 14 April 2011, the *Times of India* reported that of the Rs 82.88 lakh collected during Anna Hazare's protest fast at the Jantar Mantar, Rs 46.50 lakh came from capitalists—Jindal Aluminium and HDFC Bank among them.

Naturally, AAP never speaks of the radical systemic change that the country desperately needs. Its vision document talks about destroying the centres of authority and handing over power to the people. After making this rhetorical declaration, it gives us no idea of how the goal shall be accomplished, beyond invoking the Gandhian metaphor of swaraj, which would be violently rejected at least by dalits. To dalits who desired structural change to liberate themselves and instead found Gandhi—the status quoist reactionary—he is an anathema, and all his saintly posturing repellent. The vision document of AAP speaks about the growing divide between the rich and the poor and the loot of natural resources by big businesses and politicians, unemployment, price rise, and, of course, corruption, but never faults their source—the neo-liberal policies followed by the state. It is more comfortable with the pretence that endless tinkering with the nuts and bolts will overcome all limitations, and the old machine will generate a whole new product.

Expectedly, AAP under Kejriwal does not see any need to deal with the structural injustice embedded in Indian society. The exploitation of adivasis, dalits, Muslims and women does not ring any alarm bells in its schema. His national ambitions drove Kejriwal to protest the institutional murder of Rohith Vemula, and to speak about the atrocities on dalits in the wake of Una. During the Punjab election of February–March 2017, AAP spoke about a 'dalit manifesto' and declared that a dalit would be made Deputy CM if AAP formed the government. At the same time, the vacuity of AAP stands exposed time and again. In Punjab, the iconic Bant Singh—the CPI-ML activist and balladeer who lost his arms and a leg in a deadly assault by jats while fighting for justice for his eldest daughter who had been gang-raped in Burj Jhabbar village in the Mansa district in 2006—joined AAP. But it turned out that his attacker, Navdeep Singh, and the eyewitness in the case, Surjit Singh, had both also joined the party (though in a damage-control exercise, Navdeep was expelled the day after the story broke). All of Kejriwal's overtures to dalits are election centric and hence indistinguishable from those of other parties.

AAP made a serious bid in the elections to the Goa and Punjab state assemblies but failed to make a mark. While election results in India do not necessarily correlate with the governance record of parties, as other factors often overwhelm performance, the latter cannot be ignored. If AAP focuses on distinguishing itself by delivering on its promises to people and does not resort to populist gimmicks that would make it indistinguishable from the usual lot of political operatives, it could hope to gain in the long term. After all, even limited remedies implemented in a time-bound manner would be an improvement on the current situation. There is also a chance that progress with piecemeal solutions might make it unavoidable to recognise the underlying problem. Failing that, AAP can only serve history as a live demonstration of what ails the present system.

AAP is unsurprisingly silent on the global processes of neo-imperialism that have a huge influence on our economy, politics and society. It is absurd, though sadly not unusual, for a party born in the 21st century to appear oblivious to the imperialist workings of capital. Likewise, the leadership of AAP—which is often just Kejriwal, the ideology-free man of ideas—shows no concern for the people of Kashmir or Manipur who resist India's colonial occupation. When senior leader and human rights advocate Prashant Bhushan expressed his opinion that a referendum should be conducted regarding the continuance of the Armed Forces (Special Powers) Act in Jammu and Kashmir, he had to face violent reactions not only from jingoistic far-right circles but also sharp disapproval from fellow-AAP members. The party was quick to distance itself from Bhushan's statement. Whether this shows the craven appeasement of an electoral constituency or the personal beliefs of every other AAP leader may not be known; what does show clearly is an ideological underpinning of nationalism with its restrictive correlates—such as limited freedom of expression, fear of open debate, and unquestioning adherence to the state's official line.

In the same way, rousing calls of Vande Mataram from the AAP podium are not culturally neutral signifiers of an inclusive charter of citizenship, but coded markers of preference and identitarian affiliation. Or, just as the everyman implied by the name of the Aam Aadmi Party is a fictional being, not to be found on the ground—where, moreover, half the population is female. We have to ask what qualities are identified with this construct, this homo civicus, apart from annoyance at corruption. When we work out the cultural coordinates of AAP from these indications, its centre of gravity becomes clearer, and 'non-ideological politics' is exposed for the oxymoron it is. We begin to notice the studied silence of an outspoken party on the hegemonic caste structure that underlies the khap panchayat—even as the party speaks of 'engaging' khap panchayats in dialogue—or when a film (say, *Padmaavat*) comes under attack by caste mobs. In politics, silence is never neutral; and cultural conservatism with a free-market bias and socialist window dressing is the oldest bromide, never mind that it sounds new on Twitter.

Cultural change has a much longer gestation than political change. AAP has not done badly in terms of its performance in Delhi, but in terms of political culture, it has certainly faltered. It could not present an alternate model of politics to distinguish itself from other parties, and has fallen into the same trap it had once endeavoured to combat. Kejriwal, the face of AAP, showed himself as vulnerable as any other politician to political ambition and expediency. As a matter of fact, the politics of AAP has been devoid of any deeper understanding of India's problems, viz., the neoliberal ethos of power, the rise of hindutva fascism and the consequent rapid marginalisation of the masses. Kejriwal has never expressed a problem with any of these. His agenda has been superficial. He and his team would have been expected to learn, to deepen their understanding which could happen only with democratic processes within the party. However, those have been the first casualty in AAP.

AAP is an app to cleanse governance of its filth. But it proved to be beset with bugs. It is time the app had an update, even if the gains are to be provisional in terms of a cult of Kejriwal countering the more reactionary cult of Modi. If not, forget the hope of being an able opposition in 2019, even the sole seat of power in Delhi will be gone in 2020. And history could well be left asking, What's AAP?

REFERENCES

Ahmad, Aijaz. 1992. *In Theory: Classes, Nations, Literatures*. London: Verso.

Allen, Robert L. 1969. *Black Awakening in Capitalist America: An Analytic History.* New York: Anchor Books.

Ambani, Mukesh and Birla, Kumarmangalam, 2000. *Report on a Policy Frame Work for Reforms in Education*. New Delhi: Prime Minister's Council on Trade and Industry, Government of India. http://ispepune.org.in/PDF%20ISSUE/2003/JISPE403/2038DOCU-3.PDF. Accessed 17 February 2018.

Ambedkar, B.R. 1979a. "Castes in India: Their Mechanism, Genesis and Development." *BAWS* 1. Edited by Vasant Moon. Bombay: Education Department, Government of Maharashtra. 3–22.

——. 1979b. "Ranade, Gandhi and Jinnah." *BAWS* 1. Edited by Vasant Moon. Bombay: Education Department, Government of Maharashtra. 205–240.

——. 1982. *BAWS* 2. Edited by Vasant Moon. Bombay: Education Department, Government of Maharashtra.

——. 1987. "Philosophy of Hinduism." *BAWS* 3. Edited by Vasant Moon. Bombay: Education Department, Government of Maharashtra. 8–92.

——. 1987. "Pakistan or the Partition of India." *BAWS* 3. Edited by Vasant Moon. Bombay: Education Department, Government of Maharashtra.

——. 1988. *What Path to Salvation?* Translated by Vasant Moon (1988). Edited by Eleanor Zelliot. http://www.columbia.edu/itc/mealac/pritchett/00ambedkar/txt_ambedkar_salvation.html. Accessed 15 February 2018.

——. 1989. *BAWS* 5. Edited by Vasant Moon. Bombay: Education Department, Government of Maharashtra.

——. 1991. *BAWS* 9. Edited by Vasant Moon. Bombay: Education Department, Government of Maharashtra.

——. 2003. *BAWS* 17. Edited by Vasant Moon. Bombay: Education Department, Government of Maharashtra.

Archer, David. 2006. "The Impact of the World Bank and IMF on Education Rights." *Convergence*. Vol. 39, No. 2–3. 7–18.

Bahadur, Sayyid Ahmed Khan. 1873. *The Causes of the Indian Revolt*. Benares: Medical Hall Press. http://www.columbia.edu/itc/mealac/pritchett/00urdu/asbab/translation1873.html. Accessed 1 February 2018.

——. 1888. "Speech of Sir Syed Ahmed at Lucknow." Sir *Syed Ahmed on the Present State of Indian Politics, Consisting of Speeches and Letters Reprinted from the "Pioneer"*. Allahabad: The Pioneer Press. 1–24.

Baradaran, Mehrsa. 2017. *The Color of Money: Black Banks and the Racial Wealth Gap*. Massachusetts: Harvard University Press.

Baxi, Upendra. 1995. "Emancipation and Justice: Babasaheb Ambedkar's Legacy and Vision." *Crisis and Change in Contemporary India*. Edited by Upendra Baxi and Bhikhu Parekh. New Delhi: Sage. 124–30.

Biswas, A. K. 2016. "Sorry, Mr Das: Merit, caste... a tale of two IAS candidates." *Outlook*. 30 May. https://www.outlookindia.com/magazine/story/sorry-mr-das/297174. Accessed 16 February 2018.

Bukharin, Nikolai. 1925. *Historical Materialism: A System of Sociology*. New York: International Publishers.

Cháirez-Garza, Jesús Francisco. 2017. "'Bound hand and foot and handed over to the caste Hindus': Ambedkar, Untouchability and the Politics of Partition." *Indian Economic and Social History Review*. http://eprints.whiterose.ac.uk/123470/3/ambedkar%20churchill%20ieshr%20chairez%20final%20version-1.pdf. Accessed 15 February 2018.

Chhapia, Hemali. 2013. "Twinning courses gain currency as foreign education costs soar." Times of India. August 19.

Claeys, Gregory. 2000. "The 'Survival of the Fittest' and the Origins of Social Darwinism." *Journal of the History of Ideas*. Vol. 61. 223–240.

Coffey, Diane and Spears, Dean. 2017. *Where India Goes: Abandoned Toilets, Stunted Development and the Costs of Caste*. New Delhi: HarperCollins.

Cros, Jacques. 1950. *Le 'Néo-libéralisme' et la révision du libéralisme*. Doctoral Thesis. Toulouse: Université de Toulouse.

Dangle, Arjun. 1992. *Poisoned Bread: Modern Marathi Dalit Literature*. Hyderabad: Orient Longman.

——. 1994. *Homeless in My Land: Translations from Modern Marathi Dalit Short Stories*. Hyderabad: Orient Longman.

Das, Bhagwan. 2009. *In Pursuit of Ambedkar: A Memoir*. Translated by Isha. New Delhi: Navayana.

——. 2010. *Thus Spoke Ambedkar: A Stake in the Nation*. Vol. 1. New Delhi: Navayana.

Delgado-Ramos, Gian Carlo and Saxe-Fernández, John. 2005. "The World Bank and the Privatization of Public Education: A Mexican Perspective." *Journal for Critical Education Policy Studies*. Vol. 3, No. 1. http://firgoa.usc.es/drupal/node/24314. Accessed 16 February 2018.

Dewey, John. 2001. *Democracy and Education*. Penn State Electronic Classics Series Publication.

"The Dalit Panther Manifesto." 1972. In *The Exercise of Freedom: An Introduction to Dalit Writing* (2013). Edited by K. Satyanarayana and Susie Tharu. New Delhi: Navayana.

Dongre, Amol R. and Deshmukh, Pradeep R. 2012. "Farmers' suicides in the Vidarbha region of Maharashtra, India: A qualitative exploration of their causes." *Journal of Injury and Violence Research*. Vol. 4, No. 1 Tehran: Kermanshah University of Medical Sciences. 2–6.

Dutta, Manas. 2013. "Revisiting the Historiography of the Madras Presidency Army, 1801–1858." *IOSR Journal of Humanities and Social Science*. Vol. 13, No. 4. 46–9.

Engels, Friedrich. 1934. "Engels to Borgius: London, January 25, 1894." Translated by Sidney Hook. *New International*. Vol.1, No.3. 81–5.

——. 1972. "Engels to J. Bloch In Königsberg: London, September 21, 1890." *Historical Materialism (Marx, Engels, Lenin)*. Moscow: Progress Publishers. 294–96.

Ervin, Lorenzo Kom'boa. 2001. *Black Capitalism*. Online Resource: The Anarchist Library. https://theanarchistlibrary.org/library/lorenzo-kom-boa-ervin-black-capitalism. Accessed 17 February 2018.

Ghildiyal, Sidhartha Subodh. 2011. "UPA govt set to make 4% of its yearly buy from dalit-run firms." *The Economic Times*. 12 September.

Government of India. 2012. *Twelfth Five-Year Plan 2012-17 (Draft)*. New Delhi: Planning Commission.

Harrison, Selig S. 1960. *India: The Most Dangerous Decades*. Princeton: Princeton University Press. 190–1.

Harvey, David. 2005. *A Brief History of Neoliberalism*. Oxford: Oxford University Press.

Haygunde, Chandan Shantaram. 2017. "Two tales of two very different murder trials, a Dalit and a Maratha." *The Indian Express*. 29 November.

Hillerbrand, Hans J. 2004. *The Encyclopedia of Protestantism*. Vol. 2. New York: Routledge.

Iyer, Lakshmi, Khanna, Tarun and Varshney, Ashutosh. 2013. "Caste and Entrepreneurship in India." *Economic and Political Weekly*. Vol. 48, No. 6. 52–60.

Jaffrelot, Christophe. 2000. "The Rise of the Other Backward Classes in the Hindi Belt." *The Journal of Asian Studies*. Vol. 59, No. 1. 86–108.

——. 2005a. "The Politics of OBCs." *Seminar* 549. 191–2.

——. 2005b. *Dr. Ambedkar and Untouchability: Analyzing and Fighting Caste*. New Delhi: Permanent Black.

——. 2017. "Gujarat Model?" *The Indian Express*. 20 November.

Jamison, Stephanie W. 1996. *Sacrificed Wife/Sacrificer's Wife: Women, Ritual, and Hospitality in Ancient India*. Oxford: Oxford University Press.

Jayadev, A., Motiram, S., and Vakulabharanam, V. 2007. "Patterns of Wealth Disparities in India during the Liberalisation Era." *Economic and Political Weekly* 42. No. 38. 22–28.

Jones, Daniel Stedman. 2012. *Masters of the Universe: Hayek, Friedman, and the Birth of Neoliberal Politics*. Princeton: Princeton University Press.

Kadam, K.N. 1997. "Dr. Ambedkar's Philosophy of Emancipation and the Impact of John Dewey." *The Meaning of Ambedkarite Conversion to Buddhism and Other Essays*. Mumbai: Popular Prakashan. 1–33.

Keer, Dhananjay. 1990. *Dr Ambedkar: Life and Mission*. Bombay: Popular Prakashan. (Orig. publ. 1954.)

Knipe, David M. 2015. *Vedic Voices: Intimate Narratives of a Living Andhra Tradition*. Oxford: Oxford University Press.

Krishnan, Shri. 2005. *Political Mobilization and Identity in Western India, 1934–47*. Vol. 7, Sage Series in Modern Indian History. New Delhi: Sage.

Kshirsagar, Ramachandra. 1994. *Dalit Movement in India and its Leaders, 1857–1956*. New Delhi: MD Publications.

Lawton, William and Katsomitros, Alex. 2012. *International Branch Campuses: Data and Developments*. Surrey: The Observatory on Borderless Higher Education. http://www.obhe.ac.uk/documents/view_details?id=894. Accessed 16 February 2018.

Lenin, V. I. 1965. *V. I. Lenin Collected Works*. Vol. 29. Translated and Edited by George Hanna. Moscow: Progress Publishers.

Leo, Benjamin and Barmeier, Julia. 2010. Who Are the MDG Trailblazers? A New MDG Progress Index." Working Paper 222: Center for Global Development. https://www.cgdev.org/publication/who-are-mdg-trailblazers-new-mdg-progress-index-working-paper-222. Accessed 5 November 2017.

Mandal, Jagadis Chandra. 1999. *Poona Pact and Depressed Classes*. Calcutta: Sujan Publications.

Marx, Karl. 1853. "India." *New York Daily Tribune*. 5 August. https://www.marxists.org/archive/marx/works/1853/08/05.htm. Accessed 17 February 2018.

——. 1853. "The Future Results of British Rule in India." *New York Daily Tribune*.

22 July. https://marxists.catbull.com/archive/marx/works/1853/07/22.htm. Accessed 26 March 2018.

——. 1955. *The Poverty of Philosophy*. Moscow: Progress Publishers.

——. 1968. *The German Ideology*. Moscow: Progress Publishers.

——. 1970. *A Contribution to the Critique of Political Economy*. Moscow: Progress Publishers.

——. 1974. *Capital: A Critique of Political Economy*. Vol. 1. Translated by Samuel Moore and Edward Aveling. Moscow: Progress Publishers.

Mayhew, Arthur. 1998. *Christianity in India*. Delhi: Gian Publishing House.

Meyer, H. 1959. "Marx on Bakunin: A Neglected Text." *Etudes de Marxologie*. Edited by M. Rubel. Paris: Cahiers de l'Institut de science économique appliquée.

Ministry of Education. 1985. *Challenge of Education: A Policy Perspective*. New Delhi: Ministry of Education.

Ministry of Human Resource Development. 2011. *Statistics of Higher Technical Education, 2007–08*. New Delhi: Bureau of Planning, Monitoring and Statistics.

Mishra, Narayan. 2001. *Scheduled Castes Education: Issues and Aspects*. New Delhi: Kalpaz Publications.

Mitta, Manoj. 2014. *Modi and Godhra: The Fiction of Fact Finding*. Noida: HarperCollins.

Mohammad, Noor. 2018. "Modi Government Has Near 'Zero Effect' in Meeting Procurement Quota From Dalit, Adivasi Enterprises." *The Wire*. 9 February. thewire.in/222399/modi-government-near-zero-effect-meeting-procurement-quota-dalit-adivasi-enterprises/. Accessed 17 February 2018.

Morkhandikar, R. S. 1990. "Dilemmas of Dalit Movement in Maharashtra–Unity Moves and After." *Economic and Political Weekly* 25. No. 12. 586–90.

Mukherjee, Arun P. 2009. "B.R. Ambedkar, John Dewey, and the Meaning of Democracy." *New Literary History*. Vol. 40, No. 2. 345–70.

Nanda, Meera. 2004. *Prophets Facing Backward: Postmodernism, Science, and Hindu Nationalism*. New Delhi: Permanent Black.

Narain, Siddharth and Seshu, Geeta. 2016. "Sedition goes viral." *The Hoot*. 19 August. http://www.thehoot.org/free-speech/media-freedom/sedition-goes-viral-9578. Accessed 17 February 2018.

Navsarjan Trust. 2010. *Understanding Untouchability*. Robert F. Kennedy Center for Justice & Human Rights. https://navsarjantrust.org/2010/01/28/navsarjan-trust-releases-study-on-untouchability-in-gujarat/. Accessed 17 February 2018.

Neill, Stephen. 1986. *A History of Christian Missions*. Harmondsworth: Penguin.

NUEPA (National University of Educational Planning and Administration). 2013. *District Information System for Education: Elementary Education in India 2012-13*. Vol. 1 and 2. New Delhi: NUEPA. http://www.dise.in/. Accessed 11 Dec 2017.

Pal, Yash. 2009. Report of The Committee to Advise on Renovation and Rejuvenation of Higher Education in India. New Delhi Government of India. https://www.aicte-india.org/downloads/Yashpal-committee-report.pdf. Accessed 16 February 2018.

Pathak, Binay Kumar. 2014. "Critical Look at the Narayana Murthy Recommendations on Higher Education." *Economic and Political Weekly* 49, No. 3. 72–4.

Patil, Shalaka. 2011. "Push button parliament–why India needs a non-partisan, recorded vote system." *Anuario Colombiano de Derecho Internacional*. No. 4. 163-241.

People's Union for Democratic Rights and Association for Democratic Rights. 2012. *This Village Is Mine Too: Dalit Assertion, Land Rights and Social Boycott in Bhagana*. http://www.pudr.org/sites/default/files/final%20bhagana%20 pdf.pdf. Accessed 16 February 2018.

Phule, Jotirao. 2002. *Selected Writings of Jotirao Phule*. Edited by Govind P. Deshpande. New Delhi: LeftWord Books.

Plekhanov, Georgi. 1974. *The Development of the Monist View of History*. Moscow: Progress Publishers.

——. 1976. "Fundamental Problems of Marxism." *Selected Philosophical Works*. Vol. 3. Moscow: Progress Publishers.

Pradhan, V. 2009. "Karl Marx che Majuri Kam va Bhandwal" (Series 1–9, 1931–32). *Janata*. Edited by Pradip Gaikwad. Nagpur. 269–342.

Prasad, Chandra Bhan and Kamble, Milind. 2012. "To Empower Dalits, Do Away with India's Antiquated Retail Trading System." *The Times of India*. 5 December.

Prasad, Chandra Bhan, Devesh Kapur, D. Shyam Babu. 2014. *Defying the Odds: The Rise of Dalit Entrepreneurs*. New Delhi: Random House India.

PricewaterhouseCoopers Private Limited. 2012. *India - Higher Education Sector: Opportunities for Private Participation*. New Delhi: PricewaterhouseCoopers Private Limited. https://www.pwc.in/assets/pdfs/industries/education-services.pdf. Accessed on 16 February 2018.

Proudhon, Pierre-Joseph. 1847. *The System of Economic Contradictions, or The Philosophy of Poverty*. From Rod Hay's Archive for the History of Economic

Thought, McMaster University, Canada. https://www.marxists.org/reference/subject/economics/proudhon/philosophy/. Accessed 17 February 2018.

Pugh, Patricia M. 1984. *Educate, Agitate, Organise: 100 Years of Fabian Socialism*. London and New York: Methuen.

Rao, P. V. Narasimha. 2000. *The Insider*. New Delhi: Penguin.

Sadgopal, A. 2008. "Education Bill: Dismantling Rights." *The Financial Express*. 9 November.

Santos, Boaventura de Sousa. 2004. *A universidade no século XXI*. Cortez : Brazil. 17–18.

Sardesai, Rajdeep. 2015. *2014: The Election that Changed India*. New Delhi: Penguin.

Sekher, T.V. 2009. *Catastrophic Health Expenditure and Poor in India: Health Insurance is the Answer?* Marrakech: International Union for the Scientific Study of Population. https://iussp.org/sites/default/files/event_call_for_papers/T.V%20Sekher-IUSSP%20pdf.pdf. Accessed 20 Nov 2017.

Sharda, Ratan. 2015. "Selective Amnesia." *Organiser*. 20 October. http://organiser.org//Encyc/2015/10/20/Cover-Story---Selective-Amnesia.aspx. Accessed 17 February 2018.

Shetty, Sukanya. 2014. "40 months on, court acquits 'Naxal activist' Sudhir Dhawale." *The Indian Express*. 23 May.

Singh, Vijaita. 2017. "Foreign funds surge under NDA rule." *The Hindu*. 20 February.

Stroud, Scott R. 2016. "Pragmatism and the Pursuit of Social Justice in India: Bhimrao Ambedkar and the Rhetoric of Religious Reorientation." *Rhetoric Society Quarterly*. Vol. 46, Issue 1. 5–27.

Teltumbde, Anand. 2003. *Ambedkar on Muslims: Myths and Facts*. Mumbai: Vikas Adhyayan Kendra.

——. 2009. *Khairlanji: A Strange and Bitter Crop*. New Delhi: Navayana.

——. 2011. *The Persistence of Caste: The Khairlanji Murders & India's Hidden Apartheid*. New Delhi: Navayana.

Thompson, E. P. 1965. "The Peculiarities of the English." *The Socialist Register*. 311–62.

Thorat, Sukhdeo and Newman, Katherine S. 2010. *Blocked by Caste: Economic Discrimination in Modern India*. New Delhi: Oxford University Press.

Thorsen, Dag Einar and Lie, Amund. 2011. *What is Neoliberalism?* Department of Political Science: University of Oslo.

University Grants Commission. 2015. *UGC Annual Report 2014–15*. New Delhi:

University Grants Commission. https://www.ugc.ac.in/pdfnews/2465555_Annual-Report-2014-15.pdf. Accessed 16 February 2018.

Vivekananda, Swami. 1899. "On the Bounds of Hinduism." *Prabuddha Bharata*. http://www.ramakrishnavivekananda.info/vivekananda/volume_5/interviews/on_the_bounds_of_hinduism.htm. Accessed 20 August 2013.

Weber, Max. 2015. "The Distribution of Power Within the *Gemeinschaft*: Classes, *Stände*, Parties, by Max Weber." *Weber's Rationalism and Modern Society: New Translations on Politics, Bureaucracy, and Social Stratification*. Edited and Translated by Tony Waters and Dagmar Waters. New York: Palgrave Macmillan. 37–57.

White, Gillian B. 2017. "The Unfulfilled Promise of Black Capitalism." *The Atlantic*. 21 September. https://www.theatlantic.com/business/archive/2017/09/black-capitalism-baradaran/540522/. Accessed 17 February 2018.

White, Richard B. 1994. "The Mahar Movement's Military Component." *South Asia Graduate Research Journal*. Vol. 1, No. 1. Austin: University of Texas. 39–59.

Wood, Ellen Meiksins. 2007. *Democracy Against Capitalism: Renewing Historical Materialism*. Cambridge: Cambridge University Press.

World Bank. 1994. *Higher Education: The Lessons of Experience*. Washington DC: World Bank Publications.

Yagnik, Achyut. 2002. "Search for Dalit Self-Identity in Gujarat." *The Other Gujarat: Social Transformations Among Weaker Sections*. Edited by Takashi Shinoda. Mumbai: Popular Prakashan.

Zelliot, Eleanor. 1992. *From Untouchable to Dalit: Essays on the Ambedkar Movement*. New Delhi: Manohar Publications.

——. 2010. "Learning the Use of Political Means: The Mahars of Maharashtra." *Caste in Indian Politics*. Edited by Rajni Kothari. New Delhi: Allied. 29–69.

——. 2013. *Ambedkar's World: The Making of Babasaheb and the Dalit Movement*. New Delhi: Navayana.

ABBREVIATIONS

AAP	Aam Aadmi Party
ABVP	Akhil Bharatiya Vidyarthi Parishad
AJGAR	ahir, jat, gujar and rajput
APSC	Ambedkar–Periyar Study Circle
Bamcef	The All India Backward and Minority Communities Employees Federation
BAWS	*Dr Babasaheb Ambedkar Writings and Speeches*
BBM	Bharatiya Bouddha Mahasabha
BC	Backward Class
BJP	Bharatiya Janata Party
BMC	Brihanmumbai Municipal Corporation
BPL	Below Poverty Line
BSP	Bahujan Samaj Party
CA	Constituent Assembly
CAG	Comptroller and Auditor General of India
CASI	Centre for the Advanced Study of India
CBI	Central Bureau of Investigation
CID	Crime Investigation Department
CPDR	Committee for Protection of Democratic Rights
CPI	Communist Party of India
CPI-M	Communist Party of India–Maoist
CPI (ML)	Communist Party of India (Marxist–Leninist)
CSJ	Council for Social Justice
CSPSA	Chhattisgarh Special Public Security Act
DICCI	Dalit Indian Chamber of Commerce and Industry
DS4	Dalit Shoshit Samaj Sangharsh Samiti
EBC	Extremely Backward Class
EPW	*Economic and Political Weekly*
ERDL	Explosive Research and Development Laboratory
FDI	Foreign Direct Investment
FICCI	Federation of Indian Chambers of Commerce and Industry
FIR	First Information Report
GATS	General Agreement on Trade in Services
GHI	Global Hunger Index
IAS	Indian Administrative Service
ILP	Independent Labour Party
IMF	International Monetary Fund
IPC	Indian Penal Code
JNU	Jawaharlal Nehru University
KHAM	kshatriya, harijan, adivasi and Muslim (alliance)
KKM	Kabir Kala Manch
LF	Left Front
LSE	London School of Economics

MBC	More Backward Class
MDG	Millennium Development Goals
MLA	Member of Legislative Assembly
MSME	Micro Small and Medium Enterprises
NCBC	National Commission for Backward Classes
NCP	Nationalist Congress Party
NCRB	National Crime Records Bureau
NCSC	National Commission for Scheduled Castes
NCST	National Commission for Scheduled Tribes
NDA	National Democratic Alliance
NGT	National Green Tribunal
OBC	Other Backward Class
OMBE	Office of Minority Business Enterprises
OWS	Occupy Wall Street
PIL	Public Interest Litigation
PoA	Prevention of Atrocities Act
PPP	Public–Private Partnership
PSU	Public Sector Undertaking
RPI	Republican Party of India
RSS	Rashtriya Swayamsevak Sangh
RTE	Right to Education
SBM	Swachh Bharat Mission
SC	Scheduled Caste
SCF	Scheduled Castes Federation
SEBC	Socially and Economically Backward Classes
SEBI	Securities and Exchange Board of India
SEZ	Special Economic Zone
SKA	Safai Karamchari Aandolan
SSD	Samata Sainik Dal
ST	Scheduled Tribe
TRIPS	Trade Related Aspects of Intellectual Property Rights Agreement
UAPA	Unlawful Activities (Prevention) Act
UGC	University Grants Commission
UN	United Nations
UPA	United Progressive Alliance
UPSC	Union Public Service Commission
VHP	Vishva Hindu Parishad
WSF	World Social Forum
WTO	World Trade Organization

INDEX